# GROWING A LIFE

## TEEN GARDENERS HARVEST FOOD, HEALTH, AND JOY

ILLÈNE PEVEC

newvillagePRESS

Published in the United States by
New Village Press
bookorders@newvillagepress.net
www.newvillagepress.net

New Village Press is a public-benefit, not-for-profit publishing division of Architects Designers Planners for Social Responsibility.

Grateful acknowledgment is made to the Foundation for Sustainability and Innovation for support of this publication.

In support of the Greenpress Initiative, New Village Press is committed to the preservation of endangered forests globally and advancing best practices within the book and paper industries. The printing papers used in this book are 100% recycled fiber, acid-free (Process Chlorine Free), and have been certified with the Forest Stewardship Council (FSC).

Original paperback ISBN 9781613320174
Publication Date: September 2016
First Edition

Library of Congress Cataloging-in-Publication Data

Names: Pevec, Illène, 1948- , author.
Title: Growing a life : teen gardeners harvest food, health, and joy / Illène Pevec, PhD.
Description: First edition. | New York, NY : New Village Press, 2016.
|Includes bibliographical references.
Identifiers: LCCN 2016015942 | ISBN 9781613320174 (pbk. : alk. paper)
Subjects: LCSH: Gardening for teenagers--United States. |Gardening--Psychological aspects. |
Adolescent psychology. | Community gardens--United States..
Classification: LCC SB457.4.T44 P48 2016 | DDC 635.0835--dc23.
LC record available at https://lccn.loc.gov/2016015942

Front cover photo of Neo in apple tree by Javier
Back cover author photo by Raphael Baker
Cover design by Lynne Elizabeth
Interior design and composition by Jordan Wannemacher

# CONTENTS

*This book is dedicated to the memory of Tracy Penner, landscape architect and dear friend. Tracy's knowledge of design, native plants, and participatory planning and her delightful good humor made our partnership in the Spirit of Nature Garden at Grandview/ʔuuqinakʼuuh Elementary School in Vancouver, Canada, a joy and a delight. Our partnership is what prepared me to make more gardens with children and youth and write this book.*

# GRATITUDE

Thank you to each young gardener and garden mentor who so candidly shared their feelings, photographs, and food-growing experiences. You are this book. You all inspire me. I hope your words inspire the whole world to choose a spot to cultivate.

Thank you to all the programs that welcomed me to meet their gardeners and record their stories: ¡Cultiva!, Colorado Rocky Mountain School, Roaring Fork High School, Yampah Mountain High School, Green Machine, People United for a Better Life in Oakland (PUEBLO), Game Theory Academy and West Oakland Woods (WOW) Farm, Oakland Leaf Love Cultivating Schoolyards, Taos County Economic Development Corporation, New Mexico Acequia Association, and Project Feed the Hood in Albuquerque, New Mexico.

I had superb guidance while researching in Colorado from Dr. Willem van Vliet and Dr. Louise Chawla, with the Community Engagement and Design and Research Resource Center my advisors for my doctorate at the University of Colorado, and from the rest of my wonderful committee as well: Dr. Pamela Wridt at the Children's Environments Research Group at the Graduate Center of the City University of New York; Dr. Samuel Dennis, Jr. in the Department of Landscape Architecture at the University of Wisconsin–Madison; and David Driskell, the executive director of planning, housing, and sustainability for the City of Boulder, Colorado. Thank you so much for the several years you devoted to guiding me.

I thank my friends and colleagues who read chapters and gave me suggestions: Maryam Schutz, Halimah Van Tuyl, Christopher Juniper, Jane Katz, Louise Chawla, and Myra Margolin.

I thank Maude Pervere and Sam Miller for welcoming me to their home in Oakland so I could do research there, and my sister, Ruth Lawyer, and my brother-in-law, Don Sunderland, for giving me a New York base so I could interview the Green Bronx Machine gardeners. I also want to thank Jane Katz for driving me throughout New Mexico to visit Taos, Chamisal, and Albuquerque. What a delight to share that time and those gardens. Adam and Melony Lewis, thank you for supporting Fat City Farmers with grants in 2013 and 2014 so that I could work with that organization and help the Roaring Fork Valley youth continue to grow gardens while I wrote this book. I thank Dr. Inga Newmann, Dr. Shelley Taylor, Dr. Christopher Lowry, and Dr. Kelly Lambert for their clarifying responses to my emails regarding their research which I cite. Dr. Mark Dubin, I thank you for encouraging me to follow my intuition into this inquiry.

I so very much appreciate Laura Leone's excellent editor's eye for finding all my errors; any that remain are my responsibility entirely. Thank you, Jordan Wannemacher, for your excellent design and layout. How grateful I am to Lynne Elizabeth at New Village Press for giving me this opportunity to share these young people's stories. Thank you to all who helped this book come to life.

# PREFACE

## DO OUR BRAINS CHANGE WHILE WE GARDEN?

*I think that is what promotes the joy, just all your senses coming in as one; that is what helps promote the joy.* —GEORGE, 17, ¡CULTIVA!

I began this research because I wanted to discover how working in a garden impacts young people. What happens emotionally, mentally, and physically to a youth during digging, planting, watering, weeding, tending, and harvesting? Does the caring a young gardener gives to living things benefit the gardener? Do those experiences support learning and well-being? Could gardening's sensory input—the smells, sights, sounds, feelings, and tastes—be connected to the internal changes felt during and after gardening? When I began this research, I discovered that many scholars around the world were investigating the impact nature has on children and adults, but their research presented in the following pages provides a context for what I learned from all the young people interviewed for this book.

In school gardens, I have observed that hyperactive young boys who can't sit still in class become focused and productive when their help is needed to move a pile of dirt with a wheelbarrow to a garden bed. I have seen gruff preadolescent boys become caring and helpful when aiding a six-year-old to plant a tender seedling. What causes these attitude and behavior changes?

I have no background in neuroscience, but my intuition and personal gardening experiences tell me that something happens in the brain and body when we garden that affects our sense of well-being. I began this inquiry because I wanted to discover what might be happening to our senses while gardening and how those sensorial experiences impact us. As I was doing my doctorate, my advisor, Dr. Willem Van Vliet, referred me to Dr. Mark Dubin, neuroscientist, author of *How the Brain Works*, and professor emeritus at the University of Colorado Boulder. After hearing my hunch regarding the garden's sensory input affecting the brain and body, Dr. Dubin encouraged me to pursue this line of questioning regarding the senses. He suggested that perhaps all the senses stimulate the pleasure center in the brain and that what the young gardeners would reveal would not only answer my questions, but could also help neuroscientists in their pursuit to understand brain and body connections.

I began this exploration to see what the young gardeners, their mentors, and I could all discover together. I structured my interviews with the youth by asking them to describe to me their experiences with these two questions for each sense: "what do you smell (taste, etc.) while gardening?" and "how does that make you feel?" I also asked them about their ability to focus during and after gardening, if their eating habits and environmental attitudes had changed, and if they did other things that made them feel similarly. Their answers provide the kale chips, fresh garden salad greens, boiled new baby potatoes, steamed asparagus, and apple tart you are about to consume.

I include positive psychology and positive youth development research to create a matrix for understanding the value that these gardening experiences have for adolescents. I also include some relevant neuroscience and human and nature relationship research to provide further context for what the young gardeners reveal in their lush descriptions. I do not claim to provide any conclusive evidence regarding brain and body connections beyond the young gardeners' words. I did not give them cognitive tests or test their blood or saliva for physical evidence of changes after or during gardening.

I began interviewing gardeners ages fourteen to nineteen at ¡Cultiva!, an urban after-school and summer market gardening program in Boulder, Colorado, in 2006. In 2007 and 2008, I interviewed students at Colorado Rocky Mountain School, an independent day and boarding school with a vegetable gardening program in rural Carbondale, Colorado. In 2009, I committed to helping Roaring Fork High School, the public high school in Carbondale, start a gardening program. I also volunteered my time to Yampah Mountain High School, a public alternative high school in Glenwood Springs, Colorado, with a new dome greenhouse and a teen-mother program, where I codeveloped and taught a horticulture class to the teen mothers as a volunteer. Some students at those schools also participated in my research. I successfully defended my dissertation in October of 2011 and thought I was done with writing for a while.

When I saw Stephen Ritz's live TED Talk in January of 2012 on the work he does with youth in the South Bronx via the Green Bronx Machine, I was so inspired by him that I knew I had to write this book so that articulate, passionate, and persuasive youth voices could reach the greater public. I expanded the geographical, ethnic, and cultural diversity of my dissertation to include the New York youth that garden with Ritz and also diverse young gardeners from California and New Mexico, whom I interviewed in 2012 and 2013, respectively.

I met and interviewed the youth gardeners in their school and after-school gardens (twelve distinct programs in all). Ninety young gardeners spoke with me for a half hour or more during individual interviews. These youth are Caucasian, American Indian, African American, Hispanic, Samoan, Filipino, Hawaiian, South Korean, and Danish. Some gardeners came from Puerto Rico, Mexico, Argentina, Antigua, and the Dominican Republic. My research interview questions were approved by the University of Colorado Denver's internal review board and used at all research locations. Though I was no longer under university supervision once I finished my dissertation, I still used the same protocols for all youth interviewed in California, New York, and New Mexico, and had consent forms from parents for all interviewees under eighteen and assent forms from all participating youth.

After the first six interviews, I asked students to take photographs of their favorite places in their gardens. Their photographs and some of mine illustrate this book. I paid all the students for their time given to me for interviews with a $10 gift card to a local grocery store or similar payment to the nonprofit that employed them to add to their paychecks with the exception of Colorado Rocky Mountain School, where the garden was a school-required work crew. Those students got an organic dark chocolate bar for their time, and I gave $100 to the garden program fund. All interviewees received an eight-by-eleven-inch print of the garden photo they took.

I include some interviews in their entirety and some in portion to illustrate themes the youth discuss. Occasionally, I have chosen phrases from what the individual said and ordered their words into poem form to reflect an essence of what was expressed. I have not changed word choice, grammar, or speech patterns; they are an integral part of personal expression. Occasionally, I edited to add clarification or edited out some things that seemed extraneous. I use pseudonyms for all the Colorado youth because they were part of my doctoral research and the university required anonymity for young research subjects. All of the rest of the young gardeners are identified with pseudonyms if they are under eighteen and with their own first names if they are eighteen or over. What a humbling experience it has been to hear so many young people share their feelings so openly so that others can understand the importance of gardens for youth.

May their journeys shared here bring delight and understanding to you!

# INTRODUCTION

## WHY TEENS? WHY GARDENS?

*A garden is kind of like putting a little bit of yourself back into the earth and just be-ing helpful and not just taking all the time—just like giving something back to not just the earth, but to other people too. It's kind of making sense of life. You're giving life. It's really nice. And I think it's exciting to see things grow that you've planted.*
—DENISE, 17, ROARING FORK HIGH SCHOOL

Denise's family moved to Colorado for her senior year of high school in order to aid her dying grandmother. The school garden and agricultural biology class offered at Roaring Fork High School provided a life-supporting environment for her while she worked with classmates to grow produce for the school salad bar. The garden gave her a space and time to contemplate life at that critical juncture—as high school ends and youth start to contemplate what comes next.

My own early childhood in a small Colorado mountain town provided constant, easy access to playing in nature, which lead to my lifelong passion for the outdoors. This, in turn, compelled me to explore gardens as a place for young people to grow their own lives. I experienced nature as a wonderful place to discover life's vast diversity and beauty: holes to dig, worms to touch, trees to climb, streams to wade, and wild raspberries to pick and eat. Even as a young child, I realized how lucky I was to be in such close proximity to nature.

Engagement with nature as children often has older family members playing important introductory roles. When I was three, my grandmother and I stooped together as she held up a tiny flower on its short stem to show me the blossom. "This is a Johnny-jump-up," said Grandma as she introduced us. When I was five, my mother taught me how to plant the hard, round seeds that would produce heavenly fragranced sweet peas that grew up our back fence.

When I was seven, we left the small mountain town that had easy access to trees to climb and moved to a Denver suburb that had no trees. I was painfully aware of what I had lost. Fortunately, a short bike ride from our new home allowed me to play on the banks of Cherry Creek, where huge old cottonwoods grew and where I could gather tadpoles to bring home and watch turn into frogs (I always returned the fully developed frogs to the creek).

In that suburban backyard, my father taught me how to plant corn and carrots in a small vegetable garden. When the corn was ready to pick, he taught me how important it was to boil the water first and then go out and pick the corn so that it went directly from the stalk to the pot to retain its fresh sweetness. Each spring, my parents took me to the local hardware store, where I had the fun of choosing the colorful pansies we would plant by our back door. Though my parents were not devoted gardeners, they introduced me to the pleasures of planting and the power of personal choice when I was young.

I believe it was the loss of living surrounded by nature when I was only seven that propelled me to create access to nature for children when I became an adult. I wanted to share outdoor exploration, discovery, and joy with children. After college, I returned to the mountains and ran a summer preschool in 1970 and 1971 entirely out-of-doors near the Crystal River in western Colorado. With only a MASH tent for shelter, three- and four-year-old students hiked, sculpted shore mud, threw stones in the river, painted with wild grass seed heads, and planted tomato seeds in coffee cans with some soil to take home and transplant. Thus began my work of planting with children as a way to link them with nature.

Not everyone has rivers and forests in their immediate surroundings, but usually there is open land somewhere nearby—whether it is the strip between a sidewalk and the street or a park. Even in cities, a garden can be made where plants can attract wildlife and a child's curiosity. Children who live in an urbanizing world need more, not less, access to nature. When asked what they need in their communities, urban children most frequently respond with a request for more parks with natural features (Chawla, 2002).

In 1973, I got married, and in the next ten years, had five children and immigrated to Vancouver, Canada. In Vancouver, we moved to a neighborhood defined by coastal mountains and an ocean inlet. During those years of raising children, my outdoor education energy went into planning summer camping trips involving anywhere from five to twenty-five families. I also worked in arts education, and I loved that creative environment. I frequently visited inner-city schools to deliver art workshops.

In 1998, the year I turned fifty, I decided to go to graduate school to do something to address the enormous social inequity I witnessed in the public school system. The poorer parents did not have the business connections to get donations for their children's schools or the ability to write grants, and so the children who most needed enriched environments at school didn't have them. I wanted to do something about that. I also wanted to study creativity, particularly to understand the spark that inspires scientists and artists to discover and create.

The summer before I started graduate school, I attended a Society for Values in Higher Education conference and met a woman whose work in youth gardens changed my life. Dr. Anna Wasecha founded Farm in the City, a horticulture and fine arts program for inner-city children in St. Paul, Minnesota. When she described the ways in which she used horticulture-wedded-to-art activities to engage children in discovering the world through science, art, cooking, and fun, her words rang inside me like tinkling bells. I found my own garden path. I realized that I could make gardens with children and observe what happened to them and me as we planned, dug, planted, and harvested.

Fortunately for the scope and success of what we were eventually able to do, I found a landscape architecture student at the University of British Columbia, Tracy Penner, who was looking for a garden project to design as part of her own studies. We joined forces to collaborate with Grandview/ʔuuqinakʼuuh Elementary School in inner-city Vancouver to create the Spirit of Nature Gardens—a name that was chosen by the children. The school population was primarily First Nations[1] and also included many refugees from outside of Canada. These children and their families at the elementary school and daycare center on the same school grounds became codesigners and gardeners along with their teachers in an action research project that created multiple gardens and public arts projects.

We used a participatory planning process for planning public spaces developed by a Vancouver architect with this neighborhood that included public housing (King, 1989). Many adults wanted a community garden where they could grow food as well. Nonprofits and foundations came together to work with us, and the Mennonite Central Committee of Canada and the Environmental Youth Alliance both joined in with labor and expertise. This school community had almost no fathers, and so local carpenters, both men and women, volunteered to help the children build the garden boxes for the school garden. The children were as excited at learning to pound a nail properly as they were at learning to plant seeds and transplant seedlings. Thus began my experience with multiage community gardeners transforming school grounds into biologically and culturally rich environments. That garden won multiple awards, including the Creating Healthy Communities for Children and Youth Award from the Canadian Society for Children

---

1. A term used to describe Aboriginal peoples of Canada who are ethnically neither Métis nor Inuit.

and Youth, and was named one of the five best school gardens in Canada by Evergreen Canada.

Engaging so many different groups in developing gardens changed the way I saw public land use: so often relegated to grass, public land had far more potential to grow healthy communities than I had previously imagined. Anna Wasecha also introduced me to the American Community Gardening Association (ACGA), and I began attending their annual general meetings that bring together community and school garden activists from across the country to share experiences, challenges, and abundant knowledge. The very first workshop I attended at the 1998 ACGA national meeting was entitled "School Garden Sustainability." It is easy to plant a garden, but maintaining it and keeping it sustainable and integrated in the educational process over decades presents greater challenges.

I began my research, in part, to gain evidence to show those who develop education and public land policy just how important gardens can be as learning laboratories for curiosity and sustainability and as places that grow good health. What began for me as a deep desire to give children access to nature in their daily school life to explore, learn, and play grew to encompass multiple explorations in nutrition, transformative education, child and community health, child and nature relationships, and land use planning and public policy.

The test-driven educational system of the United States grew out of an effort to improve learning outcomes for all children and to close the achievement gaps between social and economic groups, but test-driven schools can create a great deal of stress for students and teachers, especially for youth who struggle with test taking. Are we losing essential elements for healthy human development in the hunt for high test scores above all other achievements?

How might school gardens transform the educational process for students and teachers? What could youth and their teachers learn from hands-on contact with the earth and its seasonal cycles as they grow food, flowers, and trees? Could engagement in natural life processes lead to more sustainable communities in multiple ways? This book provides some answers and more questions from those most able to respond: the youth who garden and their mentors who work with them.

## ADOLESCENT DEVELOPMENT AND GROWING GARDENS

In their teen years, adolescents engage in one of life's major developmental tasks: identity formation (Erikson, 1968). During this process, youth embrace ideals and seek leadership. Identity building can result in volatile feelings as youth seek to understand the changes brought on by puberty. Investigating the role a garden plays at this critical life juncture became my goal when I once again returned to graduate school in 2005 to get a doctorate degree. Since adolescents' "developing brains, coupled with hormonal changes, make them more prone to depression and more likely to engage in risky and thrill-seeking behavior than either younger children or adults" (Swarz, 2009, 1), this book also investigates the mental health benefits of gardening for youth.

A national United States house-to-house survey with 9,282 adults (eighteen or older) revealed an estimated 46.2 percent lifetime likelihood of developing a mental health disorder involving mood, anxiety, impulse control, or substance abuse (Kessler et al. 2005, 593). Diagnosable mental health disorders are present in approximately 21 percent of adolescents, and it is common for the first symptoms of an anxiety, mood, or impulse control problem to occur during adolescence before the age of fourteen, with three quarters of mental health disorders appearing by age twenty-four (National Alliance for Mental Illness, 2016).

The high school drop-out rate for teens with a mental illness is 50 percent, higher than any other disability. Youth who end up in juvenile detention have an extremely high rate of undiagnosed mental illness, 65 percent of boys and 75 percent of girls. Twenty percent of these disorders are so serious that the youth's functioning is severely impaired (Skowyra and Cocozza, 2006, 1). According to the National Alliance on Mental Illness (2016, 1): Suicide is the second leading cause of death in youth ages ten to twenty-four. Homicide is the third leading cause of death in youth fifteen to twenty-four (ibid.). More teenagers and young adults die from suicide than from cancer, heart disease, AIDS, birth defects, stroke, pneumonia, influenza, and chronic lung disease combined (Centers for Disease Control and Prevention, 2013). Over 90 percent of children and adolescents who commit suicide have a mental disorder (National Alliance on Mental Illness 2016, 1).

When I began my research with gardening youth, I was not aware of how frequently mental health disorders occur in adolescence. The most recently available statistics on health risk factors for Colorado, where my research began, come from the 2011 Colorado Department of Public Health and Environment (CDPHE) Youth Risk Behavior Survey. The survey was administered to 1,449 students in grades 9 to 12 in thirty-six Colorado public high schools considered representative of all Colorado youth. The survey revealed that 21.9 percent of high school students "felt so sad or hopeless almost every day for two weeks or more in a row that they stopped doing some usual activities during the past 12 months" (Colorado Department of Public Health and Environment [CDPHE], 2011). This percentage is an average of both boys and girls, however, and when considered separately, girls were found to be ten percentage points (27.1 percent) sadder than boys (16.9 percent) (CDPHE, 2011).

Kessler et al. (2005, 593) recommend preventative and early treatment interventions to target youth. A school district on Colorado's rural Western Slope (the geographical region where I did about one third of this book's interviews) opened a public health clinic inside a middle school in 2013 to make affordable health care available to all students. In the first six months, half the visits were for mental health reasons; double what the clinic director had expected according to information shared with me when I joined the advisory committee to open a similar clinic at Roaring Fork High School, where twenty-four of the youth in this book were students.

Could gardens at schools play active roles in promoting both physical and mental health? Knowing how gardening affects young people could help school policy makers and designers consider a garden's role in supporting positive youth development. It could help health and education professionals to understand the role gardens can play in diet, learning, and well-being. This knowledge could help planners consider how to best use public land for growing community health. This book presents my research with youth on how gardening impacts their well-being, eating habits, environmental attitudes, and ability to focus.

I offer these youth voices to inform and enlighten the adults who guide, plan, and direct the world. I hope the evidence presented here will implant gardens as firmly in schools as the three Rs: reading, writing, and arithmetic. May these young gardeners' voices reach other youth and unite with them as a force for growing gardens around the globe: places for health, happiness, and intergenerational well-being. Welcome to the transformative environment that these young people create together wherever they garden!

# 1

# THE GREEN BRONX MACHINE

Stephen Ritz and the grow towers he uses inside classrooms.
Credit: Green Bronx Machine

I first saw Stephen Ritz on a projector screen at Colorado Mountain College (CMC) in Carbondale, Colorado, in January of 2012. I was attending a live stream of a TED Talks on food at the college, which had attracted a large audience of local sustainable food advocates, when Ritz danced onto the screen. A former professional basketball player from the Bronx, he bopped and jumped animatedly about the stage as a myriad of photos showing high school students in the South Bronx planting living walls of food in their schools and outdoor gardens were projected behind him. Ritz spoke passionately about the Green Bronx Machine, a not-for-profit program he founded that teaches inner-city youth green job skills, including food growing in school and after-school programs. Throughout the presentation, Ritz embodied the Energizer Bunny on kale. His total enthusiasm for the New York City youth he mentors in food growing made me realize I had to meet him and his Green Bronx Machine gardeners.

The students who grow food in the South Bronx have different stories to tell than those who live and plant in the nature-rich Colorado foothills and mountains where my research was previously based—but, together, all these youth voices could be a book. Stephen Ritz's TED Talk on a snowy Saturday in January launched me on a delightful journey!

Fortunately, the next month, I was presenting at the National Green Schools Conference in Denver, and so was Ritz. I found him at his booth demonstrating the vertical growing system he uses to create indoor living walls at schools and in corporate offices, and while I normally would not mention a person's outward appearance, when I met Ritz in person, I saw that he had lost a lot of weight since the TED Talk only a month earlier. Ritz told me that he had changed his own eating habits because of gardening with his students and had lost weight as a result. He had realized that he needed to eat what he taught his students to grow—now kale rather than french fries powered his energetic drive to turn around inner-city youth's lives with green community projects. Ritz's weight-loss experience through gardening demonstrates one reason why school gardens have had a renaissance in recent decades: through gardening, individuals can fight against the obesity epidemic that affects people of all ages by growing fresh ingredients and eating more vegetables and fruits rather than processed foods (Alaimo et al. 2008; Heim, Stang, and Ireland, 2009). Gardens are quickly being seen as viable interventions to improve health.

Ritz has taught many years in New York City public schools, but on the weekends and in the summers, he has worked under the auspices of the Green Bronx Machine, a not-for-profit that he founded. The Green Bronx Machine's multiple facets combine teaching gardening and green construction skills, including green roof installation, to high school students. The prior summer, his young workers had completed two green roofs on homes in the Hamptons with Ritz and his family there as mentors. These diverse trainings prepare the participating youth for employment with contractors doing professional building renovations in their own South Bronx neighborhoods. Ritz blends education with business savvy and good partnerships to prepare these young people to graduate from high school and find green jobs and perhaps even careers.

At the high school in the South Bronx where the Green Bronx Machine began, Ritz helped students grow food for the school lunches and for community elders. With little space in the urban school to plant a traditional outdoor garden, Ritz began using manufactured metal compartmentalized wall systems that hold one plant per small box and look a bit like a plant book-shelf. These wall systems make vertical growing possible both indoors with growing lights and outdoors in sunshine. Ritz understood that not all schools have the open ground for outdoor planting and found a way to make food growing possible even in the multistoried school build-ings typical of New York City. (He switched to white PVC pipe grow towers for indoor garden-ing for the same purpose in 2015.)

Ritz himself grew up in the Bronx and did not come to gardening with the same attitude of "the outdoors is great!" that one encounters in Colorado gardeners. A star high school and college bas-ketball player who thought he would devote his life to his favorite sport, Ritz had only turned to teaching after a serious injury made him change directions. He sought out gardening as a way to save the students whom the school system often sidelined into special education classes, where their innate intelligence went unrecognized and often got smothered in a one-size-fits-all system. I was even more inspired once I met Ritz, and I wanted to meet the youth he serves.

I did not have a research grant or even a job to help me pay for my expenses to travel and interview youth, but I had enough air miles for a ticket to New York. Luckily, my sister lived a one-hour walk away from the charter high school in East Harlem where Ritz was teaching. We agreed I would come meet the youth gardeners to interview and learn from them. I arrived in early May of 2012 with the city in full bloom. The red admiral butterflies hovered over seemingly every blossom that New York City's public gardens offered. Amidst the towering buildings, many large and tiny gardens grow, filled with diverse life and beauty—a softening to the hard edges and deep shadows the skyscrapers make.

As I made the trek to the charter high school to interview Ritz's students, I walked under Central Park's towering trees and across its large meadows and then wove my way through twelve blocks of hospitals and public housing. The charter high school serves youth who had been fail-ing at other schools and who were in danger of dropping out without special programs geared to their learning styles and needs. When I entered the building that housed the high school on its upper floors and a middle school below, I had to show my driver's license. Ritz was required to meet me at the guard's desk, a level of security I had not seen in the rural Colorado schools where I had previously done my research.

Ritz had lost so much weight since I had met him in February that he could hardly keep his pants up with a belt. As I observed him work with his students during class and with the Green Bronx Machine after school that week, I quickly realized that he was far too busy to take time out to go buy a new pair of pants to fit his trimmer body. He only had time to tighten his belt.

I visited during Ritz's two-hour Sustainable Technologies class, where he combined science with gardening. The class's lab portion, held in the garden, took place on the school's sixth-floor roof. The day that I arrived happened to be the first day the students would devote the whole class period to planting. Before the class came in from lunch, Mateo, aged sixteen, came in early to meet and speak with me.

**MATEO:** The teachers actually put me in the class because I had missed more than one hundred days of school, sometimes weeks out of school, just like failing. I'll say that straight-up. They put me in the program because it gives you an extra two or three credits at the end of each marking period, just to boost my grade up, basically. They put me in the gardening program because I am a green-thumb type of person, basically. I helped out in several GreenThumb[1]-type community gardens in my neighborhood. I even built several hydroponic systems in my apartment.

**ILLÈNE:** So how did you get involved in GreenThumb programs here in New York?

**MATEO:** It wasn't in a program exactly. It was just a community person coming around needing help. Like elderly people, these people who own these GreenThumb community gardens are like over fifty or over sixty, and they don't have the physical stamina to lift an eighty-pound bag of dirt, so they used to call on me to help them out.

**ILLÈNE:** And you liked it?

**MATEO:** Yeah! Free tomato plants and everything. Yeah, like nurturing the plant in a week's time, the next thing you know the seeds grow so big, it's getting so big. How big did my tomato plant grow? Like six or seven feet tall! *My* tomato plant! A sense of responsibility kicks in. I don't know how to explain it. I get a little proud. You really put effort into taking care of something and you really succeeded. You really went through.

**ILLÈNE:** And you see your plants grow because you're taking care of them, and you said you're helping people because they need help, they couldn't garden without your help? What makes you enjoy it? Is helping part of it? Is helping people an important element?

**MATEO:** Helping and also being outside, actually being dirty, like getting dirty. I really do like being dirty. I am not no little clean-cut New Yorker. I actually like being, getting dirty. I don't care about nothing. Bugs crawling on my foot, I don't care. I just wipe 'em off. There

---

1. GreenThumb provides programming and material support to over six hundred community gardens in New York City.

is just that every day repetition, like walking to the bus stop, getting on the bus, going to school. You know, everything is nothing but technology and media and technology wanting you to buy things, go places and stuff, but there is nothing really truly saying, "Sit back and relax and get some dirt under your feet" unless it's a Home Depot ad. I just like it. I like being outside… no real toxins, a true area of greenness, no dirt from just regular air pollution. I like it that when I come home, and I have to shower because I got myself dirty from walking around the neighborhood. Come home and next thing you know, there is two pounds of dirt on the floor just from me walking around the neighborhood.

ILLÈNE: So you like to engage with the natural world, get dirty by really being in it?

MATEO: Yeah, my English sucks. [Mateo is a native Spanish speaker.]

ILLÈNE: You express yourself very well. Your English is very good. Did you see anyone in your family garden, your parents or grandparents?

MATEO: Yeah, my mom. She is a real gardening-head type of person. She doesn't really garden such as we have a garden at our house. But we have a really large amount of garden in our house. But I like outdoor gardening. Every now and then, some summers, I would get a box, a GreenThumb community garden, but it just depends on my schedule. If I have time to garden, I will, but if I don't, I will just plant a tomato seed in a pot out in front of my window.

ILLÈNE: I am curious about your sensory experiences when you garden and how that affects you. When you garden, are you aware of any smells you don't normally smell?

MATEO: Well, I have been playing around in dirt and with plants and everything since I was three years old. I am used to all the smells and fragrances, whatever.

ILLÈNE: How do those smells make you feel? Like when the lilacs come into bloom as they are now.

MATEO: You actually get, like me, like I get real proud if I am the one maintaining it. I succeeded. I want to see them bloom and I want to see them live. Some people harvest them, some people don't. But I just feel proud of them.

ILLÈNE: How does your physical body feel when you are out there? Like tomatoes, they have a very specific smell. Does it change the way you feel? How do you feel when you come out of school?

MATEO: After school, I am exhausted. But then after gardening, it depends on the day ahead of you when you are gardening. But after gardening and everything, on a day I am gardening, pretty decent. You don't waste time; you don't waste energy as long as you know what you are doing, [I feel] perfectly fine.

ILLÈNE: Does it change your ability to focus on something? Does it change your capacity to pay attention when you go into a garden, does it shift what you feel?

MATEO: You mean like in the regular world? Yes, very much, very much. When I go to a job, I mean when I go to a garden, my whole entire stamina changes. The whole entire point is to be green, to make sure the plant grows, lives. Don't do nothing stupid like break a branch, break a root.

ILLÈNE: Does it change your stress level?

MATEO: Yes. It calms me down. I'm breathing in more oxygen rather than the toxins from the cars and stuff like that from a daily regular stroll. I would say the cold, the cold wetness from the dirt and the ground. A majority of time, if you are really truly a gardener, you should be on your knees, which I would say honestly, unless you are a florist or something.

ILLÈNE: What is that like to be in touch with the earth, to be down on your knees on the earth with your hands in the moist earth?

MATEO: It's relaxing a little bit. Sometimes it's a little awkward in some situations. It's relaxing, calming. No stress. No real nothing. No one is arguing around you. No real problems, just regular things going on, just plants and dirt and that's it.

ILLÈNE: What is it like to see a seed sprout that you planted yourself?

MATEO: Well, now that I am used to it, nothing, but back then, I was just so, I used to jump up and down, I was so excited, "My God, my God, it's only been two days, my God!" [*He demonstrates his excitement very animatedly for me*]. You just start jumping up and down. If you want to get a true reaction out of a youngster, little kids when they first see something sprout, they jump up and down. That's how I actually felt. I think the first time was in kindergarten. Yeah, kindergarten. We did it the old fashioned way: where you take a piece of paper towel and the seed, and it's wet and it just cracks open, and then you just plant it.

ILLÈNE: So you soaked it ahead of time?

MATEO: Yeah. All my seeds, that's what I always do. You take a seed and you put it in a wet paper towel, some people use jars, but I prefer a Ziploc bag to keep it moist, [and put it] in a dark place, doesn't matter the temperature as long as it's not too hot or cold.

ILLÈNE: Do you think gardening itself has given you more environmental awareness?

MATEO: Yes, a lot. In pollution ways 'cause Ritz almost every day brings us how many cans the school uses, how many bottles and how much paper this one school uses each day, and there are no recycling bins. This school wastes so much. The school has no recycling bins, no bottles with bottles, paper with papers.

ILLÈNE: I would have thought that in New York City, it would be required. Maybe it is single-stream recycling? It would be good to find out if the school recycles.

MATEO: I've never seen separation in the garbage. You could spend one week in the school and see how many bottles you could kick.

ILLÈNE: Do you think it has made you more environmentally responsible to be learning these things?

MATEO: Yes, very much. I like this program not just because of the TV shows we get to be on. I don't care about that camera stuff. I am a green-thumb person and I am here for the experience. I want to learn about better and newer ways to grow any plant.

ILLÈNE: Is agriculture something you want to be in for work?

MATEO: Yeah, 'cause everyone has to eat. That's the smartest thing. I never thought about that. Growing up in New York City, everyone wants to be a basketball player, actor, singer, song writer, president. It never comes to mind. I might open a food store; nobody ever thinks about that. Maximum production of tomatoes; nobody thinks about it because nobody supports young people in New York City behind that. The majority of time, they have programs to be a movie director or car repairman. There is no real support for agriculture.

ILLÈNE: Do you have a tradition in your family, like were your grandparents farmers?

MATEO: My stepfather. My grandfather on my stepfather's side has land in Puerto Rico that they farm for their own consumption. That's it. My grandfather had a little farm—carrots, corn, beets.

ILLÈNE: Did you ever visit it?

MATEO: No. We visited it, but since my grandfather died and my father left his land with his ex-wife, they didn't maintain it; bamboo grew up all over it. If it was up to me, I would have gone up there with machetes and made a little hut out of the bamboo, made a little water reservoir, but it was a decent size, about a half acre, one New York City block.

ILLÈNE: Do you think that growing vegetables has influenced your food choices?

MATEO: Yes, a lot. I don't eat that much junk food no more.

ILLÈNE: Is that because you have tasted a tomato from the vine?

MATEO: Not just that, but it is also because of… you don't know this about me, but when I was nine years old, I was getting chest pains from high cholesterol and high blood pressure. Yep. I was a big ol' fat boy at nine years old. From nine to thirteen, I kept jumping from 180 to 210 pounds. I was between four and five feet tall!

ILLÈNE: Oh, my gosh! Do you mind me asking how much you weigh now because you look like you have a totally fit body? You lost all that? Did Mr. Ritz tell you he did too?

MATEO: Yeah, we saw those videos. I am 150 or 160 [pounds] now.

ILLÈNE: So, that is amazing! Did your mom put you on a diet?

MATEO: I did it myself. I did it all myself recently, honestly. My body growth, my change of diet, my change of my ways—it all helped out in the long run.

ILLÈNE: So you completely turned your health around by the way you eat!

MATEO: It's just, you know those days when you are bored and you get the munchies, where you want to eat a full meal? Instead of grabbing the Doritos and chips, grab a banana and water, a fruit and water. That's all it is. The little things count.

ILLÈNE: Do you like carrots when you want to munch?

MATEO: No, raw mint, raspberries, blueberries. All the berries; mainly mint also.

ILLÈNE: What is the meaning of gardening for you, the process of gardening?

MATEO: Creating and maintaining a food supply. Without gardening, there wouldn't be no veggies.

ILLÈNE: Is there anything I didn't ask you about gardening that you want me to know?

MATEO: Gardening comes with a large responsibility. That is one. You have to have respect for the plants. If you are stressed up, the plants are going to suffer.

ILLÈNE: So it is important the state of being you bring to the plants? How did you learn that?

MATEO: 'cause my eggplants kept dying 'cause I wasn't being sensitive to them. I had twenty, and then they died. They were turning yellow and brown. I found out the pH of the water was wrong. That's what I messed up on. I fixed that problem. Then they didn't bloom. I bought some of what I call blooming steroids, nutrients, you mix it up with water, and I just fed them those nutrients and they started blooming. To me, I was proud of myself because I made them bloom. But I was disappointed in myself because I had to force them to bloom. I wanted them to bloom naturally. But Olga, the garden store owner, she said to make them bloom now because when it is time to harvest, you will have a larger yield. So I figured I might as well try it. I got an eighteen-ounce eggplant. My mom made it.

ILLÈNE: That's fantastic. Thank you for sharing all this.

## TRANSFORMATION

Mateo's pride in his accomplishments growing plants animates him. He has taken control of his eating habits and now eats healthy, and has pride in this too. He and his teacher, Mr. Ritz, have gone through similar personal transformations in relation to their bodies and eating habits; they are digging the same things, literally and figuratively. Mateo engaged in community service even before he began the school gardening program because he chose to help the elderly people who needed him to lift heavy things at their GreenThumb gardens. He comes to school now because he is doing something he loves that he wants to master. He has personal motivation driving him that is not something external. Gardening may have begun for Mateo as a way to get some science credits or make some money through the weekend jobs that the Green Bronx Machine can provide, but it has developed into something that gives him a sense of identity and focus.

Mateo helped me save his interview on the borrowed iPod I had for recording. I have minimal technical skills, and I am so grateful for the help from Mateo and the several other students who also aided me. I am sincerely grateful for their assistance and what they shared with me. They are the only people who can tell their stories. They are the experts.

Ritz introduced me to the whole class when everyone returned from lunch. He had already given them permission slips so that I could interview them with their parents' consent as well as their own. Together, we climbed the stairs to their sixth-floor rooftop garden boxes. The roof offers a spectacular view over Manhattan where the East and Harlem Rivers wind their way through the maze of buildings. One of the other schools sharing the building had built raised-bed planting boxes in a previous year, and these already had some spring flowers blooming, attracting various pollinators. A twelve-foot-high fence surrounded the entire roof. Ritz's class was planting in the vertical steel structures he uses for vertical growing and also in large plastic pots for the vines, such as cucumbers and grapes. The pots were placed where the plants could eventually climb the towering fence. A bench provided a perfect place to interview students while the class worked nearby.

I thought I had mastered the iPod recording process, but was very disappointed in myself for failing to properly record the next interview with Bradley, aged sixteen. He spoke so enthusiastically about the responsibility and teamwork that gardening with his classmates taught him. He felt school gardens had a very important role to play in young people's thriving. I successfully recorded only a few minutes of all he shared.

BRADLEY: You can use the plants that you grow to feed the school for lunch. It could generate money for your school, and you could help people in the community around you near the school, and it would be a good activity for the kids to take up in their schools. It gives them something to take their mind off whatever is going on and detox their stress levels because school can be stressing sometimes. Starting something new gives you that new spark and you want to do it because it gives you a motivation because it's new instead of old and boring to you. Just the fact that we are working outside in an open environment getting fresh air as opposed to staying inside all day doing school work, and we can work apart from that and can come up here and plant.

## STRESS RELIEF THROUGH GARDENING

The stress related to school and the need for time outside during a school day was something I heard expressed spontaneously by almost every youth I interviewed. Bradley made it very clear how important he finds being outside and planting to be.

Access to nature has been shown to restore people's capacity for attention (Kaplan and Kaplan, 1990; Kaplan, 1995; Hartig et al. 2003; Kaplan and Berman, 2010), which is something important for school architects and personnel to know. A series of medical studies are currently being performed at Legacy Hospital in Portland, Oregon, to see how access to a garden relieves stress for women in labor, family members of patients in intensive care, and for medical staff caring for patients (Beresford, 2014). There is a pattern of evidence that suggests that well-designed gardens can "reduce stress, lower blood pressure, and relax people" (Open Voices, 2013).

My next interviewee Manuela, aged sixteen, soft-spoken and smiling, expressed immense pleasure regarding gardening. She was one of only two female youth gardeners that I interviewed in New York. The class had almost all male students.

MANUELA: To be honest, I didn't know that I was going to be in this program. But when I first started it, I loved it because I used to do community service work, and for community service, we used to go planting, and it was lovely.

ILLÈNE: What sort of planting did you do before?

MANUELA: Trees of all kinds... we did a million trees!

ILLÈNE: Wow! You were part of the MillionTrees Project to make sure there were a million trees in New York? So what do you like about doing that?

MANUELA: I guess it was just to be outside, and what we were doing was going to benefit the world in a way. It seems like such a small thing to do, but then once you look at in the long run, it definitely pays off. You see all the problems with global warming. They say to do your part. Well, I have tried!

ILLÈNE: What else is nice about planting trees?

MANUELA: Well, they just look very pretty in general when they finally blossom if they flower or when they are fully grown.

ILLÈNE: Do you like sitting in the shade under a big tree?

MANUELA: There is nothing better to do when you live in New York.

ILLÈNE: I am curious if you have ever planted vegetables before or will this be your first time?

MANUELA: It will be my first time. I usually just plant flowers.

ILLÈNE: Have you ever seen anyone in your family garden?

MANUELA: Yeah, my mom. She loves flowers. She does house plants. My grandma has plenty of plants.

ILLÈNE: So you have a tradition in your family of planting?

MANUELA: Yeah, I guess.

ILLÈNE: What plants do they have?

MANUELA: It's hard to say because I don't remember them too well, but she gave me a plant of my own called a snapdragon. It's pink. I am not typically a pink person. And we had something called parade roses and they were really pretty too. It's kind of hard to remember all the plants, but my mom is thinking of buying some herbs now too.

ILLÈNE: For cooking?

MANUELA: Yes.

ILLÈNE: Have you done much cooking from scratch with your mom?

MANUELA: Umm, not really, but I guess we are going to find out how that goes.

ILLÈNE: I am curious about the sensory experiences that young people have when they are gardening. When you are planting trees, which sense do you notice that you pay the most attention to: your sense of smell or sight or touch?

MANUELA: It's more like the way it looks and smells up here because some of these flower and since we have herbs and they smell really nice. And it's just beautiful to see everything so green.

ILLÈNE: How does it make your body feel to see so much green?

MANUELA: It makes me feel calmer, I guess. It makes me feel happier, more pleasant.

ILLÈNE: When you were doing community service planting trees, did you notice if it made you focus more or less while you were doing it?

MANUELA: I had to focus more during planting. I had to focus more towards the beginning because we were using some pretty dangerous stuff, I guess. And we had to use teamwork because these plants, we were thinking they would be as big as a grape vine, but they were pretty big plants.

ILLÈNE: Do you notice that your stress levels change when you are gardening?

MANUELA: Yeah, I feel happier because I guess it is nice to be around something so pretty. Technically, plants clean the air.

ILLÈNE: Well, yes, and you are working and that makes you breathe more. This is going to be your first time planting vegetables. One of the things I am curious about is whether planting vegetables makes kids eat more vegetables?

MANUELA: I guess so because I am kind of curious. You never really see how things are grown and transported.

ILLÈNE: You just see them in the grocery store. You don't know their history? Now, you will know their history. Do you have a cooking class here at school? There are onions here ready to harvest.

MANUELA: No, but we probably might start one.

ILLÈNE: Do you have a kitchen here you can use?

MANUELA: No, but we probably can go to the lunchroom.

ILLÈNE: Do you notice which sense you pay the most attention to when you are planting? What affects you the most?

MANUELA: Since we are right next to the highway, you don't really want to pay too much attention to the sound.

ILLÈNE: So what would you say you pay more attention to when you are planting?

East Harlem school rooftop garden where the Sustainable Technologies class plants.
Credit: Illène Pevec

MANUELA: I would say my sight because when I have to look at what I am planting, I have to be careful with what I am planting so I don't crush the plant or end up burying it too deep. Then I look at the dirt, and then once I am finished, I would be looking at what I planted.

ILLÈNE: When you finish planting something and you step back and look at it, what do you feel?

MANUELA: I remember when I did it for the MillionTrees [Project]. It made me feel lovely, especially since they gave us a tag to put on our tree to know that we planted it.

ILLÈNE: Oh, that's wonderful! Were you proud?

MANUELA: I guess I could say so.

ILLÈNE: And what is the meaning of gardening to you?

MANUELA: The meaning of gardening to me would be, I guess, the obvious meaning would be planting, but the meaning for me would be, I guess, some time to relax. I would pretty much rather be up here than inside writing an essay with five paragraphs.

ILLÈNE: Do you think that doing tree planting has given you more environmental awareness?

MANUELA: I'd say so. We have seen how plants grow and what happens in certain temperatures. Like when it was really hot, when we were not up here for a couple of days, we saw that some of the plants were dying because they didn't have water. But then we saw we could water them and bring them back to life.

ILLÈNE: So that is very empowering to go get water for something that can't get it for itself. Do you think that planting has made you more likely or less likely to be an environmental activist?

MANUELA: I kind of always was because I was for animal rights, so I guess I could add this to that.

ILLÈNE: Yes, animal rights and tree rights go together. Is there something I have not asked you that is important to you about gardening?

MANUELA: There are a lot of things that matter. Well, there is something I have been thinking about because I know I won't be at this school for very long, but these plants will definitely be here, so I was wondering if I were to come back in five years, will they still be like this? Because without us, these plants would not be here.

ILLÈNE: That's true. Do you think you will be able to pass on to the next class the sense of caring for them?

MANUELA: There are always people who care and love planting, so I really hope that someone will keep them alive. It would be really nice to visit the school in ten, forty years from now and see what I have done so long ago still here.

ILLÈNE: Yes, what about the trees you have planted?

MANUELA: That would be lovely, especially forty years from now. They would be gigantic.

ILLÈNE: One of the challenges with annuals, and almost all these [plants they are planting on the roof] are annuals, is that they live one year. The oregano is a perennial. What you are going to be passing on is not so much the plant, but the legacy of doing this.

MANUELA: It would be the legacy or the knowledge of planting and keeping them alive, which is the important part.

ILLÈNE: Would you like to be able to teach someone younger than you to do this so they can do that when you leave?

MANUELA: I would love to, like my little nephew. I would love for him to be planting. It would be so cute to me. I don't know why, but I would just love it! [*Expressed with great enthusiasm*].

ILLÈNE: Maybe you can. Is there a community garden near your house?

MANUELA: I don't think so. And to do a million trees, we had to go to outside the city, a long ways away.

ILLÈNE: But your mom plants inside the house. Maybe you can teach your nephew to plant something in the window.

MANUELA: That sounds very, very good.

❧

Manuela has already begun considering her legacy—the trees and plants she has transplanted and the nephew she can teach to plant. Considering the lifetime of a tree has helped her consider her own contributions on a larger scale.

# 2

## PLANTING TREES, TOMATOES, AND TRANSFORMATION

When the school day ended, Stephen Ritz's students clambered down the six flights of stairs to go home, and he and I left to see some community development projects in the South Bronx and meet one of his students who lives in that community. We went to Hunts Point Riverside Park, an area where Majora Carter, founder of the environmental justice not-for-profit, Sustainable South Bronx, initiated and developed a waterfront green belt on the Bronx River to transform a blighted area and reconnect the South Bronx to the river. I had seen Carter present on her work in the Hunts Point area at the National Green Schools Conference where I also first met Ritz, and Hunts Point Riverside Park had since become a symbol of Sustainable South Bronx's efforts to improve lives in that borough. Ritz's greening efforts with youth link up with many organizations like Sustainable South Bronx that serve young people's need for dynamic after-school education.

The South Bronx is the poorest congressional district in the United States according to the 2014 US census. The Hunts Point neighborhood in the South Bronx is on a peninsula where the East and Bronx Rivers meet. It has a long tradition of boat building and fishing. We visited several projects serving local youth, including Rocking the Boat, where young people learn to build boats and become linked to the area's history. The project is located within a larger center serving the community called José E. Serrano Riverside Campus for Arts and the Environment. Strawberries were flowering at the building's entrance, a welcoming promise to all who enter. Other projects housed within the community center also include a photography center for youth, which offers nutritious snacks to the participants, and programs that involve youth in preparing the food they will eat together during their after-school or weekend activities. The programs exist to provide creative opportunities to youth and create more social justice in the South Bronx.

Ritz works primarily with Hispanic and African American youth because they attend the schools where he teaches in the South Bronx and in East Harlem. Poverty makes their health outlooks worse than those of the general New York populace. The poorest people live in the most environmentally challenged neighborhoods that we were seeing. To clarify, the Bronx is a New York City borough and Hunts Point is a neighborhood within it. East Harlem is a neighborhood within the borough of Manhattan. Ritz made it clear that the work he does teaching youth to plant, care for, harvest, and eat vegetables is both to improve learning outcomes and to support better health habits through healthier eating and the exercise required to grow food.

Mural painted by youth at the José E. Serrano Riverside Campus for Arts and the Environment. Credit: Illène Pevec

As we drove through the South Bronx, Ritz described the high incidence of diabetes and asthma there. He told me that he learned from many public health and planning meetings that the asthma is due, at least in part, to air pollution from heavy truck traffic to the riverside docks, where goods and fresh food go from truck to ship and vice-versa. The Hunts Point Food Distribution Center has three massive components: the Hunts Point Cooperative Meat Market, which occupies forty acres and is the largest meat distribution center in the world; the Hunts Point Terminal Produce Market, which occupies 105 acres; and the Fulton Fish Market, which occupies a 430,000-square-foot facility and is the largest and oldest fresh fish market in the nation (New York City Economic Development Corporation, 2015).

The New York City Department of Health and Mental Hygiene (2013) statistics put numbers to the local problems Ritz described, showing severe health discrepancies between the Bronx and the rest of New York City. The information on cockroaches in the home and pesticides released into the air are included in the health department statistics due to their use being correlated with asthma attacks.

The population in the Bronx is 66 percent Hispanic and 38 percent African American (Bronx-Lebanon Hospital Center, 2013). Nationwide research on diabetes rates for those twenty years and older show that Hispanics have a rate of 12.8 percent, African Americans have a rate of 13.2 percent, and non-Hispanic whites have a rate of 7.6 percent. Native Americans have the highest average adult rate of diabetes at 15.9 percent average (Centers for Disease Control and Prevention, 2014).

**TABLE 2.1.** Poverty Rates and Pest and Pesticide Statistics in New York City and Hunts Point, the Bronx, and East Harlem Boroughs

| Topic | Indicator | Hunts Point | Bronx | East Harlem | New York City |
|---|---|---|---|---|---|
| Social Environment | Population living below twice the poverty level (percent) – 2000 | 69.7 | 51.7 | 63.1 | 39.8 |
| Pests and Pesticide Use | Cockroaches in the home (percent of homes) – 2011 | 47.9 | 37.7 | 42 | 24 |
| | Personal use of pesticide sprays, bombs, or foggers (percent of homes) – 2003 | 55.6 | 44.3 | 56.5 | 34.6 |

© New York City Department of Health and Mental Hygiene (2013)

**TABLE 2.2.** Asthma Hospitalization Statistics in New York City and Hunts Point, the Bronx, and East Harlem Boroughs

| Topic | Indicator | Hunts Point | Bronx | East Harlem | New York City |
|---|---|---|---|---|---|
| Chronic Health Conditions | Asthma hospitalizations among children 0 to 4 years old (rate per 10,000) – 2010 | 201.8 | 144 | 152.6 | 73.7 |
| | Asthma hospitalizations among children 5 to 14 years old (rate per 10,000) – 2010 | 72 | 54.4 | 83.1 | 31.2 |
| | Asthma hospitalizations among youths and adults 15 years and older (age-adjusted rate per 10,000) – 2010 | 70.5 | 51.7 | 74.3 | 24.9 |

© New York City Department of Health and Mental Hygiene (2013)

The mental health statistics also show cause for alarm. In New York City, a self-reporting anonymous health department survey revealed "40% of girls and 24% of boys reported feeling persistently sad for at least two weeks within the past year" (New York City Department of Health and Mental Hygiene, 2008). The survey also reported a racial and ethnic difference in depression rates. Persistent sadness is reported more often among Hispanic girls than girls of other racial or ethnic groups (46 percent versus less than 40 percent). While not as striking as among girls, persistent sadness is also reported more often by Hispanic boys (27 percent) compared to white (20 percent) or black (21 percent) boys (New York City Department of Health and Mental Hygiene, 2008).

A New York City Department of Health and Mental Hygiene (2007) report on diabetes cites these statistics showing the city's health disparities:

- New Yorkers in East Harlem, Williamsburg-Bushwick, and certain parts of the South Bronx are hospitalized for diabetes at ten times the rate of people living on the Upper East Side.
- Residents in the most affected areas also die from diabetes at seven times the rate of New Yorkers in the least affected neighborhoods.
- Among racial and ethnic groups, black New Yorkers have the highest death rate from diabetes, dying at three times the rate of white New Yorkers.

- Approximately 40 percent of New York children are overweight and at risk for diabetes.
- People in lower-income neighborhoods are twice as likely as those in upper-income neighborhoods to have diabetes.

New York declared diabetes an epidemic when the 2011 health department statistics became available in 2013: "5,695 people died from diabetes and related causes in 2011. . . . That amounts to one death every 90 minutes, 16 deaths every day" (Durkin, 2013).

In Chapter 1, Mateo already described his successful efforts to transform his health through gardening. Another young gardener who managed to change his eating habits and health as a result of working with Ritz for several years is Darrell. He was nineteen and in his last year of high school in the Bronx when I met him. He continued working with Ritz after school and on the weekends through the Green Bronx Machine after Ritz left teaching in the Bronx and was teaching in East Harlem. We picked up Darrell after our South Bronx tour. It's the first interview I have done in a car and also the first time another adult has been part of the interview. Ritz was listening and adding information while he drove us in a steady rain to Bissel Park, a place where the Green Bronx Machine transformed a dangerous wasteland into an urban oasis.

ILLÈNE: I'm interested in the experiences young people have when they are gardening and how gardening impacts young people. How do your experiences affect you?

DARRELL: They seem to impact me in a very good way really. For most young people that would actually do this sort of stuff, they may not really be interested, but I say if you actually give it a chance, it can really change not only your life, but the way you see things. I am going to tell you the truth. Before I met Mr. Ritz and did all this green technology stuff, I was just a regular dude, smoking weed, doing a lot of other stuff, just being normal kind of, but when I met Mr. Ritz and got into his program, all that kind of changed. I started eating healthier and started doing things differently; quit the stuff I needed to quit. I am nineteen now; I was sixteen then. Now, it seems to be a work in progress; the results are as you can see me now. It can really change a lot in people.

RITZ: Darrell is graduating from high school. I am so proud of him. He recently got a ninety-two on a state exam [the New York State Regents Exam]. We aspire for a sixty-five, but Darrell got a ninety-two. Sorry to interject, but I am the proud stepparent.

ILLÈNE: Congratulations!

DARRELL: Thank you.

ILLÈNE: One of the things that has interested me about gardening is how your senses engage in gardening because people talk about the changes that happen inside them and I wonder if part of it has do with our senses. Do you notice, for instance, if you smell more when you are gardening?

DARRELL: Well, that is a very good question to ask. I haven't really wondered that myself to tell you the truth, but now that you mentioned it, ever since I started gardening, I noticed that I was able to smell more things that I don't usually smell, try more things that I don't usually try, and that would be in the category of taste or seeing, and we actually saw more beautiful gardens and other things that we have been doing in our past programs and stuff.

ILLÈNE: And what about touching things? You are working with your hands when you garden.

DARRELL: We usually touch, like there would be a few times we were gardening and we would touch things that we had not touched before. Like if we are gardening and planting flowers, we would touch certain seeds that we never touched before, and there would be soil we had never touched before and these bat feces that you put in the soil to make the plants grow faster and easier. I thought that was pretty fascinating.

ILLÈNE: When you have a little plant that you are going to transplant and put in the ground and you dig a hole and put in a plant and pat the soil, what is the emotional response that you have to that planting experience?

DARRELL: My emotional response is that I feel great and I am relieved that I got that done, and I feel that I did a good job and that, in a way, I feel that I changed something that is going to alternate the future in a way.

RITZ: He is one of the most prolific planters, and I am going to interject here because Darrell is so humble, but what Darrell can do now in an hour, five or six of those kids can't do in two hours. He is that prolific. Darrell planted green walls in Dr. Oz's office.

ILLÈNE: Really, did you get to meet Dr. Oz? Was that fun?

DARRELL: Yeah, he was very fun actually. He is a very interesting man. Very interesting.

RITZ: Darrell plants with a degree of love and accuracy that is really wild. You can do it and knock it out or you can do it with love and it looks really outrageous. He is my go-to planter guy.

ILLÈNE: Would you say you do it with love?

DARRELL: Actually, yeah, at this point, I would use that word. All living things, plants in a way are living things, and we should treat them with love and care. And I think that is a good thing to learn. We had to learn it and we needed to learn it so that we would get the job done better. Because I heard that if you do things with love and care on the job, you get things done faster and better. That makes me feel that I am doing a good job, a job well done. And I hope I do many more the same way.

RITZ: Tell her about the green, man. You can be honest.

DARRELL: Well, yeah, we mostly do this not only to change the environment, but we also do it for the money in our own pockets because this economy is about money, and we got to do what we can to contribute and do what we gotta do.

RITZ: Darrell does the kind of quality work that you can really command a wage for. He has built apartments with Jim [a contractor with whom Ritz collaborates to get job training for the youth]. He has renovated housing, put in windows, flooring, glass work. And that is the blessing of it for me. Listen, I don't expect him to be a farmer, but I am thrilled that when he has to farm, he does a great job that I can depend upon him to represent the kind of work we do well. More importantly, he has gotten the skill set that really enables him enough to go out and make a living wage because he does a good enough job, because he cares enough about it to do it well. He really loves the construction work that he does with Jim and some of the people who work with him in Harlem and the Bronx that really are changing not only landscapes, but mindsets and lives because they are building housing from what was once abandoned and forlorn and desolate for affordable housing for more New Yorkers, so that is amazing and what it is all about, but that is a whole other preaching.

ILLÈNE: So you have learned a lot of job skills from getting engaged with the gardening and with this building work? Do you find that it's a similar process for you because you are working with your hands with living plants and then with the boards from what was once a living plant or is it pretty different?

DARRELL: Yeah, it's kind of like a little bit of both. If you look at it, you were to have, say you are working with construction, like we work with Jim to build apartments. It's kind of like the same process as planting with the dirt, the soil, as in construction. We get the tools and the other things, and we get to work, but once the job is done, they are both pretty much done and completed. But I think they are both pretty much the same, but it is a different job set.

ILLÈNE: But you still need to take care of a plant.

DARRELL: Yeah, sure, but if you build something, you have to take care of it, protect it from damage.

ILLÈNE: Of course. I am going to focus on the gardening because my book is on gardening. Do you notice that when you are gardening, whether it changes your capacity to focus?

DARRELL: Not only does it change my capacity to focus, but it actually makes me more eligible to actually do it and get it done in a certain amount of time.

ILLÈNE: Do you think you focus more when you are gardening?

DARRELL: Yeah, of course. Usually when I garden, I focus a lot more and I seem to catch things that other people would not catch for some reason. It isn't some reason, I just know what I am doing. I have had a lot of practice. We went through training, advanced training, to get to where we are today.

ILLÈNE: Do you notice that it carries over into the next thing you do. Say you have been planting a living wall and then you have to go home and do homework because you have a test the next day, do you find it carries over to your homework?

DARRELL: Yeah, exactly, that is exactly what it does. Farming takes a lot of precision and thinking. It takes a lot of strategizing as well. As for homework, it's kind of like the same principle, but you don't need as much focus as when you are gardening or filling a green wall, for instance. It kind of improves my thinking a lot, so when I go to school and I do my work, it's just easy.

ILLÈNE: Have you noticed how gardening impacts your stress levels?

DARRELL: Not exactly. I have not really been thinking about that. The only thing I do is when I go gardening, the only thing I think, "I have to get the job done and do it right."

ILLÈNE: Some people when they feel pressure to get a job done, they feel stressed.

DARRELL: I am not really going to lie. Sometimes I do feel a little bit of stress because we got to represent and do what we have to do and make sure people recognize it and know how good we are. If you were to plant something horribly and then present it to somebody, that is going to make you look kind of bad and make people think that you don't know how to do your job right even though you have been doing it for a lot of years. And that same thing a lot of people would worry about, doing your job right. That is a lot of pressure and it is common for a lot of people depending on what job they do.

ILLÈNE: What are your relaxation levels when you are gardening compared to when you are not?

DARRELL: Relaxation levels would be quite different because when we are actually working, my relaxation level is kind of low because we got to make sure we do it right. It takes a lot of energy and focus, so we don't really have that much time to relax. But then when we are done, relaxation levels go up, and then we leave and carry on and relax.

ILLÈNE: Now, when you did this with Mr. Ritz, was it during school or after school?

DARRELL: It was an after-school program and sometimes during school when events would come. Now, it's just after school because Mr. Ritz is not there anymore.

RITZ: I want to give you some context [*indicates to the old neighborhood that we are driving through*]. This is Wakefield, one of the more forlorn areas. It was all factories, but those have been abandoned for years. It is the North Bronx, borders the poor side of Westchester. What is a felony in Westchester is a misdemeanor here. So people did egregious things here. There is a bunch of liquor, crack, and prostitution. This is Bissel Avenue, a discontinued street. Over four hundred people were living here. We took out thirty containers of garbage and all this was abandoned and burnt. But now it has become the better side of town. I wish I had bought a house here. We changed everything here. We took fire hydrants and broke them open. After 9/11, the city put in a sixteen-foot-high fence, and now that I know about vertical farming, I have big plans for a big garden.

*[We arrive at Bissel Park. We get out in the rain to look at the living walls Ritz, Darrell, and other youth have planted. Chickens scratch in their safe pen in the park area resplendent with a gazebo and blooming fruit trees. We examine a huge fence that begs for vertical farming and for now, just separates the community garden from an outdoor storage facility for old Metro railway cars. I continue to speak with Darrell.]*

ILLÈNE: Do you think gardening has changed your environmental awareness?

DARRELL: Actually, yeah, it actually did. I think it is going to change a lot of other people's awareness as well. When they go out of their house and when they go anywhere, they actually see something. It may be different, but once they get used to it, they are going to like it.

ILLÈNE: You mean a garden?

DARRELL: Yeah, a garden.

ILLÈNE: So if someone threatened what you planted there, would you write the mayor and stand up for it?

DARRELL: Yeah, of course. Me and Mr. Ritz are going to tear down the walls. We worked too hard for someone to come and take it all away. I mean, that's just one: being selfish, and two: not thinking about it. If you can't give it a chance, you are just ignorant! You have to give something a chance, and you might like it. If you don't like it, get used to it.

ILLÈNE: Are there any other activities you do that give you a similar feeling, like the sense of accomplishment, that you have been discussing with me?

DARRELL: Well, in between gardening and the program Mr. Ritz explained to you about construction, I actually get that same exact feelings when I am building in windows and screwing in light bulbs and doing other things because that used to be an old abandoned building. Now, we turned it into an actual building where people can go in there and live their lives like normal people do, give them a roof over their heads.

ILLÈNE: If someone from the New York school board had asked if they should put gardening and construction programs into other schools, what would you say?

DARRELL: Most definitely; 100 percent yes. I think the schools need it! The kids need it! Obesity is a very serious thing. Diabetes is even worse. But this can actually change that. It can change obesity rates, crime rates, diabetes rates, etc. I think that if they put this in high schools, a lot more children would be happy with what they have and what they eat.

ILLÈNE: You talked about how you changed your eating habits. Did you used to eat a lot of junk food?

DARRELL: Yep. I used to eat a lot of junk food. I used to be a fan of pizza, chocolate, especially chocolate, mostly chocolate. I used to eat a lot of chocolate, chips, all that kind of stuff back in the day. I mean, all that shit. I used to eat it every day. But now I eat it once a month.

ILLÈNE: So what do you eat now?

DARRELL: I eat more fruits, vegetables. I would tell my mom to go outside and buy me apples, pears, oranges, broccoli, well, sometimes broccoli, but you know I got to get the greens.

ILLÈNE: So have your mom's eating habits changed too?

DARRELL: Oh yeah, of course. She is always drinking water, always thinking about the healthy stuff. She wants me to do the same thing, I mean.

ILLÈNE: Did you influence her or did she influence you?

DARRELL: It was a little bit of both. I kind of told her more things. Then she told me things. It was kind of a switch thing. But back then, she told me to always eat healthy. Diabetes is a serious thing. You don't want to get that because it is going to mess up your life. I am now aware of that 100 percent because of this program. If it wasn't for Mr. Ritz, I would still be at home now sitting in my bed eating me some chocolate and drinking some hot chocolate.

ILLÈNE: So the two of you have changed together?

DARRELL: Yeah. We learned from each other and that is what makes us as powerful as we are now.

RITZ: I do not want to be called fat by the kids. That is what it came to for me. Well, there are a lot of things.

ILLÈNE: What is it like for you to see a grownup totally change his eating habits?

DARRELL: I mean, it's like, yeah, man! You gotta do what you gotta do. That's awesome right there. Plus, Mr. Ritz lost a lot of weight. He bring sexy back, you know what I say.

RITZ: I am bringing sexy back! [Laughs.]

ILLÈNE: Have you lost weight? [Darrell looks very healthy.]

DARRELL: Yeah, of course. I drink water every day. I mostly hit the gym four times a week mostly. The gym is in my school, so you can say every day. You know, I am just trying to lose weight, be healthy, and change a lot of things.

ILLÈNE: How are your energy levels? Have you noticed a difference?

DARRELL: I noticed a huge amount because back then if you eat a lot of junk food, it reduces your energy; you can't do a lot because you have that weight on you. But if you get rid of that weight and start eating healthy, your energy, your stamina, will increase dramastically! [*Darrell invents this word to emphasize his point.*]

ILLÈNE: How about your thinking capacity?

DARRELL: My thinking capacity has increased a lot. I mean, more than usual I would say. I would say it is all because of the eating habits. The eating habits can change so many things.

ILLÈNE: And exercise? They go together.

DARRELL: Eating and exercise; that's two components that everyone needs.

ILLÈNE: So have you ever seen anyone in your family garden?

DARRELL: Well, we are mostly a Caribbean family. When I went to my home country, Antigua, they used to plant a whole bunch of stuff to make coffee. They used to plant other stuff as well. I have seen a lot of people in my home country plant stuff to eat or to make their yard look nice.

ILLÈNE: Did you see anyone in your family plant, like your grandparents?

DARRELL: I seen my uncle, mostly my uncles really, and my older cousins. I used to see them go outside every morning to check the plants, make sure everything is good. They take a few beans off to make coffee. In the afternoon, they check it again. Then they water every few weeks or once a week depending on what they are planting. I see it, and then I learned from it as well. I actually picked up some things before I met Mr. Ritz about planting and stuff, but I never really applied it to my mind till I met him, you know.

ILLÈNE: So then he gave you a way to do it here in New York. We were talking a little about teaching other kids. When you have new kids come into the program, do you teach them?

DARRELL: When we have new kids come into the program, I will be glad to show them what to do so that then they can pass it on from generation to generation.

RITZ: A few weeks ago, he came and taught some of the kids that you met today. He was kind enough and some of the kids in the first cohort were kind enough and came and met us in Brook Park and also planted those walls that are up here now. If those kids saw those, they would be shocked. We planted those tomatoes and they were this big [*shows me with his hands a plant a few inches tall and points to the plants that are now perhaps fifteen inches tall*].

ILLÈNE: That was three weeks ago! What do you feed your plants?

RITZ: Kelp and seagull and bat guano. That's the beauty of it.

ILLÈNE: Wow! I have been feeding my plants kelp, but I better get to a cave!

RITZ: Elephant poop too. I have a hook up with the Bronx Zoo for elephant poop.

ILLÈNE: I have noticed that you and Mr. Ritz have a close relationship. Has this gardening work connected you with other people too? Has it helped your connections to others working with him?

DARRELL: It has, I will say this. It has improved my connections with other human beings. Before this program, I was not really connecting to anyone really. But ever since this program, I have been connecting to other people, getting to know them, teaching them how to do this right with love and care and determination. Eventually, it will pass on from person to person, people to people, group to group.

ILLÈNE: So it has been very profound for you then. It has connected you to plants and people?

DARRELL: Yeah, plants, people, that is for sure!

Tomatoes planted by the East Harlem students in Bissel Park living wall.
Credit: Illène Pevec

ILLÈNE: What is the meaning of gardening for you?

DARRELL: The meaning of gardening for me is just change, revolution, and evolution! I mean, mostly evolution. Because the plants will grow, expand, and eventually the world will be green as long as we do what we have to do and we do it right!

ILLÈNE: Is there anything I have not asked you about that you have gained from this experience?

DARRELL: What I need to say is something I learned from another person: "Don't knock it till you try it." So with that said, I think that people should try this, and I know without a doubt, I would actually put money on it, that you would actually not only be healthier, but you will gain more skills and you will want to teach others depending on if you want to or not. But I would suggest that if you do so, that it will expand. So I think this would actually be a very good thing for other people to know; not only young people, but older people as well who have not attempted to do this. Being healthy is a very important thing. It's a hard process, but you gotta do what you gotta do.

☙

Darrell touched me deeply as he openly shared his personal life transformations. He and his mother have improved their eating habits together as a result of Darrell's engagement with gardening. The energy Ritz pours out to Darrell and in creating gardens that support a dynamic learning environment for Darrell and the other youth to discover their talents and develop their abilities has helped Darrell move from feeling disconnected from people and the natural world to feeling well connected to both people and nature and responsible to both. His academic success has been dramatic and probably speaks in part to the benefits of collaborative learning (Willis, 2007) as well as to having a terrific mentor and teacher in Ritz.

We made a quick visit in pouring rain to Brook Park, where the East Harlem students planted trees during their spring intensive week with Darrell and Ritz and some of the other Green Bronx Machine youth. Since I give each youth I interview a $10 gift card to a full-service grocery store as a thank you to them for their time and there is not a full-service grocery store near the East Harlem high school, Ritz drove me to a Super Target to buy the gift cards. I gave one to Darrell to thank him, and Ritz and Darrell took me to a subway station, where I plunged from the world of parks and gardens and into the underground. The intense New York noise, traffic, trains, and horns makes the quiet in Bissel and Brook Parks even more precious to anyone lucky enough to spend time helping create and then enjoy their peace and beauty.

# 3
# THE SUSTAINABLE TECHNOLOGY EFFECT

The following day, I walked across the park again to East Harlem to interview several more students in Ritz's class. For two boys that I interviewed, Eduardo and Damian, both aged seventeen, I decided to order their phrases into a poem format. These poems express in the students' exact words, minus my questions, what they said to me in their roof-top garden. Until their experience working with Ritz and their classmates over the last few weeks, these boys had no prior gardening experience.

The Green Bronx Machine chickens that Eduardo fed. **Credit: Illène Pevec**

## Trying to Make Our Living and City Better than How It Is Now

*Doing my part, which is planting*
*As many plants as I can plant, either me*
*Helping myself or helping the young kids*
*Coming up to do the same things as I am doing.*
*Immersion week, I planted three trees,*
*And I fed the chickens.*
*I felt accomplished that I actually*
*Planted one tree in my whole life.*
*There's more fresh air because plants give you oxygen.*
*You don't feel as tired as you do in the classroom*
*Where you just feel like sleeping,*
*It's so hot or something!*
*When you are with the plants, like cool.*
*I am actually working.*
*I work in a restaurant called McVern's on 101st*
*I actually want to be a chef when I grow up.*
*Gardening is a great preparation*
*To be a chef, very practical.*
*When you are outside, there is more fresh air*
*So you feel relaxed.*
*When you are in class,*
*There is no air, just artificial air.*
*So it is pretty much better to be outside.*
*We have like twenty-three containers of these,*
*Whereas on other roofs, there are none.*
*So maybe we can then plant that roof over there,*
*And then some more, and cover the whole United States.*
*—Eduardo, 17*

## Yes, I Like Getting Involved with the Planet, the Earth.

*When I am planting, I make sure*
*I am seeing how to make everything*
*All together into one,*
*And then actually do it.*
*I felt good. I was actually doing something with the group*
*And for the school, and it makes you feel good. Yeah,*
*We have more of a bond 'cause we all are together*
*Doing the same thing, the same job,*
*So we actually connect more.*
*I get calm. You can't rush into things when you are planting.*
*You have to wait and let it grow and all that with patience.*
*I was already calm from doing all the planting. That's why,*
*When I go to do my homework,*
*I just go do it.*
*I am learning how to actually get*
*Everything together like planting-wise*
*For the planting wall. I am learning*
*How to actually put the plants*
*Into the wall without hurting myself*
*Or doing anything wrong,*
*And I won't mess it up!*
*I think it is going to help me change eating.*
*I have seen Steve [Ritz] before he started*
*Eating vegetables, and he was really big.*
*And now he is really skinny. I want to be like that:*
*Stop eating fast food, getting more*
*Involved in eating more fruits and vegetables*
*Because I like doing more sports,*
*And I am hoping that will help*
*With my stamina and my agility*
*To move around quicker.*

*Around where people have plants*
*And trees, it looks so peaceful.*
*And when you are somewhere else,*
*It looks like everything is loud and like it is crazy.*
*To me, gardening means creating*
*Something that was never there before.*
*Like starting something totally new*
*And changing peoples' lives.*
*The more you garden, when you sell*
*The fruits and vegetables,*
*The people get healthier.*
*Like making big meals with those,*
*Like figuring out ways how to make meals*
*That are similar to meat, but are healthy for you.*
*And we will have a greener planet.*
*Ever since I started doing this,*
*I started being more careful*
*With how I sort the garbage*
*And all that. When I see people*
*Littering around, I notice that is*
*Bad for the planet.*
*—Damian, age 17*

## VALUING LIFE

Damian and Eduardo, similarly to Darrell, Mateo, Bradley, and Manuela, now care more for their community and their planet's well-being. They enjoy working with their peers, want to eat better food, and want to plant vegetables and trees in parks, on rooftops, and along tall fences to change lives! They experience peace as they participate in transformation.

Weinstein, Przybylski, and Ryan (2009) conducted four separate experiments to measure the psychological impact on people of exposure to nature and exposure to urban, human-made environments. These studies measured individuals' intrinsic aspirations, which are goals that value inner meaning, such as caring for other living beings; extrinsic aspirations, such as gaining power and money; and autonomy, the ability to speak up and make decisions in harmony with one's values. The studies done in laboratory environments used slides of nature, slides of urban or human-built scenes, questionnaires to measure intrinsic and extrinsic aspirations and autonomy, and a game involving giving away money to measure generosity. When people saw slides of nature or were in a room with plants, the studies showed that exposure to nature actually promoted intrinsic aspiration and, therefore, more concern for caring for nature and others, making connections, and being generous to others (Weinstein, Przybylski, and Ryan, 2009, 1326). Exposure to urban environments was shown to do the opposite: people showed increased extrinsic aspirations, or a valuing of money and power, when exposed to environments lacking nature (ibid.). More specifically, Weinstein, Przybylski, and Ryan (2009, 1327) found:

> Those more immersed in natural settings were more generous, whereas those immersed in non-natural settings were less likely to give. Feelings of autonomy and nature relatedness were responsible for the willingness to give to others, indicating that these experiences facilitated a willingness to promote others' interests as well as one's own. In other words, autonomy and relatedness encouraged participants to focus on their intrinsic values for relationships and community rather than on personal gain.

The urban gardening students confirm those four studies' findings in a real-world setting. The youth relate that working with Ritz and plants and creating parks and growing plant walls have increased their ability and desire to connect with and value life and health for themselves and others. Their laboratory is the inner city and they are making it a more caring place to occupy. And, as they have said, this opportunity also helps them to graduate.

Graduation rates in New York City were expected to take a dive in 2012 when the city instituted a graduation requirement wherein all students must pass five Regents Exams with a minimum score of sixty-five in different subject areas. This is the exam that Ritz referred to when he proudly told me that Darrell got a score of ninety-two. According to the *New York Times*, the rate of high school students completing graduation requirements within four years actually remained relatively steady, dropping only one percent in 2012 (Gogolak, 2013).

The New York City public school system requires competitive exams and interviews for entry into the best public high schools. Ritz works with students who do not get into those "best" schools and who are failing or in danger of dropping out. His Sustainable Technologies class combines science with a green job orientation and incorporates practical skills with basic biology and ecology. He designed the program to give students an experience with successfully growing food and also to support healthy eating.

Anthony, aged seventeen, discussed his hopes for the future and why Ritz has been such a good teacher for him. Like Darrell, he was failing before he entered the Sustainable Technologies class that includes gardening. Anthony candidly assessed Ritz's teaching effectiveness in this next interview. Anthony spoke volumes about what youth need in order to move from failure to success. Research in positive youth development supports Ritz's efficacy with students: he provides mutual respect and positive expectations for good performance (Catalano et al. 2004). Ritz's class had begun with a week's intensive gardening at Bissel and Brook Parks.

ANTHONY: Right now, the way everything is going, I am enjoying it. I am having fun. I am getting to watch, like, plants grow. I am learning how they grow as well. I am learning new stuff about plants. And you know, Steve [Ritz], he is a good teacher.

ILLÈNE: What makes a good teacher?

ANTHONY: He is respectful towards children, and I have respect for him. He is funny. He has a good sense of humor. He likes to joke around, but when it is time to get serious, he gets serious. When it is time to work, we get working.

ILLÈNE: Why did you sign up for this class?

ANTHONY: I thought it would be good for me to work with my friends, my peers, to stay off the streets doing negative things. That is why I signed up for this.

ILLÈNE: Were you interested before you signed up in learning how to plant? Is it something you had ever thought about before, learning how to plant trees and vegetables and flowers?

ANTHONY: Not exactly. I wasn't really interested. At first, I was like, "What are we going to be doing?" When he told me, I thought I could give it a shot. It's something new for me. I never grew no plants of any kind. And it's fun by the looks of it. I don't know how to put it, I feel good about myself, yeah, for planting things, and for staying off the streets and from doing bad stuff on the streets.

ILLÈNE: Had you been getting into some things that would get you into trouble?

ANTHONY: No, not at all. But it will prevent me from going to those.

ILLÈNE: Did you start in the first week when everyone went over to plant trees?

ANTHONY: Yeah.

ILLÈNE: Was that the first time you ever planted a tree? What did that feel like?

ANTHONY: Yeah. It felt like a whole lot of work. Digging a hole to then, like… I didn't know there were so many steps to plant a tree. I thought it was just dig a hole and put the tree in and just watch it grow and plant it. That's what I thought. I learned you have to keep the tree in a certain way so that it can grow straight. Make sure the roots spread out. Make sure the hole is not like that deep or wide. And yeah, I have to treat the tree with respect basically, yeah.

ILLÈNE: Has being in this program given you the opportunity to know your classmates in a new way, your peers?

ANTHONY: In some ways, yeah, because there were some students I had not talked to, but now I talk to them. But in other ways, no, because there are some friends of mine that are already here that I talk to. So it is kind of in the middle.

ILLÈNE: Is there any other class that you have where you all work together on a single goal like planting?

ANTHONY: Not a class, more like the school because we are all working on graduating from high school. That could be sort of an answer to your question as well. I think everybody would like to finish high school and go off to college and get a degree and get a successful job and have a successful life 'cause that is something I would like to do right now. I would like to have a successful life, start a family of my own when I get older, finish high school and college. Yeah, I would like to have a successful life, a successful job, money in my pockets and when I have a family, support my children.

ILLÈNE: Has this experience of planting a tree and learning all there is to help a tree to grow given you better perspective on what it takes to have a successful life too?

ANTHONY: Yeah. It helps me because it takes dedication. And I care for the tree so it has, like, helped me in a way for my future children. I will have to treat them with care and dedication. I will have to dedicate myself to them. Anything that they want, I will have to go and get for them. That is basically it.

ILLÈNE: Have you seen anyone in your family garden before you took this class? Your parents or grandparents?

ANTHONY: No, not really. Nobody from my family.

ILLÈNE: So you are the first one. You can teach your family. Do you feel like you are learning new skills from this class?

ANTHONY: Yeah. I am learning how to take dedication and care for the trees. I am learning how to work together with my peers. We all have our eyes set to one goal: hopefully, to graduate high school and go off to college.

ILLÈNE: Do you notice when you are gardening, whether your senses are engaged when you are gardening? Your sense of smell or sight or touch?

ANTHONY: With my eye senses, I see beautiful plants and trees. With my sense of smell, not really that much. I haven't smelled the flowers and plants.

ILLÈNE: Because you just have not bent down and put your nose in them?

ANTHONY: That and also my nose senses have been kind of fooling around with me so I don't have a good sense of smell when the seasons change. I have a cold or I get sick sometimes. Once I start getting better, I will be able to smell the plants. Tasting the plants, I am not really sure I will be tasting any plants.

ILLÈNE: But what about what you just planted? You just planted a lot of cucumbers and broccoli today.

ANTHONY: Well, I will eat it when it's fully grown, but not now at the moment because it is not fully there. Then it will be healthy and make me healthy.

ILLÈNE: Do you talk about food in this class and the difference between eating vegetables and junk food?

ANTHONY: Well, yeah. We talk about how many calories it takes for you to get sick off of junk food and how healthy these plants can be when they are fully grown.

ILLÈNE: Has it influenced your eating habits even though you have not yet eaten what you are growing?

ANTHONY: Yes, in some sort of way, yeah, because I started eating more salad. My family, we're Hispanic. So I have to eat, like, chicken at some point, some junk food at some point.

ILLÈNE: What do you mean by "have to?"

ANTHONY: I don't mean have to; I would like to want to. I was born eating junk food, basically. So I don't know how to put it. I have to, like, eat it sometimes because it just tastes good. But I get to burn the calories down. I exercise. Keep myself fit and in good shape. And these plants, I can't wait till they are fully grown so I can take a little bite out of one of them. Broccoli is my favorite kind of vegetables. Yeah, I love broccoli.

ILLÈNE: And it is one of the healthiest vegetables.

ANTHONY: Yeah, so I have heard. I didn't know that. It is something I have learned also.

ILLÈNE: Broccoli has a lot of antioxidants. So, in general, how do you feel when you are done gardening?

ANTHONY: I feel like a mess because my hair is all messed up and I am sweatier. But if I would not feel like that, I would feel I haven't done nothing. I feel good when I feel like this because that means I did a lot of work. I took my time making these plants as well with my peers, and we just all took the time and dedication to make these plants and to stay off the streets and, like, do nothing bad that we will regret.

ILLÈNE: Does Mr. Ritz talk to you about the importance of staying off the streets and not getting involved in gangs?

ANTHONY: Yeah, sometimes he does. He hasn't talked about it that much. He wants to keep us in a positive mood. He doesn't want it to escalate and get into an argument. It's, like, a yes and a no at the same time.

ILLÈNE: That's an interesting way to put it, "a yes and a no at the same time." I like that expression. He is giving you something "yes" to do so you won't do something "no."

ANTHONY: Yeah.

ILLÈNE: Do you find that gardening outside affects your stress levels?

ANTHONY: It actually keeps me calm. It's been a while that I have been, like, happy, happy because I have been stressed at school. I have been stressed out, depressed because of school because I heard I was not passing. But this class is helping me with my school, and so, like, I am hoping I can pass to the 11th grade and, like, go on to finishing high school and go to college.

ILLÈNE: So it helps you to feel calm and…

ANTHONY: Peaceful and somewhere where I can be myself.

ILLÈNE: Someplace where you can be yourself, that's important, isn't it? Just to be who you are

ANTHONY: And have self-control.

ILLÈNE: Do you find it helps you with your self-control? Do you know why? Can you tell why?

ANTHONY: I really don't know. It's probably because I am outside and not trapped in the classroom. Maybe I am on the roof and it's next to the water, so it keeps me cool on a warm day. And I can just keep myself normal and be normal for a change.

ILLÈNE: Do you have a problem staying calm?

ANTHONY: Yeah, at a young age I had, I still have an anger issue. I first got my anger when my mom and my father separated when I was very young. That was what forced me to get left back in 2nd grade 'cause I started misbehaving at school. I got into a lot of fights.

ILLÈNE: Because you were upset about your parents separating?

ANTHONY: Yeah. I wanted my… I wanted a perfect family. And it was when I was really young. I was in 2nd grade. I was really mad at my mother for throwing him out of the house. And, like, you know, I got over it, but I still get into those moods sometimes 'cause sometimes I think about it; it kind of hurts me because I just want my mother and father to get back.

ILLÈNE: But this has helped you?

ANTHONY: It has helped me and it clears my conscience of doing anything negative.

ILLÈNE: That is very powerful. There is something I studied in environmental psychology called attention restoration theory. What environmental psychologists are learning is that when people have access to plants, to walking in someplace like Central Park, it helps them calm down and relax.

ANTHONY: And it's quiet; it's peaceful.

ILLÈNE: And it helps executive function. What executive function means is decision making, self-control. So you have just explained exactly what these psychologists study; that by doing this work, you feel better, you feel peaceful, and you have more self-control. Do you think that is what happens to you when you are gardening up here?

ANTHONY: Yeah…Yeah!

ILLÈNE: Do you find that carries over after you are done gardening? This is the end of the school day, you don't go to another class, but perhaps you go home to do homework. Do you find this helps you to do your homework if you have been outside?

ANTHONY: Yeah, but sometimes I do my homework before this class. I get to do my homework in class and I get to finish my work and everything. So, basically, I go home and get to relax after a long day at school.

ILLÈNE: What do you do to relax when you go home?

ANTHONY: Basically, I go home, take a shower, watch TV sometimes, play some video games, go on the computer, spend some time with my grandmother. I am living with my grandmother at the moment because I moved out of my mom's house for a little bit because the house was too small, and it was full of women. I am, like, the only boy out of three kids and I am the middle child as well, so it is kind of a pain in the butt dealing with my older sister and my little sister. I like being on my own at points, just me by myself. I like solitude. I don't like the light shining over me. I like to be cool; I like to be in the shadows.

ILLÈNE: Do you ever go to Central Park and walk in the shade?

ANTHONY: Yes, sometimes. When I get the chance to and sometimes I just hang out with friends.

ILLÈNE: You might remember this about attention restoration theory; that when you are not up here working, but you want to feel the calm and happy, it might help to go to Central Park and just take a walk.

ANTHONY: Yeah. I think it is not just Central Park. Parks that are forests, stuff that has plants and trees helps clear the mind of people.

ILLÈNE: It does indeed! What is the meaning of gardening for you?

ANTHONY: I really don't know what the meaning of gardening is for me.

ILLÈNE: What does it mean for you to do this?

ANTHONY: I can't say. Like, what I can say is I think gardening is just like planting plants, making myself feel better, making myself happy, working with peers, working with teachers, having a certain bond with peers and teachers and even sometimes with the plants you can have a bond with.

ILLÈNE: Have you experienced that? Feeling attached to a plant you have worked with?

ANTHONY: No, not yet. But I am guessing that I will sometime in the future.

ILLÈNE: What about the tree you planted?

ANTHONY: Since it is the first tree I have grown, I can say I have some sort of bond with it. It kind of makes me happy.

ILLÈNE: Do you think that planting a tree or these plants has changed your environmental awareness?

ANTHONY: Umm, I think so. I think it has. I am more aware of myself and aware of where I am.

ILLÈNE: Do you think you care more about the environment now?

ANTHONY: Yeah, I care more about the environment. I want to, like, clean up the streets, make this world a better place than it is now, make it a healthier place. Central Park is a historical monument. People go there to, like, stay away, to have their alone time. If they have a pet, they go to a place where they can have fun with their pet.

ILLÈNE: So you would want to protect a natural place that you thought was important?

ANTHONY: Yeah, I would.

ILLÈNE: Do you think you would have had the courage to do this before you took this class?

ANTHONY: I think I wouldn't because I am just one person. I am growing a bond with my peers and my teacher. I think we now are much stronger as a group than alone.

ILLÈNE: If someone from the school board came to talk to you about your experiences gardening because they are thinking of putting in a garden at another school and they asked you if you thought it would be beneficial for other kids, what do you think you would say?

ANTHONY: I would say, yes, because more people would get into it and the more the merrier. Like, if you just make more gardens in other schools, I think more kids would be involved. The world would be a safer, healthier environment.

ILLÈNE: Do you think gardening makes you happy?

ANTHONY: I think it does in some way because it is just fun doing all this hard work because the cause is a good cause. And it's a good—how do you say it?—it is not a waste of time. It is beneficial.

**ILLÈNE:** Have you always lived in the city?

**ANTHONY:** Yeah, always lived in a city.

**ILLÈNE:** Do you have a view of a tree out the window in the apartment where you live now?

**ANTHONY:** Not exactly. I seen other buildings, I seen a little bit of trees, just probably, like, three on our block. In the current house that I am living in right now with my grandmother, we have a little garden for ourselves. It's like grass and trees there. I just like looking out the window sometimes.

**ILLÈNE:** So you can see those things from your window?

**ANTHONY:** I can see the insects go through the trees. I like to study the environment sometimes.

**ILLÈNE:** With this program giving you training, do you think that this is work you might enjoy doing?

**ANTHONY:** I think it would be work I might like doing, yeah. I like to do this.

One pink dianthus in a school roof-garden box. Credit: Anthony

Anthony discusses in the latter part of the interview how he has gained some autonomy, or the ability to act on his values, through this gardening experience that is a real-life version of the university studies on nature exposure relayed earlier (Weinstein, Przybylski, and Ryan, 2009). Anthony mentioned that he experienced feeling calmer and having better self-control due to engaging in the gardening program. Good self-discipline has been shown to predict school success better than IQ scores (Duckworth and Seligman, 2005). Why would time outside working with plants help with self-control?

Psychoevolutionary theory suggests that people experience stress release when in nature or viewing a natural setting perhaps because humans evolved with nature and our parasympathetic system responds to nature positively because we have developed within nature throughout our time on earth. Roger Ulrich (1981), one of the first researchers of psychoevolutionary theory, studied people's stress and recuperative responses when in urban and natural environments by measuring their physiological indicators like blood pressure and need for pain medication post-surgery. The restorative influences of nature, as Ulrich et al. (1991, 201) explain, "involve a shift towards a more positively-toned emotional state, positive changes in physiological activity levels, and these changes are accompanied by sustained attention/intake." This is very important information for those who design and run schools to understand as the physical environment in which children are expected to learn influences their behavior and ability to focus.

Exposure to nature, such as walks in parks or forests, the view outside a window, or even viewing photos of natural areas, has been shown to restore the capacity to focus while urban views and walks have been shown to deplete directed attention (Berman, Jonides, and Kaplan, 2008; Faber Taylor and Kuo, 2008; Hartig et al. 2003; Kaplan, 1995). The brain's executive function area is involved with both directed attention and self-regulation. A recent study by Kaplan and Berman (2010) showed that when directed attention is fatigued, self-regulation also does not work as well. Time outside during the school day could restore both executive function and self-regulation for tired youth and support them in completing a day's work more successfully.

Self-regulation is one of the most important attributes for optimal human flourishing (Seligman, 2011) and an important trait for children to succeed in school, along with perseverance, curiosity, conscientiousness, and optimism (Duckworth and Seligman, 2005). Each of these young gardeners discuss experiencing some or all of these important traits for success as they work collectively to plant trees and vegetables to improve their communities and give new purpose and meaning to their own lives.

Research in the Netherlands with adult gardeners showed that cortisol, the hormone related to stress, decreased after a half hour spent gardening. The gardeners reported positive moods, offering "experimental evidence that gardening can promote relief from acute stress" (van den Berg and Custers, 2011, 3). Given that many students interviewed report experiencing high stress levels at school, we need similar physiological research with youth gardeners. If adolescent gardeners showed less cortisol post-gardening, as could be expected, this evidence could influence school systems to provide access to gardening during the school day. If time outside in green space were made possible, perhaps improvements in health and learning would ensue.

A study of nine hundred Massachusetts schools adjusted for socioeconomic status showed that schools with greener environments around them have higher performing students (Wu et al. 2014). Research in England in poor urban environments, such as those encountered in East Harlem and the South Bronx, has shown that cortisol levels in adults correlate to access or lack of access to green space and can be a good biomarker for judging how human stress levels fluctuate in relation to different physical environments, with urban environments stimulating higher stress hormone levels (Ward Thompson et al. 2012).

These New York City youth all live in high-density, poor urban areas. They are especially in need of access to green areas to help them relax and focus their attention. Anthony discussed feeling relieved and happier in the park and while gardening, as did his other classmates. What Stephen Ritz offers these young students is not only a Sustainable Technologies class, but a time for breathing deeply and working with their hands with living plants—a pathway to feeling calm and accomplishing what they need to do to succeed.

East Harlem charter school students in roof garden. Credit: Illène Pevec

# 4

# THE CHALLENGES THESE GARDENERS FACE

Being an adolescent has many challenges, and being a youth of color in the United States has even more. In 2013, only 39 percent of black children under seventeen lived with two parents compared to 65 percent of Hispanic children, 77 percent of white, and 85 percent of Asian. The statistics for children living with only a mother and no father present are 51 percent of black children, 28 percent of Hispanic, 15 percent of white, and 11 percent of Asian. Moreover, statistics in the United States show a direct correlation between single-mother households and poverty. In 2013, the median income for families led by a single mother was about $35,154, about 46 percent the median national income ($76,509) for married-couple families (DeNavas-Walt and Proctor, 2014, 6). In 2013, 45.3 million Americans lived in poverty, 14.5 percent of the total population and 19.9 percent of all children (ibid., 13).

The young New Yorkers in Stephen Ritz's Sustainable Technologies class are all Hispanic or African American, and none have a father at home. There are 21 million children being raised in the United States without a father (Vespa, Lewis, and Kreider, 2013, 23), and poverty rates are highest for families led by mothers of color with no father present: 42.5 percent for African Americans (DeNavas-Walt and Proctor, 2014, 47) and 41.6 percent for Hispanics (ibid, 49). Poverty has a negative effect on graduation rates with only 70 percent of youth living in poverty graduating from high school (National Center for Educational Statistics, 2015a). Ritz's program addresses a myriad of social and economic challenges to help youth in this demographic to graduate.

Jamal, aged seventeen, joined me on the roof garden bench while the class continued planting and described the common ground he shares with his classmates.

The view from the East Harlem school garden on the roof.  Credit: Illène Pevec

**ILLÈNE:** How did you decide to be in this Sustainable Technologies class?

**JAMAL:** Well, I talked with my principal, but I didn't actually decide. He told me about it and said that sustainable careers is helping you get a career, that you would like it, and we would be planting, and it would help us with our grades and stuff like that. I decided I am going to look it out, and I actually like it. School wise, it's helping me with my grades. It's easier.

**ILLÈNE:** School is easier now that you are doing this? Why do you think that is the case?

**JAMAL:** I don't know. For some reason, for the past school years that I have been going to school, I have been in small groups like this. I work better because everybody in my group, we all are the same—people who all have problems with school. We don't threaten nobody. We work together as a team. It's helpful actually. It's helpful for a lot of people because a lot of people's grades are messed up. In this program, our grades have gone up very high. And we do more work than in any other class.

**ILLÈNE:** Do you like the physical hands-on engagement with work?

**JAMAL:** Yeah, I like hands-on work. I learn better like that.

ILLÈNE: Most people learn better like that. That's great you have a chance to do it that way. You have only been doing this for a few weeks, is that right?

JAMAL: Actually, in the garden, today is only my second day.

ILLÈNE: You didn't take part in the one-week immersion earlier this spring?

JAMAL: In enrichment [week]? No! I was in math for enrichment week. And that was cool. Math is everywhere. We did the math on animals. We watched movies that had math. What else? We did class work inside. We had this competition to see who could make it to the last stage before enrichment week is over and everybody didn't make it. Nobody made it to ten. People made it to seven, nine, eight.

ILLÈNE: Can you see any opportunities to learn math in the garden?

JAMAL: Yeah, a lot of ways. How tall the plants are supposed to be, what angles the plants are supposed to be in, how far apart the plants are supposed to be from each other. You can start weighing the food once you start harvesting. That will be exciting.

ILLÈNE: So this is only your second day?

JAMAL: With the gardening, but I have been in the class for a couple of weeks.

ILLÈNE: Have you ever done gardening somewhere else?

JAMAL: Yeah, with my stepgrandma. She has plants all over the house. I help her water the plants. Or if she buys new plants, I help her plant them.

ILLÈNE: How does it make you feel when you plant?

JAMAL: Open because plants are not like locked in anywhere. They are open and wild. They are open outdoors. They are not trapped in a box or trapped in a cage where they can't get out like animals are. They can grow. I see plants as life. Like, they are open. They can do anything they want. They can die if they feel like it, or they can grow. I see that. I see plants as life actually. I see plants as life itself.

ILLÈNE: How does it affect you to work with life itself?

JAMAL: In a good way. It is okay.

ILLÈNE: When you are gardening, do you notice the things you smell?

JAMAL: Yeah, certain smells of the plants that are strong, that are light, or certain smells of plants smell funny, they smell good, they stink. The sizes of the plants; certain plants are very small, certain plants are very big.

ILLÈNE: How do the different smells make you feel?

JAMAL: Emotion-wise, it makes me feel happy sometimes. If I smell plants that don't smell right, it makes me wonder what kind of plant this is. If I smell plants that stink, I have a stink attitude afterwards. Yeah, I don't know, it just makes me upset because if I smell something that makes my stomach work, it don't make me feel right.

ILLÈNE: You said that all of this helps you work together. Is it kind of like team building?

JAMAL: Yeah. This here is like a program my dad started before he passed away. It's called Youth Build. They come together and get children and, like, wronged kids that had a hard time in their life and don't want to go to school anymore, and they send them there. They help you—help get a job; get a house; they help you get your high school diploma; they help you do a lot of things that you can't do on your own at the time. I think this is sort of like that. And, like, everybody had a hard time in life, and it seems like gardening is helping them with it. So if they had a hard time in their life and they have friends or somebody they know who had a hard time, then they come together and do stuff like this.

ILLÈNE: So your dad started a program similar to this to help kids, here in Harlem?

JAMAL: It's actually everywhere. He started it in Indiana where he lived with his wife, my step-mom, and then it branched off to other states, like [Washington,] DC, New York, Virginia.

ILLÈNE: You must be very proud of your dad.

JAMAL: Uh huh. He's smart. A smart guy, very smart.

ILLÈNE: And it sounds like he is very caring also to do this.

JAMAL: Plus, he had been in prison. So after I was born, he changed his life around. I am glad he did it.

ILLÈNE: That's wonderful! Have you found that working with your classmates helps you to know them in a different way than just sitting at a desk?

JAMAL: Uh huh. It's a very big difference. I can see it. People who work in class, it seems that they are not focused. But we up here, everybody is focused. There is nothin', there isn't something that nobody is not focused on. Everyone is always doing something up here that they are supposed to be doing.

ILLÈNE: And have you noticed that you connect better with adults that you garden with than with adults who help you with something, like, say, writing?

JAMAL: There is. I can't explain it, but to me it's a big difference. It's a very big difference 'cause it feels like Steve is telling us to open your minds with the plants and, like, feel what they want. That's how I take it. And the teachers that we have, the teachers for math, science, the math, English, global, it's difficult—they want us to just do work, work, work, all the time instead of doing hands-on stuff. Last year, we did a lot of hands-on stuff, but this year, we are not doing anything like that anymore. But I am not mad. That is the way school works.

They change it up every year. Last year, everyone was passing with high grades. But this year, a lot of kids is failing. There is going to be a lot of kids who quit this year. But here is a big difference.

ILLÈNE: But in this class, you do hands-on and that supports you?

JAMAL: We do hands-on and read and write.

ILLÈNE: What is the meaning of gardening?

JAMAL: I don't know. No one ever asked me that question. What it means to me is I am being free. It's like I am not trapped nowhere. I don't have to take orders from nobody. Like plants, they don't have to take orders from nobody. They can die if they want to, they can survive if they want to. They just have someone to guide them. So that's how I can relate to it in a certain way.

ILLÈNE: Do you feel you have someone to guide you in this process?

JAMAL: Well, yeah, Steve with this [*speaking very animatedly*]. But in my other classes, I feel trapped. I feel like I can't get out. I have to stay there, and I can't go nowhere.

ILLÈNE: Do you feel like you can grow like the plants in this program?

JAMAL: Yeah [*chuckles*].

ILLÈNE: Is that a good feeling?

JAMAL: Yeah.

ILLÈNE: Do you think that working in a garden has helped you become more environmentally aware of what's going on around you in the bigger scope of the environment?

JAMAL: Yes! When I came into this program and we talked about global warming and all this other crap, I feel like this is more important than anything I am doing in my life. In the next thirty or twenty years, we don't know what will happen in this world. And I don't want it to happen while I am still alive.

ILLÈNE: Well, you are indeed helping. The more plants you put in the ground, the less carbon dioxide there is in the atmosphere. If someone came to you from the school board and asked if you thought they should put gardens in at more schools, what would you say?

JAMAL: Yes, you should do that. Why? Because of the carbon dioxide. There is too much carbon dioxide in the air and not enough oxygen. And if you do that [put in more gardens], the more carbon dioxide is gone, the less global warming.

ILLÈNE: And what about to support kids' learning?

JAMAL: Science-wise, to support kids learning, actually, that is a good way to do that. You can talk about plants in science, and the kids can go to wherever the school board planted the plants and do work there. Instead of being in class doing work, they can go outside and talk about plants and stuff like this. If this actually does happen, I think I stand for it—that more schools should have gardening.

ILLÈNE: I hope you get a chance to tell someone at the school board that. Maybe at the end of the year, your whole class should write the school board letters to tell them what it is like to garden in school.

JAMAL: Actually, I am going to tell Steve that.

ILLÈNE: Is there any other activity that gives you this feeling of freedom that gardening gives you and allows you to be yourself?

JAMAL: Actually, there are several. I draw, I rap, I dance, and I make beads. I don't know, rappin'-wise, makin' beads-wise, after my dad passed, that type of energy came into me. Because, like, before, I didn't know how to rap or make beads. I don't know. I feel like when my dad passed away, his spirit of those types of things came into me. So I feel that is more important than any other thing that I do. He used to rap a lot. He had songs that he wrote. So much of that is not recorded. He had seventeen books that he wrote, that he didn't rap yet, that he just had.

ILLÈNE: Did you learn his words?

JAMAL: Yeah, I learned a couple of my dad's lyrics that I can take and rap it. My dad is amazing. He talked about stuff that rappers don't talk about. Like, the world is so, what's going on in the world with the racism or countries doing things they are not supposed to be doing, how the government is messing up the economy, and stuff like that. That's what my dad raps about. He don't rap about drugs and women and money and killing. He don't rap about stuff like that.

ILLÈNE: He raps about social issues?

JAMAL: Yeah, social issues that people will really sit down and listen to and see if they can make a change of what he is rapping about.

ILLÈNE: So when you rap, you feel this freedom and the ability to be yourself that you feel when you are outside?

JAMAL: Yeah. That is actually true. And my dad draws too. I get that from him too and from my mom too. They do graffiti. My mom, she doesn't do rap. My family is talented, very talented.

Jamal finds that the garden frees him to be himself—to open up to life around him and to work in a productive way with his peers. He feels confident in the work he accomplishes, both in the hands-on gardening and the academics required. He continues to feel connected to his deceased father by doing the creative things his father once did and serving the community as he remembers his father doing.

I am surprised at how frequently young people tell me things in these interviews that I don't ask about, things that are probably difficult for them. Two of out nine students in this East Harlem class, including Jamal, told me about a parent's death. In New York, all the youth I interviewed lived without a father in their household. Since children in single-parent families face more economic, social, and health challenges than those with two parents at home (Bianchi, 1994), working in a collaborative environment with a caring adult is particularly important for them.

Jamal's father had been imprisoned. People of color end up in jail or have family members in jail far more than Caucasians in the United States. The 2010 US Bureau of Justice Statistics show the imbalanced incarceration rate: seven times as many black men as white men are jailed and almost three times as many Hispanic men. For every 100,000 men in jail, there are 3,074 African Americans, 1,252 Latinos, and only 456 white men (Guerino, Harrison, and Sabol, 2011, 27). African Americans represent only 13.2 percent of the American population (US Census, 2014a). For each one of those men in jail, there are many family members impacted.

For youth who may have a family member dead or incarcerated, a positive adult role model who engages and guides them in contributing to their communities helps provide meaning to their lives. Ritz plays an extremely important role as a guide to his students. Despite their various personal, social, and economic challenges, when these young gardeners discussed their strong connection to Ritz and their gardening classmates, they mentioned all the factors considered necessary by sociologists for positive youth development (Catalano et al. 2004).

The next interview also reveals family loss and pain and the courage this young girl developed to cope with it. Ritz was very eager for me to interview Itzel, a sixteen-year-old whose petite stature disguised a strong young woman. He considered her a very hard worker in his class and willing to tackle any job. Like most students, Itzel had participated in the week of immersion that started in the spring term. English is her second language.

ILLÈNE: What made you decide to take this class with Mr. Ritz?
ITZEL: One, because I like plants. Two, because we get to be outdoors. And, three, because we get to plant at our school; we get to make it more alive.

ILLÈNE: So you have experience planting before?

ITZEL: Yes, my mom loves plants.

ILLÈNE: Does she plant indoors or does she have a plot at a community garden nearby?

ITZEL: Inside. Ever since I was little, I used to help her. Every Sunday, she would start planting different plants. I didn't know what she would plant, but she always told me to start planting with her.

ILLÈNE: Did you grow food inside or some herbs?

ITZEL: Well, she wanted to, but when every time we tried to, my dog would eat it. So that's why we really couldn't plant edible plants.

ILLÈNE: Have you gotten to plant trees with this class?

ITZEL: Yeah.

ILLÈNE: Is that the first time you have ever planted a tree?

ITZEL: Yeah, but it was lighter than I thought it would be. It was fun to plant.

ILLÈNE: How did you feel when you planted your first tree?

ITZEL: We acting like, "I actually planted my first tree ever!" It was quite exciting!

ILLÈNE: It was exciting? Did it give you a feeling of accomplishment?

ITZEL: Yes, because we could plant trees outside and actually change the community.

ILLÈNE: Is that important to you to have an effect on the broader community?

ITZEL: Yes, because mostly if you actually walk around, you don't actually see trees in the forest, all you see is garbage. All you see is bad stuff in the community. We have children running around and they are getting sick. People need to know that they should actually start helping the community instead of dirtying it more.

ILLÈNE: So it sounds like even though you only just started planting out in the community, you actually have increased your environmental awareness? Is that true?

ITZEL: Yes, it changed a lot. At first, I really didn't care because my mom really wouldn't tell me about this, and I really didn't see that much. But once I started doing this program, Steve started telling me that kids get sick, families get worse, like, if they are sick, they get more worse, but if we plant trees, it gives us better… [searches for the word she wants]

ILLÈNE: Better air?

ITZEL: Yes.

ILLÈNE: So besides getting exercise for yourself, the community gets cleaner air. Trees actually clean the air a lot.

ITZEL: I actually didn't know that until Steve told me that.

ILLÈNE: So you are already contributing in a positive way to your community!

ITZEL: Yes!

ILLÈNE: So do you think that as a result of this, you would be more likely to stand up for another environmental cause to protect the environment? Like write a letter or do an action to help protect the environment as a result of doing this?

ITZEL: We already wrote a letter to, I forgot what program was it, showing them that we are doing the same thing as them because they are also trying to help the earth and their community too. And we are showing them; we are writing to them telling them we are doing the same and we are trying to help our community too.

ILLÈNE: Was it nice to be able to write to other people that care about these things?

ITZEL: Yes.

ILLÈNE: Yes, and you are being an example. What you are doing is an example to people. How long have you been in this class with Mr. Ritz?

ITZEL: I think this is our fourth week.

ILLÈNE: In four weeks, you have learned enough to change your own awareness. That is very powerful! I think that is really remarkable. Four weeks is a very short time for so much change to happen inside someone in personal awareness and knowledge. Do you think you can carry the skills you are learning in this program into other things?

ITZEL: I do think so 'cause this is also like a job where we have to stay on point. We have to do exactly what the boss says. This is gonna teach us about the jobs when we get older. If we manage for someone to tell us to do something, we already know the experience. Or when we get older, we... some of them right now are being leaders and showing the others what to do. And maybe when they get older, they are experienced in how to be a leader.

ILLÈNE: So it might help you to be a leader out in the community or in the job team or both?

ITZEL: Yes.

ILLÈNE: Do you notice when you are working on planting things up here or out in the community, that it changes your ability to focus? Do you notice if you focus more or you focus less when you are doing this work?

ITZEL: I focus more because, like, at first, when I would plant with my mom, I really would not focus, I would daze off, but now, I have to stay on point in what they tell me how to do it and when to do it. I really have to listen to them to get it right.

ILLÈNE: So it is changing your ability to being more focused?

ITZEL: Yes.

ILLÈNE: Do you know how to focus your mind better now as a result of doing this?

ITZEL: Yes. Just finding it better to come out here, plant, and smell the fresh air instead of being downstairs in the classroom being stuck in one room for an hour.

ILLÈNE: Do you find that being outside affects your stress levels?

ITZEL: Yes, because mostly inside, everybody gets mad. We all have our tempers. Being outside relaxes us. We get to walk around more. We get to do stuff more. We really don't have to fight or anything. We are with our friends. And, like, being out here is better than being stuck in the classroom.

ILLÈNE: Do you find that this sort of work helps your team develop a team-like attitude towards each other more than sitting in the classroom?

ITZEL: I do. When we are in a classroom, they can't take it. They just start talking, yelling at teachers… not yelling, but, like, speaking back. I feel like they are getting pressured 'cause of being stuck in a classroom for one hour. But being out here, they just start laughing, talking, joking around. And so they don't have to sit down. We can walk around.

ILLÈNE: So the physical activity helps a lot?

ITZEL: Yes.

ILLÈNE: You are saying "they." So you are talking about your fellow classmates. But what about you? Do you feel more relaxed out here? Do you feel your mind and your body relax out here?

ITZEL: Yes, because I am mostly used to working instead of being in a classroom, like, sitting down and focusing on one thing. I mostly like the experience of doing something with my hands and working mostly.

ILLÈNE: Do you have a job after school?

ITZEL: I used to. I used to work with my brother.

ILLÈNE: Doing what?

ITZEL: He used to have different jobs. One of them was being a chef. And one day, he took me to work and from there, I started going on with them and he would pay me. Not as much, but at least he will pay me. And from there, I …

ILLÈNE: Do you like cooking?

ITZEL: Yes, I want to become a chef when I grow up.

ILLÈNE: Gardening is very good preparation for being a chef. Did you know a lot of chefs are now growing their own gardens? Some are on the roofs of their restaurants, some in the back or nearby. There are a lot of chefs who want the best, freshest food and so they grow it themselves.

ITZEL: Over here, I don't know how they do it, but I do know that they have fresh foods.

ILLÈNE: I imagine there might be some chefs in New York with their own gardens. I am not sure, but maybe some, and other places where land is not so expensive. But good food builds good health. There is no price for that. Has growing good food changed your eating habits?

ITZEL: Well, I used to eat junk food when I was little. But now, it seems junk food could get you, like, make you sick. I used to eat at least three times or four times a week from outside. And so my brother made me see that could be bad.

ILLÈNE: Your brother taught you?

ITZEL: Yes. They showed us a video in school for kids. I forget what it was called. About a guy who was everyday eating at McDonalds.

ILLÈNE: That is Super Size Me.

ITZEL: Yes, there we go. That. I saw that and I don't want to eat no more. Ever since then, my brother has been telling me to eat healthy. And since I am always, like, playing outside, it's better to eat healthy than to eat junk food.

ILLÈNE: It's lucky you have a brother who cares about your health. Who does the food shopping for your family?

ITZEL: Well, there is me and my mom because my brother does not live with us anymore.

ILLÈNE: Has your brother influenced your mother the way he influenced you?

ITZEL: Well, she taught him.

ILLÈNE: But she has not taught you yet?

ITZEL: No, she hasn't taught me because she still thinks I am too little. She wants me to mostly focus on work, I mean, school. But my brother wants me to do at least both so I have experience when I grow up—how to get to work on time and to listen when they tell me what to do. And if I do become a chef, at least I know some stuff, some recipes to do and I can make it.

ILLÈNE: It's nice to have a big brother giving you advice like that. You mentioned the good smells when you work outside planting. Do you notice if the smells of plants affect you in any way?

ITZEL: Yes, because when I was little and my father was still alive, he used to take us to a park that had more trees, more grass, and I will always remember the smell because I used to be more active. I would run to the trees.

ILLÈNE: Was that here or in the country you came from before you lived here?

ITZEL: It was here. It was around New Jersey, I think. He would take us to one specific park. I forget the name. But that park was all green. Everything was green. And then that smell stayed with me ever since because we went there almost every day. It stayed with me. And now, since because we used to live different places, we just used to visit New Jersey for the park, but since we…

ILLÈNE: How did you get there?

ITZEL: By car. My father used to drive. Really, out here, there is no trees, nothing, just buildings; that smell type went away. But so, every single time I see trees or I am near something green, I can start smelling the same smell as when I was little. It starts reminding me about the park.

ILLÈNE: So it brings back memories of being in that park with your father?

ITZEL: Yes.

ILLÈNE: Our sense of smell goes into a part of the brain involved with memory making and that is why smells bring back such clear memories. Are you aware of your other senses when you are gardening: your seeing, touching, tasting, hearing, as well as smelling? What sense gives you the most information when you are gardening?

ITZEL: Mostly all of them. Because, like, there are different types of plants that I never felt before. And hearing, I can hear a lot of stuff I never knew of.

ILLÈNE: When you are planting outside?

ITZEL: Yes.

ILLÈNE: How does all this sensory experience make you feel? Just inside yourself?

ITZEL: It makes me feel good that we are putting trees; we are planting, putting green out in the world to make it better for everyone and for ourselves too. It is better because, at least now, we can have fresh air. We won't always have to see only these buildings. It's always going to stay there, I think. But at least we know the trees are going to stay there and they can actually help us more than we thought.

ILLÈNE: So the social aspect of making a contribution sounds very important to you. Had you thought about that before you took this class?

ITZEL: Actually, no. I never pictured myself doing this because I thought this is something my mom would like. At first, I didn't really think about no community, no nothing because everyone always says they live for themselves, they die for themselves.

ILLÈNE: You hear that a lot?

ITZEL: Yes. This is Manhattan, and in Manhattan, there is nothing but gangbangers. You hear that a lot on different blocks. All I thought about was myself. I didn't care about anyone else. Then Steve showed us a movie about babies getting sick and the woman breastfeeding them. It is making the woman and baby sick also.

ILLÈNE: Because the breast milk is polluted?

ITZEL: Yes. And then I started caring. I never knew that until I saw that video and I started thinking: if more babies die, then that is horrible because my baby sister died.

ILLÈNE: I am sorry.

ITZEL: She was older than all of us. She was supposed to be born first. But knowing that she died when she was born because she had the cord around her neck.

ILLÈNE: Oh, that is so sad. Your poor mother and father!

ITZEL: I didn't want to relive that day. Steve showed us the video, and seeing that kids could die, I didn't want that to happen. So once Steve said we have to do better for the community, that stayed in my mind. I started thinking I would rather save a life than kill it. So that is why I started caring more and I started doing more than I thought.

ILLÈNE: So it has had a profound impact to learn these things, especially concerning babies and younger children.

ITZEL: Yeah.

ILLÈNE: I have never had to live around active gangs because I live in rural Colorado and it is a gentle environment, lots of farms. People are friendly. But even here in New York, there are lots of people who do care, people like Mr. Ritz and lots of people doing good work with kids. You are becoming one of those people now. You are becoming one of those people who cares. Each thing you do, the more people care about people and the environment; it makes a positive difference. You are already changing the world and you are only sixteen. Remember that. Do you think this gardening program has allowed you to connect with people in a new way?

ITZEL: Yes, 'cause I used to speak to some of them. I really didn't speak to all of them, but now that I know all of them, we actually come together, and sometime in class, we speak about what we want in the room, our imaginations. The group that I did not know, they became my friends. Everybody here knows each other. Everybody just, if one is gone, we take their positions. Everything has to be dealt with, everything has to be done.

ILLÈNE: Oh! Look at the butterfly up here on the roof. Hey, kids, can you go tell Mr. Ritz? That is amazing that it is on the roof. There it is. It had to come up six floors. Look at the butterfly! [I don't live in a city with tall buildings and I am amazed to see a butterfly fly so high to find some flower nectar.]

RITZ: They are already coming. It's amazing, absolutely amazing. [Ritz is with the rest of the class directing their planting activities about fifteen feet from where Itzel and I are sitting as we talk. He, too, is very excited to see a butterfly find its way to the sixth floor.]

ILLÈNE: There are so many butterflies in Central Park like that now. That one came up sixth roof.

That is part of the miracle you all are creating. So you all care about each other now?

ITZEL: Yes.

ILLÈNE: You are creating a community of caring amongst each other now as you plant these plants and try to improve things in the school?

ITZEL: Yes.

ILLÈNE: How does that make you feel?

ITZEL: It's different than what I expected. At first, I thought that the kids that I did not know, that supposedly they want to become popular or are popular. I thought they would say that they don't want this program or they want nothing to do with this program. And yet, knowing that they actually are interested to even know and learn about what we are going to do; it shocked me.

ILLÈNE: So you are seeing people in a new way. Do you think that they are seeing you in a new way too because you are participating?

ITZEL: Well, I don't know 'cause we talked, but we really don't talk about ourselves. We talk about different things and what we like.

ILLÈNE: Do you talk about what you want in your futures now that you are in this program?

ITZEL: I only talked to some of them because they didn't really ask me that question.

ILLÈNE: Well, you could ask them since you are already creating a new future doing this work. What is the meaning of gardening to you?

ITZEL: The meaning is hearing green, like, seeing, smelling, touching! Flowers are green. They could be different colors. But mostly green for me is fresh air. Like new stuff, new stuff that we are participating in.

ILLÈNE: Is there anything else that you do in your life that gives you the same kind of feeling that gardening does? Relaxed and focused.

ITZEL: We have an after-school program in soccer. I have mostly been playing soccer since my father passed way.

ILLÈNE: Did that happen a long time ago?

ITZEL: Yes, about eleven years ago. He passed away when I was five years old.

ILLÈNE: I am sorry. That is hard.

ITZEL: Since I have been growing up, my brother, I looked at him as a father. And he taught me what to do. He saw the way we used to live, and it was really hard. So he raised me to play more like boys even though he knows I am not one. He raised me to at least see and feel and do some of the boy stuff that they do. I learned a lot of stuff that some boys in this school have not seen any girls do. If I don't play soccer, if I don't play it, I skateboard or I graffiti. And that just, like, relaxed me.

ILLÈNE: So those are things you do outdoors.

ITZEL: I can play any sport basically.

ILLÈNE: Is that important to you to get a lot of exercise?

ITZEL: Yes.

ILLÈNE: Did you always live in a city?

ITZEL: Well, I lived in Mexico before.

ILLÈNE: Your family is from Mexico? From the south?

ITZEL: From Puebla.

ILLÈNE: Oh, I know Puebla. Did you know the people of Puebla developed corn?

ITZEL: I didn't.

ILLÈNE: More than six thousand years ago, the people around Puebla selected seeds from grass called teosinte to plant the ones with the biggest seed heads and developed corn. Anthropologists have found the first corncobs in caves near Puebla and Oaxaca.

ITZEL: I have learned something new.

ILLÈNE: That is the exciting thing about gardening. There are so many plants in the world; there is something new to learn every day. Do you have views of trees from your apartment window where you live now?

ITZEL: I have a big tree outside my window. Every single time there is a storm, you can actually hear the tree knocking on the window. And that wakes me up sometimes. But at least I get to see the trees. And once they are wet, you can actually smell them.

ILLÈNE: Do you like having a view of the trees?

ITZEL: Yes.

ILLÈNE: There was a study done in Chicago that showed that people who have a view of trees outside their windows have less violence in their households. And if there were views of trees in the apartment building, people had more hope. That is pretty powerful, isn't it?

ITZEL: Yes, it is. That is another thing I learned.

ILLÈNE: Say someone from the school board came to talk to you and said, "We are thinking of putting in a garden at another school," what do you think of that and what would you say to them?

ITZEL: I would say I do not have a problem with it as long as we get more trees and more plants, like, out there. I know that some kids would actually like it, would like doing it. I would agree with it. I would tell them to go to every school and try to make a garden on their roof or outside, anywhere, so at least the kids could feel how it is to garden and what they could do to change everything.

ILLÈNE: Is there anything I haven't asked you about this experience of planting trees, flowers, and food that I could put in this book about how gardens might benefit young people? Is there something you would like people to know?

ITZEL: For everyone, not everyone, but at least the people who are viewing this, watching this, for them to at least try to go outside and plant trees—at least one. One plant can change everything.

ℛ

When Itzel learned in class about babies getting sick due to pollutants in their mother's milk, she was so distressed that she became empathic. She changed her disengaged attitude that she had learned from the uncaring norm she perceived in the neighborhood gangs to one of caring about life around her as she was taught how to plant trees and vegetables. Even a single plant in a classroom window can bring caring into the class as children take turns watering it (Noddings, 1992). It seems clear from listening to so many youth discuss how much they feel they are contributing to community well-being by planting a tree and growing food, that these gardening activities stimulate caring for their broader environment and each other.

A few moments after Itzel and I finished talking, I witnessed her courage, caring, and strength when an altercation broke out between two boys and she grabbed and hung onto a boy much larger than herself to restrain him from fighting. I had never witnessed a petite girl hold back an angry boy from a physical fight. She talked to him quietly directly in his ear as she held his arms back and persuaded him to calm down and not get himself into trouble by fighting. I did not witness what started the argument nor did I feel it was my business to ask. The school day was almost over. Ritz brought everyone down from the roof for dismissal, but kept the two boys involved in the altercation to help them sort out their disagreement.

All of these youngsters had personal life and learning challenges they candidly revealed. These challenges had made them candidates for this charter school and the Sustainable Technologies class. I witnessed their ability to work together as a team on a common goal, and I interviewed about half the class (all those who brought signed consent forms from their parents).

Gardening in the South Bronx parks where they spent their immersion week and on their school rooftop in East Harlem engaged them with life in a positive way and linked them to each other. They had found a mentor in a teacher who sincerely believes in every youth's ability to completely engage in learning, work, and community contribution.

Stephen Kaplan (2000), who has spent many years researching the human and nature relationship, proposes that to support pro-environmental behavior and overcome the sense of helplessness that seems to be common in the face of the ever-increasing environmental problems, people can engage in participatory problem solving and take action where they are likely to be successful. He suggests: "Engage the powerful motivations for competence, being needed, making a difference, and forging a better life" (Kaplan, 505). Stephen Ritz's Sustainable Technologies class has a toolkit that reflects this advice. It includes growing food in local communities to help make youth and their neighborhoods healthier. For the older youth on weekends, the Green Bronx Machine provides the chance to learn carpentry skills and to rehabilitate old buildings for pay—experiences that prepare them for a professional life after graduation. The toolkit that Ritz employs helps positive change grow in these youths' lives.

# 5

## CHOOSING HIGHER EDUCATION

After Ritz and the two boys resolved the dispute that Itzel helped to break up during class, the boys left. Ritz drove me to the Bronx to meet Nathli, aged nineteen, another member of the original Green Bronx Machine team. Nathli and I went to a nearby restaurant for our interview as it was raining and the college he attends only allows their students and faculty in the college building. Nathli was a bit shy as we began talking. I was, after all, a stranger, and Ritz had gone on to another appointment, but Nathli relaxed more and more as he shared his stories about what being on the Green Bronx Machine team means to him and the life choices it opened to him.

ILLÈNE: Did you ever see anyone in your family garden?

NATHLI: My grandmother. I never, like, paid attention to it or got into it, only when I got to my junior year in high school I did.

ILLÈNE: So now do you help your grandmother?

NATHLI: She lives in the Dominican Republic!

ILLÈNE: So how did you get involved with Ritz's program in gardening and building projects?

NATHLI: One morning in my senior year, I went into his classroom, and it happened that he was giving a training in gardening that weekend for Martin Luther King weekend. So I approached him. I used to go to his classroom every morning and he gave me the training. That was the day it all started.

ILLÈNE: That was an auspicious day to begin. Was Ritz your teacher? Were you taking a class from him as well?

NATHLI: Actually, he helped me with science reading. He gave me a little tutoring, but he wasn't like my full teacher. But we always kept in contact with the school to write and all.

ILLÈNE: How old were you when you came to the US?

NATHLI: I came when I was three. Yeah, I actually grew up here.

ILLÈNE: What are you studying?

NATHLI: Criminal justice.

ILLÈNE: Does gardening have anything to do with you studying criminal justice?

NATHLI: Actually, a little bit because I want to help the community. Criminal justice has to do with helping the community with crimes.

ILLÈNE: Do you still work with Ritz?

NATHLI: Yes, of course! We went to Philadelphia not too long ago, actually last month. I went with the other members, the other crew, my brothers, and we went over there and we spoke about our project, and we had a great time. It was a conference at the Sheraton Hotel [called] Green Jobs, on creating green jobs, so we spoke at the conference.

ILLÈNE: So do you remember when you first got involved? You are nineteen now, so you were sixteen or seventeen when you got started. Do you remember if it changed your perspective on things to start learning how to plant things?

NATHLI: It did a little bit. It did. It made me more aware and conscious of the small things, not to take them for granted, like trees, pollution. It made me more environmentally aware.

ILLÈNE: Did you notice that you felt physically or emotionally different after you gardened than when you started?

NATHLI: Emotionally, because I started to interact with people I never interacted with before. So with this program, we created a brotherhood with three other kids, which I call my brothers now. I felt emotionally better because we spent the weekend together, we went on trips together. So, basically, emotionally, we were better.

ILLÈNE: So was Darrell one of them?

NATHLI: Darrell, Nige, and Jonathon.

ILLÈNE: I met Darrell yesterday. Did you have different sorts of relationships with the boys you were working with than with the kids at school?

NATHLI: Yeah.

ILLÈNE: Did you notice that gardening changed your ability to focus?

NATHLI: In a sense, yeah, because, like I said, it made me more aware of stuff. Like, okay, we would plant this tree, but we don't know what that tree does. So you got to have that concentration to know what that tree does, and it made me more concentrate on everything. I feel more relaxed. I enjoy nature. Stuff like that.

ILLÈNE: Had you ever spent much time in nature before you started gardening?

NATHLI: Never, never, never. I mean, I wasn't that environmentally aware. I was just being me, being myself.

ILLÈNE: Well, you were being you in a city. It's hard to be in nature when you live in a city full of cement.

NATHLI: That is the beauty of our program—that we are creating that type of colony in the city. We are bringing the country to the urban area.

ILLÈNE: I was over at Bissel Park yesterday by the place where the trains all go that used to be a road, over by where they work on all the Metro trains, but now it has chickens. Did you help plant that?

NATHLI: You were with Ritz? Yeah. Over the summer, we went over there. Before I joined the program, the kids before, they had already done big projects: the Empire State Building,

Bissel Gardens mural painted by youth. Credit: Illène Pevec

the NBC store; that was the first kids that started the program, they were doing that project. We are just following their footsteps. We took it to another level, but they left the blueprint for us.

ILLÈNE: Well, everyone that does something is taking it to another level, but each group that does something has an impact, changes the community where they are doing it.

NATHLI: Yeah.

ILLÈNE: Did you notice that your sensory awareness changed when you were outside gardening?

NATHLI: Uh huh. I always ask, "Why do some streets in the city smell this way? How would they smell if we plant something different?" A couple of projects we have done, I can see now the difference in those areas. In Harlem, we have a little lot that we transformed. It was a parking lot. Now, we have a garden. You can see the difference, and it has a different vibe. Vibes! And that is what it is all about, vibes and peaceful feelings.

ILLÈNE: Vibe as in vibrations?

NATHLI: Yes, so you can feel it. For me, it made me more relaxed. It made me more think about stuff. It sent me to the right path. For me, I was on the right path, but gardening made me more sensitive to stuff and sensitive to nature and [want to] take care of it. It made me more relaxed.

ILLÈNE: Do you think there is a connection between caring for nature and the social justice issues you are studying now?

NATHLI: Yeah, of course, because if you look at it, there is a lot of injustice human beings do to nature. It goes from corporations abusing it to people abusing it. Like I said, it's a maze what I am studying. This program, it makes me interact with nature. In criminal justice, I am providing justice for my community, which, in the long run, will help nature.

ILLÈNE: The crimes against the earth affect poor people more than rich people because they usually live next to the crimes against the earth.

NATHLI: That is one of the things we talk about. We come from one of the poorest districts in the world in New York, the Bronx. For us to be homegrown, we were grown here in the Bronx, and to spread it around New York, that says a lot. We could easily say, "Nobody is going to listen to us because we come from the Bronx," but they listen to us, and it's nice.

ILLÈNE: Now, people invite you to conferences to speak. How does that make you feel that people invite you to speak at a conference?

NATHLI: It makes me feel that people care. They are supporting the youth and they support the movement that we are trying to do. And they support the Bronx. Not for nothing, but our main focus is in the Bronx.

ILLÈNE: Your main focus is here at home. And that is physically where you are doing the transformations. Do you think you have changed a lot because of this?

NATHLI: Uh huh. I was a community person because I used to play baseball and I used to be in community leagues, but I was never into it. Oh, now, I am feeding homeless people. Now, I am providing food, I am providing a lot of food for people. I am providing a different atmosphere for children and stuff like that. So it changed me. It changed me and for the better.

ILLÈNE: Do you have a sense of accomplishment from what you and your brothers have done?

NATHLI: Absolutely. Absolutely. On a personal level and on a, what our goal is: on a personal level, each one of us is in college.

ILLÈNE: That's fantastic. I know Mr. Ritz is so proud of you all.

NATHLI: I am sure if it had not been for the program, our mindset might not have been in college. We might just be hanging out. It gave us a sense of family.

ILLÈNE: That's fabulous! You have gotten really close to these boys while you have been working with Mr. Ritz. Have you gotten to know other young people as you work in different communities?

NATHLI: When I first started with the program on Martin Luther King weekend, we went to a school in Harlem. We met with a couple of program students and with other students from other schools and they liked the concept, but for some reason or another, they haven't taken it. Their program is there, the concept is there, but they have not expanded it. They talk to us and we work in collaboration with them.

ILLÈNE: Do you think that having Mr. Ritz as a mentor, an adult mentor, has been a big part of what you have accomplished together?

NATHLI: I look at Steve as a father. I even tell him that; we talk and I say, "Oh, you're my father." And for most of my brothers too. Anytime, we call him; he does a lot. No matter what day, no matter what hours, we can call and ask advice. We always go out to eat. I never see anyone more devoted to the youth like Steve and his wife.

ILLÈNE: That certainly seems to be the case from what I have observed. It's amazing!

NATHLI: Yeah.

ILLÈNE: Do you think that gardening itself has been an important part of this transformation in your own personal life in terms of rich relationships and the very clear goal setting that has resulted in you being in college? Are these connections to Mr. Ritz and your brothers because you are working with things that are alive or do you think anything you did as a group would have done the same for you?

NATHLI: I think that we came with a specific goal. I think that we jumped right to that goal. Our goal was to make gardens for schools, make gardens as classrooms. Our goal was to feed people. I think that we did it with a lot of energy. We did it with a lot of emotion. It was great. But I think if it was anything? No, it was not going to be the same. We came up with a goal and we accomplished it. We continue to look at that goal.

ILLÈNE: So it was important that the goal had to do with living things and food and serving the community? You could have collected books for that, but it's different working with soil and living things.

NATHLI: It's different. Most people say, "Oh, working with soil, how is that going to change the community?" It's mind-boggling to see the amount of people at the events where we get invited. And it's only soil and doing plants and stuff like that, but people see the unity between us and the community. For me, that is fantastic.

ILLÈNE: So it has allowed you to meet lots of people you would not have met otherwise?

NATHLI: It would have taken me longer to meet all the people I have met in a period of two years.

ILLÈNE: It's clear that all of your accomplishments in that specific goal of creating school gardens and feeding people have spilled over into your life. Would you like to tell me about that? I know you graduated from high school and you are in college.

NATHLI: The influential part of it is that we meet people that are very successful. In the education level, they are successful in their lives. That makes us proud and makes us say, "I want to be like that!" It has spilled over. I want to be successful in the future. If it wasn't for the program, the motivation might be there, but it wouldn't be the same.

ILLÈNE: You have met a lot of people who are role models.

NATHLI: Of course, starting with Stephen Ritz. That is my first influential role model that I had. Then, we have met other people along the way that have inspired me to be more successful.

ILLÈNE: So you have learned not only gardening, but you have learned business things with Ritz.

NATHLI: We are a like a not-for-profit, but our mindset is kind of business.

ILLÈNE: And you get paid now that you are not in the classroom?

NATHLI: Yeah. Over the summer, we did a couple of paid gigs, as Steve likes to call it: paid gigs. We did a couple of those, but mostly volunteer work. It deals with our curriculum. Yeah. A lot, a lot of volunteer work. The way I look at it, yeah, we could get paid for our work or whatever, but for the amount of fun and the amount of experience we get, there is no price. When we do community work, that is priceless.

ILLÈNE: Did you work on that green roof in Connecticut?

NATHLI: Yeah, in the Hamptons. And we stayed in a private house and we worked on a private house.

ILLÈNE: You got to go to the beach too. Didn't you stay on the beach?

NATHLI: Yeah. On the last day, we went to the beach. We could have got paid too! We did get paid!

ILLÈNE: Ritz has a great ability to find people who understand what he is trying to do with young people to make it possible for you to learn all these things and get paid too. Green roofs are a big deal now.

NATHLI: It all started with a lot of support too from great big institutions. I'd like to give them the thanks.

ILLÈNE: Do you know who was supporting it when your team started working with Ritz?

NATHLI: The reason that we are on the map is Trinity Wall Street. They are big landowners and they saw the concept and they said, "Okay," and we are successful, in part, because of them.

ILLÈNE: Did gardening change your eating habits?

NATHLI: Yeah. I was a little more chubby than I am now. [Nathli is slender now, but he didn't show me a photo of himself before.] Now, I am a little more active, more exercise now. I eat my little french fries now and then, but not regular. Now, I watch out what I am eating. I throw a lot of fruits and vegetables on my plate, but before, if you got me food, I am eating it. Now, I am more aware. It has to be something savvy.

ILLÈNE: Have you influenced your mom's eating habits?

NATHLI: Yeah. My mom, she jokes around. She has this distinctive shape. She's eating more healthy. We are eating more organic in the house. We are buying more organics.

ILLÈNE: What is the meaning of gardening itself to you?

NATHLI: For me, it is like growing organic stuff, growing new stuff. For me, I am growing food for the food bank, and it helps to feed people who may not have it, and if they know how to garden, growing stuff, that's how they can survive. That is how I look at it. For me, I always go to the food. That is what I put my emphasis on: food. And that is what gardening for me means. If people don't have much money, if they know how to grow food, they can survive.

ILLÈNE: Where you grew up in New York as a child, did you have a view of trees?

NATHLI: I grew up in New York projects. It's sort of about tall buildings—skyscrapers—and it had a green area. It had trees, beautiful trees.

ILLÈNE: Did you have a view from your apartment of trees?

NATHLI: Yeah. Not all the projects are bad. Mine was in the middle. The condition of living in some of the projects is not as good. I grew up in a green area and I saw trees, but, oh, it's just another tree, whatever, but I never paid too much mind on it.

ILLÈNE: But you played outside on the playground?

NATHLI: I played outside on the playground. I played baseball all day, but I never felt, oh, there are so many trees, but now I am, oh, look at this tree.

ILLÈNE: Is there anything else you have done that gives you the same feeling of relaxation and accomplishment that you have gotten from working with Mr. Ritz and your brothers on gardening projects? Do you have other activities that give you similar feelings?

NATHLI: Not even close. Just for the fact that I know that I travel to explain to people what we are doing to change the mentality of people, to change laws to environmentally friendly concepts. Not even close. I mean, I think that the closest I have come is playing baseball because, for me, it united a community that went to cheer for the youth, but not even close, I mean, not even close! They set up a three-day event and then they have us speak!

ILLÈNE: If someone from the school board came and asked you what you thought about putting in more gardens at more schools, what would you say?

NATHLI: Well, go ahead! Go ahead because I would say, "Think outside the box!" It's not only a, "We are doing this just for the garden in the school." You got to consider the camaraderie you are going to build. For us who built that, most of the students, we thought we would not graduate from high school. Just coming to that program changed our whole mentality, our whole paradigm. I would say, "Go ahead because it's thinking outside the box. It's not only thinking of a garden program, you are just going to grow stuff, but it will build brotherhood and it's nice."

ILLÈNE: Mr. Ritz told me that Darrell did not used to talk. Did you know him then?

NATHLI: Yep. What's funny with Darrell, we used to take music classes and his was piano.

ILLÈNE: He plays piano?

NATHLI: Yeah, a little bit. He used to, he wasn't that chit-chat type of person. He used to be him and his piano in a corner, just quiet. Once I met him in the gardening program, he was more extroverted, more socializing, more talking. Now, he is a more social person, and he has a nice sense of humor, and people get ahead for that.

ILLÈNE: Did you see other similar changes with other members of your group?

NATHLI: All the other members. They all have their own disappointments, even me. Ones didn't see high school as a thing to do, ones had problems at home, ones were not social, ones were not on the right path, but it all clicked and it all changed once we started expanding our horizons. We started getting out of the Bronx, we started meeting people, and people started talking to us. Yeah!

ILLÈNE: So you think all of you changed?

NATHLI: Absolutely, absolutely! One way or another! One way or another!

ILLÈNE: That is very powerful. Is there anything I have not asked you relevant to this experience with Mr. Ritz and your brothers gardening and building that you think people should know about? What these activities can do for a young person?

NATHLI: What have they done for me? Expand my mentality; make me more ambitious in being somebody, being somebody in life, in my community. Taking matters into our own hands.

ILLÈNE: You mean accepting responsibility for things to happen for yourself?

NATHLI: Becoming more responsible. They may not click at a certain age. I am young, whatever; I am going to do this. But things are happening and you grow. For me, I grew. The program really helped me. Now, I am more aware of my surroundings, my environment. Now, I am protecting my environment because if we continue to destroy it, we might not have it. So, yeah!

ILLÈNE: What is the main emotion you would ascribe to how you feel when you're gardening and working with your brothers?

NATHLI: Energetic and positive. I don't feel no negativity. I don't feel no "I can't do this." I just feel positive. For me, it hits me, "Oh, I am building something with my own hands and it is going to be here for a long time. Yeah!"

⚘

Thanks to Ritz helping Nathli with science reading and giving him the opportunity on Martin Luther King, Jr. Day to find a purpose and focus for the rest of his high school career through the Green Bronx Machine community gardening activities, Nathli now pursues his personal interest in criminal justice in college. His desire to improve his own community that began with planting green walls with food has expanded to social justice. The community service work he does, the close camaraderie he experiences with his "brothers" while he does it, the mentorship from Ritz that makes Nathli see him as a father, and the mutual caring in the group reflect all the elements that researchers have identified as key to pro-social development (Berman, 1997; Lantieri, 1999).

Berman (1997) identified four elements necessary for youth to develop social responsibility in *Children's Social Consciousness and the Development of Social Responsibility*:

1. A caring, nurturing environment,
2. Pro-social and ethical behavior modeled,
3. Development of effective ways to confront an injustice and handle conflict effectively, and
4. Developing the ability to gain perspective on situations.

Ritz's work with youth contains all four elements. These youth feel cared for by their mentor and can see the difference they are making in each green leaf that grows under their care. These experiences empower them and give them a shared goal of continuing their educations in which they support each other to succeed.

With our interview over, Nathli kindly led me through the maze of busy rush-hour streets to the correct subway for me to return to my sister's house in Manhattan. I felt the kindness and concern from him to ensure that I did not get lost. The next day, I interviewed the youngest student in Ritz's current class, Justin, aged fifteen, new to the experience that Nathli has now had for several years.

ILLÈNE: How did you get involved in this class?

JUSTIN: The principal told me that he would put me in a program for my interim week and we would do a lot of gardening work. We did a lot of project work in the South Bronx.

ILLÈNE: What made you decide to do it?

JUSTIN: Well, to be honest, once they said, "pay," I said, "Oh, yeah." The teacher told me and the principal told me that pay was one of the things that might happen, that might take place, so I was, like, "Yeah, I'd like do it." I like doing it! I like doing hands-on work on the ground. You use a lot of muscle. It just feels good. Some cucumbers might be growing and a lot of things. It feels good to know that I contributed to that or strawberries or something like that.

ILLÈNE: Do you like contributing to something growing or to people having something to eat?

JUSTIN: Both, actually. Yeah.

ILLÈNE: Have you ever gardened before you started doing this?

JUSTIN: No, I had a plant, but I just watered it before.

ILLÈNE: Have you seen anyone in your family garden before?

JUSTIN: No.

ILLÈNE: So you are the first person in your family? So how do you like it?

JUSTIN: It's really good 'cause I am doing it with a lot of friends, like a lot of gardening work. It's just fun.

ILLÈNE: Do you like collaborating?

JUSTIN: Yeah, and I just like a lot of hands-on work. That's one of those things I have been working on, you know, those little flowers [*indicates to a growing wall filled with marigolds*]. I did the whole thing. I like doing it. It's just fun. I feel more peaceful. It calms me down.

ILLÈNE: Do you know that almost every single young person I have talked to says to me, "It calms me down, makes me peaceful." What do you suppose that is all about?

JUSTIN: I don't know if it is the nice cool aroma. I guess [it's] the cool, the feng shui, I don't know the words to use for it. The vibe, the good vibe, I guess. It's just, like, calm. But you do stuff at your own pace. Like Ritz, he is cool [and lets you] work at your own pace. If we are fooling around, he might tell us to stop playing around. We do it at a nice pace. It's calm, really calm. It's simple, nothing too difficult, nothing too heavy.

ILLÈNE: Do you notice that your state of being changes when you are doing it, like between lunch and now? You came to this class right after lunch. Do you feel different now that you have planted a bunch of boxes with marigolds?

JUSTIN: Like, from lunch till now I feel more calm, more relaxed. I feel good, different in a good way.

ILLÈNE: Did that happen when you were planting trees out in the Bronx?

JUSTIN: Yeah, but the trees in the Bronx, that was like really hot, and that was a lot of trees we planted, and there were a lot of bugs. It was more work, but it was fine. The heat and the bugs were annoying, but besides that, it was really calm. But it was a nice exercise, too. Like, right now, those flowers were no exercise. The trees I planted were more exercise.

ILLÈNE: So you like to use your body?

Student planting marigolds in a living wall. **Credit:** Justin

JUSTIN: Yeah, active. Real active.

ILLÈNE: Do you notice when you are gardening which one of your senses gives you the most information?

JUSTIN: I want to say it's like all five senses. We were smelling a plant that tastes like mint. And it actually smelled like double-mint gum.

ILLÈNE: It is mint. They take the mint extract and put it in gum. So when you have all these senses being stimulated, do you notice if you feel differently than when you are somewhere where you don't get sensory stimulation, like when you are sitting in a classroom?

JUSTIN: You mean like my emotions?

ILLÈNE: Yeah.

JUSTIN: The smell is just, like, so like refreshing, so like air. I don't know. I guess, you know, people say the plants give off oxygen? My guess is that fresh air. I guess it just is that fresh air, that fresh oxygen, makes you feel better, more calm, that fresh air. There's a lot of fresh air around plants.

ILLÈNE: They breathe out oxygen. That is part of photosynthesis; plants breathing out oxygen.

JUSTIN: That's probably why that smell is so refreshing. Some of them have that special smell like mint. Overall, it smells refreshing, especially that breeze coming by, it smells refreshing.

ILLÈNE: Do you think planting trees and planting things up here has made you more environmentally aware than you were before?

JUSTIN: Yes, a whole lot. I actually started to appreciate many things. I appreciate what the gardener is doing 'cause this is a lot of work. It is fun, but it is still a lot of work, so I appreciate what they are doing. I didn't know it was really a job. I appreciate the knowledge I got from this. Like, I learn more about plants, about plant life, you know. I learned about planting and the people who plant in a garden. This teaches you a lot. Like, from little plants, it teaches you a lot.

ILLÈNE: Do you think you would be more likely to get environmentally engaged as a result of this experience? Would you reach out and protect the environment as a result of this?

JUSTIN: Like global warming, something like that?

ILLÈNE: Say if some part of the Central Park was threatened, would you be more likely to write the mayor or stand up to protect it as a result of this experience?

JUSTIN: Yeah, because literally green, because everything you see around you is green. When I smell the smell, I feel refreshed, so I think of green. Everything has got me going green now. So, yeah.

ILLÈNE: One of the things I ask kids is whether gardening changes how they eat, but you haven't had the chance to eat what you have grown yet, so do you think you might change your food choices as a result of growing food?

JUSTIN: I haven't been eating at McDonalds a lot. I haven't been for a while. I kind of eat more, like, vegetables, you know, salad. I don't know what it is called, that crunchy part of the salad?

ILLÈNE: You mean a cucumber?

JUSTIN: No, it's actually part of the salad.

ILLÈNE: Lettuce? You mean the crunchy ends at the bottom of the plant?

JUSTIN: Yeah, the lettuce, the ends, I don't know, that tastes good. Everything has got to be more like salad.

ILLÈNE: Do you know that it's extremely good for you to eat salads?

JUSTIN: But I like salad dressing on it. Is that cheating?

ILLÈNE: Cheating? No. It depends on what kind of salad dressing you use and how much.

JUSTIN: Like olive oil and vinegar?

ILLÈNE: Olive oil and vinegar are good for you. Olive oil is good for the body because it does not have saturated fats. It's extremely good for you to eat a lot of vegetables. What is the meaning of gardening for you?

JUSTIN: The meaning of gardening? That's a good question, actually. The meaning of gardening for me is, like, going green, not even going green, but being green—planting a lot of good vegetables, plants, trees. That's what gardening means to me: planting, making good choices.

ILLÈNE: What is the meaning for you? What is the meaning behind your actions?

JUSTIN: Meaning, like, how do I feel when I am planting something? I feel good when I am planting. I know how plants grow. I am planting life. That is what gardening is. I am planting life.

ILLÈNE: What would you tell someone who is in a younger grade about this experience? If someone asked, "Should I sign up for this class next year?" What would you say?

JUSTIN: You will actually start making better choices. You will understand. You should really go in this class because you will make better life choices. You will get actually to eventually eat a lot of good stuff in this class because the kids who start in September will get to eat what we planted that will be all grown. You will make a lot of good choices and you can eat while you work. Not all the jobs allow you to eat while you work. And while you work, you will plant more food for the future. And especially kids in the school I am in now, if you mention, "get pay for it." We haven't been paid yet.

ILLÈNE: Do you think you would consider working in this area or in something related to gardening?

JUSTIN: You mean, like, a summer job? Of course! Of course!

ILLÈNE: Is there something you don't like about gardening?

JUSTIN: The bugs. Like, sometimes the heat, but sometimes I wear a hat to protect me from the hot sun, and if the sun bothers me, I will put a hat on. It's just that the bugs are noisy sometimes. Sometimes, the bugs I work around with, they are really little. Like, today, they didn't bother me today, and I know they are good for the plants, so I just kept them in there. But sometimes, I am around those huge bugs, like those huge centipedes, I don't do that. They are, like, huge and so many legs, but aside from that, nothing really bugs me.

ILLÈNE: If someone on the school board came to you and asked if they should put in a garden at every school, what would you say to them?

JUSTIN: I would say, "Yeah!" For one, they could save money on the lunch here. Some of the food at some schools is really nasty, and the food from a garden is freshly grown, so they could save money on buying nasty canned food. Mostly, it's not really fresh. They could just plant it for themselves, and seeds don't really cost a lot. All you need is to have patience with it.

ILLÈNE: And what about the opportunity for other kids to learn like you?

JUSTIN: The opportunity is, like, they have a lot of opportunities; better, healthier food choices, better life choices, like, I mean more active choices. Like me, I am an active person. They will make better choices, you know.

Planting life! Better choices! Fresh food! A lot in the human condition hangs on the ability to make good choices; choices that make our lives healthy and gratifying. After only four weeks in the Sustainable Technologies class greening the poorer and less-than-healthy neighborhoods in New York City, Justin has gained more appreciation for the environment. He says that what other youth will get from this approach to learning is the ability to make better choices by working with a mentor and one's peers to care for the environment collaboratively.

# 6

## SOWING SEEDS FOR SUCCESS

Justin emphasized the healthy choices that planting gardens offers him, both in his activities and his food consumption. Ritz gives his students opportunities to learn to make good choices and discusses their options and the possible results. Researcher Elaine Harper (2007, 23) writes, "Autonomy is a basic human need having influence on motivation... Quality programming for troubled and troubling youth considers the ingredients of choice, control, and motivation in creating autonomy supportive environments for students to develop integrated emotional and behavioral changes." This dovetails with Stephen Kaplan's (2000) suggestion discussed previously that giving people the chance to plan actions to benefit the environment and carry those out provides the autonomy necessary to become proactive rather than passive when confronted with environmental problems.

I heard all of Ritz's students discussing the positive changes for themselves and the environment resulting from their Green Bronx Machine work. Ritz introduces students to basic skills required for planting and caring properly for plants and then gives them a job to do. He supervises and supports the process until they are ready to function autonomously. Their community work gives youth the chance to teach younger children as well, which reinforces their own learning and confidence. As Ritz emphasized when speaking about Darrell's ability to plant a beautiful green wall, he knows that Darrell now functions professionally on his own. Ritz no longer needs to tell him what plant to put where or how to plant. These youth develop autonomy under supportive guidance. On a personal behavior level, the youth working with Ritz have also seen him change his own choices from junk food to healthy food and watched his body transform, thus inspiring similar new food choices for themselves and similar body and health transformations.

The last New York interview I did was with Jonathon, aged nineteen, another one of the "brothers," the tight knit group of boys that have worked with Ritz for the last three years. His story illustrates how important it is to gain real skills and then use them for meaningful action to improve one's community. Jonathon's Green Bronx Machine experience inspired him to complete high school and find a personal goal. He kindly came from the South Bronx to meet me in Ritz's classroom during the lunch hour so I could hear his story. (I paid for his Metro fare as he made a long trip across town to save me the same trip and expense for myself.)

JONATHON: One day in high school, I had a living environment class. I was really low in credits back at that time. I got introduced to a teacher named Steve Ritz, and he explained to me how my life could be if I just worked hard. So, little by little, I started hanging with him. After school, I started working with him. One day, he introduced us to a man named George Irwin. He showed us an edible wall, a free stand. So I wanted to learn more. So one day, George gave us the chance to learn more and get certified. We took a bus out to Boston and we stayed in a five-star hotel called the Lenox, and we got trained to do an edible wall, and we did a ten-foot wall. It was a crazy day, but we got it done.

ILLÈNE: In one day?

JONATHON: It actually took us a couple of days. We had to drill it, everything. If you don't know what you are doing, you can get hurt. The boxes are really sharp and they can cut you. That's why you always wear gloves on the job. Then we came back to the Bronx, and, little by little, I just started hanging with him. That's how I got started.

ILLÈNE: Have you been part of this team that put in a green roof?

JONATHON: In the Hamptons? Yeah. I actually put in two green roofs in the Hamptons. And I actually did the NBC wall!

ILLÈNE: NBC television in New York?

JONATHON: Yeah, in the store where you can buy all *The Office* [the television show] stuff.

ILLÈNE: So it is inside the store?

JONATHON: Yeah. Well, I believe it is still inside the store. I also did a wall at a little high school in Harlem. That's about all the work I have done. And I have also been to some parks, and I helped in Brook Park and helped clean up the yard and plant more. And I try to do as much as I can to help my community. It's hard out here in New York.

ILLÈNE: I can tell. Everyone is struggling for space.

JONATHON: We try to do as much as we can to show kids that not everything is about candy and chips. You don't want to eat none of that stuff. If you want to eat chips, eat organic chips or vegetable chips. Don't eat like cheese doodles because they are seventy calories for a little bag, just a little bag, and you are paying fifty cents for air because that is what it is, basically.

ILLÈNE: Air and chemicals

JONATHON: Yeah, that's all it is, just to keep it fresh.

ILLÈNE: It sounds like this program of learning how to do the edible walls has made you think about what you eat. Is that true?

JONATHON: Yes. I used to eat a lot of bacon, and then I cut it down. I try not to eat it as much. I also cut down a lot on greased food. I bake my chicken now. I don't fry it. I also eat more salad, things that are healthier. Also, I try to show kids that eating this can help you. You know being in the Bronx where everything is number one, you know: poverty, asthma, sickness, diabetes, everything like that. It is really tough and really hard for kids to learn how to be healthy and stay healthy. I am lucky to be one of those people who can show them how to be healthy.

ILLÈNE: So you are being a role model?

JONATHON: I am trying to be the best I can be.

ILLÈNE: Do you feel better now that you have changed the way you eat?

JONATHON: Yeah, I feel much better. I am lighter on my feet and everything.

ILLÈNE: Have you lost weight eating more vegetables and less greasy food?

JONATHON: Yeah, a lot of weight, about twenty pounds.

ILLÈNE: You know changing human behavior is one of the hardest things to do.

JONATHON: Tell me about it [*laughs*].

ILLÈNE: I congratulate you that you have tackled your own behavior in a way that benefits you.

JONATHON: Yeah. I like to show kids that staying active and helping out your community makes your community! Your community is your home. Make it nice! Don't throw garbage on the floor. Recycle. Do what you gotta do to make it clean, nice, not only for yourself, but for other people to look at because people judge you by how your neighborhood looks. You don't want people to think you are a hoodlum because the neighborhood looks ugly. I try and tell the kids to keep it clean, stay positive, go to school, and do what you gotta do. There are a lot of things in the world of things going bad. You got to get what you want because if not, you are not going to be able to do what you want to do.

ILLÈNE: You are showing them that you can make a difference in the reality around you.

JONATHON: Mr. Ritz tells me to tell the kids my story—how when I first met Mr. Ritz, I was seventeen and I only had three credits.

ILLÈNE: You only had three credits in high school?

JONATHON: Yeah, that's why I first went [to Mr. Ritz's class]: because I didn't want to go to school. When I met Mr. Ritz, he motivated me to go to school. That's when I started doing night classes, afternoon sessions, Saturday school, trying to do the best I could do so I could graduate. So, little by little, I pushed forward and I graduated.

ILLÈNE: Fantastic! Congratulations! That's wonderful. Had you ever planted anything in the ground before you met Mr. Ritz?

JONATHON: Never! [*Said very emphatically!*]

ILLÈNE: Had you ever seen anyone in your family plant something—your grandmother, for example?

JONATHON: My grandmother, yeah. She's got plants all over her apartment.

ILLENE: So this was your introduction to planting things with Mr. Ritz?

JONATHON: Never in a million years would I have gotten into planting. Never!

ILLÈNE: So how do you feel now when you are planting something?

JONATHON: It makes me feel good, just bringing the world alive. Actually, making my community look better, it makes me feel like I am doing something positive rather than something negative. I try to stay positive. The more I plant, the more food we grow, the more we get to give away to kids, to homeless shelters. We actually give food to a homeless shelter called Part of the Solution on Webster Avenue. We try to give as much food as we can. I have been there a few times. It's not the greatest thing you want to see. We've got mothers and children eating there. It's really something tough to look at. It makes your eyes open and realize that I'm a very fortunate kid, so I really try my best to help others. Whether it's food or clothing, I try my best.

ILLÈNE: Where do you grow the food? Which one of the gardens? I saw two gardens. Ritz showed me Brook Park and Bissel Park. Does food grow in both places?

JONATHON: Yeah. We put our seedlings in Bissel, and then when they are fully grown enough to put inside the ground, we bring them to Brook.

ILLÈNE: You sprout in that greenhouse?

JONATHON: Yes. We actually had a farmers' market and we raised a couple hundred dollars that was going towards the children of Haiti when the earthquake happened. We actually donated, like, gifts. It's not much, but it's something.

ILLÈNE: It's something important for them. The poverty in Haiti makes poverty in New York look easy. They were actually eating dirt in Haiti to get the minerals out of it because they don't have food.

JONATHON: Rough! That's what I tell the kids, "You guys got it made compared to other kids in other countries." Some believe me and some don't. You are always going to have those type of kids, like, that don't care, don't want to listen to you. But sooner or later, reality hits.

ILLÈNE: Do you have younger siblings?

JONATHON: I have a younger brother, Daniel. He is ten. So I try to tell him, "You go to school, and if kids bother you, don't pay no mind to them, you do what you got to do for yourself. When you get older, that kid is not going to be there no more." I tell him, I say, "Stop playing video games! Go outside!" And he goes outside now. I try to keep him as positive as I can. I tell him to do his homework whenever he has a test, to study. I try to do everything I can to motivate him. I tell him, "I know there are kids out there, but I don't care what they do. I am here to care for you because you are my little brother." That's what I try to keep it positive.

ILLÈNE: Does he listen?

JONATHON: Yeah, most of the time. The video game part, he don't listen that much. Can't do much about that. Take it away and when you give it back, he gets back on it.

ILLÈNE: Does he ever come planting with you when you go with Mr. Ritz?

JONATHON: No, but he, when I go outside to play, he comes with me. When I go to the park to run around, he runs around with me. If I play basketball, he plays basketball. If I play football, he tries to catch the ball. I want him to look at me like a role model for him. That way, he notices and he thinks, "I want to be like my brother, Jonathon. I don't want to want to be like the kid next to me in class. I want to be like my big brother, Jonathon." I try to keep him motivated.

ILLÈNE: That's one of the things I wanted to ask you about gardening. Did it help you to focus?

JONATHON: Yes, because when you are planting, you do not want to put the seed too deep or too high. It has to be just right. It's like taking care of a life.

ILLÈNE: It is taking care of a life.

JONATHON: If you don't do it right, it's not going to grow. I learned my lesson one time. I was in a hurry and I decided to plant fast, so I threw some seeds on the ground and threw some dirt over them and they never grew. Mr. Ritz said, "See, that is what happens when you rush." So I said, "All right," and I took my time the next time and they grew. The free stand wall was the first wall I did. And a lot of people wanted to see it. Carrying that wall is really heavy, especially when it is filled with plants and you have to take it off. You have to put it on the roof and strap it down. I said one day to Mr. Ritz, "I can't do it no more. You have to put this on wheels." Then the mobile unit came out and that was the greatest thing ever.

ILLÈNE: I bet! What kind of wheels did you find for it to hold the weight?

JONATHON: I think they are four-inch rubber wheels. That way, they can hold up. If we used plastic, they would just break. If it breaks, then there are all sorts of problems and I have to lift it up again. I am trying to avoid that. I am trying my best. A lot of kids think that planting that stuff in the wall is easy. When you got to pick it up, that's the roughest part. The panel alone is about thirty pounds, but when you put soil and plants in it, especially when the soil has water in it, it expands. Then it dries. People don't realize that. They all laugh, like, "Oh, that's easy, you just drop it and you shake it and it comes out." It doesn't because the roots expand. You shake it and shake it, and it doesn't come out. People don't believe me, so I say, "Here, you try it," and so they try it and shake it and it won't come out. Living walls are probably the greatest invention.

ILLÈNE: That's amazing. Urban farmers are exploring vertical agriculture like you all have been doing for cities. There is this place in Chicago that I was reading about where they have converted a slaughterhouse to vertical growing walls for food. I have not seen it, but have just read about it. What you all have been doing is exciting. Did you go to Discovery High School where Mr. Ritz was teaching? Did you have vertical walls in your classroom there?

JONATHON: We had about four there. Each one I assembled, I planted, and I helped the plants to grow.

ILLÈNE: So did you harvest the food to take to the lunchroom?

JONATHON: I never went to the lunchroom because I didn't really like the lunch. So I brought in a piece of baked chicken, cut some lettuce off the wall, and we actually grew some cherry tomatoes, so I would pull some off and eat them, and they are free.

ILLÈNE: Well, they are the result of your labor, the sun's labor, the plant's labor.

JONATHON: That is what it actually teaches you. They teach you how far a plant will go to get sunlight. When we had the wall, you see the plants going up towards the sun. Mr. Ritz taught us about how the plant goes up the wall towards the sun, he taught us about the life cycles with the wall. It helped me out a lot—life cycles, photosynthesis, and all that. Of course, Mr. Ritz taught us more. The wall can't teach us everything, but it can teach you about plant life.

ILLÈNE: It sounds like it taught you about collaboration too.

JONATHON: Actually, all the food we grew, we fed 450 students inside the school, gave them a healthier menu for the day. All the kids ate the salad. All the kids liked it. Sometimes, not everyone agrees with you, but you just do the work.

ILLÈNE: Have you found in all the work you do with Mr. Ritz and the students that you formed different relationships with them than in your other classes?

JONATHON: Darrell, Nathli, they are my brothers.

ILLÈNE: That's what Nathli said too.

JONATHON: They my brothers. We've been through everything together, you know. Taken Regents [Exams] together, doing all the work, picking up bags of soil, picking up the panels, they been through it all. Also, we help each other too. My friend, Darrell, he is in high school now, and we tell him, "Do what you gotta do, man, don't be there no more. Do what you gotta do to move on to college." We try to keep Darrell the most positive. He is the youngest. If you don't do what you gotta do for yourself, things ain't going to come easy; things are going to get harder. Sooner or later you not going to be doing what you want to do. You end up working at McDonalds, and you don't want to work at McDonalds." He laughs and says, "Yeah, I understand." Those are my brothers. We call each other, text each other to see how we are doing. It's great!

ILLÈNE: So if someone from the school board came to you and said, "We are thinking of putting in gardens at other schools, but we don't know if they really teach students anything," what would you say to them?

JONATHON: I would tell them, "Let's have an assembly and you can talk to us and the guys. And we talk to the kids and we tell them our stories, and hopefully, they be inspired, and hopefully, you be inspired, and hopefully, you get the garden done." If it works, it works, but sometimes not everything happens, and then you just got to move on from there.

ILLÈNE: Were you a good science student before you started learning science by developing growing walls?

JONATHON: I was like this. I never really liked the science. I did what I had to do to pass, but when the wall came about, it was like, man, I just wanted to learn more and more and more. The wall is not just about the living environment. It's about math. You gotta know how much. When you do a roof, you gotta know how much soil you use goin' in there. You have to know how you got to cut it. You have to know the measurements for all that. So people think, "It's a living environment, you just have to put it up." But no, it is a lot harder than that. We actually did a job training at that high school in Harlem that I told you about.

Other kids got involved in research.

ILLÈNE: You trained them?

JONATHON: Yeah, I trained them. If you see a dead plant, you should cut it out because you don't want another dead plant and another one 'cause that is going to escalate. So I try to tell them, I tell them that all you have to do is water once a week. Just 'cause it is dry in front, does not means it isn't moist in back. So I took it out and showed them, and they believed me. A lot of the kids, they listen to me and trust me and believe me.

ILLÈNE: So what is that like for you to teach younger kids things you have been learning?

JONATHON: Great! It makes me feel like a role model, someone they can look up to and learn from. I don't want kids thinking, "Oh, here comes some kid telling us what to do." I want them to see and say, "Yeah," you know. I want to try to do as much as I can and be something like that or something more. I don't even want them to be like me. I want them to be better than me. Whatever you want, do what you gotta do. If you let everybody tell you, "You can't do this," you will never get it done. So I try to tell them, "Just go for it. If you don't succeed, then you don't succeed. If you do succeed, then keep movin', keep movin'."

ILLÈNE: This has clearly given you a lot of self-esteem to help other kids and do all this work with the walls and planting trees and see your success. Have you found that this kind of work changes your stress levels?

JONATHON: Yeah. In a way, it makes me relaxed and calm, not agitated. Because before, when I used to go to school in the morning, I be, "Man, I don't want to be here." I am angry a little bit. When I start working on a wall, I get focused and you smell the peppers and spearmint and everything like that. It just makes you feel calm and relaxed and you just keep going about your day calm and relaxed.

ILLÈNE: Do you think that part of calming down is getting to smell these plants' essential oils?

JONATHON: I think so. It works for me. If it doesn't work for the next person, then I am sorry. It happens all the time.

ILLÈNE: So it relaxes you? Does it carry over? Say, after you are done planting, you have to go do homework; does it carry over to the next thing and help you do it?

JONATHON: Yeah. When I used to have class with Mr. Ritz, smelling all the plants and stuff, it made me calm and relaxed and just focus on what I had to do so I would always be the first one done, and I tried to keep my grades up high. So I find it very relaxing, all the smells. It just makes me calm. If I really focus on the plants, it makes me just think and just relaxed, peaceful, just thinking all about the plants, and that is all I do.

ILLÈNE: Do you think that this will influence what you will do professionally? Are you in college now?

JONATHON: I actually am trying to do something with agriculture.

ILLÈNE: And what do you want to do with agriculture?

JONATHON: I want to learn more than just about the edible walls. I want to know how it all works. What soil can you use besides Pro-Mix. The way different plants function. How much water this plant should get, how much water the next plant should get. Right now, I am just learning about the walls, but I want to learn more. I want to learn about everything. I want to learn how to farm in the field. I want to learn how to use a tractor. Everything!

ILLÈNE: You have had a huge opportunity to connect with Mr. Ritz, your brothers, younger students! Have you had the chance to connect with other people too?

JONATHON: Yes. When I was in Philly, I forget what the event was called, but I actually had to learn how to speak. Mr. Ritz said to just pretend no one is there and you are just talking. So that is what I try to do. I tell them that I came to class one day and I met Ritz, and that is the start of the story. I also try to explain to people how the program works, how I got involved, what this unit is for, how it works. I just try to not be too shy. Only when the camera is on, then I get a little nervous and I see the light, oh, man. I tell them everything they want to know about how I came to be a mobile edible farmer.

ILLÈNE: It's given you a lot of opportunities.

JONATHON: Yeah. I try to keep on going because I know I have learned a lot, but sometimes, I feel there is something I am missing. I try to figure out what I need to learn more to figure that out, and when I figure it out, I am amazed, and I want to learn something more about that. Then I turn to Mr. Ritz, and he talks with me and he tells me this is what I can do, this is how I can learn it, to look at this website and read these articles, and I do it.

ILLÈNE: You know, we need a whole new generation of farmers because the average age of farmers is about fifty-eight in the US. It's wonderful that you have an interest because we are going to need new and intelligent young farmers like you. We need young people like you who have learned how to work collaboratively to restore agriculture to something healthier. Did you grow up in an apartment or house with a view of trees or nature?

JONATHON: I grew up in an apartment. I think, in my whole neighborhood, there were maybe four trees.

ILLÈNE: So you did not have any exposure to a green environment?

JONATHON: When I look out one window, I see the alley, and when I look out the other window,

I see the other building across the street. When you go to a park, you don't see no trees in the park either. It's just a basketball court, the swings, and the little playground. So I try to go to parks further out, like Central Park or, whenever Ritz calls me, I go to Brooks Park.

**ILLÈNE:** So now that you plant trees, it's a whole new world?

**JONATHON:** People think that planting trees is easy, but it's really hard. You have to dig a hole two- or three-feet deep. You have to take up all the soil and moisten it. The tree itself is heavy. I want people to see my neighborhood as a clean environmental neighborhood. I don't want them to see it as just a neighborhood of drugs and prostitution and sex, nothing like that. I want them to see an environmental, sustainable environment. I don't want to see just another neighborhood in the Bronx. I want them to say, "Oh, this part looks nice." We try to keep it looking as environmentally friendly as we can. We can only do so much, so we try.

Once Jonathon met Ritz, he chose to work hard to go from three credits to graduation. He has thrived while contributing to improving his community. He, along with his other "brothers," encourages Darrell to graduate, and Darrell is succeeding. People graduating from high school have better earning potential in their futures than those who do not: "High school dropouts earn $9,200 less per year on average than those who graduate. Over the course of their lifetimes, they will earn an average of $375,000 less than high school graduates, and roughly $1 million less than college graduates" (Burrus and Roberts, 2012, 1). Dropouts are also more likely to have bad health (ibid.).

The average national graduation rate in 2011–2012, the most recently published statistics, was 81 percent (National Center for Education Statistics, 2015b). The Asian/Pacific-Islander graduation rate was 93 percent in comparison to a graduation rate of 85 percent for whites, 76 percent for Hispanics, and 68 percent for American Indians, Alaskan Aboriginals, and African Americans (ibid.). The dropout rate was similarly disproportionate for different ethnicities: with an average national dropout rate of 7 percent in 2012–2013, the dropout rate was 5 percent for whites, 7 percent for African Americans, and 12 percent for Hispanics (National Center for Education Statistics, 2015a). While Ritz's students who stayed working with him for several years (the "brothers") were statistically far more likely to drop out of school, they did not. They graduated.

The affection and respect these adolescent boys feel for each other helped them all complete school. The Green Bronx Machine team members all say that they are brothers. They shine with their mutual regard, reflecting the caring they experience with Stephen Ritz. Each acknowledges the opportunities that Ritz has given to them to learn, grow, and succeed. They mirror his caring in how they live and work as mentors to younger children. A meta-analysis examined fifty-five evaluations of mentoring programs for youth and showed that those serving at-risk youth were the most effective and that forming close relationships between mentor and youth was a significant factor in their success (Dubois et al. 2002). In observing these young people work with Stephen Ritz, I witnessed very close personal relationships.

A six-year study done in Spain with high school students who were failing and in danger of dropping out (a similar profile to Ritz's students) used a garden-based program to give students hands-on learning in science, cultural studies, and music (Ruiz-Gallardo, Verde, and Valdés, 2013). Those students' graduation rates and behavior improved significantly. Since gardening is, in itself, an act of caring, I posit that young people working in a caring environment with a caring adult are in an optimal environment for positive youth development.

Ritz's students in East Harlem and the South Bronx have gained confidence as they have gained skills that make them able to improve their community's health, their own health, and their employability. They are proud and grateful for all these opportunities. When Stephen Ritz calls on them to do something with the Green Bronx Machine, they respond with pleasure and skill!

Darrell and Michaela harvest vegetables in Bissel Park. Credit: Green Bronx Machine

# 7

## GARDENS GROW HEALTHY YOUTH

*I seem more in tuned to everything. I like hearing the wind between the trees and the plants, the laughter from the other people working. I'm surrounded by so many things that are organic and trying to grow and bring new life.*
—ROSEMARY, 18, COLORADO ROCKY MOUNTAIN SCHOOL

The garden programs portrayed in this book support youth in gaining the skills and knowledge they need not only for gardening but also for life. As the adult mentors and youth work together towards the common goal of nurturing the soil and plants to harvest food for themselves and their broader communities, the young gardeners also grow good health in themselves, both physically and mentally. They also improve the social and physical environments in the communities where they garden, as we have already heard.

What makes a garden a good environment for growing youth into mature, responsible, caring adults? The natural processes that happen in a garden—the seed sprouting and reaching for light, leaves gathering energy from the sun for photosynthesis, roots stretching down to find water and nutrients and anchoring the plant, flowers opening for pollination, and fruit maturing in the sunshine—all mirror the development of a young person who also seeks to discover and fulfill personal potential and live as a contributing community member connected to others in a common goal of mutual thriving. The health of a biological ecosystem depends on all members of that system doing well and playing their interrelated part in the whole—in a garden, the humans are the members who have the capacity to strengthen the well-being of all other elements by providing water, nutrients, and caring.

This chapter presents some research and theory in psychology, sociology, and how the garden setting itself may enable healthy youth development. These theories and research create a trellis to support the information the youth share with us about their experiences. This framework will enable us to see and understand how the garden helps the youth harvest mature fruits within themselves while gardening together with their peers and mentors. Positive youth development, positive psychology, and ecological psychology form this framework.

The psychological and social field known as positive youth development uses research-based evidence to identify the social and psychological elements that support optimum youth development. Positive psychology identifies and explores the psychological traits that help people thrive. Whereas ecology identifies the niches within ecosystems that different organisms occupy, ecological psychology describes the social and physical elements in the diverse environments humans inhabit. These environments are often called behavior settings.

Behavior settings influence people's behaviors and relationships and make some things more possible than others. For instance, a garden makes digging a possible behavior whereas a classroom often requires sitting. Research within these fields explains why the first-hand experiences related to youth growing food are so important to understanding youth development.

## POSITIVE YOUTH DEVELOPMENT IN AN ORGANIC GARDEN

Elements considered important for positive youth development include these conditions: "physical and psychological safety, appropriate structure with clear boundaries and expectations, and supportive relationships where clear behavior expectations for cooperation can be met" (Eccles and Gootman, 2002, 90). Through an extensive literature review and broad consultation, Catalano et al. (2004, 101) identified the following goals and indicated that positive youth development programs needed to "seek to achieve" at least one:

1. Promotes bonding
2. Fosters resilience
3. Promotes social competence
4. Promotes emotional competence
5. Promotes cognitive competence
6. Promotes behavioral competence
7. Promotes moral competence
8. Fosters self-determination
9. Fosters spirituality
10. Fosters self-efficacy
11. Fosters clear and positive identity

12. Fosters belief in the future
13. Provides recognition for positive behavior
14. Provides opportunities for pro-social involvement
15. Fosters pro-social norms

The youth from New York discussed all of these directly or indirectly as benefits from their immersion in their program to grow food. As you read what each youth has to say about their experiences in the next ten programs across three more states, you will see that all the programs are fully committed to youth well-being. Peer bonding and adult-youth bonding develop naturally through teamwork once the behavior expectations are made clear to all participants. The youth describe their pride in their new skills and their sense of contribution to their local community. By providing food and planting trees to reduce global warming, they find hope for themselves and their communities through their own agency. The opportunities for pro-social development abound in the garden setting. The youth often call their gardens sanctuaries, a place where they experience peace and safety from the problems some of their communities hold outside the garden fence. Many of them have harvested knowledge and demonstrate their cognitive competence as they pass on this knowledge to younger children and the general public. They show their moral clarity by giving their time to making a positive contribution to their communities. Please consider what they say throughout the following chapters in light of these fifteen goals for positive youth development.

Each program has its own clearly defined structure that the youth know and respect, and each garden leader has a distinctive way to organize the participants. In some gardens, youth volunteer for certain tasks, and, at others, they do what the leader says needs to be done. Some youth even assign tasks to peers when they serve as leaders. The act of gardening models the act of nurturing a growing child as each gardener provides the plant with the support it needs to grow.

All of the gardens profiled utilize organic gardening methods. By learning and practicing organic soil development and pest control, the youth can see how important it is for plants to be fed naturally rather than chemically. They see the healthy worms wiggling in soil that is free of chemicals and the many beneficial insects playing their important roles in pollination and in predation on destructive insects. These gardening teachers do not lecture youth on the dangers of taking drugs, using alcohol, or smoking tobacco, but the conversations about how to nurture plants organically have obvious parallels to human health. The youth can taste the difference in what they grow organically. Ana, a seventeen-year-old from Roaring Fork High School in Colorado, explains how she feels about what she picks and eats from the school garden:

I don't have to worry about rinsing it because I know there's no chemical and everything is pretty clean. If it has dirt on it, I will probably rinse it, but I also just wipe it a little bit. For the energy, I guess it makes me feel better to eat something that we have produced in the greenhouse because it is not, I guess, manufactured. It feels fresher and crispier than when you go to the store. It feels better.

Researchers focusing on the quality of engagement that youth have with shaping their environments conclude that interaction with a setting matters (Larson, 2000), a conclusion that concurs with ecological psychology's premises regarding the developmental need for direct experience with the environment (Reed, 1996). Building on this capacity for interaction, Larson (2000, 170) analyzes initiative as a key factor for positive youth development and defines initiative as "the ability to be motivated from within to direct attention and effort toward a challenging goal." Agency, or the ability to act on one's own, develops as students gain gardening skills and ecosystem knowledge.

## INTRINSIC MOTIVATION

Intrinsic motivation, or the desire to be doing something while also being invested in it, needs to happen in "concerted engagement in the environment, with exertion of constructive attention in a field of action involving the types of constraints, rules, challenge, and complexity that characterize external reality" (Larson, 2000, 172). We have already heard Darrell, Nathli, and Jonathon describe what they experienced by joining in the Green Bronx Machine gardening program and how they found the motivation within themselves to volunteer their time to community food growing and tree planting, and also to graduate.

Kayla, a senior at Roaring Fork High School in Carbondale, Colorado, spoke eloquently at a 2013 regional Farm to School meeting. She described an Earth Day event that her environmental science class organized and carried to completion building soil in the school's young orchard.

It wasn't a trip. It wasn't a vacation. It wasn't getting out of the classroom. It was doing something real and being in control of it, which you do not see a lot of in school. In school, students are not put in a position to make decisions. So this was a very different experience for all of us. This was something real. I was part of the team and I was blown away by how well it went. And how significant it was. It was profound for me, personally.

Kayla had spent the day with her environmental science classmates filling wheelbarrows with leaves and semicomposted horse manure. The twenty students and about ten adult volunteers needed to cover about one quarter of an acre with biological matter that would break down to enrich the poor soil around the young saplings. What she was doing mattered to her because she and her classmates planned and executed this endeavor themselves to nurture this nascent forest garden before they all graduated. It was the first time in Kayla's school life that youth were put in charge of something and expected to plan and accomplish it as a group. The experience incorporated collaboration, intrinsic motivation, and concerted engagement towards a challenging goal—all necessary elements for positive youth development.

At all but one site I studied, youth chose to participate in gardening by signing up for the class or work activity (the teen-parent horticulture program, where the program was required for science credit, was the one exception). When youth choose to take the class or participate in gardening over other choices, it has much in common with what Larson (2000, 174) calls "structured voluntary activities," where youth work with adults to accomplish something they want to do. Such voluntary activities require "concerted effort over time toward an outcome" (ibid.). A garden provides a perfect opportunity for concerted effort over time. One might get a radish in twenty-five days, but most plants take longer to provide an edible result. Fruit trees provide a big test: waiting for that first apple to grow and ripen may take a few years of fertilizing, mulching, watering, and patience.

Research has found that voluntary activities, such as sports and after-school arts programs, have higher intrinsic motivation for youth and higher concentration levels than schoolwork. And for some youth, such as those I met in the South Bronx and East Harlem, the success they experienced in gardening showed them how capable they were and helped transform failing grades into academic success.

## ECOLOGICAL PSYCHOLOGY

One theorist, James J. Gibson (1979), proposes that we perceive and relate to our environment through our senses; that our senses seek information from what they perceive. In a garden, we are immersed in our senses and one with our experience. Multiple times, youth told me that they felt one with nature. I inquired into youth's sensory experiences in gardens before I heard of Gibson's theories, but knowing his theories helps me to understand what the youth describe. "One perceives the environment and co-perceives oneself," Gibson (1979, 126) stated.

What does it mean to co-perceive oneself? Examining a tomato plant gives a person the chance to use the senses in multiple ways: see a beautiful vine with a brightly colored fruit, smell the distinctive tomato scent, touch the smooth fruit and the fuzzy branches, hear the sound of the stem break as one plucks the tomato, and taste the fruit's sweet juiciness. All of these perceptions make the perceiver very self-aware and present. As all the senses feed information to us, we bask in the pleasure they cause.

## AFFORDANCES

Gibson (1979) invented the word "affordance" and the theory of affordances to describe the possibilities of interaction—all that an environment makes possible for an animal, including humans, to do. He expands the definition of an animal's ecological niche to include all that it is possible to do in that niche. Architects and landscape architects use the theory of affordances to analyze potential or existing actions and interactions within spaces, such as buildings, gardens, plazas, sidewalks, and parks. This information on affordances helps them to design places better suited to human needs. Of course, gardens also afford behaviors for wild animals to find food that the natural environment does not provide. This is why school gardens often need deer fences to keep animals out of the lunch crop.

Just as ecology studies all the parts of an ecosystem, animate and inanimate, as an interdependent system, ecological psychology examines the interrelationship between the person having an experience and the elements of the environment the person inhabits. What affordances do youth discover in the gardens where they work, how do they react to these affordances, and how do these affordances serve their developmental needs?

A wheelbarrow affords hauling compost to a garden bed or carrying a heavy apple sapling to where one will plant it, but one can also give a friend a ride in a wheelbarrow or lean back in it for an interview. Aaron, over six feet tall, was clearly far more comfortable reclining in the big wheelbarrow that he chose to occupy for our conversation than in the small school desk he had occupied prior to our discussion. He told me that the first thing he thinks about in relationship to a garden is flowers: "They make you feel good, you know. It's like when you go over to your girlfriend's house, you bring her a flower." A flower affords the opportunity to smell, pick, give as a gift, or even eat if it is edible. You will hear young people in this book talk about all these possible interactions without ever using the word affordance.

## BEHAVIOR SETTINGS

Roger G. Barker (1968) developed the concept of behavior settings. As Aaron illustrated by relaxing in a wheelbarrow to speak with me, the garden provides a very different behavior setting than a classroom. It is also a place where conversations between people of diverse generations seem to be on more equal footing than in a classroom where a teacher maintains authority. Barker (1968) explains that particular behaviors expected in certain settings offer a way to view and analyze the human-environment relationship, something important to consider when planning a school to best serve the developmental needs of children and adolescents.

A classroom behavior setting consists of a teacher, classmates, four walls, a whiteboard, books, computers, a pencil and paper, and a set of rules. These rules often demonstrate that the expected behavior is primarily sitting, listening, discussing, and answering questions. A garden opens an entirely different range of expected behaviors that include direct experience via the senses with nature. A garden can also include math for measuring, weighing, counting, estimating, and problem solving for the best way to measure and organically improve the soil's nitrogen content. It is a place to draw from life, sing a song for pure pleasure, or simply enjoy the peace and quiet. A living environment offers more potential behaviors and affordances than a static one, and that is something the youth I interviewed often bring up themselves. Isabella in Colorado explains her own agency in gardening:

> It's being with nature, and it also helps me a lot. Like, it's a good time to think when you need to be alone or you need to express yourself because you are just out there doing it. Nobody else has told you, "No, you have to do this and you do it like that or you're wrong." You can actually just make up your own way for gardening, and it's a really fun experience.

Barker (1968) explains that people perceive and conform to the expected behaviors that different settings require. He considers the optimum learning environment to be one where people can actively have some control and decision-making authority over what happens in the setting. Viewed through the lens of affordances and behavior settings, a garden offers a wide range of activities not allowed in a building. Digging a hole to plant a tree affords a student some physical exercise and perhaps a choice in what shovel to use, what tree to plant, what kind of soil amendment to use, and with whom to accomplish the task. Tree planting opens the possibility of a long-term relationship with a living being to help it thrive and a step towards community sustainability wherever that tree grows. In this way, the youth develop knowledge and competence in caring for the environment, a sustainable human behavior that supports the community's future as well as its present (Heft and Chawla, 2005).

The garden behavior setting affords youth agency, choice, creative problem solving, and a collaborative application of practical knowledge. The Green Bronx Machine youth have already made clear how important making good choices and taking action to improve their community is. In the Bronx and East Harlem, Stephen Ritz's students also do gardening indoors in the garden walls they install, which create a new affordance and behavior setting within a schoolroom, figuratively expanding the learning environment.

Teaching long-term sustainability practices is integrated into the curriculum in all the garden programs discussed here. They encompass the three E's of sustainability by transforming school grounds into organic gardens growing food for school lunch and neighbors: environment, economics, and equity. They are not growing food only for themselves, but are transforming land and people into a partnership solution for healthy, affordable food for all community members for the long term. Those people who may not be able to buy organic produce in the grocery store, can access it affordably at their school salad bar or in a youth-run farmers' market.

Life processes not clearly evident in a schoolroom permeate a garden—gardeners witness death, decay, and resurrection when a plant dies and rots into the ground and when new shoots emerge anew from old roots come spring. Sometimes, a seedling dies because the gardener forgot to water it or it froze when temperatures fell—natural consequences related to a plant's basic needs for water and warmth. A gardener learns by witnessing a plant's life cycle that what they do matters and that there is always another chance to replant even if you have to wait a season.

Gardening youth discover many ways to perceive, interact, and behave within a garden. Many of these physical interactions teach them about personal development. Jonathon from New York related that when he planted seeds carelessly, without attention to what they needed, they failed to sprout. When he planted the seeds with care and awareness, they grew. What a profound life lesson he learned that he now applies to other endeavors.

## THE HIGH SCHOOL BEHAVIOR SETTING

School forms a major part of the social context, the behavior setting, for most North American adolescents; they spend about seven hours a day, five days a week, in school buildings. Some developmental psychologists argue that the changes youth experience beginning in early adolescence do not fit well within the social environment of many schools, where the behavior setting and the restricting rules leave little room for choice. School settings can conflict with the growing need the adolescent has for autonomy. The warmth of a grade school teacher-student relationship changes to a less personal one just at the time adolescents need to have more personal support and care from adults. At this time, they need help as they find their way through the turbulence brought on by puberty when they seek independence of thought and action (Eccles et al. 1993).

A teacher or adult mentor in the less formal environment a garden affords at a school or after-school site can provide meaningful guidance and personal care to adolescents in this critical developmental period. The three young men who had worked with the Green Bronx Machine for several years all have managed to graduate from high school thanks to being involved in gardening with a devoted mentor. How many youth would be more likely to graduate if their schools or neighborhoods offered them gardening programs with mentors?

Williams and Brown (2012) use the word pedology to explain the importance of including gardens at schools to enliven education and children's capacity to contribute to life's sustainability. In the 2015 online Merriam-Webster's Dictionary, pedology has a double meaning: "1. soil science; and 2. the scientific study of the life and development of children." With this one word, we see how school gardens unite children and youth in learning about the Earth (planet and soil) and how to care for it effectively while they build soil organically and grow their own knowledge.

To summarize, we develop in relation to our settings. Different settings provide different opportunities. A garden is a particular behavior setting that affords young people the opportunity to use their senses to perceive their surroundings and to respond. It affords collaborative action for youth and adults to work towards a common goal of environmental improvement and food growing. It demands a moderate level of physical activity, and the fresh food harvested tastes great and supports good health. Gardens provide a behavior setting that supports initiative, choice making, and behavior conducive to the planet's and the human community's well-being (Williams and Brown, 2012).

Gardens offer the human brain a more suitable environment for its own growth than buildings. John Medina, a neuroscientist at the University of Washington, challenged the entire concept of school buildings at a keynote speech he gave to the US Green Building Council Colorado Chapter's Green School Summit in November 2014, where I listened attentively. He brought neuroscience and ecological psychology together in his opening statement, paraphrased here: "I am not sure why you all brought me here when you build schools. The brain evolved in the out-of-doors, in always-changing meteorological conditions to problem solve in a state of constant motion." If that is how our brains evolved, why would we impair continued brain evolution by indoor confinement five days a week? School gardens offer a behavior setting the brain needs.

## FLOURISHING: HUMAN WELL-BEING THEORY

Positive youth development theory identifies the social structure that young people need to grow successfully through adolescence and into adulthood. Ecological psychology describes behavior settings, their affordances, and why they matter for human perception and development. To relate to the reader the many personal feelings the youth expressed to me in relation to their healthy development, I turned to positive psychology for a framework.

Dr. Martin Seligman, a past president of the American Psychological Association, is a founder of the positive psychology movement that dedicates its research to discovering what makes people thrive. His book, *Flourish*, appeared in 2011 just as I was reading and rereading the first fifty-two interviews I did with these young gardeners. Seligman's (2011) theory helped me organize these youth's experiences with a construct he calls PERMA: **P**ositive emotion, **E**ngagement, Positive **R**elationships, **M**eaning, and **A**chievement.

Positive emotion describes what we experience from pleasurable physical sensations, such as warmth, comfort, ecstasy, and delight, to name a few. Engagement relates to absorption in what one does and is often described as flow, a complete concentration on a task; whether it is making music, discovering a mathematical theorem, drawing, or gardening, the person loses track of time and does not feel anything until the task is completed or paused and then experiences deep satisfaction, even elation, from this total focus (Csikszentmihalyi, 1997).

Positive human relationships form the basis for our most memorable life experiences, such as a wedding, a birth, a death of someone close to us, or creating a garden with others. Meaning arises from "serving something that is bigger than the self" (Seligman, 2011, 12). Humans have created many institutions that meet this need, such as the Boy and Girl Scouts of America and similar organizations, religion, politics, and the family, and clearly for these youth, creating gardens serves something bigger than themselves: their communities. Finally, achievement comes from the delight in seeing a result, accomplishing a task one has set out to do, such as planting, caring for, and harvesting a garden.

People choose to pursue mastery and success for their own sakes and not just for what they get. The thrill of harvesting food that one has planted comes from seeing the transformation of a seed into something new, colorful, and edible and filled with taste, and then being able to share it with others. Interwoven with achievement is an engagement with the process in which it takes to get to achievement, which is a characteristic of the flow state. It is actually quite difficult to separate flow and achievement. For flow to occur, it requires some sort of process towards mastery (Csikszentmihalyi, 1997). Achievements on behalf of the common good are elements for flourishing in life (Seligman, 2011).

One of Seligman's colleagues, Stephen Post, tells a story to illustrate the importance the common good. When Post was a child, if he was in a bad mood, his mother would say to him, "Stephen, you are looking piqued. Why don't you go out and help someone?" (Seligman, 2011, 20). Seligman now routinely assigns his students to do a kindness and has them report back about how being kind makes them feel. Research has shown that doing something kind or expressing gratitude will make a person feel better not just briefly, but for a month (Seligman, 2011). Imagine the benefits to the students who plant and harvest the carrots and lettuce for the school lunchroom's salad bar when they realize that their efforts help many youth have a better lunch every day at school. The young gardeners' experiences reflect these five categories of well-being, and I will reference them in the following chapters.

# 8

# ¡CULTIVA! A MARKET AND YOUTH LEADERSHIP GARDEN

*I just feel kind of like I have, it's kind of like I have a new task, but it's not a task that's a burden. It feels like I have a new joy and it feels like putting my work efforts, and especially getting paid for something I love to do, it's just, it's great.* —BASIL, 14, ¡CULTIVA!

*I like the garden because it gets people working on the same thing. That way you can connect with people. It's a good way of getting people together doing something positive.* —DIANA, 17, ¡CULTIVA!

Basil, aged fourteen, and Diana, aged seventeen, work as peer leaders at ¡Cultiva!, a youth market garden and leadership program that is part of a larger, Boulder county gardening nonprofit focused on food sustainability called Growing Gardens. ¡Cultiva!'s $157,000 annual budget comes from a fall fundraising harvest dinner ($40,000), the profits made from the youth selling the food they grow at the Boulder Farmers' Market ($15,000 to $20,000) , and a myriad of small grants, including county funds for Fresh Food for Families and Fitness ($20,000)[1].

Boulder county sits on the eastern edge of the Rocky Mountains, where the mountains meet the plains, and the city of Boulder is the county seat. The city of Boulder has a median household income of $56,312 (2009–2013), with 22.8 percent of the population living below the poverty line (US Census, 2014b). ¡Cultiva! recruits youth from all income brackets and ethnic backgrounds for its program.

I bought some tomatoes from the young ¡Cultiva! farmers manning their Boulder Farmers' Market stand in the fall of 2006. Their enthusiasm as they told me about their program intrigued

---

1. In 2010, the food sold at the farmers' market brought in around $14,000 (Growing Gardens of Boulder County, 2011).

me and led to me interviewing several youth farmers for a class research paper. I so enjoyed learning from them that I expanded my inquiry to three more Colorado youth gardening sites over a four-year period for my doctoral dissertation. For this book, I included three more states and eight more programs through 2013.

The ¡Cultiva! youth inspired me to dig further, plant the research seeds, and harvest a dissertation and a book all rooted in young people's experiences growing food. They were the only farmers I interviewed in Colorado programs who gardened during all four seasons and who were paid for their efforts. The ¡Cultiva! youth also receive leadership training and work with younger children as garden leaders. The youth have adult mentors and serve as mentors themselves.

## HOW ¡CULTIVA! WORKS

¡Cultiva! is a youth-operated organic market garden where youth participants plant and nurture a two-acre garden, harvest the produce weekly to sell at the farmers' market, and donate a portion of what is harvested to those in need in the local community. The program's mission during this time is for youth to learn how to care for and protect the environment, operate a small business, and take part in a variety of activities that create positive change for the community, the environment, and themselves. The two-acre site is located behind the North Boulder Recreation Center and next to a large community garden, where adult gardeners work on their own garden plots within sight of the youth. For a starting pay of $7.25 per hour for summer participants (aged fourteen to nineteen) or $5 per day for apprentices (aged eleven to thirteen), youth work ten to fifteen hours per week, "tending the garden, selling at the farmer's market, delivering and preparing produce for homeless shelter residents, seniors, and families in need, and working on a variety of community projects focusing on food and hunger issues" (Growing Gardens of Boulder County, 2011).

¡Cultiva! began in 1999 and involves a great number of young people, especially when compared to school garden programs, with the greatest number of hours per week spent raising food from seed to table year round. Each summer, ¡Cultiva! hires ten high school-aged youth leaders between the ages of fourteen and nineteen who work three or four days per week for six-and-a-half hours per day. The forty other employed youth work two or three days per week in the summers for ten to fifteen hours per week. The youth at ¡Cultiva! work longer hours than those at school gardens, and the youth leaders work at least a full year, participating in all gardening tasks from planning to harvest. About one hundred youth apply each summer for the forty open positions, with youth leaders often returning throughout high school, as was the case with the five youth I interviewed. As a nonprofit, community-based program, ¡Cultiva! includes youth aged eleven to nineteen, but I only interviewed those between the ages of fourteen and eighteen, the age group I had chosen for my research.

The food that ¡Cultiva! youth harvest goes to several destinations: 70 percent goes to the local farmers' market and the remaining 30 percent (about 1,200 pounds) is donated to low-income families in nearby public housing communities, the local homeless shelter, and two local charities (Growing Gardens of Boulder County, 2011). Spring through fall, ¡Cultiva! runs a Children's Peace Garden right next to their row crops, where youth gardeners guide seven to eight hundred preschool to high school visitors each year through the garden and lead nature and gardening activities. The visiting children pay four dollars in the off-season and six dollars in the summer—money that goes toward maintaining these experiential learning opportunities.

The ¡Cultiva! garden and the other three rural Colorado school gardens included in this book all lie within hiking distance of mountains. The more-than-mile-high altitude they have makes the growing season relatively short, so the gardens all have at least one greenhouse to protect cold-sensitive crops, such as tomatoes and basil, and provide a place for the youth to

Entry to the ¡Cultiva! Children's Peace Garden. **Credit: Erin**

work in the colder months. The two acres of land that the ¡Cultiva! and the Boulder community gardens occupy offer a quiet retreat from the busy traffic on the west side of the farm fields.

I interviewed four girls and three boys, ages fourteen to seventeen, at ¡Cultiva!, as well as the program director, Vanessa. Two of the youth were Hispanic while the rest were of European-American descent. The youth answered questions regarding their sensory experiences while gardening and how gardening affects them personally. This included their environmental attitudes, their capacity to focus post gardening, and their eating habits. Basil, aged fourteen, was the youngest gardener I interviewed there. It was Basil's second year gardening in the program and his first year as a youth leader. Rose, aged sixteen, was the only youth I interviewed there who was a volunteer gardener and not a youth leader. She had been a paid worker in the summer and she continued without pay that fall to fulfill a high school community service requirement. She chose ¡Cultiva! and gardening over any other place she could have gone to do her service.

These young gardeners' answers reflect intimate feelings in relation to nature and their personal development. I felt privileged to hear them speak so movingly about how growing food communally makes them feel they are doing something positive for their broader community and for themselves personally. When I consider a more than forty-year age difference between us, their willingness to share so much humbled me and kept me interviewing more youth in more places. I wanted to see if location or socioeconomic status made any difference to the experiences youth had while gardening or if the experiences were intrinsic to gardening and a well-run program (I encountered no badly run youth gardens!). I conducted my interviews at ¡Cultiva! during the school year when the gardeners on site were mostly the youth leaders.

## DEVELOPING YOUTH LEADERSHIP CAPACITY

Vanessa, one of the five adults who supervise work with ¡Cultiva!, directs the program. She was starting her seventh gardening season when I interviewed her in the spring of 2008 after I had completed the youth interviews. Vanessa explained ¡Cultiva!'s purpose to me on a sunny spring day while we sat on the grass, her infant son playing beside us while youth nearby planted kale, chard, and spinach.

> There actually are a number of different philosophies behind it. The first, the most basic, is to get them [the youth] outside and get their hands in the dirt, trying to get them to experience this agricultural past that we have. I think that's sort of the core of the project; just to have people outside, doing whatever part they like most, and finding their own connection to it. There's also

a leadership component to the program, which is fairly important, which is getting the kids to take responsibility and ownership over the garden and find things they feel they'd like to contribute to and make their own and take leadership in developing and running that part of it.

¡Cultiva! hosts a big, annual harvest dinner that has become a community rallying point for local food and is a major program fundraiser. The youth leaders have the job in the summer to supervise work teams comprised of five to seven young people, ages eleven to nineteen, to accomplish all the daily food growing jobs: planting, weeding, irrigating, and harvesting. These work teams change in membership a couple of times a week, enabling all youth to get to know each other. The constant changing of work team membership is done intentionally to prevent cliques from forming, Vanessa explained to me. The leaders earn one dollar more per hour than the other youth participants. Each young person has a variety of ways to engage with the garden, according to Vanessa.

> Everybody finds something different. The bee program has been something that really connects and resonates with very few, but when it resonates, it really does; the people that do the beekeeping really like it. We've also had people that really like just the figuring out part of irrigating and constructing the shelves; the people that are very mechanically inclined do that. And then there are people that like to just be in the garden with the plants on a very peaceful level. Then there are people who like to work with the little kids and help to teach them what they've learned about gardening, trying to get the younger generation involved. Because we have so many different components of the program, everybody can find their own little niche in those main categories. The other one is cooking and that really sparks the kids too. We do cooking classes once or twice a month where we bring vegetables from the garden, and local chefs will lead cooking classes on how to make those into food, and that really hits home with the kids. They really like the cooking part, and it opens up all sorts of stories of what their parents have cooked or what they've never tasted. The chefs really share their background and the kids share their background.

The adult leaders present leadership and conflict resolution classes to the ¡Cultiva! youth leaders to prepare them to supervise their peers. All youth gardeners participate in four nutrition classes each summer and four cooking classes on site, as well as three classes at restaurants with professional chefs. In the winter, the youth leaders evaluate all of these seminars to advise the adult leaders and themselves as youth leaders in how to make the seminars better for the following year and which new topics to explore. The program, though not school-based, has many components to inform the youth and develop communication, critical thinking, and educational leadership capacities.

These youth do not have to take tests on what they learn, but they share their newly harvested knowledge by teaching younger children who come to summer camps or visit on field trips in the Children's Peace Garden next to the ¡Cultiva! row crops. The youth leaders also develop seminars for the youth gardeners on such topics as the health impacts of what we eat and the carbon footprint for standard industrial agriculture compared to local, organic agriculture. None of the other teens I interviewed at school gardening programs were involved in educating others as actively and broadly as the teens at ¡Cultiva!.

Since the ¡Cultiva! youth leaders have the responsibility of supervising other youth gardeners, they use a variety of capacities, including their senses, to assess what needs to be done. Marie, aged fifteen, explains how she looks for what to do before she gives instructions to her day's crew:

> When we went out every morning, we would look at the garden, figure out what we were going to do that day, and I would key into what rows had more weeds and what rows had more things we needed to work on, what rows needed mulching. Mostly that was what I was looking for, I'd say; the weeds and how the plants looked themselves.

Barclay, aged sixteen, thrived in his role as a gardening mentor to younger children. The mentoring at ¡Cultiva! is done in teams on specific topics that can be delivered several times in one day as visitors rotate through various workshops. Workshops include planting, cooking with the solar oven, and playing games oriented to teaching botany and environmental awareness. Barclay did not enjoy his work as much when supervising the volunteers or paid youth workers who were not part of the leadership group:

> People who don't want to be gardening are doing it because they're being forced to by their parents or they feel like they have to be there. As a youth leader, you're really opened up to that. It's really hard because some people don't want to work.

Over one hundred youth apply and are interviewed by the ¡Cultiva! staff to get the paid gardening jobs. Some people can also volunteer without receiving pay. More than a year after Barclay told me how difficult it was to supervise a reluctant youth gardener, I met a mother who told me that she indeed forced her son to get up and go volunteer at the garden so that he would learn the value of physical labor and how to grow food. He had hated it, but a year later, he applied for a job and was hired, and now, a year older and paid for his labor, he told me that he is proud of what he is doing. One can understand the challenges that a sixteen-year-old faces trying to persuade an unwilling twelve-year-old to work hard. Marie also commented on the challenges she encountered as a youth leader who needs to inspire her peers:

> The days are getting long and it's getting hot out and you've been there a couple of hours. You want to keep doing work, but you want to motivate others. I think that is the hardest part 'cause you want to talk to them and get their interest, but you don't want to be talking all the time, but it's a hard thing to try to find a balance.

## FAMILY EXPOSURE TO GARDENING

As with all of my research sites, I asked the young people whether anyone in their family gardened. All of the ¡Cultiva! participants had grown up with access to nature and trees around their homes. Family exposure to gardening was a big factor in choosing gardening as an activity for ¡Cultiva! youth. Five of these seven had at least one actively gardening parent. Rose had a mother, grandmother, and great-grandmother who gardened, and her grandmother displays a large picture of Rose peeking into a birdhouse when she was a small child. George, aged seventeen, and his family formerly lived in the German countryside and have a garden plot at the same community garden where ¡Cultiva! is located. He felt that growing food held happy childhood memories for him. Marie relayed, "If my mom didn't garden, I don't know if I would even be here today." Her mother was the one who told her about ¡Cultiva!.

Diana said that she had tried to have a garden at home once before, but no one in her family gardened and she had not been particularly committed to that first start. Heather, aged seventeen, answered that her brother influenced her to garden as he is also a youth garden leader at ¡Cultiva!. Basil's dad both gardens and cooks, and Basil helps his father with his garden.

Barclay said that once he started at ¡Cultiva!, he influenced his family to plant vegetables so that they would have plenty of fresh food at home:

> There are very few things that I show extreme amounts of passion for, but robotics and gardens

are something I really show passion for, and I don't know how I did it, but my mom had flower gardens, but I said it would be so cool if we had a [vegetable] garden, and we put it in. I think that they have told me several times they wouldn't have put in a garden if it wasn't for me.

## CONNECTING TO NATURE AND BEAUTY THROUGH THE SENSES

One day, Marie had a delightful reward for taking a closer look at things while she assessed what work needed to be done:

> We were working with the flowers in the morning and then there would be little baby bees sleeping inside the flowers. They are really small and they would just kind of be sleeping in there, and you'd be kind of afraid to pick the flower because you would be taking its home away, but then it would stretch its wings and fly away. It was really sweet.

These were probably wild bees smaller than the honeybees that Marie is used to seeing in the garden. A study done by the Museum of Natural History at the University of Colorado in Boulder identified 946 distinct bee species in Colorado (Scott et al. 2011). One can easily relate to her enchantment with a tiny bee seemingly napping in a flower. Using the senses in many different ways gives a rich texture to the youths' lives and many felt deeply rewarded by their sensory experiences. The only sensory experiences mentioned by them that they did not like (three of seven in this group) was getting dirt underneath their fingernails, being dirty, or feeling really hot midday in the summer. But those who mentioned these discomforts also said in the same breath that they can always wash their hands or take a shower when they are done and it's just part of the gardening job. In the end, they feel really good about what they have accomplished. The sense of achievement far outweighed the minor discomforts for all youth I spoke with in four states.

Basil bubbled over with enthusiasm for his sensory experiences and confessed that after gardening, he doesn't want to have to come back inside:

> The smells of the garden, they can't be matched. It's just, it's great! Starting my day in the summer with the smells of the garden, it's just really, it's great! I just love it! It's such a beautiful place, especially in the ¡Cultiva! garden. There's always the mountain backdrop, and it's just, it's gorgeous to be around.

George found special pleasure in what he heard in the garden: "The sound of birds, and in the summer, when the creek is running, and also wind connect me with nature, calm me down."

## FEELING CARING, CALM, RELAXED, AND PEACEFUL

Whether it is nature's song, her vibrant colors, her variety, or her specificity of form, the youth working in the ¡Cultiva! garden all expressed the calm and peace they experience while gardening and a deep appreciation for these feelings that often contrasted with the hectic feelings they encounter at school or in everyday life. Marie related her understanding of the link between nature, growing food, and a feeling of peace:

> I think it's kind of just something that being outdoors in nature brings you back sort of where, you know, without technology. It brings us back to where we are all from. Because you just get caught up in all this technology, but gardening is like this essential thing that has to be done by somebody because you know you don't get food [any other way]. In that way, it's a very essential part of life. Sometimes, we don't see that; we just go to the grocery store and buy it. But then, actually being able to say, "I made food or I grew food for myself," it just brings it all back together, and I think that's why I think that it is peaceful and enjoyable.

The youth come here straight from school, which, for some, involves a long, crowded bus ride or a bike ride on busy streets. After the hectic commute, the garden becomes a sanctuary, a word used by both Rose and Barclay. Barclay explains:

> Whenever I come to the garden, there's always this kind of calming presence. There's always like a small amount of dew; it's very calm. It's nice to be able to touch the dirt and be with the plants; it's just this connection that we as humans have lost over thousands of years. It goes back to our basic instincts that we used to be in the dirt.

In her interview with me, Rose described vividly how gardening enhances her well-being. She may not be paid in dollars, but she certainly gains a great deal:

ROSE: I just picture myself in a little pathway at the beginning of it [the garden] and having plants all around me. I don't know what it is, but I kind of relax right when I see that. Creating things, you're making things happen. I guess I've never really thought of how scents make me feel, but if I could put it into words, I'd say energized and relaxed at the same time—a balance between the two. It's just very peaceful, and the smells, they just, it's hard to put this in the words, I just really like all of it combined—all of my senses being used all at once. I'm mostly into the touch of it and the sight; touching and sight are the most prominent for me: the different variations of color and the reflections of light on the plants, the size of the plants and what I can see when I am going through the plants, like the different bugs and the different sizes of the fruit they produce if they do produce fruit and the colors that they produce. Just the texture is really, really cool. 'cause I also like to draw, so I always like focusing on the light source all the time and the individual-like sides and views I can get, how this leaf looks by itself and in a group. And when you touch things, you can kind of see them in a sense because you are getting the texture and you're, you know, feeling the temperature of it.

ILLÈNE: Has growing food changed your eating preferences?

ROSE: We've actually made food from the garden and it's really good. Yeah, it's a lot more fresh, more flavorful obviously because it hasn't traveled miles and miles to the grocery store. It just, it's a lot more satisfying. I'm not really a huge vegetable person either, but when I come here, I go, "Yeah!" and I taste garlic because it tastes so good. We did this program called Slow Foods where we just got a bunch of the vegetables from our garden and we cooked meals with these chefs from a restaurant. It was really, really good.

ILLÈNE: How does gardening impact your feelings?

ROSE: I always think about a lot of things that are going on with me. And I come out; I'm just so much more relaxed, like, after I do it. It just slows me down, it makes me think for a second, helps me relax. When I leave here, I'm like, "Oh, I'll make it." I'm just really optimistic and happy. It's really therapeutic.

ILLÈNE: Do you notice if gardening affects your ability to focus?

ROSE: I can get focused. It helps me focus and, like, slows everything down. It makes me able to concentrate on one thing, not several things at a time like I have to at school, like due dates and tests and stuff like that. It brings, it just kind of lets me slow down and focus on one particular thing that needs to get done, and when I do it, I move on to the next thing and I focus on that for however long I need to.

ILLÈNE: Has gardening changed your environmental awareness?

ROSE: I don't really see as much an environmental thing in gardening as I see a sustainable thing. It seems like gardening is more for people and environmental is more for creatures and the plant life.

ILLÈNE: Are there other benefits you experience from gardening?

ROSE: I can get something done and I can see my work right in front of me. I can see what I have accomplished. Just that I know I am helping these plants keep going. I'm harvesting and I'm weeding. I'm just helping with the up-keep with it all. I'm doing something good for myself because if I wasn't doing this, if no one was doing this, nothing would really be happening here! I guess I was saying how I think it's really therapeutic. I have clinical depression and so I'm always really anxious and don't get a lot of sleep and, you know, I'm down a lot of the time, but when I come here, and after I come here, I feel like more complete and more, I feel happier. I feel like I can do things, like I'm doing something good for myself and I'm doing something good for someone else and it makes me feel like a good person overall. I just, I don't know, it's really, I guess to sum it up, it's really therapeutic. Just going to therapy and talking to someone about problems is really not the same as being able to focus in the silent space, you know, and think to yourself about what is going on with yourself. Do some self-medication instead of relying on, like, medication or, you know, other people! It makes me feel really self-reliable, like, in a good way.

Diana did not garden when she was a child, but her feelings about what she gains from gardening echo Rose's:

DIANA: I like it because we're out in the air. I like the moist smell of earth and I just like the outside feeling. It's nice working in a garden, but you get dirty. I don't like it when the bugs buzz in your ear. This is your job. It's a good thing.

ILLÈNE: Are there things you find difficult in your gardening job?

DIANA: A lot of times, I confuse things: dandelion leaf and an arugula leaf; they're very similar. At first, it's frustrating because there are so many weeds, but then, when you're done, you realize that you did all that work, so it's a sense of accomplishment.

ILLÈNE: Does the food from the garden taste different from what you buy at the store?

DIANA: Like the carrots from the garden, they have a better taste, such a better taste than if you go to Safeway and buy some. My family, when we buy it, we don't eat organic things. That's just how it is. It's more expensive. But when I am in the garden, like, when I try it, it actually tastes better. I was, like, surprised!

ILLÈNE: Are there other things you enjoy about gardening?

DIANA: I like it because I get time to think about my life. I think about my problems or things, but then, at the same time, I am busy with something. I am actually doing something productive, so it's good.

ILLÈNE: Does gardening affect your ability to focus?

DIANA: It gives me more focus, like, it relaxes me. And since you're actually doing something, it's not like you're just sitting there and thinking, you're actually focusing on something and that's a nice part. Since I am actually doing something with my hands and, like, just being there with the plants and, like, outside, it makes me feel a little bit happier than I was before, like I'm doing something good, something good for my life.

ILLÈNE: Has your environmental awareness changed?

DIANA: We are part of the earth. Why not do things for the earth? We get food from it!

ILLÈNE: Does gardening outside impact your feelings?

DIANA: When we see tomatoes and strawberries, it just makes you feel like you should do things. Also, it's nice in the summer just being outside with the trees. It gets your mind off things. You have time to reflect on your life. It's not like you're sitting at home thinking. You kind of work them out because you're doing more physical work! You come to a solution. You reach a kind of peace.

Basil echoes Diana's feelings about the garden bringing peace to the gardener: "It's something that you can come to and it can just take away any of your worries." The youth clearly found relief from life's stresses through the gardening process. All seven brought up the value of self-reflection and the peace they experience. The focus they relate while gardening reflects deep engagement with their tasks. They take pleasure in seeing what they have accomplished. Diana notices that the shared labor brings people together on common ground. Growing good food for the community gives their work meaning.

Marie uses the word "we" to discuss the shared accomplishment:

The harvesting, this is what we have all been working to, and then you look at the food, the tomatoes and lettuce, and, wow, this is what we've been working so hard to get, here it is, and it's a physical thing I can touch and it's there. So I think for me that is, yeah, the most pleasurable part. I think definitely part of it is seeing, the physical, visual part of seeing it all, packing it all into the coolers and the bags and seeing just how much it is. It's really great to say, "Wow, we've put this much work into and here it is. Here is all this food."

Several gardeners also mentioned renewed energy. Barclay used the word energy in his interview sixteen times, indicating how much gardening impacts his personal energy levels:

I'm so tired. I feel like I've done twenty hours of homework this week, but I've noticed that since I've been here [in the garden], I feel better. I've had some hard days at school, but it's nice here; people are laughing. I think it's a great input and output of energy. I think it outputs stress, but inputs positive energy, so it balances it out. So, positive energy pushes out that negative energy when you get here.

## SERVICE AND RECIPROCITY

Vanessa, the program director, noticed significant changes in the youth garden leaders over time, including their increased peacefulness that she attributes to their mentoring roles:

With the mentoring role that we put the teenagers in when they work with the children, you see a big change in those kids. They become a lot more patient, they become a lot more peaceful because they have to be that role model. It's a powerful place to put teenagers in that role where they're not kids, they're not just goofing off, they're being looked up to. And I think over time, keeping them in that role often is really neat to see how they change and become those kind of people, become those people that are mentors not just when they're in front of kids, but more it's part of their life.

Just as gardening provided something inwardly satisfying related to deeply personal experiences, the youth also expressed pleasure in what they could give others through their efforts. Barclay feels that gardening and mentoring younger children has given him a new career direction:

I want to go into agriculture after I get out of high school and part of that is that I want to help to feed as many people as possible and that includes children too. I've seen the videos of children starving and I just want to help not only those kids, but as many kids as possible because I think they are our future. They may not take something away from it immediately, it may take a couple years to set in, a couple of months, but I think it's something they'll remember their whole life, being in the garden. Once you know about something like this, your curiosity really grows. Before this, I wanted to go into pharmaceuticals, but now I want to go into agriculture.

The youth at ¡Cultiva! feel a sense of service to both people and nature. Marie explained that that "this is going to be good for other people too, [which] makes it even more enjoyable." George

¡Cultiva! youth leader harvests carrots.  Credit: ¡Cultiva! youth gardener

expressed this feeling of unity also: "It all connects one way or another, so I figure that I'm help-ing the environment, it's helping the garden, I'm helping myself. It's not that everything is about me, it's that everything is about everything else."

## ENVIRONMENTAL AWARENESS AND ACTIVISM

That "everything else" leads to how gardening affects the young gardener's relationship to the whole environment. Being one with the earth found expression in diverse ways among the youth I interviewed. I asked them all directly if gardening had affected their environmental awareness and attitudes. Five of the seven found that gardening had changed their outlooks. Two felt they came into gardening because they already had a positive attitude towards the environment, were already engaging in other environmental activist activities, and knew they wanted to spend more time outdoors. Basil found that gardening had made him more environmentally aware on a very basic level: "It's really affected me, especially when I see littering or contamination of water. It just feels like that's just going to come back to us and haunt us. It really makes me want to put a stop to all of this [polluting]." He is studying ecology at school and said he wanted to work with younger children to help them become more environmentally conscientious.

Heather said she doesn't know if gardening, school, or just maturing had made her more aware, but that she definitely noticed she was more attuned to environmental issues now, especially those related to food: "The where-your-food-comes-from thing, it makes so much more sense, like going local, buying at the farmers' market instead of buying something a little bit cheaper at the grocery store. You know that a truck has wasted I don't know how many gallons of gas to bring it here, crowded the highways or whatever."

Barclay says he's learning how to be more conscientious in his behavior as a result of participating in ¡Cultiva!: "I would say maybe a little, but I came in already aware. I've always ridden my bike. I would say maybe it has trickled in. I'm more cautious of the water I use. It's the biggest thing that I have come away with that I hadn't come with is water usage." Barclay does environmental restoration work as a volunteer and finds his feelings in that work similar to gardening and considers both to have great value: "I just think that these two things the most are going to help me out the rest of my life as far as having the skills I need." Since Barclay is also involved in building robots, a modern, high-tech undertaking quite different than gardening, it seems significant that he feels the work he does outdoors with and for nature has the most importance for him. Robotics potentially would offer a well-paid career to him while stream restoration and gardening will not, but he values working with nature more than the glamour of a high-tech career.

Hearing the word calm used in relationship to garden accomplishment bears further investigation and will be discussed by many of the youth in this book. With gardening, they see an immediate result to their work: weeds picked and tossed in the compost, a row of seedlings transplanted and watered, and vegetables harvested, washed, and ready to sell. They can see, smell, taste, and touch what they have done. Though I never asked them about school, most brought it up and discussed their stress, not their achievements. There is no competition in a garden, but there is a great deal of collaboration towards a mutual goal: the harvest. Not one young gardener said, "I want to grow the prettiest flower or the most lettuce or the biggest pumpkin." However, school stresses competition for grades, SAT scores, sports, and style. Gardening requires collaboration with fellow gardeners and nature. When I asked Rose, who travels about thirty minutes from her high school to ¡Cultiva!, if she felt it would be good to have a garden at a high school, she responded unequivocally:

I guess I would say that normal high school life is very, very hectic and rushed and very stressful, and I think that it would be good for the focus of the kids and for the happiness of the kids and, you know, the health, the overall health, for them to get out and do something that is productive and that they know they can do. I mean, anyone can do it, and they know they'll get something good out of it because it's refreshing and relaxing and you're more able to focus and it makes people so much happier from what I've seen.

## ABILITY TO FOCUS

Rose cited better focus as a benefit to her from gardening. I did not administer any cognitive tests to actually measure mental functioning pre and post gardening nor did I measure their stress hormones before and after. However, I asked all the youth whether time spent gardening changed their capacity to focus. A renewed capacity to focus could be a very good thing in the course of a school day for students with many demands on them to concentrate in one subject after another. Most of the ¡Cultiva! gardeners went from gardening to travelling home to doing homework during the school year. Six noticed that it improved focus.

George agreed with Rose: "In the garden, there's not that many distractions, so you keep on working. So, it helps you get in that mind-set so that when you do other tasks, it helps you get in that mind-set easier. It motivates me." Heather also noticed the difference for her: "I think it might [help me] be able to focus, make me focus more. Especially, like, now 'cause I had school all day, and then gardening to clear my head, and then home to do a lot of homework. I guess it's easier than going directly from school to doing homework." Marie clearly found it much easier to focus after gardening: "If I had not gardened at all, just started my homework right away, I would be, might be, more tense. But after gardening, it's like, okay, I can just get this done, it'll be okay. I can be more peaceful, bring a peaceful sense into doing that. I definitely think I focus better after I garden."

Recent research with adult gardeners in Holland has shown that gardening reduces the stress hormone cortisol and iterates the neurological benefits resulting in the relaxation that gardening produces (van den Berg and Custers, 2011). These young people have all described vividly their own experiences in this realm. While I did not measure their stress hormone levels pre and post gardening, their words certainly confirm their calm and happy states post gardening.

## NEW TASTES AND CHANGES IN EATING HABITS DUE TO GROWING FOOD

Naturally, gardening leads to tasting and what the young people eat in the garden and after gardening. I asked the youth about their changes in eating as a result of gardening, and five of seven ¡Cultiva! youth leaders say that gardening has changed their eating habits to include many more vegetables, as well as raw ones, even if they already ate quite a lot of vegetables at home. George said that since his family gardens, he already ate a lot of vegetables and loved them. He can't understand people who don't eat vegetables.

Basil also enjoys how the food tastes: "I think everything is a little more sweeter when it hasn't been really handled by as much human hands and machinery. Once it's picked off right away and you eat it, you're tasting the real plant."

Several youth commented on the energy difference they notice in garden-grown food. George explains: "There is kind of still that energy in it, like the life in the plant provides if it's fresh picked, and I think it gets into you, but if it sits around, it dissipates."

Besides the better taste in garden-fresh vegetables, there is the fun of learning to cook, which is both a gustatory and a social experience. As Rose described earlier, the Slow Foods program brings in chefs from local restaurants to cook with the youth what they have harvested in the garden. The youth take these new experiences home with them. Marie describes greater access to and diversity in vegetable consumption:

When we have a harvest, there is a lot of stuff we can take home, so I've started cooking with eggplant and zucchini. I guess tomatoes and that kind of stuff that I used before, but especially eggplant and zucchini and kale too I had never eaten before here. I guess I tasted it before, but I didn't use it when I was making salads or stuff like that or even I didn't incorporate it into my food. It's really good.

Basil also enjoys eating a greater variety of vegetables than before he began gardening at ¡Cultiva!: "I have [changed] a lot. I've really opened myself to many different types of vegetables, especially it's been a lot with basil and eggplant. Eggplant parmesan has become one of my favorite dishes. I really like it."

Marie also reports significant dietary changes:

I try to eat more vegetables. Also, I like simpler food, you know, like raw vegetables, maybe you don't have to soak it in cream and salt or something. Also, like, where the vegetables, where the food comes from 'cause this is all organic, you see that you grew it from a seed, you know. You don't just like go to Safeway and get a random apple or something. You know where it comes from.

Knowing the food's provenance seems quite significant to the young gardeners. They like to eat the things they grow. Rose admits, "The weird thing was I hated cherry tomatoes and then I came here and I love them now. Only from here though because they're so fresh."

Barclay is honest about how much he has changed his habits and the appeal of junk food.

I've stopped eating things with high fructose corn syrup in them. For the most part, I think that everything in moderation. I don't really eat fast food anymore. If it was available, I wouldn't not eat it, but I've definitely cut down on soda. I had a streak going from like March to July, but you just feel a lot more energy when you're away from junk food. It's just negative energy whereas vegetables are positive energy. It's fun to have a little junk food now and then though.

George notices that when he eats garden-grown food, it gives him "more connection with the food and stuff than just going to the store and getting something." The fact that all of the youth gardeners but one (George, who already ate a lot of vegetables) report eating more vegetables as a result of growing them will receive further discussion, as will the role school and community gardens can have in making fresh, organic food available to people who cannot afford to buy it.

## RECAPPING

For a final snapshot of the ¡Cultiva! gardeners, let us review what they shared. All of Seligman's (2011) elements appear in multiple ways. Positive emotion, engagement, meaning, and positive relationships and accomplishments (PERMA) seem to grow with the vegetables, the weeds, and the youth. Several say they experience joy. All report a pleasure and appreciation for eating the fresh vegetables they grow together—from the better taste to feeling connected to what they eat and what they grow. All report better focus or engagement and feelings of calm and peace while gardening and afterwards. Six out of seven had exposure to family members gardening before ¡Cultiva! and report positive family relationships from those memories. The youth mention positive relationships with the young children they introduce to the garden. I did not ask the youth at ¡Cultiva! about their friendships at the garden, but I noticed the collaborative and friendly way they worked and planned together when I was there. They have a commitment to caring for the environment and the community's well-being through growing food organically. This commitment would fall into the realm of meaning in Seligman's flourishing construct. They mentor younger children and lead youth work crews. They sell and donate the produce they raised. These young people are proud of their accomplishments, the A in PERMA.

People talk to any person sitting next to them weeding, which allows people to know new people in the gardening process. Vanessa said that it was not uncommon to read a year-end evaluation where a youth reported something similar to, "I've gone to school with this person for the past three years and never talked to them or thought we'd be friends, and now we're hanging out on the weekends, doing sewing projects, going to the movies."

Every youth I spoke with at ¡Cultiva! expressed a deep appreciation for what comes from growing food together. Barclay sums up the ¡Cultiva! experience this way:

Yeah, it's that energy. It forces you to be in a good mood; it's not in a forceful way, but it just happens. You come and you see people learning and having fun. But it's just cool to see people smiling, and I think a lot of that energy is from the people that are here. It's like we put energy and other people take it out, like an energy transfer, that might be taking place.

# 9

## COLORADO ROCKY MOUNTAIN SCHOOL
### WORK CREW GARDENERS

*There is something to be said about the conversation in a garden, any garden. It's usually a lot deeper and more vibrant than conversations that I have anywhere else. There is something more primal about working in a garden than conversing over at a dinner party or something. I guess these primal instincts we have really bring out the best in us.*

*Even if we are trying to discuss the same things, I find myself being more organized with my thoughts and it is easier for me to articulate myself and easier for me to formulate my own opinions [in the garden]. I have worked in the garden for about three years and I have seen people I have never really gotten along with and they haven't gotten along with me, but in the garden, all that sort of changes.*
**—STEVEN, 18, COLORADO ROCKY MOUNTAIN SCHOOL**

We heard similar statements about gardening connecting people deeply in both New York and Boulder. In 2007 and 2008, I spoke with youth at the Colorado Rocky Mountain School (CRMS), an independent college preparatory school serving approximately 155 students in 9th to 12th grades annually from all over the United States, including 16 percent (approximately twenty-four) international students each year. Local students who live at home make up 40 percent of the student body, and 60 percent board at the school (Colorado Rocky Mountain School [CRMS], 2013). CRMS was a working ranch with cattle and horses fifty years ago when it was founded. This is a completely different environment from the South Bronx and East Harlem where the Green Bronx Machine youth garden and live: at CRMS, there are no public housing high-rises nearby and no skyscrapers to block the sun. The CRMS garden has been a vital part of the school community for more than a decade.

The CRMS philosophy integrates rigorous intellectual and artistic pursuits with the daily physical work needed for the school community to function. Students and faculty also engage

Colorado Rocky Mountain School onions grow in front of a straw bale greenhouse
Credit: Colorado Rocky Mountain School student gardener

in exciting outdoor explorations in the surrounding mountains and rivers. CRMS occupies valley land on the banks of the Crystal River in Carbondale, Colorado, with a majestic mountain peak, Mount Sopris, providing inspiring views. Some of its land is now leased to a local rancher to graze grass-fed cattle, and while the school is not currently raising livestock, the one-and-a-half acre garden and three small greenhouses provide 40 percent of the produce served in the dining hall, some 11,500 pounds in 2013 (CRMS, 2013). The students weigh all harvested food before carrying it to the school kitchen, about two hundred yards from the garden.

CRMS was the only place I interviewed youth where I had a prior relationship with the organization or school. My daughter had attended the school for two years (1989–1991), and I had known the school's founders and many faculty members, though I did not have personal relationships with the current faculty when I was doing this research.

The person who developed CRMS's garden program, Linda Halloran, proposed it in 1996 not only to provide a learning environment and grow food but also to have one more work crew that could function in the winter (with a greenhouse) since work crews form one branch of the CRMS educational structure. Throughout the school year, every student does two hours on a chosen work crew twice a week after classes. Students do either two or three different work crews annually and can choose the three-month garden crews. Paid staff maintain the garden in the summer months. CRMS considers work a key component to a meaningful life; the campus jobs are real and necessary, not token. All work crews involve service and learning useful life skills, such as gardening, carpentry, electrical wiring, food preparation, childcare (at the campus preschool), and sometimes animal husbandry depending on the year and livestock on campus. Students have helped to build dorms and greenhouses and install photovoltaic panels.

CRMS awards many scholarships to local students, as was the case for my daughter. The boarding students tend to come from families with substantial economic resources. Virtually all graduates go on to university. The CRMS gardening program had the longest history of all the gardening programs in this book (eleven years then, sixteen now) and included a prior gardening program run by an organic farmer in the school's early history. The CRMS students were the most economically privileged that I interviewed. It was also the only school garden where the garden stemmed from the school's work and service philosophy. Many students perceive the garden as emblematic; they take pride in growing, harvesting, and serving to the entire school the literal fruits of their labor.

Grants funded the garden's beginnings with a greenhouse where students grow drought-tolerant perennials and vegetable plants from seed, transplant to the garden, and sell many at the annual spring garden fundraiser. The CRMS garden has continued for almost twenty years with these multiple purposes of education, community demonstration, and food provisioning. The school now covers the garden operating expenses via its annual budget.

During one of the four terms that I interviewed students, CRMS offered a Politics of Food class as a senior elective. Several interviewees took this class in addition to their gardening education and received considerable information about how the United States grows, processes, and markets food. The class used Michael Pollan's (2006) The Omnivore's Dilemma as a text, as does the public Roaring Fork High School agricultural biology program in Carbondale that is also discussed in this book.

Halloran has a teaching background, extensive gardening experience, and a year-round assistant. She mentors the four to six students she supervises in organic gardening methods during each of the two weekly work crew teams. One work crew comes Mondays and Wednesdays and the other on Tuesdays and Thursdays. Halloran plans what to plant after conferring with the school cooks, and they enthusiastically embrace the student-grown food. These students are not as involved in planning as the ¡Cultiva! youth because they commit only a few months' time to the garden rather than a full year.

I interviewed the CRMS gardeners during their work periods. I observed a respectful, focused environment where students chatted with friends, as well as with Halloran and her assistant. Halloran gave clear instructions needed to perform the day's tasks in a conversational manner. The young gardeners accomplished a lot of planting, weeding, and harvesting in their two hours. The youth also had time to themselves as they worked on assigned tasks. Over the course of two years, I interviewed sixteen students, five males and eleven females ages fifteen to nineteen, though most were eighteen as these were the students who could give consent for themselves and didn't have to mail the parent consent form home to sign. Most of the students I interviewed who were under the age of eighteen lived in the valley and saw their parents daily.

Since CRMS has a required outdoor program, most students there choose the school in part because they wish to spend a lot of time outside. The only exception I encountered was the two South Korean foreign students I interviewed, a male and female, who found spending so much time outside a completely new experience. All but two of the students interviewed chose the garden work crew, but the two who did not were glad they had ended up in it. They had become very enthusiastic despite not having chosen gardening initially. I did not find any major difference in attitudes between those who took the Politics of Food class and those who didn't except perhaps that those who took the class had slightly more interest in articulating the societal benefits of learning to grow one's own food.

Halloran told me that students occasionally complained about getting dirty, but only two students I interviewed mentioned not liking it. Both said that the pleasures of gardening outweighed feeling dirty, so maybe they like to complain to the adult in charge, but not to me, the interviewer. One girl who vehemently did not like being near insects when she gardened told me her attitudes changed quite a lot as she grew to understand the insects' role in life's interdependent web.

The interviews revealed many benefits discussed below: relaxed, happy, and invigorated students; a feeling of caring for the earth and the life it supports; an abundant harvest of fresh, delicious food that students enjoy snacking on as they harvest; and an enormous sense of accomplishment and contribution to the community when they deliver the day's harvest to the school kitchen and eat it at dinner.

Most of the students I interviewed began gardening earlier in childhood with a parent or grandparent. Thirteen of sixteen students had some exposure to gardening with parents or grandparents even if it was only observation. Several said certain garden smells took them back to childhood memories. I have turned some of their interviews into a poem format, with all the words and phrases theirs, and some interviews appear in narrative formats to eliminate my many questions and irrelevant information.

## CONNECTING TO NATURE THROUGH THE SENSES

Rosemary, aged eighteen, grew up in the Aleutian Islands with an Aboriginal Alaskan father who harvests the sea and a mother who gardens. The words are hers entirely:

## I've Never Had a Bad Time Gardening

*That smell puts me*
*In the zone of calm,*
*Cool and collected.*
*Good childhood memories*
*When I was a little girl*
*In the garden with my mom.*
*There is this different scent,*
*Like new life almost.*

*I seem more in tuned*
*To everything that's*
 *Around me.*
*The wind, the plants, the bugs.*
*I see pleasure*
*Watching things grow.*
*It's very relaxing,*
*Calming, you know.*

*Greens, orange, or red*
*Like peppers. It puts*
*A lot of people*
*At ease. Refreshed.*
 *Playing in the dirt,*
*Your blood is flowing,*
*Feeling close to nature,*
*Re-energized.*

Hana, aged eighteen, gardened at CRMS for the first time in her senior year during the spring semester and found the experience personally transformative.

HANA: I could be philosophical in the garden, but I think I am more amazed. The soil is really earthy and rich. It reminds you of clean: clean water, clean air, just new growth, life. All the smells are really fresh, like if you ate them, they would be just so fresh. It feels like there aren't any toxins in them, like pesticides, just natural. It's very important! Sometimes, I find myself going into the store. There are so many products that I don't even know the names of their ingredients, even in a simple box of crackers.

ILLÈNE: Do you think about what you are looking at when you are gardening?

HANA: You don't really think about something until you are fully involved with it. It's kind of like that with gardening. We were planting these tiny little seeds the other day. They were supposed to germinate in ten days or something. Then we came back and then there were these little tiny sprouts out there. They were like lettuce sprouts. I can't believe that something like that small can grow this big. It was just so cool. Mostly everything in the garden is new and fresh and natural and pleasant. There is nothing about it that's not to like. If I went to school all day, just sat in the classroom, if I never went outside, it would be really hard.

ILLÈNE: Do you think that this process of gardening here at school has affected your environmental attitudes?

HANA: I definitely admire the composting system. All the food we don't eat is composted and other plants as well. Just that our school has a garden is important. It's kind of like a symbol of our school, I guess.

ILLÈNE: Have you changed any of your eating habits since you began gardening?

HANA: Since I came to CRMS, I became vegetarian. I tried to go vegan for two weeks, but it was too hard. I was educated about the way our food is grown and how unnatural we choose to grow, especially meat. I had a really hard time even when I did eat meat, eating it. I just didn't like the feeling of eating another being if you know what I mean. It doesn't seem like a pleasant thought. Then there is the mass production of animals and hormones. It's not a very humane way to go about things. I went on a [CRMS] trip, and it was fly-fishing. We were up in the mountains and everything there is pretty and organic and natural, and I caught a fish. Everyone told me, "Fish can't feel! Fish can't feel!" And I was trying to get the hook out of the fish's mouth and I couldn't. Another guy had to come and help me, and I felt so bad for the fish. He killed it because I didn't want to. He put it out of its misery. And I just decided that if I couldn't kill anything, I wouldn't eat it. If I couldn't kill it myself, I would not eat it.

**ILLÈNE:** Do you find that you focus better after gardening?

**HANA:** After going to classes all day, gardening is kind of the relief block and you just go, "Phew," take that breath. And so, in a sense, you are focused because your mind is clear I think because you can think about whatever you want or you can think about nothing. You can focus your energy wherever. When you are in the garden, you are in the soil and you are with the plants. You're outside! You're working! You're making a difference! You're changing. If I'm gardening a lot, I get really inspired by it. I understand an appreciation for the world, how unique everything else is, how small this plant is now, but then it's a huge tree! How cool everything is! I have a greater appreciation for the work people do to support their environment and protect it.

Hana expresses here all the PERMA elements for flourishing (Seligman, 2011): positive emotions, engagement, an empathic relationship with other living beings, and the meaning and achievement she gains from gardening—a new life activity that has influenced how she lives her daily life and what foods she chooses to eat. The garden is also a refuge for her at the end of classes; a place to let go of all the intellectual activity and just be.

## COMPARING GARDENING TO WILDERNESS TRIPS

Since CRMS takes students on wilderness adventures several times each year, I asked these youth to compare their sensory experiences and feelings in relation to nature on wilderness trips to those experienced gardening. April, aged sixteen, explained:

> I feel like it's really specifically gardening, that kind of being one with the earth, essentially. Most people will kind of laugh at that and look down upon that as not really a true thing. It definitely is though. You definitely feel more connected; you're coming from a totally natural place that we came from, the earth. Being able to reconnect with it is a great thing; it's definitely one of my favorite things to do here.

Eve, aged eighteen, echoed April: "I think that gardening is a lot more intimate connection to the earth and your surroundings than just walking on top of it." Tom, aged seventeen, expanded on the difference between an outdoors trip and gardening for him:

When I am in the garden, I am creating something. When I am on the San Juan River, I am not really creating anything; I am just kind of going along with nature. I'd say that in the garden, you are affecting nature in a good way rather than when you are on the San Juan, you are worried about affecting nature in a wrong way. "Leave no trace" is, like, one of our morals I guess we live by on our trips, so we leave the place as good as new or better so we don't like affect it in a bad way.

Richard, aged sixteen, expressed similarly the difference between backpacking and gardening: "You are never planting a plant. You are sleeping under a tree. There is a difference between making it grow as opposed to stomping on it and destroying it."

## FEELING CARING

With the responsibility to not harm the wilderness always in their awareness and much news of environmental degradation in classes and via media, these youth discover a personal capacity for caring for nature in the garden even if they have never been exposed to such possibilities before. Sage, aged nineteen, the oldest student I interviewed at CRMS, comes from South Korea and confesses, "I wasn't very interested in plants because I don't like bugs and worms and I hate spiders, so I didn't really like them [plants] and didn't take care of them, so I didn't notice them before." She goes on to explain her personal transformation regarding small living creatures and plants as a result of working in the school garden:

### Pleasure
*Working with soil,*
*Touching bugs and worms,*
*Transplanting seedlings.*
*Calm, tranquil, peaceful.*

*If I planted the seed,*
*It's like my baby.*
*If I didn't plant it, it feels like little relatives.*
*I am more aware of live things.*

*Nurturing, gentle,*

*Eating food right out of the garden,*
*Liking raw vegetables more.*
*I like this new world of gardens and living things.*

Other students echoed this feeling that plants they tend are like one's children. Gina, aged fifteen, added that the plants in the garden are "like a kid, but a bunch of them in one place." Karen, aged sixteen, expressed empathy for the plants:

> I think it's because I think of them as living beings. I treat them as if they have feelings. It's not like I'm doing it for myself or the community even though thinking about the community is good, but I kind of do it for the plants because it's kind of like they're babies in a sense because they can't take care of themselves and they need water to live, and it's kind of for them.

These students who express so much caring for plants live with a lot of academic pressure to perform and succeed constantly and many noticed that working outside in the garden provided significant stress relief. Karen elaborated:

> When I garden, I just don't really pay attention to anything else. I just dig the holes and put them [seedlings] in and keep going. It makes me feel calm and I kind of get into the motion of doing it. I feel like I don't really have to worry about anything, like my homework or anything like that. I just have to worry about putting the plants where they go and taking care of them.

## FEELING CALM, RELAXED, AND MORE ABLE TO FOCUS

Fourteen of the sixteen CRMS students used the word calm a total of twenty-six times, more than any other word used to describe gardening's impact on their feelings. For the two students who did not actually say the word calm, Hana used the words serene and peaceful to describe how gardening made her feel. The calming effect of engaging with plants and the earth made the garden a blessing at the end of a busy academic day. As Jessie, aged sixteen, put it, "If I take care of them, they'll take care of me!" She went on to explain this feeling of reciprocity she experienced:

It helps so much when you're relaxed. I'm a day student, so I go home afterwards, and it just helps that you kind of released the tensions of the day and you can just go home, and it's easier to work on homework. You're working in a group of people in the garden, but it's almost like a solo act, where you get time to reflect and kind of think. And that carries through with you after gardening because you're really relaxed, and it definitely carries through more in the day when you go home and you're able to focus on what you have to do for the next day to be prepared because you haven't been stressed from eight o'clock in the morning to the end of the day. It's a break in between what you have to do and what you have to think about.

Time to self-reflect, connect with the earth, and let go of the day's stresses permeated these young people's conversations about gardening at school. Despite gardening being a two-hour work crew sometimes requiring quite a lot of physical work, many came out feeling re-energized and capable of focusing on the homework they inevitably had to do that evening. Sage put it this way: "It's a lot of work, but I get away from school. Two hours is fast going by. I feel pleasure afterwards."

Jessie told me that some work crews don't last the full two hours, but gardening always does. However, these gardeners don't mind that they have to work longer than classmates on other work crews because, as Tom explains, "When you come out of gardening and you have had a chance to kind of relax for a while. If you are calm, you can definitely hear, see, smell, taste, and you appreciate it more because you have had a chance to reflect in the garden."

Karen even discovered that gardening provides memory enhancement for her:

When I'm gardening, I think of the things I do and I have a bad memory. So, when I'm gardening, I think of them all so I kind of associate them while gardening. And [when I] go back and think about what I was thinking about when gardening, it seems to help.

Gina described gardening as a meditative experience:

It's almost like meditation: like my body is present, but my mind just kind of drifts off and goes someplace else and thinks about things. It's brainless tasks most of the time, so it's also, like, zenful, so you get to listen to things. I think about stuff so I don't have to go home and think about it right before bed so instead, I can just go to sleep. I just feel happier in a way and more at peace.

These meditative feelings are so common amongst the gardening work crew that students nicknamed it the "meditation crew." The school nurse even told one of the girls who went to her with a stress-related issue to go to the gardening work crew and garden because it would make her feel better. Since gardening has been shown to lower stress levels in adults (van den Berg and Custers, 2011), it most likely does in adolescents as well.

Every student I interviewed reported experiencing improved focus after gardening, an experience concurrent with attention restoration research that shows time spent in or looking at nature restores the capacity to pay attention and improves cognitive function (Hartig et al. 2003; Kaplan and Berman, 2010). Laurel, aged seventeen, related, "I'm able to complete my homework faster because I'm in a better place to do other things because I just spent an hour not worrying about my homework and my grades and my timing for anything because there's no deadline here [in the garden]."

## FOOD QUALITY, EATING HABITS, AND PRIDE IN ACCOMPLISHMENT

The general feeling of well-being from working in the garden that students expressed extended to their pleasure in having access to tasty, garden-fresh food to munch on while they work. These students provide an enormously important service to their school community by providing healthy, organically grown food to school meals that they enjoy together in the dining hall near the garden. Many discussed feelings of accomplishment and contribution. Steven, aged eighteen, commented: "A lot of the time when I am gardening, I am able to realize that my labors have paid off."

Rod, aged fifteen, experienced pride in what he grew through a unique connection to the school kitchen: "My mom works in the kitchen, and so she is always telling me about how big the carrots are and how good the onions are, and it's like, 'Mom, I know! I just picked all of it!'" Rod proudly photographed his hand with squash he had just harvested.

The quality of food they grow and eat, along with their role in community sustainability, proved very important to all these young gardeners. Rod compared what he grew to what he had eaten in the federal school lunch program: "I came from a large public school before I came here as a freshman, and, I mean, that food was really disgusting. Like, you could tell it was all frozen, that the person just threw it on the tray and put it in the oven."

Steven saw growing food as enhancing his awareness: "It gives you more appreciation for what you are growing. And appreciation leads you to not overuse what we currently have in our society." Richard increased his awareness of the food's origin that he ate:

Squash that Rod harvested and his hand.  Credit: Rod, CRMS student gardener

Each year, we have a harvest dinner that is all things from the garden, that self-sustaining dinner. I think it helps bond the community. This community created the food you are eating. You have to respect these people because they are feeding you. It sort of takes out the dissonance, maybe. You go to McDonalds and order a hamburger, and it's a disgusting hamburger. It came from a slaughterhouse, and you have no idea where it is or who works there or what all those cows do. But here, the garden is right next to the dining hall.

Carrots fresh from the garden had become Rod's preferred snack. Steven also admitted to a significant dietary change: "I've actually eaten a lot more plants because of gardening. I used to have sort of a phobia about eating something green, but now I can actually eat pretty much everything." Jessie added, "Eating in the garden, I've gotten into a more organic, natural sort of state of mind. I don't really go into the grocery store to buy Oreos anymore; it's more to buy the more organic things. I think you get a lot more satisfaction with the eating of food right here when you pick it. You're like, 'Wow!'" Richard also noticed a difference when he ate something while in the garden: "When I am sitting at the table, all I am thinking about is consuming the food and getting my energy for the day, but in the garden, when I pick something off, I just eat it. It's like, 'Cool, this is a plant, this is a living thing.'"

April could not have been more enthusiastic about the food she grew:

I like vegetables so much more. I don't think I liked vegetables that much before coming to this school. Then gardening, something about just getting a bell pepper or a radish straight from the ground; suddenly, it tasted better. I think the garden educated me to try to eat better foods and try to think more about the local foods that are grown here and try to buy local produce and stuff because I've eaten a lot healthier and it kind of changed what I craved for. Definitely, on a good day, I'm always excited to come to the garden because I'll be like, "Oh, I didn't like lunch today, but now I get to go to the garden and eat whatever we pick today." I always get excited; eating from the garden is an exciting experience that never gets old. I don't think it will ever get old.

Many students discussed the pleasure they experience grazing on the garden's bounty during work crew, walking by the raspberries between classes, or seeing their crop at the dinner table. Dwight explained how the good taste combines with a feeling of accomplishment:

When I'm in the garden, I don't know if I am hungry or not, I just eat everything, every kind of vegetable that I picked that day, like green beans and carrots. One day, I picked the green beans a lot, and that dinner they served it with the steak and I thought, "Oh, that's the green bean that I picked," and it was rewarding. I think that these days, there are many vegetarians and many people changing to vegetarians, but not many people have experience gardening, so they are eating vegetables, but they don't know where they come from. By learning to do this gardening, we can know carrots are from underground, sunflower seeds are from the flower, everything like that. It kind of makes people more comfortable and familiar with vegetables.

There is no one on the gardening work crew who does not like tasting and eating what they grow. They not only enjoy the fresh tastes, but the huge sense of accomplishment and knowledge gained from picking and eating something they grew themselves.

Eve lamented, "One hundred years ago 99 percent of the population was connected in some way to what they were eating. Now, it's like 1 percent is connected to the food cycle. I think there is something wrong with that, personally."

People's migration from rural, food-growing environments to urban environments in industrialized nations has removed them from observing how food grows. Eve's feeling that something is wrong comes from her personal experiences growing food and what she has learned. I don't ask any of the students what they think about the American industrial agriculture system, but they venture their opinions, as Eve did, that something is wrong. I do, however, ask them about their environmental awareness.

## ENVIRONMENTAL AWARENESS AND ACTIVISM

Food sustainability has significant voices in environmental awareness and activism thanks to farmer-writers Aldo Leopold and Wendell Berry, native foods researcher Gary Nabhan, activist-author Anna Lappé, and writer-gardeners Michael Pollan and Barbara Kingsolver, just to name only a few in a rapidly growing field. CRMS has had a commitment to sustainable living from its founding in the early 1950s. Students have helped to build an adobe art studio and a solar dormitory. The chemistry classes are experimenting in making photovoltaic cells with plant cells doing photosynthesis. The garden's beautiful presence at the school's entrance demonstrates that local food holds a place of honor at the school.

I asked all interviewees if the gardening experience had made them more environmentally aware. The answer actually proved difficult for them to discern since their curriculum has such a major experiential environmental education component. Also, the young people's attitudes have been formed by their family attitudes. As Rosemary explained, "I think they were already pretty shaped when I was a kid just because that is how I was raised." Two male students agreed with her that they had always been environmentally aware, but thirteen students felt that working in the garden had definitely made them more aware and conscientious.

Jessie explained her intimate connection to nature through breath itself:

It just gives me a greater kind of awe of the fact that when I breathe out, the trees breathe in, and [when] they breathe out, I breathe in. It should be working all together, but it's not. And the only reason it's not is because something unnatural happened, and the only unnatural things that have happened are from us.

When I asked Laurel if gardening had changed her environmental awareness, she answered:

Until about three years ago, I was my father's daughter, and my father is very Republican, very cowboy, very diesel. Not that that's a bad thing, but he's never concerned with throwing things out, never concerned with his fuel consumption until prices went up. Suddenly, everyone cares so much more when it affects their wallets. Suddenly, everyone's a tree-hugging hippy, as my dad calls it, because the wallet's getting thinner. So until about three years ago, I was my father's daughter in that sense, and then something happened that seemed to significantly change a lot of aspects of my life, politically and fundamentally, and then that grew. And that something that made a huge impact is that I dated a Buddhist for a while and spent a lot of time with her family and the sort of the loving atmosphere that engulfed her house, and it was hard to be stressed in her living room. And that ended, and I came out from it sort of resenting it, so I went through a bit where I also didn't care again, but it grew back. Once you get it, it comes back; it's like a weed, but a good weed. All weeds are kind of good. My grandma says, and my grandma is really big into gardening, that weeds are just plants that grow where you don't want them to. So I try to use that analogy when anybody tries to use weed in a negative connotation, and I have a grandma who actually transplants the weeds, dandelions and all, just has a garden of dandelions. Sorry, I digress. But it grows back once you establish it. Back to when I was fourteen and dating a Buddhist and then coming to this school, which has a huge impression on how you feel about the earth, being in the garden, loving it so much. This one [garden], I haven't spent a whole lot of time with, but I still love it like the one in my house. Imagining something hurting it is rather painful, which is what presses the environmentalist thing; it's not because I want to save the world, it's because I want to save these things that save me. [I'm] not trying to be selfish. It's more like, "please don't hurt the things that make me happy."

Laurel's deeply personal experiences have made her an activist who has stepped in to change how her father does business:

I run the recycling program for my dad's company, which started this year. It started out with me sitting on peoples' desks and watching them drink a soda and waiting for them to go throw the can out until they sort of moved it to the recycling. And then it's growing a bit; we have an eco-shredder that's a locked box where people come and shred paper and turn it into either paper or compost or something. It's an actual business.

## PERCEIVING THE WORLD: THE SENSES

*Today, I picked yellow green beans. I guess they're just yellow beans, but I've never seen those before and I didn't know that beans actually got that yellow. I've never seen that shade of yellow in a fruit outside a banana. The colors are just super vibrant! There's always vibrant yellow! You'll get a huge contrast; you'll get the perfect raspberry in just a bushel surrounded by green beans and you'll just have a little group of three raspberries hanging out in it. Everything is super alive.* —APRIL, 16

The sense of discovery in the garden, of seeing something for the first time or coming to a new awareness, stood out in many sensory experiences the youth described, such as Dwight feeling in contact with nature through his hearing a bird sing and the wind blowing in the garden. Jan, aged fifteen, echoes: "[I feel] happiness like when the birds sing a song. I wish I could whistle like a bird." While hearing was not a dominant experience for most, what they noticed besides the expected outdoor sounds of wind, birds, and bugs was a feeling of intrusion when an unnatural sound interrupted the quiet. Georgia, aged eighteen, explained: "It's a peaceful place, and when things go by really fast and loudly, it isn't very pleasant."

Rod detailed his fingers' encounters with touching in the garden:

> Carrots are slippery and onions are slimy and raspberry bushes hurt. And zucchinis kind of have a weird touch because they have all these little spiky furs on them and it kind of feels weird to touch. And, I don't know, it's just a fun thing to pick everything because it's so interactive.

## COMPARISONS TO SPORTS AND ART ACTIVITIES

When I asked students about other activities they did that gave them similar experiences to gardening's sensory stimulus, the answers varied from doing art to participating in competitive and noncompetitive sports, such as backpacking, rock climbing, and hiking. Their answers offer an opportunity to understand a little more about the nuanced experiences that produce positive outcomes for young people's feelings. Jessie shared her experience as a runner and rock climber:

> I'm on the cross-country running team, and I get this really good feeling of just, like, overwhelming healthiness and I get the same feeling when I come out of here [in the garden]. I've spent my time well and it's affected me well. I really like that feeling! I also rock climb, and it's the same sort of thing. At the end of the day after your work, you're just, like, "Yes, I did what I came for and I feel good now!"

Several students mentioned backpacking, hiking, and rock climbing as noncompetitive outdoor physical activity that gives them similar sensory feelings as gardening. April compares the two:

> It [backpacking] kind of relates to the garden in the sense that you're accomplishing something. It [gardening] may not be something huge like backpacking up a mountain; it's probably not going to change someone's life except your own in the large scale of things. No one is there to

congratulate you. The sense inside yourself that, "I did this," and just, like, the fulfillment of that and being accomplished in something definitely lends a hand in how that relates to the garden because every time you look around, and you're like, "I've been contributing to this space," it becomes a little bit of your own. It becomes a little bit of your own trail because you've traveled it and shared experiences with it even though it's inanimate, but you'll remember that, and it [backpacking] definitely relates to the garden in that way.

I enjoy how April moves back and forth between describing gardening and backpacking so that it's hard to discern which is which. Students also mentioned making art and playing a musical instrument as similar to gardening in the way those activities made them feel. Rosemary found that almost any activity involving being in nature made her feel the same way as gardening, evidence that, as research shows, being in nature helps our minds to relax and restore better cognitive functioning (Berman, Jonides, and Kaplan, 2008; Faber Taylor and Kuo, 2008; Hartig et al. 2003; Kaplan and Kaplan, 1990; Kaplan, 1995; Kaplan and Berman, 2010; Ulrich et al. 1991). Rosemary explained what activities were similar to gardening in how they made her feel:

Art, being able to paint something or draw, but a lot of the time, I am either looking at a picture of something in nature or I am actually outside. Cooking, because I am cooking with the materials I grew. Maybe sometimes when I go down by the water, like to the river or to the ocean, I

Colorado Rocky Mountain School garden with Mount Sopris, where students frequently climb, in the background. **Credit:** Illène Pevec

get a very calming sense, like the same type of thing I would get as gardening. So, basically, anything if I am in nature pretty much. Even digging a hole, I get the same sensation.

Richard discovered that playing music had several elements in common with gardening. The repetitions of themes in playing jazz reminded him of planting, and that "they are both senses of accomplishment, but they are different accomplishments. Gardening is more for the community and music is for myself, I think."

CRMS students had extremely full schedules and very busy lives with many required school activities, but all found refuge and meaning in the garden. Eve explained: "I think there's kind of two aspects to gardening: the aesthetics- and product-based aspect of it and there is also kind of the joy of gardening." They all expressed a desire to nurture and protect the natural environment. As we heard in New York and at ¡Cultiva!, gardening unites the individual with a collective effort to serve the community. Laurel elaborates:

> I've always been someone who wanted to actually contribute something, and I was born in the wrong day and age to do that because you can't really directly contribute to your family until you're an adult and working. I can't go chop firewood or drive the horse into town to get groceries or do anything really contributing. But that's why it's nice here [in the school garden] because there's enough, as opposed to my garden at home, that you can make a huge difference. You can bring in a fifty-pound box of potatoes that takes two people to carry in and say, "Wow, this is a lot of food." People are going to be eating this; it's going to keep people happy, healthy, and good.

Sunflower in the Colorado Rocky Mountain School. **Credit:** Illène Pevec

# 10

## ROARING FORK HIGH SCHOOL GROWS FOOD FOR LUNCH AND SUSTAINABILITY EDUCATION

*We live in a world where we really don't interact with our food at all. We just buy it and eat it. We do different jobs in all these crazy things just to make our huge complicated system work when it was really pretty great back before things got so complicated. So when we get a chance to go out, work with things and garden and get our hands dirty, it really brings us back to our roots. I don't know, maybe it's instinct. Maybe that's really the way people are supposed to be. You get back in touch with nature, your more wild side.*
**—DASH, 17, ROARING FORK HIGH SCHOOL**

Dash's hand with potting soil.  Credit: Dash

D ash, aged seventeen, is a senior in the second year of the agricultural biology program at Roaring Fork High School (RFHS) in Carbondale, Colorado, two miles from Colorado Rocky Mountain School. RFHS moved to a new building on the town's edge in 2007 and had incomplete landscaping. Two area nonprofits, Central Rocky Mountain Permaculture Institute and Fat City Farmers, had collaborated on a nearby ranch in 2007 to run an organic agriculture training program for young people wanting to start a Community Supported Agriculture (CSA) farm[1] and were seeking land to continue that effort. In 2008, I suggested to these nonprofits that a public school might consider hosting the program for the benefits that a farm on school property could bring the school during the school year.

We convened a community meeting with people interested in better food for schools and sustainable local food sources and decided to ask Dr. Clifton Colia, the high school principal, if RFHS would like help from the nonprofits to develop a garden and greenhouse as a biology learning center. He warmly welcomed the proposal. He and the biological sciences teacher, Hadley Hentschel, had already discussed starting a vegetable garden.

He agreed that the school would start an agricultural biology class and host the proposed CSA training program for the next school year in the resulting school garden. During the school year, students and Hentschel would run the garden and greenhouse as a hands-on science class. Fat City Farmers and Central Rocky Mountain Permaculture Institute would run the garden in the summer to train future farmers in how to farm organically. All of the food raised during the school year would go into the school lunch program. The principal would work with us to obtain permission from the school board to use school property to launch this program. Dr. Colia also welcomed me as a researcher with the students.

A nine-month process with the school board resulted in approval of the agricultural biology program and the proposed physical infrastructure in May of 2009. Fat City Farmers raised the funds to build the greenhouse and fences and to install irrigation, and the school district gave its land to be used free of charge. The town granted water rights it held on the bordering irrigation ditch, a valuable asset in this high, dry mountain region. (The cost of water is an important consideration in all farming.)

The school district required the nonprofits to carry liability insurance on the greenhouse. The school district pays the agricultural biology teacher's salary and the electric bill for running

---

1. CSA farm customers prepay for a season's worth of produce. These prepaid shares finance the farm operations, and the shareholders and customers assume risks for crop failures.

the greenhouse fans. The school occupies former ranch land, where cattle still graze just beyond the fence (as do deer, hence the need for an eight-foot-high fence).

I became a volunteer grant writer for the project and a coordinator for communication between the schools and the nonprofits. Besides writing multiple grants in the next two years to build the greenhouse and fence the three-fourths-acre garden, I obtained two small outreach grants from the University of Colorado at Boulder. These education-focused grants helped RFHS and Yampah Mountain High School, the two public schools collaborating with the nonprofits to engage students in agricultural production and obtain funding for books, films, and field trips to visit local organic farms and greenhouses.

These university outreach funds also gave me some paid time (about twelve hours a week for two and a half months) to support the agricultural programs at these two public schools. The nonprofits' directors, Jerome Osentoski and Michael Thompson, gave an enormous amount of professional time pro bono to make everything happen, and Thompson also wrote key grants. Collaboration made these programs take root and grow.

I have a personal stake in the programs' successes when I am giving my time to help make them happen. However, as you will see discussed by the youth, no matter who has been involved to make a program happen, the young people's experiences and responses have many similarities in all the garden sites. I do not think that my involvement at RFHS and at Yampah Mountain High School has influenced the students' interview answers, but there is no way to know that definitively. However, our shared efforts made it possible for them to have these experiences of growing food at school.

## ROARING FORK HIGH SCHOOL'S SOCIAL CONTEXT

Roaring Fork High School is the main public high school in Carbondale, a city with a population of about 6,500 and situated in a beautiful Colorado mountain valley at about 6,200 feet above sea level. Carbondale began as a coal mining and ranching town in the late nineteenth century, but the Ute Indians had used the region for fishing and hunting for more than eight hundred years. The discovery of silver in Aspen in 1879, just thirty miles away, and the influx of settlers pushing out the Ute resulted in a Ute rebellion in Meeker, Colorado, that same year. In response, the US government sent the Ute to reservations to clear the region for white settlement (Aspen Historical Society, 2015). Carbondale became the potato growing capital regionally in its early agricultural history to feed the miners and settlers arriving, and later, it became cattle-ranching country. It has experienced a huge Hispanic immigration in the last twenty years, as have many Colorado mountain towns near ski resorts. The 2010 US Census shows Carbondale as 39.3 percent Hispanic and 58.4 percent Caucasian.

RFHS serves 310 students in 9th to 12th grade and has a very friendly atmosphere. Sixty-five percent of the students are Hispanic. The school has about a 50 percent free and reduced school lunch population—meaning that about one half of the student body lives with significant financial challenges. All parent consent forms for student interviews went out in Spanish to those students that requested Spanish; I promised the parents in writing that no information would be shared with immigration officials, nor would I ask questions related to immigration status.

The 2009–2010 school year was the first year for the agricultural biology course. The class demographics reflected the school population in that first year while the 2010–2011 class was evenly divided between Hispanic and Caucasian students (these were the two years that I did interviews with the students). About seventy-five students took the course in that time and I interviewed twenty-four of them, all who volunteered. The class requires both academic and hands-in-the-dirt work. Requested enrollment for the program's third year doubled, but the instructor could only manage one class per year because he teaches all biological sciences at the school.

Dr. Colia said in my interview with him that, "Without all the community organizations, grant writing, tools, expertise, it would have been a minor project." It has been a major project with about $100,000 raised and spent, along with a likely equal amount of professional time donated for architectural design, permaculture design, curriculum support, earth moving, and labor. Without Dr. Colia's initial approval of the program, the garden could not have happened. Without Hadley Hentschel, a biology teacher willing to get dirty with his students and develop a new program, the garden would not have happened.

Carbondale used to have only a three-and-a-half-month growing season due to its high altitude, but that seems to have extended to an average of four frost-free months in recent years; although in 2014, an early frost on June 20th forced us to replant all the squashes and beans. The forty-foot geodesic dome greenhouse made by Growing Spaces, a company from Pagosa Springs, Colorado, was installed with an underground climate battery, a system of large plastic tubes buried about six feet beneath the surface. The sun heats the air in the dome greenhouse and fans blow the warm air into the tubes and keep it circulating through the soil to keep it from freezing in winter. In the summer, the cooler subsoil temperatures cool the very hot sun-heated air and send the earth-cooled air back into the greenhouse to keep the temperatures from getting too high. The Carbondale Rotary Club donated labor, cash, and machinery to dig down into the

Volunteers build the underground climate battery for the greenhouse with student-built hoop houses in the background. **Credit: Dr. Clifton Colia**

ground and install the air tubes in the foundation. There is also a back-up propane heater for winter's subzero nights.

The garden's development has been paired with community education in sustainability related to food and energy. We planted the fruit orchard inside the deer fence with community members and students on Climate Action Day in October of 2010. Parents, students, and community members delivered truckloads of manure, straw, and compost, planted trees, and attended films on the US food system shown at the school. Every major local foundation has given grants to help develop the garden. In December of 2014, an assistant secretary to the US Department of Agriculture visited the garden and commented on how well integrated the garden, academics, school lunch, and school efforts are towards sustainability.

The school Energy Club, begun by a group of students when they were in middle school with the help of their science teacher, brought together energy nonprofits and a solar installation business to accomplish the next step to sustainable living and education that the garden initiated: a 379-kilowatt solar array installed in 2015 to generate clean electricity for 100 percent of the school's electrical needs. The school did not have to buy the photovoltaic panels, but instead hosts them on the school property and buys the electricity back at a lower rate than buying from the electrical grid. It is expected to save the school $398,000 over twenty years and prevent 9,226 tons of carbon from entering the atmosphere (Grandbois, 2014). Students now see, on one side of their school, many photovoltaic panels harvesting the sun so that they can power their computers and, behind the school, a vast array of fruit trees and vegetables harvesting the sun so that they can grow their lunch. These visible steps towards climate change mitigation offer both knowledge and hope.

In 2015, Fat City Farmers invited immigrant families to use the orchard space as a community garden, and children ages three to sixteen spent the summer working alongside their parents to raise food for their families and have fun together. Creating a comprehensive agriculture and sustainable education program takes long-term commitment, and little by little, different aspects develop.

## THE AGRICULTURAL BIOLOGY CLASS

In mid-September of 2009, on the school's community work day, students from many classes and all four grades constructed and planted the school's first garden, a round keyhole garden bed with a space in the center (the keyhole) for composting materials. This inaugural activity launched the new academic and hands-on food-growing program. About ninety students participated in carrying rocks to circle the garden and layering soil, aged manure, and old straw to create the growing bed near the science classroom door. They planted hardy, dark leafy greens like kale, Swiss chard, and various lettuces. We discovered that having the young people work in a circle created an excellent conversation setting for conveying soil building and planting information easily. The salad greens grown were harvested and eaten by the agricultural biology students that fall, again the next spring, and the second year as well. A thick, white, permeable row cover cloth extended the growing season very well so that food could be harvested during freezing weather.

The agricultural biology class lasts for a full academic year and is open to juniors and seniors who have taken basic biology. The students have academic work as well as tasks pertaining to food growing during their nine-month class. They study soil science and botany, the politics and economics of the food industry, and how to plant and care for vegetables and fruits. They do spring planting and fall harvesting, though a class harvests the prior students' crops before they plant due to the school calendar. Unlike the ¡Cultiva! youth, these students do not farm in the summers because school is out. The greenhouse operates year round, and food raised in the summer primarily goes to the local food bank. Fat City Farmers raises the money to pay for a summer garden and greenhouse manager and has plans for a summer CSA internship program to take over the summer work.

The 2009–2010 students built two hoop houses to use for early spring planting before the greenhouse was built. When late spring windstorms destroyed them, the youth learned first-hand the setbacks farmers face due to extreme weather. A professional work crew built the large dome greenhouse in May of 2010. Students were not allowed to help due to the dangerous height, but they saw the process and helped with the interior bed construction.

Hentschel had never taught agricultural biology, but took on the new program with enthusiasm and found a suitable curriculum using the student version of Michael Pollan's (2009) *The Omnivore's Dilemma* and the 2010 online sustainable agriculture curricula developed by the University of California at Santa Cruz. He supplements the reading with documentary films on the industrial food system and on organic agriculture and permaculture.

In the 2010–2011 school year, three students from the first year's class served as greenhouse interns. These students assisted the greenhouse manager in harvesting crops for the school lunch program, as well as in outdoor work and whatever else needed to be done. Due to an agreement with the school board, Fat City Farmers raised the funds to pay the greenhouse manager, but the nonprofit ran out of money after three years. Hentschel found it worked better for him and the students to manage on their own without a greenhouse manager as there were more learning

Final phase in constructing the RFHS Growing Dome. Credit: Illène Pevec

opportunities to problem solve: pests, planting schedules, temperature fluctuations, etc. There has been a steady stream of tomatoes, cucumbers, herbs, and salad greens to the school lunch salad bar. Greenhouse-grown figs, oranges, and pomegranates get eaten during the agricultural biology class. Students not in the program will regularly ask which of the foods being served was grown at school.

We had a cooking class the second fall when the agricultural biology students made pesto using the greenhouse basil and a vegetarian lasagna featuring Swiss chard. I was the facilitator for making the lasagna. Aaron, a student I later interviewed, complained vociferously when we were making the vegetarian lasagna that it would taste awful without meat. We served it at our student-parent AmeriCorps sign up that night, and when he tasted it, he stood up and made a public apology to me and the other students, saying that it was really delicious. I was touched and amazed that he would make the effort to publically say he had been wrong to judge a food before he tasted it and was delighted with how much the students enjoyed cooking together.

The agricultural biology class was approved as an AmeriCorps service-learning class for 2010–2011, so seven of the students, including Aaron, took the opportunity to do three hundred hours of community service working in the school garden (class time counted) to earn $1,133 towards college. AmeriCorps does not approve this kind of service-learning at a high school level any longer, so we were lucky to get it then.

While both ¡Cultiva! and Colorado Rocky Mountain School had been growing their garden-

RFHS students prepare salad and lasagna for their parents. **Credit:** Illène Pevec

ing programs for eleven years when I interviewed their participants, RFHS was in the first two years of developing a program and garden site when I spoke with its gardeners. However, you will see from what the students say that even one or two hours a week spent tending food plants can result in profound impacts even when a program and a garden are new.

## MY RESEARCH WITHIN THE AGRICULTURAL BIOLOGY PROGRAM

I interviewed twelve students in the late spring of 2010 during the program's first year and twelve more in the late fall during the program's second year. Some students were not interested, and many forgot to bring permission forms to school signed by their parents (eleven eighteen-year-old seniors could sign for themselves). I found no significant differences from what students in the first year of the program said from those of the second year and have not divided their results by when they participated. They had some different experiences because they had a greenhouse the second year, but the impact of engaging in gardening seemed the same. Dr. Colia and Hentschel's comments are integrated where appropriate. I interviewed more youth at RFHS than at any other site because more were involved during the school year.

**TABLE 10.1.** RFHS Student Demographics (n=24) for Interviewees, 2010

| Ethnic Background | Hispanic | Caucasian | Pacific Islander | European (Exchange Student) | |
|---|---|---|---|---|---|
| Number of Male Students | | 6 | 4 | 2 | 1 |
| Number of Female Students | 6 | 5 | 0 | 0 | |

Credit: Illène Pevec

A total of thirteen males and eleven females, ages sixteen to eighteen, gave interviews. These RFHS students pioneered the garden project for their school. They did collaborative garden design projects along with their academic work and worked in the garden. Their experiential, hands-on agricultural biology class earned science credit. Even though their first crops were much smaller in quantity than those at ¡Cultiva! and Colorado Rocky Mountain School, these students still expressed an enormous sense of accomplishment and pride in their collaborative effort to grow food for the school lunch.

## FAMILY CULTURES AND GARDENING

The youth fall into two distinct ethnic groups at RFHS. I have assigned pseudonyms to these interviewees based on their Caucasian or Hispanic ethnicity to make it easier for the reader to distinguish voices because it is valuable to know if culture makes a difference in how students experience the school garden. The life experience differences between being a recent immigrant or a youth from the wealthier white culture in a small town could conceivably influence a person's perceptions.

Similar to the other Colorado youth gardeners, many at RFHS had family members who gardened. Some had grandparents who ranched in Mexico and some who ranched in Carbondale. Prior family exposure to gardening may certainly influence young people to sign up for a gardening program as only two students out of twenty-four had no one in their family who they had seen garden.

**TABLE 10.2.** RFHS Students' (n=24) Prior Gardening Exposure, 2010

| Students with Prior Gardening Exposure from Family Members | Number of Hispanic Male Students | Number of Non-Hispanic Male Students | Number of Hispanic Female Students | Number of Non-Hispanic Female Students |
|---|---|---|---|---|
| Grandparent Gardener | 3 | 1 | 3 | 1 |
| Parent Gardener | 1 | 4 | 2 | 3 |
| Both Parent and Grandparent Gardeners | 1 | 1 | 1 | 1 |
| No Family Adult Gardener | 1 | 1 | 0 | 0 |

Credit: Illène Pevec

Antonio, aged eighteen, explains why he took the class:

My grandparents have ranches and stuff in Mexico, and I thought it was pretty cool to learn about it. I'm doing it, and then my mom helps me do it [plant beans]. But I was thinking about, like, going into agriculture 'cause my dad owns forty acres of land.

Courtney, aged eighteen, shares memories involving her grandmother and her father: "I used to garden with my grandmother all the time because she loves flowers, but it was never vegetables. It was big beautiful flowers." Her father grew food in a home garden: "We used to grow cucumbers and red peppers and a bunch of spices and stuff that my dad cooked with, but I never really helped." This recognition of their families' love for their gardens suggests transference of love and respect for gardening across generations. Maria, aged eighteen, expressed family transference directly: "My grandparents and my family have been pretty much growing and farming. I think that I inherited that from them. I really enjoy it, especially when I am doing it with my grandma."

Daniela, aged 16, felt that she gets her identity from working on the land: "I guess it's the feeling of home; and that's pretty much who I am. I'm a farmer and a country girl, and that's just who I am."

Chase, aged eighteen, explained the influence he had on his family when he volunteered at a local farm dedicated to sustainable agriculture the summer before he took the agricultural biology class:

> I volunteered at Sustainable Settings, and [my parents] are really extremely surprised that I am doing this. They didn't expect me to be that kind of guy that goes outside and works on a farm or in a garden. That's what made my mom start gardening last summer. She did it when she was young and then she just hasn't done it. But, I guess, after I worked at the farm last summer, she started gardening again, so it was really fun for all of us.

Derek, aged sixteen, the Rotary Club exchange student from Denmark, told me that his parents had planted an apple tree in their yard when he was born. He appreciates the forethought his parents had to plant a tree many years ago to give him fresh apples, and he feels connected to them and the tree.

From what these youth say, it seems that there is a mutual modeling that can occur in families. When one person shows real pleasure in tending the soil and plants, other family members witness this and it may well influence them to try it. These youth have positive memories related to significant positive relationships they have in their families related to gardening. These reflect the P and R in PERMA (Seligman, 2011): positive emotions and positive relationships.

## CONNECTING TO NATURE AND RECIPROCITY

When I asked about their various sensory experiences at each research site, the youth often ended up talking about their senses bringing them in touch with nature in a pleasurable way. Rachael, aged seventeen, explains the difference for her between gardening and visiting nature on a hike or similar activity:

You are in nature and you're working with plants and you are surrounded by nature and bringing part of that into existence by being a gardener, but when you are hiking or swimming, you are enjoying what's already there instead of adding to it. When you're a gardener, it's your job to bring up the plants and help them along, but when you're hiking and swimming, you are just enjoying what's already there that kind of just takes care of itself.

All of these young people at RFHS live surrounded by nature due to Carbondale's setting. The school has beautiful mountain views out all windows and from the garden. All had extensive exposure to natural environments throughout childhood. The parents of Michaela, aged eighteen, had made sure she played outside a lot when she was a child and did not let her spend much time in front of cartoons. She and her dad kept a garden together when she was younger. She expressed gratitude for her parents' wisdom: "I know a lot of kids who are into video games. They watch TV all day on the weekends. I feel they won't appreciate Earth as much or what we actually have in our valley. I am just grateful that I am able to, like, care about it." Michaela began as a greenhouse intern the following year because she enjoyed working in it so much.

Respecting nature extends beyond the school or home garden for these young people. Learning about nature by studying plants and the food system sensitizes them to how they view nature outside the garden too. On a recent mountain hike, Chase surprised his father with his new observational capacities developed through gardening. Chase laughed as he explained his father's confusion at his son's new behavior:

Normally, we don't focus on anything; we just focus on getting to the end. But I kept stopping frequently, just looking at all the different plants, smelling the different plants. All that was because of gardening and put a different aspect on even hiking. He [my dad] said, "What are you doing?" He looked at me, like, I don't know, like I was a different person, I guess. He wasn't used to me stopping a lot on our hikes. It was kind of funny.

Denise, aged seventeen, discussed a connected feeling that was expressed by many: "I guess I realize that I'm just as much a part of this earth as any of these plants are and that kind of obligates me to do my part to take care of it." Rodrigo, aged eighteen, expressed dismay over what happens when people do not respect nature and natural processes and do not feel connected to their actions in relation to nature:

I mean, we watched movies and read books about how chickens are processed and what cows get to eat, and, honestly, all those things I believe are not correct. Chickens should be chickens. They should roam free. How can I put this? Everything should fit in normally. I think people shouldn't mess with nature or try to change it in any way. I think that is what is affecting us.

This awareness of nature as a place we go to and enjoy for the way it is and the garden as a place where we actively care for nature occurs in many young gardeners' reflections. A sense of reciprocity emerges in terms of their relationship to nature and growing things. Maria's family grows a lot of food on their acreage forty-five miles away from the school, as do her grandparents in Mexico. She expresses a very deep connection to nature and understands that nature gives to her:

Gardening helps me care more about the earth. Working with nature has helped me to see that nature works with us to give us what we need. Seeing how our food grows, we should care about our earth. We need Earth to survive and it gives us so much; we should give back.

Carlos, aged eighteen, has only been in the United States for four years. He hopes to become a chef and is taking the agricultural biology class because he would like to grow some of the food he prepares for others. He feels gratitude for plants: "Some people don't care about plants. They only want their product. And I do care for plants, and I will grow my own food in the future because plants are the more important thing in the world because they give us, they feed us."

Pedro, aged eighteen, echoes this concern: "Plants are living, so they need some kind of support from us as well as we need from them. So, by making sure they are okay, it makes us feel good about it, doing something." I had observed Pedro a few days earlier very carefully mixing water into the soil with his bare hands before transplanting. He had done this with such care that I asked him what he was feeling as he worked: "It made me feel really great 'cause the plants really needed the water since the soil was really dry. So, it made me, like, know that I was helping the plants in a way because they were gonna need the water and they were gonna be happy in the soil."

Patrick, aged eighteen, has a particularly strong interest in plants and gardening and was doing independent study in horticulture as well as taking the agricultural biology class. He remembers gardening as a small child with his mother. He no longer lives with her, but he grows food at home with his father. He continues caring for the garden with skills he has learned with both parents:

You always have the satisfaction of knowing that you produced something from nothing because all of this came from the smallest seeds or the smallest plant, and to have that satisfaction knowing that you helped something grow and live and flourish, it's just a wonderful feeling!

Pedro and Patrick echoed this awareness that we take care of nature and nature takes care of us. He and the other students express deep engagement with nature (the "E" in Seligman's (2011) PERMA acronym for flourishing) through gardening. Pedro explained:

It's just like relaxing, it's fun. You feel like you're contributing to it. It helps you out in a way 'cause the plants you are planting also give something back. Also, you are helping the environment because you are putting in plants that are taking out carbon dioxide.

Twenty-one out of twenty-four students used the words calm, relaxed, peaceful, or happy to express how gardening makes them feel. The three students who did not use those specific words used vocabulary with positive connotations, such as free, good, and energized.

Antonio discussed his feelings as being part of a large natural system: "It calms me down, relaxes me. I feel it's like a picture of being in a forest, you know, nature, but I don't think about synthetic stuff or how we are affecting it. It's just like being there, being calm, enjoying nature."

For Patrick, his own familiarity with gardening made him feel calm: "It's something I know, so I don't have to struggle to learn, and it's just something I've always had good experiences with. It's just something that makes me calmer. I like it. It's soothing."

Aaron, aged seventeen, who lettered in all the major sports at school, also helps his mother with her landscaping business and feels in touch with his identity in a garden, where he feels part of a lifecycle. He particularly likes to hear water running: "I like it because I know it all works together, just a big old complete cycle. It calms me down. It makes me feel relaxed, at ease. It reminds me of who I am, and I don't have to worry about anything else."

Rodrigo observed: "It's different because you are normally in class trying to focus hard or something. Out here, you can be freer, more relaxed." Rodrigo identifies freedom from classroom pressures as a cause for his relaxation. Michaela, a member of the school's championship girls' volleyball team, was sitting with me outside near the garden in the spring. The birds were singing, and she found that these sounds or silence in the garden affected her beneficially:

Sometimes, you don't really hear anything. Sometimes, it's just silence. Like just dead quiet silence, but if it's outside, you hear birds like that one singing or little sounds. Everything just seems a lot more peaceful. Just for it to be semi-quiet, I think is important in a garden. My school day is really not quiet or relaxing or peaceful at all. That's why it's so nice to come out here and be out in nature and kind of, like, center yourself again.

Michaela was not alone in appreciating the quiet in a natural setting in the midst of a hectic school day. Bernardo, aged sixteen, notes that the quiet in the garden could be a refuge for any student at the school, "'cause if they are having a test or something and they want to escape, just for five or ten minutes, they can go to the garden to have a time of silence to reflect."

Ashley, aged eighteen, finds that working in the garden gives her time to reflect and that relaxes her: "When I'm in here just picking the basil, then I'm thinking about whatever I want. So, yeah, I get kind of the same feelings. It's relaxing to be in here and it's fun. I like it."

Ana, aged seventeen, told me the meaning of gardening related to its capacity to relieve stress:

Gardening for me would kind of fit into a stress release because you're doing something that will distract you maybe from things that stress you or things that make you feel bad. So, if I go out and garden, it will make me feel so much better when I am done.

I asked Julieta, aged eighteen, what she looks for in a garden: "Just peace, I guess, peace and quiet. You know, it's usually, like, pretty full and happy."

Papaya blossom in RFHS greenhouse. Credit: Ashley

John, aged eighteen, discussed happiness when describing how the smells of the garden made him feel: "Happier, I guess, yeah. Definitely, they make me feel happier. Like, it's a nice environment." A few weeks later as I listened to his voice recording, I could hear the smile in his voice as he spoke. Sixteen students, two thirds of them, used the words happy or joyful a total of thirty-nine times in these interviews. Ana equated happiness and helping nature in the garden: "Happy. Peaceful. I don't know. It makes me feel that I'm helping, that I'm creating something by watering it, and over time, you'll see how your skills are, how when you help them, they develop into this great thing."

The calm and peace the youth gardeners expressed most likely came from their complete concentration on something that enthralls, what Seligman (2011) describes as engagement. Csikszentmihalyi (1997) defines this psychological state of total concentration as flow. So, perhaps the peace they find in the garden comes from their being in tune with nature's own flow. These youths' comments represent only a small sampling from a rich cornucopia filled with the ways they experience calm, peace, relaxation, and happiness in the garden.

## HANDS-ON LEARNING

One thing a garden science lab offers to students of any age is hands-on learning. Research with younger children (Klemmer, Walliczek, and Zajicek, 2005) and adolescents (Cammack, Waliczek, and Zajicek, 2002) has shown that science retention goes up when paired with garden activities that bring to life concepts and facts. The RFHS students frequently brought up how important this experiential learning was to them. Aaron put it quite bluntly: "In the classroom, it is not fun. Coming out here, when you're physically touching and learning, it's more fun and keeps it interesting. It helps high schoolers. It keeps them interested and focused."

Julieta plans to have a career in veterinary sciences. She knows she learns best by physical engagement with life:

It feels better to be outside doing things with the earth and, like, doing something rather than just learning about it inside and not fully experiencing the hard work and feeling what it's really all about. You can't really learn something, know how it is, until you are out there doing it. That's how I feel about things.

Pedro agrees: "You learn more than just what the teacher tells you. You learn from your experience out there in the gardening part of it. You learn so much that you would not learn in other classes." Rachael would have happily made a presentation to the school board on how important this learning process in a garden is for her and other students:

> If you have eight classes, and all seven of them are sitting in a classroom except for this one, and then you get to come outside and dig holes or plant plants and learn about how all of that works, it's definitely a lot more beneficial. And I think that kids need to know as much as they can about life, about things we need to know in life. You should know how to grow a garden and you should know how to support yourself financially and you should know how everything works in the real world. So, this prepares us for things in life, like how things grow and why you shouldn't go to McDonalds. That's knowledge that people will have to have for the rest of their lives. So, I think we need to be pushing for more things like that, that, without a doubt, we will use, instead of only pushing pre-calculus and stuff because they say it connects the neurons in your brain, but I'm not going to use calculus when I leave high school. So, I think gardening and learning how our country gets our food and how it's grown, I think that's something that someone needs to have just to be good and successful and live life to its fullest.

John saw the value in a learning process that allowed him to get up and move during school. He is a high-achieving student and an athlete participating in football and track. John explains:

> It definitely tightens you up to sit in the desk and watch a chalkboard all day. Getting outside helps to relieve a little bit of that. My physics class, that's more crunching numbers. Looking forward to a class makes it a lot easier to learn than dreading the class. So, yeah, you learn more easily [in the garden].

Looking forward to a class comes naturally when it relaxes students and gives them time outside in the fresh air to move and engage actively with their classmates in creating something tangible. Hentschel received the school's Teacher of the Year Award in 2010 and explains his philosophy of education:

> I guess experiential learning is one of my biggest desires through education. Kids still need to be exposed to textbook sources and notes and all that, but the only time they seem to really lighten up and connect with materials is when they actually get to do [it]. Outside, we can get experi-

ments going for a week, a month, even nine months, which is another benefit. A lot of it is still natural for kids. Kids still come in inquiring about how the world works. So, I think it actually takes less guiding when kids have hands-on [learning]. Maybe a little more on the management end, but as far as getting them to understand the key learning objective or understand what is going on with the lab, they can actually do what it is they are wanting to learn.

Roberto, aged seventeen, confirmed his teacher's observations: "I learn way more when I'm doing something rather than just sitting there and taking notes and just listening. It's a lot easier."

Both years that I interviewed students, Hentschel and I led a class focus group on two articles the students read that were published in the *Atlantic Monthly*: one that extolled the many benefits of youth gardens and called them a form of urban renewal (Kummer, 2008) and another that criticized school gardens as places of forced labor for immigrant children (Flanagan, 2010).

The Nuestras Raíces Farm in Holyoke, Massachusetts, which is discussed in Kummer's (2008) article, resulted from an Amherst College student undergraduate thesis. The farm has grown over the years to include thirty acres and a business incubation program, where young farmers can get microloans to grow food to sell at farmers' markets and to local restaurants, and is a place where teens can garden for free. The nonprofit developed to keep this very successful program growing food and people's skills and now has an $800,000 annual budget. Kummer (2008) writes:

The farm, a mile from downtown Holyoke,… has turned into an attraction of its own, with a petting zoo, a farm stand, summer concerts, and weekly pig roasts—a look, and a life, as close as people in the Puerto Rican community can come to the villages they and their families remember…. Farmers go through an eight-week training program during which they write a business plan that serves as their application for a plot; so far, 20 of 45 applicants have been given plots at a monthly rent of $25 a quarter-acre, and microloans to start "incubator farms."

Kummer's (2008) article described the power that engaging in an agricultural community development project has to positively transform young people's lives. In complete contrast, Flanagan (2010) lambasted the California Board of Education for going along with Alice Water's efforts to enliven science education and school lunch by starting the garden at Martin Luther King Middle School in Berkeley and daring to assume that planting, harvesting, and preparing food might help students to learn basic math and science skills. Flannagan (2010) argues:

Until our kids have a decent chance at mastering the essential skills and knowledge that they will need to graduate from high school, we should devote every resource and every moment of their academic day to helping them realize that life-changing goal. Otherwise, we become complicit—through our best intentions—in an act of theft that will not only contribute to the creation of a permanent, uneducated underclass, but will rob that group of the very force necessary to change its fate. The state, which failed these students as children and adolescents, will have to shoulder them in adulthood, for it will have created not a generation of gentleman farmers, but one of intellectual sharecroppers, whose fortunes depend on the largesse or political whim of their educated peers.

I was very curious to hear the high school students' opinions about these two articles since these youth were engaged in a program that taught botany, soil science, and horticulture with a significant hands-on component similar to the Edible Schoolyard program in Berkeley that Flannagan criticized. The students in both years that we did these focus groups responded identically: how important it was to them to learn something at school that seemed relevant to their lives now and as adults. A few said they now are considering careers in agriculture as a result of the course.

I also asked them if they felt that the sort of activities they did supported a sense of community in the class in comparison to classes that did mostly book- and lecture-based academics. All of them said that working together to build and create a garden made a positive difference in class relationships and sense of community, a confirmation of positive relationship building in the gardening program.

The students made sure I understood that they wrote papers and took tests—that they were developing academic skills in this program and not just gardening skills. They vigorously defended their right to learn in this engaged, hands-on manner. The consensus was 100 percent in favor of experiential learning's value. They don't consider themselves sharecroppers but contributors to the common good.

## WORKING TOGETHER ON SHARED GOALS

Working together on common goals, such as construction and planting, emerged as an important aspect of the students' experiences. There is not an extensive mixed-ethnic participation in town life in Carbondale: the Caucasian population dominates the running of government and civic organizations. Language differences have limited adult communication, but the immigrant youth all study English in school and quickly learn it well. The youth play on sports teams together and participate in student council, dances, plays, and classes together. I hear Spanish spoken a lot at school amongst Hispanic youth, and I hear these same youth switch to English with their Caucasian friends.

I asked Hentschel if he saw more mixing between ethnicities in this class compared to the others that he teaches. He explained that he structured work teams to have an always changing mix of students working together:

> We see a lot more, partly, I guess, integration and, partly, the whole class working together more or in larger groups, cooperative-type groups. But when we were building the hoop houses or building the garden beds, we would have six or eight kids working together on a common task, whereas in a typical lab [in a different science class], we would have two or three, and it's usually the same two or three. They wouldn't leave that group [all term]. I guess in the other classes, the non-ag classes, they isolate themselves, whereas in this class, in any given day, you look at them and they're working with different people outside.

What do the students say about this group approach to work and learning? Patrick found that gardening in a group helped him learn better because if he explained what he already knew to others, he came to understand it better himself:

> Gardening with the class of people, I am more active socially, more into the conversation and into the plants, and I am trying to connect the two. But when I am not gardening socially, I am 100 percent focused. When you add the social factor to it, I try to enrich my learning by helping other people. If I restate something in a way that someone else can understand it better, then I also understand it better. It makes it easier to go back and talk to them about it. And if you talk to them about it, and say you didn't know when to pick the tomatoes, I can go back and have a conversation with one of my peers about what should and shouldn't happen next. So, I think it's a social thing, and gardening isn't really a fast-paced thing, so you can work at it at your own pace.

Just as Patrick felt that he could offer the knowledge he already had regarding gardening to his peers, Ana felt she could ask for help when needed from a classmate:

When we are in different groups, sometimes you're with people that you don't talk to outside of that class, but you're in that class and you pretty much talk to everybody because it's teamwork, and you might need some help from someone else and you don't know how to do it, so you ask around to find someone to help you. And if it was in another class, you probably wouldn't go up to them and talk to them at all. Now, there are some people in this class I have in another class and I can go up to them and talk to them in that other class.

The gardening teamwork in larger, fluid groups enabled peer-to-peer knowledge construction and friendship formation. It also gave people the opportunity to do something they may have never done together and shifted their perspectives as Julieta describes:

I think a lot of the people that I have seen come out here are the kind of people that are like, "I don't want to do that, it's a lot of work and it's really boring." But then, those same people have come out here and are shoveling the rocks and mud out of the way and, like, you know, getting their clothes dirty to mess with the plants and, like, they're going on the field trips going, "Oh, that's cool. What's that?" And even the kids that didn't think they were excited about it, they got excited about it and they wanted to learn about it by the end of it, you know? [They] changed their attitude about it and towards the environment. That was kind of cool to see how a lot of my peers changed their attitude towards the things around them.

The opportunity to work in a collaborative way rather than in a competitive way, and to laugh and talk during a class, probably help the youth feel both excited and relaxed. Derek, as an exchange student, found it was easier to meet people and get to know them in this class: "Like when we were planting and digging, we would definitely talk more and talked different than in a math class, for example." Cynthia, aged sixteen and one of the quietest and shyest people in the class who did AmeriCorps, observed: "Yeah, I think it's really important to have other people to share with and just talk to while you're working." Perhaps creating gardens at schools can increase school safety levels by preventing alienation of students through shared contribution to caring for nature.

For Antonio, the first thing he thought of when he thought about the garden was the hoop house his class built because it was "something we accomplished as a class." Rodrigo summed up this shared experience very powerfully: "We got to do something for a good, sustainable garden. If we all work together, it helps make the world a better place." They took pride in their shared achievement in contributing to sustainability.

Students water vegetables in the hoop house they built at RFHS. **Credit: Illène Pevec**

## MAKING THE WORLD A BETTER PLACE WITH GOOD FOOD

Wendell Berry (2009, 15) suggests that sustainable agriculture "refers to a way of farming that can be continued indefinitely because it conforms to the terms imposed on it by the nature of places and the nature of people." The students have made it clear with their comments that growing food together fulfills many social and physical needs for them: it suits their nature as developing young adults. A school with empty land, good sun exposure, and access to affordable water can create a model for sustainable food growing as the schools portrayed in these pages have.

Bella, aged seventeen, pointed out: "Growing your own food helps you and people in the community because you're providing good stuff, healthy food." Maria, like the Maria in East Harlem, felt proud of leaving a food growing legacy: "I'm just proud of what we do. It's pretty exciting to see that we are doing something good to help out more students, knowing that we might not be here to eat that food, but other people are going to be able to eat it and enjoy it."

Denise concurs: "At the end of the day, when I go home and do my homework, I feel more optimistic. I think about things, like, what I do and how it's going to affect the world in a year or so. You just kind of think about all these connections."

Maria told me that even though her family has always grown food at home, having the knowledge she has gained in class about the industrialized food system has made her appreciate the actual act of gardening even more: "I feel a lot more energy. A lot of times people feel tired and they're lazy from being in the sun, but it gives me more energy to feel I am doing this to care for my family's health or my friends' health. And it's a really nice experience, and it's really beautiful to look at what you grow. I really love it. I really do."

For these youth, growing food with their own effort, knowing its origins are clean and not tainted with chemicals, picking it fresh, and eating from the source all add up to better taste and better health in their minds. The exercise from gardening combined with consuming the toxin-free nutrients in organically grown vegetables support good health. Knowing that what they are doing can help their families' health, their own health, and community health empowers them with energy as Maria so eloquently shared.

Due to the national youth obesity crisis and health concerns regarding what adolescents eat, I asked all of the students if the gardening class had changed their eating habits. Four said that it did not and twenty responded that it did. Many, like Dash, said the class makes them think before they eat:

> Well, I just try to eat less of the bad stuff. But it's still in my everyday life probably, the processed foods. But if I'm in [the market] and I look at the candy bar, I think, "Well, I could eat that candy bar. That looks pretty delicious!" But then, I think, "Well, it probably also has a lot of crap in it." Then, maybe I'll pick an apple or something instead.

Roberto has changed what he prefers quite a lot. He shares cooking responsibilities with his mother and sister, so his choices impact what his family eats:

> I used to go for the not healthy frozen foods from the store. And now I go for more healthy stuff. I like to make salad a lot. I make pasta. I eat more fish than I used to. I used to eat a lot of red meat, but I don't anymore. You can learn how to eat healthier. You can be more independent and not have to go buy stuff. You can grow your own food.

Knowledge empowers individuals to make better decisions. Ana commented that she eats more vegetables: "I feel good. I feel healthier. And I feel like I am doing the right thing, making the right choice." Students in New York also discussed making the right choice by choosing healthy food, indicating they have gained the ability to make positive choices based on the knowledge they have acquired from gardening.

## A CHANGE IN CAPACITY TO FOCUS

When I asked if gardening changed their capacity to focus, 91 percent of the students were very sure that gardening helped them to feel more refreshed and focused. Two said that it did not, but then used such words as refreshed or calm to describe how gardening made them feel. It is very difficult to know if it is the actual gardening, the time spent outdoors, or the two combined, but the students notice quite profound impacts on their capacity to focus.

Patrick and Julieta both volunteered separately that they suffer from attention deficit disorder (ADD). Their comments reflect research done with youth with ADD that shows that just a twenty-minute walk in nature can restore focus for a youth with ADHD to the same level as the drugs used to treat ADD (Faber Taylor and Kuo, 2008). Julieta explains how gardening helps her calm down and focus:

> You know, you can take energy from the earth, from the things around you. I got to spend the whole other class outside, so now, in the next class, I can kind of calm down and relax a little bit and put the energy that I got into my other work into my other class. That's a lot for me to say because I have ADD.

Patrick concurs:

> I'll leave the school [after gardening], and I'll just be in a calm state of mind, not really thinking about much, just kind of relaxed and steady in what I'm doing and whatever I'm thinking about. It's really a steady flow of thinking. When I'm leaving [on a school day with no gardening], my mind is racing, thinking about three different topics because I have ADD.

Research shows that the relaxation from time spent in nature not only relaxes a person but also improves executive function and cognition and that no drugs are necessary (Kaplan and Berman, 2010). The Centers for Disease Control and Prevention (2015a) cites these statistics: "Approximately 11% of children 4–17 years of age (6.4 million) have been diagnosed with ADHD as of 2011." A national study indicates that time outdoors in green spaces should be considered an effective, low-cost treatment with no side effects for the most common of neurological disorders affecting youth (Kuo and Faber Taylor, 2004).

If time outdoors can help students to gain an ability to focus, it would be a very important intervention for schools to integrate into the school day. The students that I interviewed used the words refreshed, energized, relaxed, peaceful, and calm when discussing how their psychological state and sense of focus changed in the garden. Antonio said it did not change his focus, but indicated that a change in focus actually did occur as he forgets his problems: "I don't think it affects me in that way. Not really. I just enjoy. It calms me down. If I am thinking about other problems, it just relaxes me and makes me not think about them that much."

Chase was certain that his focus improved:

You can definitely focus a lot easier. You don't feel as tired or just really bored at all because you just came back from outside. It stays with me for a good portion through lunch and then halfway through my next class. It's kind of a good feeling that you can't really get rid of.

Andrew, aged sixteen, observed that working with the plants could totally turn around his emotional state and makes it easier to focus.

If I get mad about, say, a grade in my first class and then I go to the greenhouse, I don't even worry about it. I just plant, water, totally relax; just no pressure at all. And then I go into my next class and it's just totally chill. So, it does balance it out. Having three hard classes in a row all day would just suck, but here, the greenhouse, just balances it out.

Maria also feels her focus becomes centered on her outside work, which changes her state of being. It matters to her that she can help:

I am happy to be doing something to help. I stop thinking about things at school. I focus on what I am doing outside. It clears my mind about anything. Yes, it carries over, makes me feel more calm [Maria's emphasis], a lot better. I get a heavy load off my back. Work is good for me. I feel better.

These statements reflect both engagement and meaning derived from gardening. These youth feel profoundly affected by working outside and caring for plants. Through work in the garden, they are more able to concentrate on their next tasks and are grateful to help nature and others.

## ENVIRONMENTAL AWARENESS AND ACTIVISM

I asked the youth whether or not their environmental awareness had changed as a result of their time in the garden and if they felt they might be more likely to take a stand on an environmental issue. Twenty-one said that working outside in the garden had expanded their awareness, and all responded that they would be more likely to take an activist's stance relevant to the environment due to what they had learned from gardening and the class. Three pointed out that because Carbondale has many environmental organizations and community support for wilderness, clean energy, clean water, and local shops, it is hard to determine just where their environmental awareness originated. Regardless of when their environmental awareness began, they felt they had definitely grown in awareness due to the class and felt capable of taking actions whether it was composting in their backyard, riding a bike rather than driving a car, or writing letters to officials to save a favorite place. Julieta felt the class empowered her to take action: "It taught me how to respect what's around me and how to build the things around me that I want."

Pedro found a new appreciation for each living thing in his surroundings: "I cannot go around stepping on plants just because I don't know what it is because every plant has its own way of working in the world." This knowledge that a living being occupies a niche in an ecosystem can be transferred to awareness that all natural systems have interrelationships that deserve respect.

Denise feels part of the larger, complex natural system: "I feel very enlightened. I feel like I'm part of something, I guess, more that I thought I was before." And Michaela feels the responsibility to behave with environmental awareness: "I definitely care more about where I am putting my trash, how I'm recycling, what I can do to lessen my dot on the earth."

Sometimes the amount of new information the young people have and need to process seems like a lot to manage. Dash mentioned that he started the class with quite a lot of awareness and actively participates in green initiatives. He also expressed a sense of feeling somewhat overwhelmed by his increased knowledge:

> We've been learning how messed up the food system is, so that's kind of changed [me]. It's kind of made me pessimistic about food because it sounds like things are so messed up that it would be really hard to fix now. And the government is not doing much in terms of helping out.

Despite the pessimism he expressed, I continued to see Dash participate in all the things he excels at and seems to enjoy: track, theater, speech meets, gardening, and working on the green team managing waste separation for the local arts festival.

Life thrives in the RFHS dome greenhouse world. Credit: Denise

## KNOWLEDGE, ACCOMPLISHMENT, AND PRIDE

Environmental activism requires efficacy, or the capacity to act on one's knowledge. Carlos delights in all that he has learned and now feels capable of using his new knowledge: "We, as a group, are doing a great job growing our own vegetables. It makes me feel happy being able to know that stuff. And we set goals. If I wanted to start my own garden, I would know how to do that." Pedro also sees himself as able to contribute by sharing with others what he has learned in this class: "It's just a good feeling. It makes you feel good inside. You can bring so much knowledge to people who don't know anything about planting, about plants. It helps you out with stuff in the world, with what you are eating and putting into your body.

Pedro advises his parents too: "I tell my parents and inform them about what's good and not good to eat." When I asked him what his parents think about having their son tell them what to eat because of what he's learned in an agricultural biology class, Pedro replied: "They actually like it. They seem to be interested and seem to cooperate, which is good."

For Chase, growing food, "Makes you realize that you are not a lazy person after all. You are doing things on your own, doing things that not a lot of people do. It makes me feel really good and accomplished." Several young women share this accomplished feeling as well. They value seeing tangible results. Ana says: "It makes me feel content, happy, that I'm doing something other than sitting down in my classroom, something that you will see over time what you have done."

Courtney's first thoughts about the garden are on, "The fresh foods you grow from it and that satisfied feeling that you can eat something you grew and loved and took care of." She takes pleasure in the new hands-on skills she has acquired:

A lot of the stuff I didn't know how to do, like building the hoop houses took a lot of effort too, and I know how to do that now. Yeah, I learned a lot with the tools that I had no idea how to use. It made me have a lot more respect for nature and the hard work people put into gardening that I really didn't see before. It's just, like, oh, you throw in a seed and you water, but it's a lot more about nurturing and caring and giving your love to the plant and making it grow and produce something.

Rachael saw how the skills she learned while gardening carried over into other areas:

Things have a set of steps that you need to do to accomplish them, and you know what those are the garden, but sometimes, there is a reason behind what you do that gives meaning to it and makes you want to do it. The steps it takes to make a real garden, it definitely takes a lot of work. So, I think it teaches you discipline in other areas of your life as well. Like if you can take a garden and start from scratch and then have fresh fruit produced in the fall or whatever, I think seeing the results of that definitely goes towards other aspects of your life: working hard and not giving up the first time a weed sprang up or something. I think the meaning of it, ultimately, you're going towards, and so that's why you're doing it and that influences other areas of life where you have a goal that you set forth and you don't just give up when something bad happens.

Aaron also gives his perspective on what students can and need to learn through a school garden:

The way the school system is now, we are losing a lot of important educational pieces that children need, you know. Like when you [referring to the adult generation] went to high school, you had home ec. We don't have that! We don't have anything like that. What agricultural biology does for students, it teaches them to be more useful. It teaches them to be independent, have pride in things that you accomplish. I think that it teaches pride. It's just another thing that teaches you to be, helps you learn who you are.

These observations come from a diverse student group. According to Dr. Colia, some excel in everything they do while others struggle at book-based learning. All find knowledge, meaning, accomplishment, engagement, positive relationships, and good feelings in the garden. They express happiness at connecting with nature, each other, and themselves. They take pride in making good personal choices in what they eat and in helping the environment and their school community by providing organically grown food to their school lunch program. Patrick expresses his love of fresh vegetables and sense of accomplishment in the garden:

You know the sound when you break open the peapod? That, like, crack of fresh, crisp vegetables? I love that sound because garden fresh vegetables are so much better than anything. Sounds [like that] always remind me of the work you've put in and the beneficial properties everything has after you're done.

# 11

## TEEN MOTHERS GARDEN AT YAMPAH MOUNTAIN HIGH SCHOOL

*The secret of life is to plant without the knowledge that you will harvest. You plant with the knowledge that others will harvest.* —DR. DON MATTERA, SOUTH AFRICAN POET

Inside the greenhouse at Yampah Mountain High School. Credit: Katia

Leigh McGowan, Yampah Mountain High School's principal, has Don Mattera's above quote beneath her e-mail signature, so it came as no surprise that she quickly embraced a science teacher's suggestion to start a gardening program and build a small dome greenhouse to introduce students to soil and botanical science. The same science teacher, Susy Ellison, had previously engaged students in successfully constructing and wiring a photovoltaic array to help power the school—and she had raised the money needed for both projects by writing the grants. The idea to build a greenhouse came from a former student who went to the Central Rocky Mountain Permaculture Institute after graduation and suggested the greenhouse for the school's science program. Ellison teaches basic high school science to students who have difficulties in traditional school settings and finds that, "You have to do something. You can't just go blah, blah, blah!"

This chapter will examine the student population served and the specific social and learning context at Yampah Mountain High School to understand what differentiates it from the other gardening programs. Yampah provides public, alternative high school education to youth who have a risk of dropping out otherwise. Yampah serves 126 full-time high school students from four school districts in a 120-mile river valley corridor in rural Colorado. It also hosts the teen-parent academic program for the region (forty-three students in 2009–2010). It sits low on a mountainside in Glenwood Spring, Colorado, overlooking the Colorado River. It is fifteen miles from Carbondale, where Colorado Rocky Mountain School and Roaring Fork High School are located. The five teen mother students' experiences gardening at their school greenhouse, along with the impacts from these experiences relative to themselves, the community of learners, and their children, make up this chapter.

## YAMPAH MOUNTAIN HIGH SCHOOL AND THE GARDENING AND HORTICULTURAL SCIENCE PROGRAM

Yampah Mountain High School students built the school's dome greenhouse in the spring of 2009. They were able to do the building themselves with help from adult mentors because of the manageable size (twenty-two feet in diameter) and the fact that it came in a kit with clear instructions. McGowan explains the impact constructing the greenhouse had on the students:

> Building the greenhouse engaged kids who don't connect in the classroom. These kids found internal motivation via building, a group effort. They worked cooperatively and they participated willingly. It was a very important project for the students. Two of the senior boys worked on the

greenhouse as their senior project. They would begin digging from the moment they got to school, and they did it all day long. They felt that, for them, building the greenhouse was a way to give back to the school on an ongoing basis. They felt it was very important for them to give a gift to the school to serve the school that would go on after they had graduated and left.

The digging referred to by McGowan was for the foundation to install the climate battery, the system of buried pipes that circulates air in the soil to keep the soil from freezing and the air temperature above freezing (the system described in detail in Chapter 10). I did not meet or interview the students who built the twenty-two-foot-diameter-dome greenhouse because I had my first direct contact with the school at the greenhouse dedication in the spring of 2009 and not during the construction phase. The dedication ceremony included a barbecue with locally raised, grass-fed beef burgers donated and grilled by the man who raised the cattle and a huge salad from the greenhouse run by the permaculture instructor who advised on the greenhouse and was also directly involved in building the one at Roaring Fork High School too.

That following fall, eight of the forty-three teen mothers at the school enrolled in the semester-long horticulture science class. The teen-parent program occupies most of the bottom floor of the two-story building and is made up entirely of teen mothers, with the occasional teen father dropping in for a special event. Each one of the young mothers had created a life-size body portrait that included photos of their babies. These self-portraits hung in the hall and visually claimed that space. There is an infant nursery and toddler playroom and preschool off this same hall, as well as the mothers' classrooms. Once children are three and a half years old, they go to a daycare program at another school a mile away. Some of these young families have a sixty-mile school bus ride to get to Yampah; the babies have their own car seats buckled into a bus seat.

Ninety-eight percent of the young women in the teen-parent program are Hispanic and all eight in the horticultural science program are Hispanic. Some had brand new babies and some had toddlers. Marcella, a seventeen-year-old mother who participated in this study, had a four-year-old son in preschool already, but the other interviewees' babies stayed in their school's nursery.

I had my first exposure to the teen mothers after the greenhouse dedication ceremony. After we had all finished our delicious local food luncheon, a group of moms arrived back at the school with large soda pops, french fries, and hamburgers from a fast food purveyor. Their teacher identified them to me. They showed no interest at all in the free hamburgers and garden fresh salad with higher nutritional quality than what they had just spent their limited funds to buy. I did not ask the moms I interviewed a year later if they had been in that group of teens laden with junk food or if they had come to the luncheon because they were fully engaged in growing food and herbs in the greenhouse by then. Since the teen-parent population changes, it could have been an entirely different group I saw at the dedication, but the total lack of interest shown in free, good quality food illustrates the importance of this horticulture and nutrition program to introduce teen mothers to food-growing skills so that their children will also have good food. These young students already have the responsibility to raise children to be healthy.

I am impressed by the excellent support I see at Yampah for these young women, aged fourteen to eighteen, and for their children. This program had the elements defined as important for positive youth development: physical and psychological safety, appropriate structure, and supportive relationships (Eccles and Gootman, 2002, 90). The teachers are warm and affectionate with the mothers and their babies, and they do everything they can to support the students academically and emotionally. The two nurseries are bright and cheerful with staff who appear to give excellent care to all the babies. The mothers can bring their babies into class with them if they need to nurse or attend to them in some way and are encouraged to go into the nursery with them at lunchtime. The program provides this shared lunchtime so that they will see the good nutrition the program provides for their children and learn from this healthy model while they eat lunch together. I perceived no judgmental behavior by any adult at the school towards the young mothers. The girls receive not only academic instruction but also parenting-skill workshops, including intergenerational literacy and a class in child development.

I was never part of any interaction the teen mothers had with the other students on the building's upper floor. None of those students participated in the greenhouse that semester during the time I was there, and, according to Ellison, the teen-mother group dominated the greenhouse activity that term. (She was frequently gone that fall due to a family illness and this impacted her ability to bring her other classes into the greenhouse.)

Including Yampah in this research provided a unique group a voice. Not only did these teens have parenting responsibilities, but they also did not have a choice in their participation in the horticulture class. It was the only science class offered to them that term, so if they needed a science credit, this was the only class they could take. Only eight girls enrolled, though occasionally one or two others dropped in for a day. This lack of choice is an important qualifier to consider in what they say—do their experiences sound different from the students who chose a gardening class or activity?

I included this school in the outreach grant that I wrote to the University of Colorado at Boulder because the program was just beginning and needed funding. I knew Ellison slightly because she taught in a summer renewable energy program for which I had also written grants. The same permaculture and architecture team that helped to start the greenhouse at Roaring Fork High School also helped Yampah to get their dome greenhouse built. When I met Sally Kilton, the teen-parent counselor and teacher, I told her about my background in integrating gardening with academics, and she was eager for my help with the new horticulture class for the teen moms. The University of Colorado Outreach Grant provided the science teacher with $150 to buy books for the horticulture program two years in a row and money for gas for field trips for the students to see local horticultural enterprises, as well as some small funding for my own time spent at Yampah during that term.

I helped to orient Kilton to appropriate curriculum and co-taught with her and Ellison. I also taught quite a few classes that fall by myself when the teachers were at various professional trainings, so I had a different relationship with these students than at the other research sites where I had no regular responsibilities for what they were learning. However, I had nothing at all to do with grading them or giving them tests and the students knew that. I delayed interviewing them until the spring so that I was not involved in teaching them at the time that I did the interviews with them in their greenhouse. There was a five-month separation between my involvement with the class and the interviews.

The youth gardeners I interviewed at Yampah had differing levels of English fluency. Only one was born in the US and seemed to use English more than Spanish, though I also heard her converse in Spanish occasionally. I frequently explained things in Spanish to the girls because several had very little English, particularly one recent immigrant. I was very impressed to see by the end of spring term when I interviewed the five who were still at the school, that their English had improved significantly. I found that those youth with less English use fewer words and came to the point more quickly. They don't tell long stories, but they do speak openly about their gardening experiences and express their feelings quite freely if not as loquaciously as those students for whom English is a first language. In the interviews, I gave them the opportunity to speak in Spanish, but all preferred to do the interviews in English, the language spoken at the school.

Ellison found that the horticulture program offered a way to introduce the girls to the science vocabulary (words like botany, microscope, and slide) included in the Colorado English Language Acquisition (CELA) test that they all had to take. We integrated nutrition and cooking into the horticulture class so that learning to grow plants and to make vegetable soup and pesto were a part of science. We even made corn tortillas by hand, something they told me that they had never done. The school longs for a good kitchen to be able to better engage students in cooking as the current one is very small and inadequate for even a small group. This school does not participate in the federal school lunch program, which is one reason why it is not uncommon to see the students leave the school for a fast food lunch.

These young women had enormous responsibilities to care for their babies and continue their high school educations. Imagine combining the sleep deprived nights one experiences with infants and teething toddlers with attending school full time. The one girl who began the class pregnant did not attend again once her baby was born in October as she was allowed three months at home to care for her baby and get used to being a mom before she returned to school.

The horticulture class did not use a text, but we did present botanical and soil science to them in very short informational discussions that were immediately linked to hands-on work in the greenhouse. We had them look up things on the Internet related to both botany and nutrition to practice literacy and technology. When we had an aphid infestation on the tomatoes, peppers, and basil, we had them look up aphids and non-pesticide approaches to getting rid of them. They bravely tackled the aphids with water and soap in squirt bottles and helped to tear out the badly infested plants. Even though they found it rather disgusting to chase after these pests, they laughed while doing it. Ellison ordered lacewings from a local insectarium and then the girls looked for signs of the newly hatched predators that we hoped would devour the aphids.

Kilton told me that they do not give homework because these girls go home each afternoon with their babies in tow and have their hands full in fixing dinner and getting their babies bathed and to bed. The lack of a book with regular reading assignments or any written assignments to be completed independently at home meant that the program did not cover several areas of knowledge that the other school programs did, including information regarding how the industrialized food system works in the United States. The science was at a very basic level, with botany lessons focusing on plant parts and reproduction. Most other information had a practical nature for the girls to understand some basic things about soil, decomposition, worms, and plants so that by the end of the semester, they knew enough to create their own organic gardens if that was what they wanted or might want to do in the future. We focused more on nutrition when we asked them to research a fruit or vegetable on the Internet. If we were planting spinach seeds one day, we would have them look up spinach nutritional values and write those into their journals and we would discuss ways to feed spinach to their babies and when to introduce this food into an infant's diet. This was a completely practical class for imparting gardening, nutrition, and eating experiences and skills.

We did a participatory planning session in the fall to discover what plants the young gardeners most wanted to grow and what they would like specifically to learn about during the semester. They all wanted to grow strawberries and roses[1]. They liked growing the ingredients for salsa too, and those were the first plants in the greenhouse after the dedication: tomatoes, hot peppers, cilantro, and basil. Marcella pointed out that Mexicans do not eat basil, but prefer cilantro for seasoning tomatoes. I was able to get a vigorous rose donated for planting outside the greenhouse, but the strawberries were not available for planting in the fall and so the girls planted them the following spring.

One girl brought up the need to know about poisonous plants so that they could protect their babies, so we did a short class on the poisonous plants outside in Colorado (poison ivy, for example) and some poisonous houseplants that they might encounter. We also included how to call poison control for help. I shared my experience that occurred when my middle child was about two and put a piece of dieffenbachia in her mouth that was growing near a commercial hot springs swimming pool where we were swimming. She started crying and holding her tongue. I called poison control, and they told me to give her lots of water and watch her for any sign of having a more dangerous reaction. I was just one mother sharing an experience with other mothers the way that mothers do.

We incorporated as much cooking and food tasting as was practical given the very limited time and the tiny kitchen facility at the school. We were not able to take the girls to the organic fruit orchards or a permaculture farm because the drive was too long for this group that had babies waiting to be nursed, but I brought a selection of organic apples for them and their little ones and, during one class, we had an apple tasting. Until I cut up several different kinds of apples and placed them on separate plates with the apple variety names in front of each one, these girls had not realized that there were so many different kinds of apples and that each has a unique taste. They thought there were only red apples and green apples. During the apple tasting, one of the girls had her six-month-old baby on her lap who had already gotten a tooth. He very happily gnawed away at the apple piece his mom held for him. In this setting, skill building in healthy baby nutrition combined with the pleasures of good eating. He was the only baby to taste apples in class, but I sent the uncut apples home with the young mothers. We also made vegetable soup from scratch as part of our multidimensional approach to introducing vegetables as a familiar,

---

1.  Roses have a very special place in Mexican culture as they are the flower attached to the story of the Virgin of Guadalupe, the patron saint of Mexico. Her image surrounded by roses is well known to all Mexicans as is the miracle attributed to her. It has occurred to me that the girls' request to grow roses at school comes perhaps from this profound cultural tie they have to the flower, but I did not think of this when I was with the girls and could ask them.

delicious part of their diets. In my interviews many months later, several girls brought up that what they tasted in these food-tasting sessions had been new to them.

At Christmas, there was an amaryllis lily in the school hallway window. I brought it into the classroom and had the students draw the flower in their garden journals and then write the flower's anatomical names onto the drawing as I explained their function. A flower's reproductive life is very easy to see in a big amaryllis and all we lacked was a bee spreading pollen to make the picture complete. The girls seemed very interested and asked a lot of questions. I pointed out to them the similarities between a plant's reproduction and a person's and wondered if anyone had ever discussed reproduction with them before their early pregnancies.

The girls' demeanor seemed different inside the classroom than outside in the greenhouse. They were more squirmy and avoidant of work inside except when the activity involved art of some sort, such as drawing a flower, but in the greenhouse where they each had a specific hands-on task to accomplish, they were more focused and relaxed. They chatted with their teachers and each other as they worked. They would leave the greenhouse at the end of about an hour to get their kids dressed in snowsuits for the school bus drive home. This juxtaposition of activities is what mothers typically have to juggle. I felt that having three adult women mentoring these girls in gardening and cooking in a relaxed and supportive environment was a good contribution to their education and self-awareness, and I was glad the grant made it possible for me to be part of it weekly for the entire semester.

These teens, though under eighteen, signed their own interview consent forms because the school considers them liberated adults since they have the legal responsibility for their children. This class had the least amount of time spent gardening compared to other programs because the Yampah horticulture class met only once a week for about one-and-a-half hours for one semester. They had fewer opportunities to harvest food grown by their efforts as the program and greenhouse were new—the food was just getting planted for the first time. The aphid infestation that first fall made most of the tomatoes and peppers students had planted the prior spring inedible and we just had to throw out most of them. As a class, the teen mothers planted salad greens, broccoli, and carrots, and by the late fall, they had some greens and herbs growing, but not an abundance of food to taste. The fans in the greenhouse were not yet hooked up that first fall due to incomplete electrical wiring, so few plants survived the December cold. The students' exposure to both gardening and eating what they grew also suffered from the erratic attendance some had in class. On occasions, sick babies kept them home. They experienced less than a quarter of the gardening time that the other high school programs had and a tiny fraction of the time that the ¡Cultiva! youth gardened, but these five teen mothers, despite the limitations, still harvested enough to make a significant impact as you will see.

Kilton took horticulture in high school herself and was completely engaged in starting this new program. Her philosophy was that experiential learning is best for this learning population where English was a second language. (Kilton was completing a master's degree in English as a second language.) Kilton explains:

> I am a firm believer in kinesthetic learning, especially with the population of students we work with at Yampah. For the most part, they all learn by doing. By far, that is the very best way that they get it. We picked lettuce in the greenhouse for our Thanksgiving dinner. So they really get it. They get what they're learning even if there is a language barrier. So the hands-on [learning] is priceless.

Kilton noticed that sometimes the girls acted like any teenager who did not wish to make an extra effort to do something—in this case, climbing the small hill to the greenhouse. The distance from the school door to the greenhouse door is perhaps two hundred feet. The hill itself may be a thirty-feet walking distance up some stone stairs. Kilton elaborates:

> They walk up the hill like it's a tragedy to get out of the classroom, put their coats on, and get up into the greenhouse, but once they're up there, they're happier there. It creates energy for them. And some of them get into it and some of them don't, but I would say that more of them do than don't.

What did the teen-mom gardeners themselves say about hands-on learning while digging in the dirt? The rest of the chapter is dedicated to the observations from the five girls who took the class and were at the school when I did the interviews in spring.

## GARDENING AS A FAMILY HERITAGE

*My grandma, she loves plants. She would plant them beside the house, and every day, she would go out and water them, and it was nice to look at her.* —KATIA, 16

All five teen mothers have prior experience with at least one person in their families gardening to grow food. Three girls, Natalie, Delia, and Katia, all had grandparents that farmed in Mexico. Delia, aged seventeen, lived with her grandparents for a year when she was six in a small Mexican town. Her grandfather raised corn for human consumption. Currently, her mother grows hot pepper plants at home to use in cooking.

Katia, aged sixteen, finds that the smell of moist soil and the roses reminds her of her grandmother because she liked smelling the roses her grandma grew as a child. Katia said that the rose scent makes her feel, "Happy and comfortable. Like, mostly, I would relax with the smell of the roses."

Natalie, aged sixteen, left Mexico too young to remember her grandparents working the land and doesn't remember eating the food they grew, but knows they farmed and that her uncles now farm there at the place she had only visited once after immigrating. She describes the huerta at the back of the family house with oranges and bananas. She helped her mother to water flowers and says that her family wants to return to Mexico. She much prefers the more rural, small-town environment where she lives now in Colorado to the "ghetto" neighborhood in Los Angeles where she spent her childhood.

Marcella's father keeps a garden at the home where she lives with her parents along with her son. She shares the cooking responsibilities with her mother. Her father grows roses, tomatoes, and cilantro. She confesses that, "I don't like doing it [gardening] that much, but I enjoy having the things there." Like Katia, when Marcella smells a rose, she feels, "Relaxed. Like really nice smells relax me, really relaxed."

Virginia, aged seventeen, has a mother and an aunt who work in commercial organic greenhouses in a nearby town. She wanted to understand more about what her mother did professionally and that is one of the reasons that she signed up for the class even though there was no other choice in science classes. She chose this experience to better know her mother's daily work and because she wanted to learn how to do those same things. She remembers having a garden with both vegetables and fruit trees in it when she was about twelve and eating the delicious carrots that grew in it.

In some significant way, each of these young women has family members who have grown food even though no one has an active memory of doing anything to help in the family garden besides watering.

## THE SENSES, NATURE, AND RELAXATION

Virginia enjoys coming into the greenhouse both at school and where her mother works: "Everything is so green. It's pretty. It smells good too. Like fresh air, clean. It just feels alive in here!" She finds that these fresh and alive smells make her feel, "Peaceful and calm." It's the garden's peacefulness that she remembers when she is away from it. She likes the round space that the dome greenhouse provides and the feeling she gets from being surrounded by plants. She is the only student amongst twenty-nine interviewees who garden in a dome greenhouse who specifically mentioned really liking the dome shape. She attributes the peacefulness she experiences in the greenhouse to its shape: "It is just me and the plants, and I am surrounded by them."

Marcella says she receives the greatest amount of sensory information from her eyes when she gardens:

> Looking at each different plant, and when I come back, knowing what plant is what. Tomato plants I kept in my head because they grow really tall, and basil, and the mint. It's looking at them, how they look, like how the tomato plants look that they're, like, hairy, and I get that in my head, and the picture just stays in my head.

Marcella is glad that she has learned to distinguish one plant from another because, "I don't want to eat something that I don't know what it is instead of just knowing what they are and being able to see what I can eat." Marcella also appreciates what she hears in the greenhouse: "It's just good to hear nature sounds."

 Katia's nose leads her way in the garden because smell triggers her memory: "It helps me if I smell one plant and then another. It helps remind me what each one is." Besides the good scents relaxing her, she finds that when she feels upset, she seeks the quiet of the garden: "I want to be in a quiet place where there is no noise. It relaxes me."

Delia joins the chorus in appreciating the relaxation she experiences from flower smells. These scents made her happy too, and she likes the progress she witnesses in the garden: "You can see every week that they grow. If you come today and then you come next week, they are all growing and green." This growth makes Delia feel, "Happy, glad because I did it. I worked with my class." She also noticed that working in the greenhouse brought her together in a good way with her classmates: "We get more together. We talk. If I don't talk to a girl, if we come here, we get together and we talk more. I think it's 'cause it's so quiet. I t's relaxed."

When I asked Natalie how the garden smells made her feel, she responded, "It makes me feel good inside, all fresh, good." When I asked her how she felt touching the soil, she confessed to feeling slightly afraid of the worms. However, she went on to say:

I enjoy touching the soil, the plants. You can feel them. I feel part of them. It makes me feel that I can care more about things. Not to, like, be, you know how some kids are just, like, "Whatever," grabbing things, throwing it to the ground. Being more gentle, caring more, the plants are like people.

## PARALLELS BETWEEN GARDENING AND CARING FOR CHILDREN

I asked all the youth what other activities in their lives gave them similar feelings as gardening. Natalie told me that caring for her son gave her similar feelings as gardening: "Spending time with him, just playing with him, just being there." She also said that after gardening, she can focus better on certain things like writing, science, and math, but not reading. She likes to plant seeds the best, but she is afraid of transplanting because, "I am afraid I am going to kill them."

Delia also found that it was caring for her daughter that seemed to give her similar feelings as gardening: "It's the same thing. You see them grow. They get big… and seeing her, touching her."

Katia has similar feelings to Delia and Natalie and finds meaning in a garden's growth process:

For me, I like it also. For me with my daughter and being pregnant nine months and right now she is two years [old], and I have seen her grow. And it's really nice, and also for the plants. You first see a seed and you plant it, and then you see it grow. So it's really nice. I really like to see that, to be excited while it is growing. You have to be watering the plants, and for my daughter, I have to be feeding her.

Virginia added: "I like to touch the soil and feel the plants. It feels good because you are helping a plant to grow. So, it feels like you are helping someone to grow." She also compares caring for plants to caring for her son, but finds gardening, "A little more relaxing, not so stressful." We laughed together over the fact that plants don't cry.

Marcella felt that cooking was the other experience she had which gave her similar sensory experiences as gardening. She did not speak as much about her sensory feelings as the others because for her, the garden was a place to learn. She appreciated the new knowledge and skills she gained: "I accomplished learning. I learned new things."

From Kilton's observations, what the girls shared in the greenhouse with their children was vitally important:

The greenhouse environment creates a connection between the moms and their babies. And that's really big because we take the toddlers in to release ladybugs. And that's a really, really big deal! And that moment of engagement of that teenage mom seeing that discovery of that two-year-old is absolutely priceless because that magic that the toddler sees of the ladybugs being released and crawling on their hands and arms being so excited because the baby is so excited is, like, huge. That's huge!"

## FOOD CHOICES FOR THEMSELVES AND THEIR CHILDREN

Since one of the goals of the horticulture program is to influence the young mothers' food choices for themselves and their children to go in a healthy direction, we exposed them to fresh fruits and vegetables through growing, tasting, and cooking. I asked all of them about any changes in their personal food habits or the choices they made on behalf of their children that happened because of what they experienced in class. I noted a predominantly positive, self-reported behavioral impact related to food with the exception of Marcella. She acknowledged what she learned factually about nutrition when I asked her if the class had influenced what she ate or what she gave her son to eat, but our interchange puzzled me and I include it here in its entirety with my questions:

MARCELLA: They tell us what is more healthy. Like different variety of foods that are different, that are really healthy for them [babies], what vitamins they have. Yeah, it helps me to know what is better for them, what vitamins they need. I guess that's it.

ILLÈNE: So have you made some choices about what foods you give your baby based on what you learned?

MARCELLA: No, not really. I haven't because I only had that class for the semester, and I didn't come back because I had already all my science credit. So I haven't learned that much more. I don't know.

ILLÈNE: But you said you did learn about vitamins, but you are not sure that influences you in how you feed your baby?

MARCELLA: No, not really.

I did not wish to criticize Marcella's choices, so I dropped this line of questioning with her.

It sounds as if she felt she did not have enough information or that a one semester class was insufficient to actually change her food choices. I did not ask her or any of the other girls what their parent's eating habits were, but, of course, when a person lives where family cooks share duties, as was Marcella's situation with her and her mother, and not everyone is learning nutrition simultaneously, it is difficult for any one individual to change what may be unhealthy family eating patterns.

Katia did feel that the class had influenced her in terms of her child's nutrition:

It has because I have my daughter. And it really helped me when I'm giving her what she needs to be healthy, like vegetables that are good for her, and it has influenced me a lot. I was really, like, not into the vegetables, but now, for my daughter, I have. What she loves are peas. That she loves.

Delia claims that because of the apple tasting day we had, she now eats a variety of apples, something she had not thought possible before she learned there were multiple apple varieties. For her baby, Delia says: "I want her to be healthy. She eats strawberries, watermelon, everything. She likes everything!" Delia also told me that she personally likes to taste everything on the days that we cook. Natalie also feels her choices for herself and her baby have changed to become healthier. She explains her improved food choices:

Instead of chips, I choose a fruit. I try to give water instead of lots of juice or put water in the juice. I feel that I have to learn how to, how do you say, how to give him healthier things. He likes oranges. Yeah, he does, and calabacitas [zuchinni]. He likes those.

Virginia claims that she already ate a lot of vegetables before taking the class. She is the one person in this group who described the difference in taste between something home grown and store bought. She discussed the carrots she tasted from her family's garden when she was twelve. Like many other youth in the other garden sites, knowing the food's origins was important to her taste appreciation. Virginia explains:

I knew where they came from and how they were, you know, who helped them grow, you know, who helped them along the way. And they taste a lot better when you do it yourself instead of coming from the store because you don't actually know where they are from.

## CHANGES IN ENVIRONMENTAL AWARENESS AND ACTIVISM

These young women became more environmentally aware by learning to build the soil, care for the plants, and use integrated pest management rather than pesticides in the greenhouse. When I asked Virginia about her environmental awareness, she replied, "I think it's changed because you know you are helping to build something that is good for others. You feel proud of yourself." When I asked her if she would be willing to take an environmental stance, she answered very firmly: "Yeah! I've never liked people who throw their trash on the ground. I see people do it, and I usually pick it up, and, you know, when my sister does it, I make her pick it up, or my baby's dad does it, I make him pick it up."

Katia feels that gardening has directly impacted her environmental awareness, "Because it is something beautiful and you need to take care of it." She used almost identical words as Virginia to describe her activism when it comes to trash, especially in relation to her siblings when she sees them throw garbage on the ground.

Natalie felt that she could now explain to others how to plant a garden in order to improve the environment. Delia's gardening has made her committed to preservation: "We have to take care of the trees." Marcella now sees environmental issues through a food lens: "If we don't protect the environment, then we won't be producing any food for us. They [those who might pollute] need to think that they are the ones eating from there too."

## EMPOWERMENT AND CHANGE

*I was learning a new experience. I don't know how to say it, but, yeah, it helped me because I was learning to do something that I have never done, so I felt different for doing something for the first time. I get to work with plants, something I have never done before.* —MARCELLA, 17

Marcella clearly values and owns what she has learned. She has added this new knowledge to her skill set and values this. Delia also expresses confidence and some inner transformation from this gardening experience: "Yeah, I know that I can grow something and can do something with my hands. It makes me feel that I can care more about things."

The girls had seen a full year's greenhouse process when I interviewed them. Katia commented: "I remember when Susy [Ellison, the science teacher,] first told us that were going to make it. And it wasn't, like, a long time ago, and now, I am able to see all of this and what they have contributed, and it's growing. Now, everything is really nice." She found that this process also changed her personally: "Before, I wasn't interested in plants. I didn't like them. But now, I really do." This experience at school has also connected Katia to her farming grandparents in a new way: "Now, I can understand why they loved planting so much."

Virginia has found new meaning in life through learning to garden: "I don't know if I am really helping the environment, but I feel like it because you know it is here and you're just planting. I think planting on Earth is part of helping the earth."

Natalie has also found herself changed by this gardening experience: "I feel that I enjoy it. I feel very happy inside. I know that I am going to grow something." She, like several girls, expressed appreciation for the field trips they took to commercial greenhouses not only for the fun but also for the learning experience.

Kilton has watched these girls from their first introduction to planting the first tomatoes in the spring that the greenhouse was built to a full eighteen months later when I interviewed her. She shares her perspective on the gardening experiences and their meaning for the students:

> That kinesthetic kind of knowledge stays with you forever. No matter what happens, those girls that were in the horticulture class and involved in planting the plants and learning how to get rid of the aphids, that kind of knowledge will never leave their brains. In my opinion, you can teach algebraic equations, but if you don't keep doing it, eventually that knowledge leaves us. But the earth science, the knowledge that they learn in the greenhouse, that will never leave them. It will always be there. And that is what is so fabulous about it. In the career opportunities it creates for them to be thinking about also because not everybody is college bound and especially when we're dealing with students that are undocumented. What are these moms going to do? How are they going to support their families? How are they going to feed their families? So that gives them that knowledge too so they might just be able to feed their kids. You know, how important is that?

Kilton is not the only one looking to the future. Virginia told me: "I know that when I look at a plant and I see my child, and he's growing up and this world is not really pretty right now. So I try to make a difference so when he grows up, he has the same kind of world that I had when I was young." Virginia has only been on this earth seventeen years, but she perceives her childhood as a time when things were better for the planet. This is most likely because when she was a small child, she knew nothing about pollution, endangered species, or global warming—things that she certainly hears about now as a young mother worrying for her child's future.

Despite their many challenges, these teen moms all clearly describe the elements identified by researchers for positive youth development present in their shared food-growing experience in their school greenhouse: bonding, social competence, behavioral competence, a sense of self-efficacy with newly developing skills, the opportunity for prosocial involvement, and a feeling of hope for the future (Catalano et al. 2004). The bonding and social competence appears in their improved relationships with each other and their children; a sense of self-efficacy comes from acquiring new skills and practicing their use; the prosocial involvement comes with growing food to share with the whole school at a shared Thanksgiving meal; and hope for the future comes from experiencing and identifying the parallels between caring for their children and caring for plants and the earth and in taking pride in all of those.

These young mothers also express Seligman's (2011) flourishing elements: positive human relationships with their peers, teachers, and children in the garden; their engagement and focus; their positive emotions from their time spent together working in the greenhouse; the broader meaning of caring for the environment and making the world a better place for their children; and their sense of achievement in learning to grow food, prepare it, and feed their children well.

# 12

## ADOLESCENT HEALTH AND THE FOOD ENVIRONMENT
### WHAT DIFFERENCE CAN A GARDEN MAKE?

*I never ate vegetables very much until I started doing this [gardening]. It started open-
ing my mind to eating something I had grown myself, to eating locally grown. I never
really ate salads myself until this. I was never a big vegetable guy. I always love to eat
meat and that's all I ever eat. I never ate salads or vegetables until the greenhouse, until they started growing and I started trying them. And I thought, "Hey, this is good!"*
**—ANDREW, 16, ROARING FORK HIGH SCHOOL**

Freshly harvested vegetables at ¡Cultiva! in Boulder, Colorado. Credit: Illène Pevec

I magining Andrew and all youth gardeners discovering the flavor, crunch, zing, and fun in the vegetables they grow themselves brings hope to anyone working to improve young people's food choices. Why does food choice matter? This chapter will examine adolescent health issues in the US and the possible impacts on health from school policies, the National School Lunch Program, time spent with electronic media, and the agribusiness, fast food, and advertising industries.

## YOUTH HEALTH IN THE US

We are in a health crisis. In 2008, more than one third of children aged six to nineteen were overweight or obese (a body mass index (BMI) of 95 percent or higher) (Ogden et al. 2010). In 2010–2011, 17 percent of American youth aged twelve to seventeen, or approximately 12.7 million individuals, were considered obese by the Centers for Disease Control and Prevention (2015b), a rate that has more than tripled from 5 percent in 1980. A study by Ng et al. (2014, 770) revealed that, "Worldwide, prevalence of overweight and obesity combined rose by 27.5% for adults and 47.1% for children between 1980 and 2013. The number of overweight and obese individuals increased from 857 million in 1980, to 2.1 billion in 2013." This same study analyzed more than 1,700 medical reports and studies and could not identify a single country that has lowered the obesity rate in the past thirty-three years. Death from obesity worldwide is estimated at 3.4 million for 2010 (Ng et al. 2014).

Research indicates that weight increase comes in large part from higher caloric consumption and lower energy expenditure in all age groups (Brownell and Horgen, 2004). Lower consumption of vegetables and fruits and a higher consumption of carbohydrates and fats exacerbates expanding waist lines (Dennison, Rockwell, and Baker, 1998; Newby, 2007).

The statistics presented here will focus on the US, with some Canadian and European references, because the youth in this book live in the US. It is possible that what the young American gardeners say about their personal experiences may well reflect what international youth might say. From my work creating youth gardens in Canada, Brazil, and Mexico, I have heard young gardeners in those countries say similar things to the voices here, but I did not interview internationally for this book.[1]

Food purchasing habits in the United States have changed dramatically—since 1970, there

---

1. For a glimpse at youth gardeners in Brazil, see Illène Pevec's (2005) documentary film, *A Child's Garden of Peace*, on PBS's Natural Heroes series Web site.

has been an eighteen-fold increase in spending on fast food (Brownell and Horgen, 2004, 8). French fries are sold in more fast food outlets and restaurants than any other food item (Schlosser, 2001, 115). Potatoes are the most widely sold vegetable in the US, accounting for 15 percent of all sales. Fifty percent of potatoes are consumed as processed food: french fries, potato chips, and other potato products (Economic Research Service, 2016). When McDonalds first started serving french fries in 1955, the serving weighed two ounces; supersize portions are now almost seven ounces (Brownell and Horgen, 2004, 181). The issue in the US is not just what we eat but how much we eat. Americans consume on average four servings of french fries per week (Schlosser, 2001, 294).

"About half of all American adults—117 million individuals—have one or more preventable, chronic diseases that are related to poor quality dietary patterns and physical inactivity, including cardiovascular disease, hypertension, type 2 diabetes, and diet-related cancers" (Office of Disease Prevention and Health Promotion, 2015a, 1). The US Surgeon General, Dr. Richard Carmona (2004), testified to a congressional committee that today's children may be the first to have shorter life spans than their parents and that a change in lifestyle to healthier foods and more physical activity could improve health dramatically. He assembled panels of experts to develop a national action plan to combat obesity, citing the risks for adults, children, and youth (Brownell and Horgen, 2004; Foster et al. 2008; Newby, 2007; Peterson and Fox, 2007).

As well as the physical health problems, an obese appearance can cause severe psychosocial consequences: low self-esteem, social alienation, discrimination, and, especially in girls, depression (Doak et al. 2006). Recent research indicates a relationship between Alzheimer's disease and both types of diabetes, a relationship so close that some scientists now refer to Alzheimer's disease as type 3 diabetes (de la Monte and Wands, 2008). Both physical and mental health problems due to obesity will likely extend into adulthood if young people do not find a way to turn around their eating and physical activity habits. These health problems threaten quality of life and life itself.

Certain non-white populations in the US show greater risk for being overweight, specifically Hispanic and Native American children, both boys and girls, and African American female children (Brownell and Horgen, 2004; Centers for Disease Control and Prevention, 2015b; US Government Printing Office, 2007; Levine, 2008; Ludwig, Peterson, and Gortmaker, 2001; New Mexico Department of Health, 2013). Poverty makes for higher rates of overweight children, and parents with low education levels have unhealthier children (Centers for Disease Control and Prevention, 2015b).

Additionally, people's ill health impacts the economy. Obesity-related hospitalization costs for children and adolescents in the US more than tripled from $35 million to $127 million between

1979 and 1999 (Centers for Disease Control and Prevention, 2009, 2). According to the Harvard School of Public Health (2014), one estimate for paying for the health expenses related to obesity in 2005 was $190 billion dollars. The US Surgeon General identified this cost as second only to tobacco-related diseases (Carmona, 2004).

What role could youth gardens play to prevent obesity and create a healthy population that is able to live vigorous lives and contribute to the national economy rather than drain it due to health care costs? Greener schoolyards with gardens offer fresh air, more exercise opportunities, and mental health benefits (Bell and Dyment, 2008). This chapter explores the health challenges and disparities youth face and the role food gardens at schools and after-school garden programs can play in creating good health through access to growing, preparing, and eating vegetables.

## WHAT FACTORS FORM THE FOOD ENVIRONMENT?

To understand a garden's full potential as a healthy food and activity environment for young people, we must examine the broader societal context that has led to ill health. What are the home, neighborhood, and public school food environments? How has media influenced what youth want and consume? Though caesarian section (Huh et al. 2012) and antibiotic use in infants (Trasande et al. 2013) have been both been linked to obesity, they will not be explored here, but both need to be considered by those seeking comprehensive solutions to the obesity crisis.

First Lady Michelle Obama has taken a national lead in modeling wellness by bringing Washington, DC, school children to the White House to plant a garden, starting her physical fitness campaign, *Let's Move*, and by championing recent improvements to nutritional content guidelines in school lunches (Henderson, 2010). A First Lady can have excellent influence on public health as Eleanor Roosevelt, Michelle Obama's inspiration, did when she asked Americans to start Victory Gardens during World War II and twenty million home gardens sprang to life filled with vegetables (Pollan, 2008; Spiering, 2015). Along with inspired First Ladies, we need broad national policy change to create comprehensive, long-lasting improvements. According to the Centers for Disease Control and Prevention's director of the Physical Activity and Nutrition Division, Dr. William H. Dietz (2011, 744), a pioneer researcher in obesity, we "do not have in place the kind of policy or environmental changes needed to reverse this epidemic just yet."

The US puts high priority on individual rights and responsibilities, but this individualistic attitude affects the American food environment in such a way that it has made obesity an individual medical problem rather than a public health issue. The World Health Organization calls on countries to address issues of social and economic equity in the design of obesity-prevention programs as obesity is higher for lower-income people with lower levels of education due, in part, to the high cost of the healthiest foods (Loring and Robertson, 2014). The American Dietetic Association also insists that food equity needs to be a primary component of public health policy: "It is the position of the American Dietetic Association (ADA) that access to adequate amounts of safe, nutritious, and culturally appropriate food at all times is a fundamental human right" (Struble and Aomari, 2003, 1046).

A complex web of political and economic factors influence weight and health, including policies for agriculture, health, economics, education, town planning, and other business practices. Several post-World-War-II developments shape the current food environment, including agribusiness, fast food outlets, the National School Lunch Program, the advertising industry, and televisions in every home. Where food outlets exist and what kind of food each sells play a role in eating habits.

Using information gathered via the National Health and Nutrition Examination Survey, Reedy and Krebs-Smith (2010) compared what foods US children aged two to eighteen said they ate with what foods are considered to be empty calories (i.e., foods that provide little or no nutritive value). They found that 40 percent of what children consumed came from grain deserts, pizza, and sugar-sweetened beverages—all high in calories and low in nutrients. In the US, fast food outlets have doubled since 1970 (Muntel, 2012).

A high concentration of fast food outlets in a neighborhood, particularly in urban poor areas, is correlated with higher obesity in preschool-aged children in that area (Newman, Howlett, and Burton, 2013). A comprehensive Canadian epidemiological study of adult health and the number of fast food restaurants in neighborhoods showed a direct correlation between weight gain and proximity to fast food outlets (Hollands et al. 2013; Hollands et al. 2014). A study of 16,810 individuals aged twelve to twenty-nine gathered and analyzed what and where young people ate in 1977–1978 and again in 1989–1991 and 1994–1996 (Nielsen, Siega-Riz, and Popkin, 2002). This study showed a significant increase over time in the number of calories eaten outside the home by this age group, particularly snacks and fast food purchases. The study's authors called for equal access to healthy options for adolescent snacks, something that after-school and school gardens provide: fruits and vegetables.

A dietary recall study involving 17,370 adults and children showed that 37 percent of the adults and 42 percent of the children had eaten fast food on at least one of the two days they recorded their food consumption (Paeratakul et al. 2003). This resulted in a "higher intake of energy, fat, saturated fat, sodium, carbonated soft drink, and lower intake of vitamins A and C, milk, fruits and vegetables" (ibid., 1332). A review of forty studies on fast food outlet proximity and obesity found that fast food outlets were more dominant in poor and multiethnic urban neighborhoods and near schools (Fleischhacker et al. 2011).

Canadian researchers suggest limiting the number of fast food restaurants allowed in communities as a potential way to limit weight gain (Hollands et al. 2013; Hollands et al. 2014). Examining the physical environment's possible impact on people's health, such as through the presence of fast food outlets or, in contrast, access to community and school gardens, represents an ecological approach to understanding health. These studies examining the negative impact on health of living in proximity to fast food outlets indicate the potential for public land-use planning and zoning policy to improve community health.

Planning can prioritize space for community gardens and walkways to reach gardens (Ashe et al. 2007; Pothukuchi, 2004). School districts can prioritize their land for educational food gardens (Williams and Brown, 2012). Agricultural policy can preserve agricultural lands close to urban centers so that more food can be grown locally, including in urban areas on public land. Community gardens, and space for them to flourish, need a place in policy, towns, and cities.

Research with adult urban community gardeners in Denver showed that community gardeners consumed fruits and vegetables 5.7 times per day compared to home gardeners who ate them 4.6 times per day and non-gardeners who reported eating 3.9 servings per day (Litt et al. 2011, 1466). A majority, or 56 percent, of the adult community gardeners met the five-times-a-day national recommendation for fruit and vegetable consumption compared to the 37 percent of home gardeners and 25 percent of non-gardeners studied (ibid.). People gardening in community gardens eat more vegetables than home gardeners who also grow vegetables (Alaimo et al. 2008; Litt et al. 2011). The conversations with other gardeners in a community garden can result in traded recipes and produce. Youth who grow food with other youth have the collective space to grow more varieties of plants and vegetables than might be possible in a home garden plot, particularly for those who live in the inner city.

## FAST FOOD ADVERTISING'S IMPACT ON CHILD AND ADOLESCENT HEALTH

Where children get their food has changed over the last forty years as has what is available to eat. Agribusiness and advertising have shifted food consumption away from fresh, home-prepared foods to many processed foods with negative nutrient values: high in salt, fat, and simple carbohydrates (Brownell and Horgen, 2004; Nestle, 2007; Schlosser, 2001). Calories consumed at fast food outlets have increased between 1977–1978 and 1994–1996 from 18 percent to 32 percent of total calories consumed (Guthrie, Lin, and Frazao, 2002, 140).

What is the role of advertising in promoting these manufactured and fast food products? Media profoundly impacts what children eat and how they spend their time (Roberts, Foehr, and Rideout, 2005; Gantz et al. 2007; Ludwig and Gortmaker, 2004; Wiecha et al. 2006). The social and economic factors influencing children's and parents' food consumption include daily television advertising inside homes (Gantz et al. 2007). Television viewing delivers a triple whammy: time spent sedentary, junk food snacking, and advertising of fast foods. A study with 4,746 middle and high school students in a metropolitan area in the American Midwest showed that youth who spent significant time watching television and playing video games ate more junk food and consumed more calories in comparison to youth who spent more time studying and reading as those youth chose healthier snacks (Utter et al. 2003, 1304). The first study to link obesity to television viewing involved more than ten thousand youth and revealed that "in 12- to 17-year-old adolescents, the prevalence of obesity increased by 2% for each additional hour of television viewed" (Dietz and Gortmaker, 1985, 807).

Americans own more televisions per family than any other nation, approximately one per person (Roberts, Foehr, and Rideout, 2005, 1). The 2010 Kaiser Family Foundation report on childhood media surveyed 2,002 nationally representative youth aged eight to eighteen in 2008 and 2009 on their television, computers, and video game use, as well as their time spent listening to music, and discovered that "over the past five years, young people have increased the amount of time they spend consuming media by an hour and seventeen minutes daily, from 6:21 to 7:38" (Rideout, Foehr, and Roberts, 2010, 2). The study showed that cell phones are used not just for talking and playing games, but for accessing television as well. The heaviest use of media was by children aged eleven to fourteen and averaged 11:53 per day (ibid., 4). Television viewing by children also reflects race and ethnic factors in the United States: "Hispanic and Black youth average about 13 hours of media exposure daily (13:00 for Hispanics and 12:59 for Blacks), compared to just over 8 1/2 hours (8:36) among Whites. Some of the biggest race related differences emerge for television time: Black youth spend nearly six hours daily watching TV and Hispanics spend 5:21, compared to 3:36 for Whites" (ibid., 5). This means that children spend more time with media than an adult spends at work or a child spends at school. The heaviest media users report lower grades and less contentment with their life and are twice as likely to get into trouble as those who use media the least (ibid., 4).

Food advertising to children has fewer regulations to comply with than toy advertising (Schor, 2004). Another Kaiser Foundation study of children's food and media habits looked at advertising on youth's favorite ten channels and discovered that annually, given the amount of television that teens aged thirteen to seventeen watch, they see an average of 28,655 ads, or 217 hours (217:37 to be more exact) (Gantz et al. 2007, 2). Half of all advertising time on children's shows is for food (ibid., 8), and "Fast food is featured in twenty-four seconds of ads per hour and soda 10 seconds per hour" (ibid., 9). Amongst all food ads aimed at youth, 34 percent are for candy and snacks, 29 percent are for cereal, and ten percent are for fast food. Only four percent are for dairy products, one percent for fruit juices or water, and none are for fruits or vegetables (ibid.).

In the early days of television in the 1950s, children were not seen as a serious market to be targeted with ads. Today, they are seen as a market to exploit: "Expenditure on marketing to children went from about $2 billion in 1999 to approximately $15 billion in 2004" (Schor and Ford, 2007, 11). In 2004, McDonalds spent $528.8 billion globally for advertising, 40 percent targeted to children (ibid.). Additionally, the advertising industry engages in sophisticated research to discover how to deliberately entice children to want what they don't need (Schor, 2004, 21). Advertising industry language mimics war: targets, aiming, collateral, "sending out a virus" (ibid.). Companies enlist children and youth as viral marketers to represent specific products and have parties to test these with their peers (Schor and Ford, 2007, 12).

Industry marketing via television has been shown to play a large role in children's health in terms of food choice (Brownell and Horgen, 2004; Schor, 2004), quantity of food consumed (Jacobson, 2005; Ludwig, Peterson, and Gortmaker, 2001; Wiecha et al. 2006), and amount of time spent being sedentary (Brownell and Horgen, 2004; Coon and Tucker, 2002; Dietz and Gortmaker, 1985; Gortmaker, 2008). Time spent watching television, playing video games, and using computers has proven to be a primary factor in childhood weight gain (Dietz and Gortmaker, 1985; Gortmaker, 2008; Ludwig and Gortmaker, 2004). Children spend ten times more hours watching television than in vigorous exercise (Ludwig and Gortmaker, 2004, 226).

The unhealthy food products' advertising climate for children has similarities to big tobacco before protective legislation stopped tobacco's direct ads to youth. Similar to the tobacco companies that refused to admit publicly the health dangers caused by their products until hit with litigation, the food industry continues to develop products that lead to unhealthy eating and drinking. In order to produce products people will crave even when the products are not healthy, scientists with Unilever and Nestlé reportedly have studied "how certain foods, such as chocolate biscuits, burgers, and snacks, make people binge-eat, thereby fueling obesity" (Schor, 2004, 125). Research shows that both animals and humans will choose food high in sugar and fat when given the option (Brownell and Horgen, 2004).

Alternatively, fruits and vegetables do not get television advertising time, but they contain the nutrients for good health: higher fiber, and water content that lead to a greater feeling of satiety (Rolls, Ello-Martin, and Tohill, 2004). Food decisions made at home depend on the parents' nutrition knowledge and having the strength to turn off the television and hand-held electronics. Framing school and after-school gardening programs for youth in the light of this media barrage advertising poor quality manufactured food products shows gardens as a powerful intervention to get youth up and moving away from television and the unhealthy eating habits it encourages. Another factor in children's weight gain could be the National School Lunch Program before the recent improvements to approved school lunch menus.

## THE NATIONAL SCHOOL LUNCH PROGRAM'S HISTORY AND OUTCOMES

The National School Lunch Program (NSLP) is one area of children's food environment that is regulated by policy. School lunch has a mixed history with uneven results, with poor quality food having been served over many decades (Levine, 2008). It is possible that if funds allocated to the Healthy, Hunger-Free Kids Act of 2010 are sufficient, that the new school lunch improved nutritional guidelines may make a positive difference in children's food environment (Hellmich, 2011), but there is a sixty-four-year history of poor quality food served in schools to counteract—foods that contain too much salt, fat, and sugar that make children crave them.

During the Great Depression of the 1930s, many children went hungry and lacked adequate caloric intake to concentrate at school. Educators and nutritionists lobbied the federal government to make a federal school lunch program available and affordable in all schools. NSLP began in 1946 to provide hungry children with food because World War II exposed how many undernourished adolescents were unfit for military duty (Levine, 2008). The United States military did not want to rely on malnourished young soldiers and brought their influence into the school lunch program's creation.

The United States Department of Agriculture (USDA) had a comprehensive intention for the NSLP that it has overseen from its inception: to guarantee a market for certain surplus US agricultural commodities. The USDA paid farmers for surplus commodities, such as corn, wheat, soy, rice, and milk, to name only a few, and fed them to the children in schools (Levine, 2008). The US government wedded hunger relief to farm subsidies during the Great Depression and after World War II and created the system that supports the agribusiness development that dominates US food production today (Pollan, 2008). Private citizens pushed for the well-being of the nation's children, but government agencies put industrial agriculture first (Levine, 2008). The USDA framed the child as a consumer primarily to eat excess commodities needing a market.

A complicated NSLP history involving inadequate access to school lunch for the nation's poorest children in the program's early years, along with poor quality food in many schools, led to private enterprise being seen as a possible way to improve school lunch and allow access to more children in the late 1960s (Levine, 2008). Fewer and fewer children bought lunch as the price for the unsubsidized lunch steadily rose and quality suffered. States did not adequately match federal expenditures to make lunches affordable. Private food corporations began entering the picture by 1969, which led to the availability of junk food in schools. Community activists even sought partnerships with private food purveyors, thinking they might strengthen inner-city job and business climates (Brownell and Horgen, 2004). Congressmen of liberal and conservative leanings thought that privatization of school lunches might solve the cost and delivery problems. Lack of government funding at state and federal levels for a quality lunch program eventually opened the doors to McDonalds, Pizza Hut, Taco Bell, and their ilk to American public school lunchrooms (Levine, 2008).

Children's exposure to poor nutrition inside public schools increased in 1972 when the National Soft Drink Association successfully achieved an amendment to the National School Lunch Act to eliminate restrictions on competitive foods (i.e., those foods not provided by the government) in schools. Beverage makers began to sign pouring-rights contracts with schools, giving certain companies, such as Coca-Cola or Pepsi, exclusive rights to students. Schools benefited by receiving not only revenue from the vending machines but also sports clothing and educational materials branded with the company logos. These contracts allowed large corporations to negatively impact children's health inside public schools nationwide by making soda pop's zero-nutrient, high-calorie presence approved by education officials and Congress (Brownell and Horgen, 2004; Levine, 2008). The power of the American Beverage Association lobby in congress is immense.

A twenty-ounce serving of Coca-Cola or Pepsi has fifteen teaspoons of sugar (Brownell and Horgen, 2004, 166). The World Health Organization dropped their recommended added sugar intake level to 5 percent of daily calorie intake, a recommended amount that equals about six teaspoons of sugar, meaning that one twenty-ounce regular soda has two and half times the recommended daily amount of sugar (Jaslow, 2014, 1). The Office of Disease Prevention and Health Promotion (2015b, 1) said in its 2015 dietary recommendations that in order to prevent obesity, diabetes, heart disease, and dental caries that food consumed should not exceed "3 to 9 percent of calories from added sugars, after meeting food group and nutrient recommendations. For the patterns appropriate for most people (1,600 to 2,400 calories), the range is 4 to 6 percent of calories from added sugars (or 4.5 to 9.4 teaspoons)." These guidelines apply to added sugar and not to what naturally occurs in a piece of fruit, vegetable, or whole grain.

For several decades before these more stringent sugar-consumption guidelines, the soft drink corporations successfully colonized US public schools like a yeast infection. Children's consumption of soft drinks doubled between 1985 and 2005 (Peterson and Fox, 2007), but when one considers that soft drinks did not exist inside schools until the 1970s, it is not surprising that placing soda pop alongside company advertising has doubled childhood intake. School systems even agreed to meet certain sales targets in their contracts with soda companies. In 1998, the Colorado Springs school district signed a multimillion dollar contract with Coca-Cola, promising to triple their sales of that company's soft drinks to 21,000 cases (Brownell and Horgen, 2004, 164). School principals were advised to give students unlimited access to vending machines throughout the day and to launch promotional events for Coca-Cola (ibid.). These sorts of contracts went into schools all across the US. Sugar-sweetened (primarily with corn syrup) soda pop consumption is a primary factor in the health crisis we now face (Jacobson, 2005; Ludwig, Peterson, and Gortmaker, 2001). In 2015, Pepsi was the second largest food conglomerate in the world and Coca-Cola was the third largest (Kell, 2015). Consider the international financial power these companies wield to sell products high in calories and low in nutrients to youth.

Several studies have shown that when people increase their consumption of calories via sweetened drinks, they do not cut down their consumption of other calories (Rabin et al. 2002). However, research involving 1,810 children aged two to eighteen across the US showed that not only do soft drinks increase calorie consumption but also displace milk consumption, reducing valuable nutrients needed by growing children (Harnack, Stang, and Story, 1999). A study of 548 ethnically diverse children aged eleven to seventeen in Massachusetts showed that sugared-drink consumption was associated with a risk of obesity (Ludwig, Peterson and Gortmaker, 2001). By caving in to the soft-drink lobby and allowing soft-drink vendors into schools without requiring scientific evidence of how sugared drinks affect growing children, Congress created policy that laid the table for obesity.

Thirty-six years after soda machines were encouraged in schools, some states and local school districts superseded federal policy and initiated bans on foods known to cause obesity. California banned soft drinks in elementary and middle schools in 2008 and in high schools in 2009 (Fudge, 2009). Colorado banned soft drinks and all high calorie drinks in schools in 2008 (Engdahl, 2008). Philadelphia banned soft drinks citywide as part of a larger comprehensive effort to improve childhood nutrition (Food Trust, 2008). Philadelphia also banned all junk-food advertising in schools, but for more than thirty years, junk food permeated school lunchrooms nationwide (Foster et al. 2008).

The United States Senate and House Committees on Agriculture write the legislation determining which foods can be served in schools in the NSLP, which commodities will receive subsidies, which farmers qualify for the subsidies, and how much direct financial support will go to feeding children (Levine, 2008). Over the last decade, the Senate committee, along with obesity experts and food service managers, called for sweeping reforms to the list of foods allowed in schools. In 2004, the Child Nutrition and WIC Reauthorization Act passed with a section in it to support Farm-to-School efforts and school gardens, but Congress failed to appropriate funds for Farm to School and school gardens (Brownell and Horgen, 2004).

The Community Food Security Coalition, Slow Food USA, and National Farm to School Network all organized campaigns to encourage an increased dollar allocation to ensure funding for fresh food in school lunches. Finally, in 2010, with bipartisan support, President Barack Obama signed the Healthy, Hunger-Free Kids Act into law (Henderson, 2010). The law has created much opposition among the Republican congressmen who resent restrictive guidelines that impact big business, such as the frozen food purveyors whose products no longer fit the healthier guidelines. Some children want their french fries back and school nutrition directors have not received enough money to meet the healthier guidelines easily (Confessore, 2014).

In 2012, more than 31.6 million children ate school lunches every day (US Department of Agriculture, 2013, 3).[2] The 2010 guidelines include a federal funding increase to bring the total amount paid from $2.72 to $2.78 per child for the 56 percent of children nationwide who meet the free and reduced-price lunch guidelines (ibid.). The 15 percent of youth who qualify for reduced-price lunches pay $.40 per lunch and the government pays the rest (US Department of Agriculture, 2015, 1). As any person who prepares meals at home knows, six cents is very little money when we need to greatly improve the quality of food served, but it is a start and the nutrition guidelines have improved.

For federal reimbursement, the school lunches must meet the new healthier guidelines: calorie minimum and maximum limits, 50 percent whole grains in any grain-based food, two vegetable servings, one fruit, 1 percent fat milk (no chocolate milk), and a protein with vegetarian options, such as nuts or beans, in each lunch. For schools in high poverty areas, there are

---

2. Free and reduced-priced lunches were 68.2 percent of the annual total (US Department of Agriculture, 2015, 1).

federal grants available for school gardens through the Child Nutrition Discretionary Grants, though these are not simple grant applications.

A majority of public schools participate in the NSLP and more than three quarters of US schools offer a School Breakfast Program as well. Over five billion school lunches were served in 2014 (US Department of Agriculture, 2015). Before the 2010 guidelines, there had been a forty-year period of vending machines, à la carte competitive foods of poor nutritional quality, and advertising of sodas and unhealthy food in public schools. Schools sold these high-calorie, low-nutrient foods to their students because they got a financial kickback from the food producers and advertisers who got advertising space in schools (Brownell and Horgen, 2004; Levine, 2008). Schools raised money to meet their shortfalls, whether for school lunches or athletic uniforms, by selling unhealthy food to their students.

## INTERVENTIONS LEADING TO HEALTHIER FOOD AND HEALTHIER PEOPLE

Removing junk food from schools requires policy changes by knowledgeable public servants and a public willing to fight for changes and adequately fund the NSLP (Finkelstein, Hill, and Whitaker, 2008). Federal policy change has begun with the Healthy, Hunger-Free Kids Act of 2010. We also need comprehensive health education campaigns that not only improve children's diets but also get youth physically active. School officials can create policy to dedicate outdoor space to gardens and curriculum to include hands-on learning in them. Food grown at school can be integrated into school lunch, modeling sustainable environmental behaviors that make it possible for food to be consumed where it is grown rather than shipped thousands of miles (Williams and Brown, 2012).

Brownell and Horgen (2004) conclude *Food Fight*, their book on the many barriers to healthy eating, with five pages of action recommendations, including suggestions to counteract the commercialization of children into market objects. They encourage celebrities and TV shows aimed at children not to advertise foods with poor nutritional value. They refer to the public food environment as toxic and remind us that individuals cannot fight this on their own. This social-ecological view of health is relatively new (Stokols, 1992) and provides a "theoretical framework for understanding the dynamic interplay among persons, groups and their sociophysical milieus" (Stokols, 1996, 283). As mentioned earlier, a social-ecological health perspective considers design interventions that include both the built and natural environment.

Children cannot make decisions on what they eat independently of their parents who buy the food served at home. Nor do they make decisions about the food served in their dominant social setting, school. To reverse the obesity epidemic, we need to view the entire health setting and devise interventions that create healthier environments for children daily. What would it take in terms of federal policy change for schools nationwide to get funding to implement a garden as the centerpiece for active engagement with healthy food and physical environments?

These changes require political will and a philosophy of education that embraces youth health. Ecology and agricultural education need to be taught in teacher-training programs and incorporated into public school curriculums (Williams and Brown, 2012). Thanks to the visionary California State Superintendent of Public Instruction Delaine Eastin, who called for a garden in every school in 1995, California passed nutrition education legislation in 2002, identifying best practices in school gardens and establishing a grant program to support them (Ozer, 2007). The California Department of Education published its curriculum guide, *A Child's Garden of Standards: Linking School Gardens to California Education Standards*, for grades 2nd through 6th for gardening and nutrition to support learning science and nutrition in garden settings (Agee and Bruton, 2002). In 2006, the California Instructional School Garden Program was established with $15 million to promote, develop, and sustain instructional school gardens (University of California Board of Regents, 2016). In 2013, the University of California put out another curriculum wedding gardens and children's nutrition entitled *Nutrition to Grow On* (Morris and Zidenberg-Cherr, 2013).[3]

## SCHOOL GARDENS RENEW APPETITES FOR FRESH FOOD AND KNOWLEDGE

School and after-school gardens have the goal of childhood health and hands-on learning about the environment, but they have not been settings for medical studies regarding the impact on children's health, per se. We need the data from medical studies to show if health improves when children have the chance to eat vegetables at school that they have grown themselves. The gardens' results have been measured in multiple ways (pounds of food raised, science scores raised in comparison to control groups, social skills learned, etc.), but not consistently in the same ways (Blair, 2009) .

---

3. These curriculums and many from other states are now free to download from the Internet.

Medical researchers could do quantitative studies—on the portions of produce consumed per child when children garden or the children's body mass index (BMI) before and after participating in a school garden—to see if gardening helps students eat more vegetables and maintain a healthy weight or even lose weight as those participating in the Green Bronx Machine have. The activity levels during gardening could be measured with precise observation techniques. The BMI of children in schools with established vegetable gardening programs could be compared with schools that do not have them.

Engaging youth in research would empower them to realize their capacity to generate important knowledge and make healthy choices based on research. Youth could participate with researchers in designing studies as part of health science education. Youth might find it exciting to investigate whether a school garden intervention that grows fresh food for the school lunch could change what their peers and they themselves choose for lunch. They could make comparisons between food choices and exercise levels for students who did gardening as part of the school day to those who joined a gardening club after school and to those who did not engage in gardening at all. Young people might enjoy measuring gardening's physical and psychological benefits.

California's statewide Garden in Every School initiative and one of its stars, the Edible Schoolyard in Berkeley, provide an admirable model of garden to kitchen to table. Ecological knowledge derived from experiential learning, place-based education, and a healthy social environment in which adults and youth together work and eat fresh, school-grown food form the basis for the Edible Schoolyard's educational philosophy (Waters, 2008). Where school gardens combine nutrition and health education with gardening education, students eat a wider variety of vegetables (McAleese and Rankin, 2007).

Newby (2007, 52) states: "Successful—and ethical—interventions should involve comprehensive nutrition programs designed to facilitate healthy behaviors and food policy interventions at local, national, and international levels to ensure that nutritious foods are affordable and accessible to children in all income levels." Except for the Healthy, Hunger-Free Kids Act of 2010, recent initiatives to improve and protect child health have come not from the federal bodies in charge of school lunch, but from states and concerned parents, citizens, nonprofits, and medical professionals. Finkelstein, Hill, and Whitaker (2008, 259) suggest in their national review of school food environments, that these groups "have the opportunity to play an important role in changing social norms" related to school food health.

## THE UNITED STATES SCHOOL GARDEN ARMY

Do we face the moral equivalent of war concerning the health of our children, the American food supply, and the food marketing system? Do past wartime initiatives offer possible solutions for today? In 1917, on the eve of the its entry into World War I, the US was consuming 90 percent of domestic agricultural production and planning to send soldiers to fight in Europe (Hayden-Smith, 2006, 4). The US government mandated the United States School Garden Army (USSGA) to engage the nation's school-age youth in producing food for consumption at home and at school as a way to ensure that the nation could be fed while commercially grown food was shipped overseas for US troops (ibid.).

The USSGA guide for the western United States proclaims: "Production is the first principle in education. The growing of plants and animals should therefore become an integral part of the school program. Such is the aim of the school garden army" (Stebbins, 1920, 40). Consider how radically different this attitude is from today: children in 1920 were seen not as consumers, but as producers, and their education as farmers was the responsibility of schools.

The US Department of Defense funded the USSGA as food production was paramount for national security. The Bureau of Education managed the USSGA with a goal to enlist youth in growing food. The USSGA curriculum, the first American effort at a national curriculum, taught youth gardening techniques and real-life problem solving, as well as attempted to synthesize the old rural values as society transitioned from rural to urban (Hayden-Smith, 2006).

Prior to writing the USSGA guide, C. A. Stebbins worked at the University of California at Berkeley in the Junior Garden Program that brought together the school district and the university in an effort to prepare urban youth to learn gardening and business skills as a way to maintain what were considered wholesome rural values in an urban context. This model purposefully developed business skills and values of hard work and thrift, and strongly influenced the USSGA's focus on citizenship development as well (Stebbins, 1920). The World War I Junior Garden Program in Berkeley eventually included a weekly farmers' market to sell their produce, as well as a bank. [4]

While the USSGA focused on urban and suburban youth, the USDA began its precursors to 4-H programs with rural children between 1900 and 1920 with the intention of educating not

---

4. Quite a few of the gardening programs described in this book also give youth the opportunity to learn some marketing skills along with the food growing, including the Green Bronx Machine, ¡Cultiva!, Love Cultivating Schoolyards, Taos Economic Development Corporation Garden, and Feed the Hood in Albuquerque.

United States School Garden Army poster for World War I. Credit: Library of Congress Archives

just the rural youth, but their parents. The USDA deemed America's farmers easier to teach through their children. During World War I, the number of young people involved in the rural programs geared to agricultural education grew to over 100,000, with the number of agricultural extension workers growing from 2,200 to 6,000 (Hayden-Smith, 2006, 7).

"He who produces is a patriot—a good citizen" and "a garden for every child, every child in a garden" were key statements in the USSGA literature (Stebbins, 1920, 40). More than 50,000 teachers and thousands more community volunteers participated. In Los Angeles alone, 14,000 students worked in 13,000 garden plots, indicating that almost every child had a plot at school (Hayden-Smith, 2006, 9). As one example of the program's success, the children at Ann Street Elementary School in Los Angeles planted, raised, and sold two tons of potatoes (ibid.). One can imagine the children proudly weighing their bags of potatoes freshly dug from the earth.

Educationally, the school-gardening curriculum reflected the move towards experiential education favored by such progressive educational leaders as John Dewey, then at Columbia University and Liberty Hyde Bailey at Cornell, who worked towards including nature study in public education. When the US and its European allies won the war, schools were encouraged to continue gardening, but the USSGA was discontinued in the 1920s. As evidence of the program's lasting efficacy, the children who were trained to be gardeners in 1917–1918 were all adults when World War II began in 1941. They knew what to do when the new Food for Freedom campaign began, and, once again, school and home gardeners shared a national responsibility for the nation's well-being (Hayden-Smith, 2006; Pollan, 2008).

The World War II home-gardening program had a national focus on improving the nation's health through growing and consuming more vegetables and fruits. When Eleanor Roosevelt worked to establish the Liberty Garden campaign in 1943 (later named the Victory Garden campaign after the armistice), she did so despite objections from the USDA that feared home gardens would hurt professional farmers' profits. The focus on America's eating habits and growing food at home resulted in a higher level of consumption of fruits and vegetables than at any other time before or since. Home gardeners produced 40 percent of the produce consumed by Americans (Pollan, 2008). A national policy for Americans to learn to grow a significant portion of their dietary intake worked during those two world wars to provide people with exercise, food production knowledge, and healthy food to eat.

We need to look to our nation's past in growing food in wartime and realize that we have many lives to save once again due to the unprecedented obesity crisis we face. The social-ecological health approach suggests that we look at the environment, public policy, and individual behavior to find a healthier way forward as these are all interrelated. Past efforts reflected in the wartime efforts have shown that when people grow food themselves, they eat it. Youth who garden learn food-growing skills and nutritional awareness as the young gardeners have told us. By working together to grow food, these youth gardeners develop personal agency and have already helped mediate this health crisis by improving their own eating habits in many cases. The United States has a long tradition of uniting farming and the cultivated person for individual and national well-being. Thomas Jefferson, a farmer as well as a statesman and president, wrote in a letter to John Jay: "Cultivators of the earth are the most valuable citizens. They are the most vigorous, the most independent, the most virtuous, and they are tied to their country and wedded to its liberty and interests by the most lasting bonds" (University of Groningen, 2012).

# 13

## OAKLAND: GANGS OR GARDENS?

*I actually was walking to work one day. I seen these young men running. There was probably three or four of them. They were walking and then they started running. I didn't know why. I didn't know what the situation was. A white pick-up truck pulls up and comes to the side, and [a man] gets out of the truck and he starts chasing after the boys. This whole time, I am thinking, "Oh, my God. This is so scary!" I am scared. I am really scared. Mind you, I am two blocks from work. I kept walking, but I noticed that the boys was running because they stomped the man's front windshield in, so he was trying to chase them down to get them. It just seemed like, piecin' it, seeing it all, piecin' it together. You can see his windshield is stomped in. It wasn't broken, but it was stomped in. Seeing them run, I am piecin' that together. He isn't chasing them for no reason. I get to work and I am waitin'. "Do you all know what just happened?" I am tellin' Suzanne and the rest of the group. "Do you all know this just happened?" But I get into the garden and I am thirty minutes into work, and I forget about it because I am in a peaceful environment now. I just forget about it all. But then I leave work, and I am thinking about it again. Oh, God... I am thinking about it and, oh, my God, I am scared!*
**—SALINA, 19, OAKLAND**

The city of Oakland, California, is scared too. According to the Urban Strategies Council (2011, 3), "Oakland averaged 110 reported incidents of murder and manslaughter per year from 2000–2009, an average rate of 26.8 homicides per 100,000 people per year. Over the 9-year period, Oakland contributed on average 84.7% of the murders in the County." A 2011 report by the Alameda County Public Health Department stated that the "violent crime rate is three times the national average, 12.9 per 1,000 compared to 4.7 per 1,000" (Alvarado et al. 2011, 14). Much of that violent crime is committed by youth against youth.

Salina, aged nineteen, joined the People United for a Better Life in Oakland (PUEBLO) youth internship gardening program in 2012. She had graduated from high school at Youth Environment School the year before, where she had participated in a gardening program to improve the school lunches. Salina describes vividly the challenging and frightening side of living in Oakland and then mentions how working in the garden—a peaceful place—mitigates the fear that the high crime rate and street violence causes her. She used the word peaceful a total of twenty-two times during the hour she spent describing her gardening experiences. But what is this broader, not-so-green context that includes the city's streets?

An Alameda County Public Health Department report on Project New Start—a program that helps youth to remove tattoos as a way of visually changing their allegiances and lives—calls youth gangs a main source of threats to young people on Oakland streets (Alvarado et al. 2011). A rapid rise in violent crime (assault, murder, rape, and burglary) in Alameda County between 2004 and 2008 was worse in Oakland than any other city, and even though it declined by 13 percent in 2009, Oakland still "exceeded the state and national rate by 60%" (Urban Strategies Council 2011, 1). A National Gang Intelligence Center (2011, 9) report on gangs and their criminal activities showed 33,000 active gangs in the United States with over 1.4 million active gang members, including juveniles and adults. In 2011, the Alameda County Public Health Department reported over 30,000 gang members in the state of California, with at least 65 organized gangs in the city of Oakland alone (Alvarado et al. 2011, 8). Of the gang members statewide, 60 percent are Hispanic, 30 percent are African American, 6 percent are Asian Pacific Islander, and 4 percent are white (ibid.).

In 2009, the Discovery Channel aired *Gang Wars*, a frightening two-part documentary that portrays youth with guns whose goal is to control turf and kill any who oppose them. The Alameda County Public Health Department cites that film's statistics in their Project New Start report: ten thousand Oakland youth are involved in gangs on Oakland streets daily (Alvarado et al. 2011, 8). The Alameda County Public Health Department is not alone in its effort to support youth resiliency with positive role models, job training, and healthy activities, and city grants also help to fund the gardening programs where the teens I interviewed work as part of green job training efforts.

I decided to go to the Bay Area in California to interview youth gardeners because I knew there were many excellent youth gardening programs there and I had friends I could stay with while I visited. I did not know how dangerous Oakland is for youth before I went. My freshman college roommate, Dr. Carol Miller, a pediatrician and professor of pediatrics at the University of Cali-

fornia at San Francisco School of Medicine, wrote glowingly in an e-mail to me about the transformative impact a gardening program in San Francisco had on one of her patients.

> Gardening has a way of balancing your soul, and seeing the results of your work is so satisfying.
> Food sustainability is becoming quite popular in the Bay Area. Many are changing their private
> landscaping into edible gardens. Even better, community gardens are cropping up, several in
> seemingly disenfranchised neighborhoods. I support a project in San Francisco creating local
> edible gardens in neglected neighborhood plots. The work force comes from young people living
> in the neighborhoods, and they learn about the nutritional value of the foods they grow, culmi-
> nating in a feast they prepare for themselves. One of my wayward teenaged patients who had a
> baby got hooked up with the project, and it literally changed her life. She would come to her
> baby's appointments and tell me all about the virtues of organic foods, a diet based on vegetables,
> all about the vegetables she was growing, the best ways to prepare them, and her resolve to feed
> her baby only from her garden of organic foods. It's been a year and she has sustained her enthu-
> siasm, her work in the garden, caring properly for her baby (without the benefit of appropriate
> role-modeling from her own mother), and she went back to school (something I had been trying
> to get her to do for the longest time). I really do believe getting involved in creating something
> from the earth made the difference in her life, which just kept building in a positive direction.
> The story has become a part of my teaching to medical students and residents to keep them from
> giving up on young people too early and to show them an example of the many resources we
> should engage to promote health. It's been about two years since this teen's transformation and
> [she and her new baby] continue to achieve (she finished high school and recently enrolled in
> junior college) and her parenting skills continue to flourish.

It did not work for me to meet with the program Carol recommended as they were too busy,
but, fortunately, I learned that another friend of mine, Rashidah Grinage, ran a community social
justice program in Oakland with a youth gardening component. It was through this program,
PUEBLO, that I met Salina who described so vividly her spring and summer experience working
as an intern there.

Rashidah put me in touch with Grey Kolevzon, the program coordinator that oversees
PUEBLO's youth gardeners, Green Pioneers. Kolevzon gave me other garden programs' contacts
in Oakland, and I interviewed eleven young gardeners, ages fourteen to nineteen, in three distinct
programs: PUEBLO, Oakland Leaf, and West Oakland Woods. Each has a slightly different focus,

but all teach organic agriculture, leadership, and job skills.

These young food growers eagerly shared their gardening experiences and described how they learned to care for their environment, grow, prepare, and eat healthy foods and to work collaboratively to make their community a safer, healthier place for everyone. None have criminal or gang backgrounds. All have chosen a garden path rather than the streets.

PUEBLO serves young people through several different programs—they offer trainings and internship opportunities through Pathways to Employment, promote community engagement and restorative justice through Community Peace, and expose youth to gardening and nutrition through Green Pioneers. I met Salina near where she lives not far from downtown Oakland on a sunny September day. She had finished her summer internship with PUEBLO a few weeks earlier and reflected on all she had learned and experienced and how it had changed her awareness. I asked her why she had applied to work with PUEBLO for the summer green job training—a program similar to the one offered by the Green Bronx Machine—a year after she graduated from high school.

SALINA: Because I already had experience in gardening and I wanted to basically see how much farther I could go with it because I want to build a garden when I get my own house. So, I wanted to know what to do, how to do it, what to use, how to build more gardening things, and stuff for future reference.

ILLÈNE: One of the questions I like to ask youth gardeners is about their senses. Can you look back on being in the PUEBLO garden and tell me which senses gave you the most information?

SALINA: Vision and hearing because I've seen a lot of insects. I have seen a lot of different ways to plant. I think I remember vision because I am a visual learner. For me, to see things is better for me to learn it of course; when I was able to see people plant new plants or see other types of insects that I have never seen before and touch insects. Touching, I was touching insects, and I am scared of all types of insects. I was touching worms and stuff, and I am sitting here, "ewww," but it seemed natural because I was in a garden, you know, a garden environment.

ILLÈNE: So seeing all those insects and touching insects you had never touched before, did that change your attitude towards worms and bugs?

SALINA: It actually did. I used to be scared of, like, all touching. I've seen a lot of bugs. I've seen a lot of spiders, a lot of worms. I've seen a lot of beetles, ants of course. I've seen a lot of birds and squirrels too. I was actually in the garden once all by myself, and there were these two squirrels. The trees were, like, that high [indicates tall trees with her hands] and there were a whole lot of them. I saw these two squirrels chasing each other back and forth and, I didn't know, it seemed like they were flying. I didn't know squirrels could run that fast. I think me just seeing a lot of stuff and just listening to everything.

We were at Stonehurst gardens when I seen a lot of these things, which was one of the main gardens we worked at. Stonehurst is a school garden. The factory was next to it, and we could hear the factory boom, doing its stuff. But if you take the factory out of your head and ignore those sounds, you can actually hear a lot of birds. I seen a lot of like hummingbirds. I seen a lot of dragonflies. There was a lot of bumble bees. I planted, I want to say, ten or fifteen sunflowers. Bumblebees was over there all the time. The sunflowers grew six feet high or so. The garden experience was really fun to me. I actually planted a lot of things. I planted the sunflowers by myself, which grew to be beautiful. I planted tomatoes, which grew to be big and beautiful. Everything was just big and beautiful, you know. I wasn't expecting it to grow that big because, usually, if I tried to plant something on my own, it would die real soon.

I just had a love for it [gardening]. I didn't think I was going to have that much of love for it, but I actually just grew a lot of love for it. It kind of made me happier inside, you know. And just to be able to taste the things that I planted, it was like, "I can't believe I planted this. I can't believe I grew this since it was like a baby and I took care of it. I can't believe I grew this." I would be there every day to work from ten to two and then leave on the weekend and come back Monday. It grew in two days. It grew that fast. It was just a happy experience. I really liked the garden. I wouldn't mind trying it again with PUEBLO all over again.

I actually graduated in 2011. I graduated when I turned eighteen in May. Since I am nineteen now, I would have thought maybe I was not going to be able to join the program because it is a summer job and they only take certain ages. I actually started before the summer job came around. I was one of those people that were there before everyone else came in. It was just me and this other boy. We had to hustle to start the garden. By the time everybody else did come in, there wasn't that much more to plant. It was more like fixing up the garden, just making the aisles and stuff.

I remember working at the zoo. When you drive into the zoo, it's a hill, and we had to plant 150 trees in like a week or two. We had to dig holes, and the ground up there was like cement. It was so hard that we had to bring in a mechanical shovel to dig those holes for us. We had to dig the holes and then we had to plant the trees of course. Planting trees is easy. You get the wire and you just put the tree in the wire. You put the dirt in.

We brought buckets of compost. It was a steep hill and in the sun, it was so hot up there. Everything that we needed we brought up the hill before we started up the hill so that we wouldn't have to go up and down. We had to plant trees along the hill. Basically, when we finished planting a tree, we had to put a mound around it and put mulch inside the mound so that when they water it or it rains, the mound would stop the water from going down the hill and the mulch would hold the water in the mound.

I liked that experience. I caught a couple of lizards. They have some native lizards around there. So working at the zoo, I seen a lot, a whole lot of lizards. It was actually a fun experience. We tried to catch these lizards after we were done planting at the end of the day getting ready to leave. It was the biggest lizard I had seen up there. I want to say it was as long as a ruler. It was more fat than long. I just remember trying to find it. They were fast. I didn't know lizards were that fast. Just being able to see new insects, new reptiles.

The thing that amazed me the most about gardening was just seeing a lot of insects and stuff like that. It just amazed me how much I was not scared. When I first got in there, of course, I was scared, but I got over that real fast. I am just amazed about that because I never thought I would get over insects.

ILLÈNE: So this was a whole new experience for you, seeing a big diversity of animal life?

SALINA: Yes. Yes, that was a big part of the gardening thing. To me, the experience exposed me to other life. That was a big part of my experience. Thinking back on it, I was exposed to nature. Just being a human, and I see all these insects and stuff, like, "Don't kill them, just let them go outside." If I see an insect in my house, I am going to try my hardest not to kill it, depending on how big it is. Noticing that everything has a life, everybody has a life. Noticing that plants have lives.

There was this one time, maybe within the last three weeks of the program that we were out there, there were seven of us and there was this other man who was working with us who brought his group up there. He wasn't necessarily a gardener, he was the handyman. There were maybe ten or fifteen of them, and he brought his group up there to build a compost bin. They were moving a compost bin from the front of the garden to the back of the garden. We had everything planted out, and everything was looking nice. Everything was in place and they were walking through the aisles. The lady we were working with, Suzanne, she was big on the aisles: "Do not step on the plants. Step on the aisles. This is why the aisle is here." And they stepped on our plants. They stepped on our plants! I wanted to kill them [laughs]. I was upset. I was upset! We planted these nice flowers for the bumblebees and the butterflies too because we had a lot of butterflies, and they stepped on them. "How could you all be so careless about stepping on our plant system?" I was actually saying a lot of other things because I was really mad. I'm like, 'cause it was a back area, so the garden, when you drive past the school, you can see the garden right there in front. But there is a back area where there is nothing planted; it is nothing but hay. You could walk through there easily. They decided to walk through the garden and destroy half of the garden. It really got to me. "Whoa! You all are not the ones that planted this. We are, and you are sitting here trying to move this compost bin! You are destroying everything we did, everything that we planted. You all can't say sorry? Nothing, nothing to show that you guys care about our garden too?"

ILLÈNE: So what did they say?

SALINA: They didn't say anything. They just walked on by. They took the compost bin to the back of the garden and left. Did they really just destroy our garden when they could have gone the other way? Well, gosh, your whole group just destroyed everything we just built. We had, what is that stuff you put in your…, it starts with a c, the stuff that you put in your salsa?

ILLÈNE: Cilantro.

SALINA: Yes, cilantro. We had cilantro planted, and then when you walk down, and I want to say there was squash on the other side, so when you walk down, you've got the cilantro, then you've got the squash and then the sunflowers. And then towards the back we didn't really plant anything back there because we were still working on it, but the cilantro, the squash, and sunflowers, and everything else that was planted, they just stepped on it all. I had been working there for probably three months, and everything that's planted I seen getting planted or I was a part of it getting planted. Just to see it getting taken away that fast over footsteps. Not because an animal was hungry and he wanted to come and eat it; that would have been acceptable. Not because an insect was hungry and he wanted to eat it. It was because humans was trying to do something that would have been so simple and so easy to avoid. Just to see humans come by and destroy everything we had worked hard on in the sun over a three-months period, just to die that fast. They were all men and they are heavier than women. There were a lot of ups and downs in the garden. Suzanne, who I believe she still goes up to the garden every day, was our supervisor. She checks on everything. I believe she replants every year. She was actually there. I don't think that she noticed it, but once everything calmed down and everything was back to normal, we did bring it up. "Do you know they stepped on everything?" And the way Suzanne was, she was, "Oh

God!" She really took it to the point to where it was, "I can't believe they did that either! You guys worked on it and I worked on it. We put our time and our hearts and minds on it. They came just one day and they destroyed everything." It was really frustrating. It was really frustrating.

ILLÈNE: So you really came to love the garden?

SALINA: I did. I expected the plants to be destroyed by animals and insects, not humans.

ILLÈNE: It sounds like gardening has been a real immersion in ecology for you and in caring.

Do you think your environmental awareness and attitudes have changed? It sounds like they have.

SALINA: Yes, they have. They have. Working in a garden, it actually opened my eyes to see. When I walk around and I am walking down the street or wherever in my environment and I see a garden, it makes me want to meet, want to jump in and meet, whoever made this garden and say, "Hey, can I help you sometime?" And, "Do you know if you do this it will make your plants grow faster or better."

I want to say one thing that really stood out to me while working with PUEBLO. We had a man named Eric come and work with us for a week at Castlemont High School. We spent a week learning how to make hydroponic gardens: how to build them, how to take care of your plants. It had fish. We had a fish tank at the bottom. We had a big box at the top. We had rocks inside. We had lights going over the rocks for the sun. We had the fish in the water with the plants in it. Just learning how to build it [the hydroponic system] and seeing how fast everything grows, it just was, like, this could really come in handy if we could get it out to the community and teach everybody how. I think that stood out to me. The environment we live in with all the fast food and everything, basically, all the fast food, I feel the fast food has to go. Building a hydroponic garden, once it comes down to the point where people need to grow their own food and people should start growing their own food, I believe a hydroponic garden would be perfect. It was really easy to build. Everything grew within a week. We already had little plants coming up.

I think that every school should have a gardening class because this fast food is not good at all. Everybody needs to learn how to garden. At least every young person should. So, I am pretty sure there are a couple of older people who know how to do it, but they don't do it. They say young people are the future. If everyone knew how to grow a garden, everything would be able to change. It would be, basically, everyone growing his or her own food. You know where your food comes from. You know it hasn't been shipped from Alaska or something, you know, and traveling for weeks and days and getting old. I really hate to go into a grocery store and buy some grapes and I see a lot of bad grapes on the bottom, I hate that.

For me just to have the knowledge on planting and gardening and have an area, that would be perfect. I really think every school should have a gardening class. Not a gardening class to where it is, like, optional that you should take it or not; a class where you have to take it. I think times are going to change. The weather now is really kind of crappy. So, to learn how to garden, to learn how to build hydroponic gardens and just to learn how to take care of a gardening environment, I really think it would change a lot of people because it brings peace. If you have something to bring peace in and it changes everybody's emotions and everybody's thoughts on how to care for people, I think that it would change the world, you know.

ILLÈNE: Tell me a little bit more about how gardening brings peace for you. How did you experience that?

SALINA: [*Sits quietly for a while considering her answer before responding.*] I think it was the quietness. Sitting there gardening and sitting there just digging holes or, you know, counting seeds. Sitting there, it's a peaceful environment. When you walk into a garden, it is a peaceful environment. You don't want to be loud. You don't want to say curse words. It actually made me change my style of music. I don't want to listen to rap music. I'd rather listen to some slow music or some other kind of music. There was one day that we were in the Stonehurst garden with Suzanne, and I was digging holes in some mounds for beans she was going to plant. She had an iPod and she put on Bob Marley. She said, "I don't know if you guys are going to like my music." We sat there for about two hours and we were just planting and listening to Bob Marley, and it was just being peaceful for me. Being able to be quiet, being able to see like bugs and insects, and being able to see the birds fly around. Just being able to see the squirrels fly around, I mean, run around. Just being in a peaceful environment, period. I noticed that if you are in a garden, you don't see a lot of cars drive by, which was perfect, you know. It was just perfect. I just felt like that was real peaceful. In Oakland, people have their cars, which have these loud speakers. They listen to their music real loud. It is kind of annoying. Now that I live by the lake and I go around [where the cars park], that is so annoying. To be in a garden and not hear any of that, just being able just to plant in the quiet or have this nice music, it brought peace to me. I felt I was able to talk however, express myself however, and nobody would get mad. It was real, real peaceful. I believe that it would bring peace to a lot of people. If they took the time out to sit in a garden and participate, participate in the things, you know, that you do in the garden; it just brings a lot of peace. I believe it would bring a lot of peace to everybody, everybody. No matter where you come from, no matter where you goin', no matter what race, what age. It just brings peace because there are not a lot of things going on around you and you can tune everybody else out so it can be just you in the garden, which was, "Alright, this is my quiet zone." Now, you have this time where you can think about whatever you have on your mind or whatever you want to do later. It's just real peaceful. It helps you think. It helps me think. I am going to speak for myself. It helps me focus on whatever I need to focus on. If I feel like I need to do something later in the week, I can think about how I can fit that in my schedule, how I am going to get around that. It just makes me feel better. Now, when I leave the garden and I get into this other environment, it just brings back things where I am like, "Okay, I can't really focus on what I was thinking about in the garden because all these things are happening and I have to watch my surroundings now." Everywhere, you have to watch your surroundings, but in the garden, you really don't because it is a peaceful environment.

ILLÈNE: It's a safe environment?

SALINA: Yeah, a safe place. I believe if people had a garden behind their house or a neighborhood garden or, you know, not necessarily a neighborhood park, but a neighborhood garden…

ILLÈNE: A place to garden, a community garden?

SALINA: Yeah. If every neighborhood, if you have one of those every five blocks, it would change a lot of people.

ILLÈNE: You said your focus is different when you are in the garden. Can you describe to me how your focus changes when you are in the garden? How is it different from when you are in class or walking down the street?

SALINA: It's different because whatever I am thinking about, I can fully think it through. Say I am walking home, I am watching my surroundings because there are a lot of things that happen in Oakland. For me, I feel like I am never too safe to take my mind off of the streets. When I am in the garden, I feel I can do that. I feel like I can just not worry about who is walking past the garden because they are just walking past the garden. A lot of people walking past the garden, they really look. They are, "Oh, this is nice. How long have you guys been here? Can we come by and help?" "Yeah, you can." And that's that. If I am walking down the street and somebody walks past and they have to ask you this type of a question and if you don't answer it the way they want you to answer it, it could lead to other things. And it's just a lot of things that you try to avoid when you are not in the garden, and I feel like if I am in the garden, you can just have peace and everything will be peaceful.

ILLÈNE: I have heard from all the kids here in Oakland about the danger they feel here in the city and that the garden is a sanctuary from all that. Do you think that because of these experiences where you found peace in the garden that you would seek out other opportunities to be involved with youth gardens or community gardens?

SALINA: I actually wouldn't mind. There was a lady named Frankie [a PUEBLO garden manager]. I talked to Frankie a couple of weeks ago and I basically told her, "Yeah, I am pregnant now. If there are any more job opportunities that I could work with you guys, I would like to do it. If anything come up, it could be anywhere." Especially now that I have more knowledge and know what to do now, I would not mind workin' in the garden with anybody. I wouldn't mind startin' a garden, comin' into a garden that is already goin'. Just workin' in a garden would be very peaceful to me. I want to build my own garden, like I told you, when I get older. When I have my own house, I want to have a garden in my front or backyard. To be able to get enough experience in it right now before that time comes would be lovely—it would be perfect. It would be perfect because by that time, I would know everything I need. I would know how to plant certain plants. It would be perfect.

ILLÈNE: As far as junk food goes, has being a gardener changed your personal eating habits?

SALINA: Yes. I don't eat McDonalds anymore, which is something I have stopped maybe a year ago. I used to eat Taco Bell. I don't eat Taco Bell anymore. Burger King, I don't eat Burger King. A lot of places that people talk about are bad, I don't eat there. I would probably go to Subway, eat pizza, but that's on rare occasions.

ILLÈNE: Do you eat more vegetables now?

SALINA: I have a lot of fruit and vegetables at the house now. I actually just went out a couple of weeks ago to get it. My refrigerator you would never see any fruits and vegetables, nothing. We used to go the grocery store and buy mixed vegetables and never eat it. It would be in the freezer for months and then we would throw it out. Now, I have a big thing of apples. I have plums I just got done eating. I have nectarines I just got done eating. I have carrots that I am still eating. I don't drink soda anymore. I drink juice and water now. And junk food, I cut that out. I would eat candy every once in a while, but I don't eat candy now that I am pregnant and stuff. I don't eat hot chips. I used to eat hot chips all the time.

ILLÈNE: Tell me what the meaning of gardening is for you.

SALINA: The meaning of gardening is… I never thought about that question. Let me see… When I hear gardening, I hear, "Hey, Salina. It's time for you to come here, get into a peaceful environment, clear your mind. Let's plant a couple of things." That is what gardening means to me. It means: "Clear your mind and come into this peaceful environment!" I just always had that feeling every time I went into the garden. It was time for me. There would be a couple of times I would be on the way to work and I would be in an argument with my boyfriend or something, and by the time I walked into the garden, my mind was clear. I was okay for the day. It's just peacefulness. I feel like nobody is banned from the garden. Everybody can come in here. Everybody can come work with us. Everybody can help us out. And so that is just what it means to me. Anybody come. Everybody, sit here and clear your mind.

At this quiet, profound conclusion to our conversation that covered peace and inclusivity while working in a garden, I boarded the Oakland bus that would take me back to where I was staying. Salina waved good-bye me as she walked home. I reflected on how much Salina valued the awareness and experiences gardening gave her: the myriad life forms that she discovered in the gardens, the better food she learned to eat, and, most of all, the peace she found through the process of planting and nurturing gardens. It is fortunate that she discovered gardening and healthy food before she became pregnant. Her buying choices had filled her refrigerator with good food for her and her developing baby.

Salina's experiences reflected those of the gardeners in East Harlem, the Bronx, and Colorado. Whether it was a city or rural area, youth were finding time to think and let go of their worries in the garden—whether those worries were homework or gang activity. Positive emotions dominated; engagement with all the life forms that she encountered helped Salina feel her connection to other living beings; her mentor introduced her to new, quieter music; she gained meaning by understanding how valuable urban gardens were to community health; and she harvested achievement through all of her experiences. She found a peaceful haven in a city.

# 14

## CHANGING THE URBAN FOOD DESERT

Neo waters edible nasturtiums in the Castlemont High School garden. Credit: Javier

The People United for a Better Life in Oakland's (PUEBLO) executive director, Rashidah Grinage, drove me on a Monday after school to meet PUEBLO's Fall 2012 Green Pioneers student interns in the garden behind Castlemont High School in East Oakland, where they work twice a week. I asked Rashidah where I could buy $10 gift cards from a full-service grocery store near the high school for my thank you to each youth I would interview. She could think of no supermarket nearby, and, as we drove, I saw none. I had been to an Oakland farmers' market on the previous Saturday morning and was impressed with its large size and diverse food and plant offerings, but, evidently, a great deal of Oakland is a food desert with little access to fresh foods, including the Castlemont High School area (Greenaway, 2012). The Oakland Food Policy Council (2015) defines a food desert as "an area with little or no access to foods needed to maintain a healthy diet. Often those areas have a higher presence of fast food restaurants. Access can be limited by distance, lack of transportation, or affordability."

The United States Department of Agriculture (USDA) designates an area a food desert when more than five hundred people live more than a mile from a full-service market with healthy food (Ver Ploeg et al. 2009,1). In the US, the USDA estimates that 2.3 million households live more than one mile from a full-service grocery store and more than half of those, 11.5 million individuals, are low income (ibid, 2). Food deserts often have corner stores that sell candy bars, chips, and soda pop, making the easiest, closest food to buy also the unhealthiest. After many years working and living in the area, Grinage calls the entire East Bay a "junk food jungle." That afternoon in 2012, I asked the four youth gardening at Castlemont what kind of food store was nearby so that I knew where to buy their thank-you gift cards. They gave me the name of a franchise that sells fruit and vegetable smoothies, which seemed like a reasonably healthy way for them to access healthy food, and so that is where I went.

Student-created compost directions sign. Credit: Illène Pevec

The Castlemont garden that PUEBLO manages is fully fenced and has quite a few different varieties of fruit trees—all with student-made signs to designate each variety—lining its borders. Inside the garden, there are about twenty-five to thirty raised beds planted with vegetables, flowers, and herbs, an old shed, a new shed, a chicken coop with a variety of chickens, a composting area, a small greenhouse, and many signs students have made explaining various garden aspects, such as compost making.

We arrived just after school when Grey Kolevzon, the program coordinator, was orienting the youth to their garden jobs for the week. They were all sitting on benches in a tree-shaded semicircle near the garden's center. Kolevzon, who also teaches ecology at Castlemont, explained that their regular garden supervisor was recovering from surgery and the young gardeners were going to need to take a lot of personal responsibility for getting work done over the next two weeks on their own.

Kolevzon led the discussion in such a way that the youth themselves identified the various daily jobs that needed to be done during the two afternoons per week they came to fulfil their paid internships. Neo, Javier, Rosanna, and Sione, the four PUEBLO interns, had all worked with PUEBLO in the summer, so they knew the garden well and took pride in how it looked. Each volunteered for a daily job: weeding the garden beds, cleaning up the falling leaves and getting them into the compost, harvesting each day's bounty (including the now ripe apples), and turning the compost and spreading the completed compost. We arranged that I would meet the youth interns at the garden again on their two work days that week to interview them.

The next day before returning to Castlemont to start the interviews, I met my friend Dr. Carol Miller (introduced in Chapter 13) for lunch. She told me that her husband, Dr. Ron Miller, had been the principal at Castlemont and warned me that the area was dangerous, advising me to be very careful on the street near the school. Somewhat concerned, I paid close attention to my surroundings on each visit, but nothing alarmed me. It all seemed very quiet to me in terms of people on the street. The garden sat behind the school away from the street. I heard a lot of sirens while I was there, but I felt no personal danger.

Neo was at the garden raking leaves when I arrived. After the other three gardeners arrived, we decided the interview order and they began their work. I was very impressed that each went directly to the task agreed upon at their meeting. In over seven years of visiting youth gardens, this was the only time where there was no adult present to supervise the young people working (I was there to interview them, not to supervise them). No one fooled around. Is that because I was there and they wanted to make a good impression? I don't know, but I noticed their responsible attitudes and actions. The weather was late-September warm, pleasant for working outside.

I interviewed Neo first because he had an online class he also had to attend that afternoon. He was the oldest, aged eighteen, and dressed very neatly. He has a pierced lip with a piercing that had a curved arrow going up and around the pierce point. He is very polite. We sat on a bench watching the bees that had taken over an old shed nearby and Neo explained his name to me.

NEO: I joined this class where we had to choose our warrior name. I still hadn't chosen what my name was and I was, like, frustrated because everyone else had but me. At the very last second, I just said, "Neo." I didn't even think about it. It just came out.

ILLÈNE: How did you get involved with this program?

NEO: How I got involved in this program [PUEBLO] is mainly because of my brother, Javier. He is younger than me. This is not the first high school I attended. I went to two others. This is my second year here. The main reason I decided to join the garden is that my brother was very active with after-school programs and I was always interested in gardening. That was one thing that I was really interested in when I was a small kid as well. I would love to climb trees and be outside. I loved to just plant stuff and watch it grow. So, I have been involved in a lot of garden programs. It was after school and it was summer.

In my own free time, I had a garden at my house and just planted whatever I wanted. I would help my mom too. So, we would have our own gardens and stuff. So, when I heard that my brother was really involved in a garden and he would bring vegetables home, I was really interested in doing stuff like that. That's what I wanted to do. So, I transferred mainly just to join the program. That was something I really wanted to do, so it didn't matter what type of school I was attending just as long as I joined the gardening program.

ILLÈNE: When you gardened with your mom, did she plant vegetables?

NEO: Yeah. She would mainly have me, like, do all the hard labor, soften up the soil and get deep into the ground so we could dig in the fertilizer. Once we moved into our house that had a backyard that was big enough for a garden—the thing with the area was that it had gone through a lot of construction, so there was a lot of, like, concrete, rocks, and a whole bunch of sheet rock mixed into the soil. So nothing would grow. The dirt was just solid and flat and really dusty. So, I had to completely renew everything. It was really hard because the soil was just really dry, dry grey dirt, so I dug in really, really deep into the soil so I would make sure and I wouldn't have to redo it again. It was a lot of hard labor. It took me about a week to do the whole area, and after school, I would go home and just dig all day.

ILLÈNE: Do you know why gardening appeals to you so much?

NEO: For me, I feel like I am really connected to any natural organism. Just that I feel like my body is really sensitive so when I touch it, I feel when I touch something, like really pure, I feel part of it. It's kind of cleansing me as well and makes me feel more peaceful.

ILLÈNE: What kind of information do you get from your sense of smell?

NEO: So, for my sense of smell, I feel, I feel like really, really energized. When I take a nice deep breath of fresh air, that fresh oxygen the plants give out, it just like puts me at ease because even in the roughest days, if I just go where there are just a lot of plants, I know that I can relax and get myself together. To me, I like the color green because it looks really rich and it's bright. It's a very vibrant color. It's a really nice mood color. Green, it feels, like, energized. It gives you energy just looking at it. I feel more awake! I feel more awake!

ILLÈNE: When you come out here, you have had a full day of school?

NEO: A full day of staying in class and suffering through all the closed-in areas that I have to be in. I come out here and I feel fresh and I feel like more relaxed. For me, it makes a huge difference because I have lupus. For me to be in a closed-off area, puts a lot of stress on my body so my body tenses up, like on accident. Not on purpose! It just tenses up. That's what it does. I could try as much as I could, as much as possible, to try to relax, but it makes very little difference how much effort I put into trying to ease myself in the really closed-off environment that school is. So for me to transfer from a really closed-off environment to a more open, fresh environment that this garden is, I feel like it does a lot for my health.

ILLÈNE: To have a serious disease and to discover what helps, that's an important discovery to make. What about taste? You said you watched your brother bring fresh vegetables home. So now you get to bring vegetables home from the garden. How do you like the taste of vegetables you have grown yourself?

NEO: To me, I've never really liked the taste of vegetables. I love the taste of fruit. But no matter the taste of vegetables, I know because even though they taste very bitter sometimes, just very unpleasant, I still eat them for the fact that they are really nutritious. I tell this to everyone: that sometimes, it is not for taste, but you think about the benefit of eating something really nutritious; because I have been a vegan, but not anymore. There is a long story behind why I stopped being a vegan. I wish I still was. I was a vegan about two years ago. The reason I became a vegan was because I was tired of just watching, like, my family eat a lot of unhealthy food. And every day, there would be more statistics on diabetic people and people coming up with, like, younger children becoming diabetic. I felt like it was really sad that a lot of people conform to just being satisfied with eating junk food and people would be really vicious without their junk food because I would test people and people would be, "No! I need my Cheetos." I thought it was kind of sad. I wanted to be an example of the powerful things you can accomplish and how having a good nutrition could be beneficial. I completely stopped eating meat. For me, it wasn't that hard because ever since I was little, I loved eating fruits and vegetables, but I also would eat meat and junk food and just mix it in. But then I went solid just eating raw fruits and vegetables—all raw food. So, when I was doing that, as days went by, people noticed this bold action that I took: that I was not going to stand for being a person who walks around with chips and hot Cheetos every day and has a need to drink sugary drinks and artificial stuff. So, a lot of people felt influenced by what I did. Even though I did not reach out to a lot of people, I did change perspective to a lot of people at my old school, at Arise [High School]. So, some people decided to quit eating junk food and, out of nowhere, everybody started trying to join me. I started a little movement. Even though it did not last very long, I felt like it definitely affected people. Unfortunately, they felt like they could not do it. It was too hard of a challenge for them, so they gave up. But I kept going, and people saw how important it was to, like, eat fruits and vegetables. So, as time went by, I was an example of what would happen if you eat a lot of vegetables. So, over time, just eating raw foods, it increased my hearing. It increased all my senses.

Yeah, just out of nowhere, it just hit me. Like all my senses burst into this sensitive mode where... This happened while I was riding my bike home, and I was just riding my bike and out of nowhere, I felt like this huge flash of light just hit me in the face and I was just... I am trying to, like, get myself back together, right? But there wasn't any light that hit me in the face and I noticed that everything got a whole lot brighter. Like nothing changed, nothing physical outside my body changed, just that I felt like I could see and I could focus my eyes a lot better. I was riding my bike. I was, like, tripping out, right? I was like, "Wow, what is happening?" Right?

So, I heard a car right behind me, so I go towards the sidewalk so they could pass by. I am right there and I am waiting for the car to pass by, but it wasn't passing, so I looked back, and it was so far behind me! Wow! I heard that car from so many blocks behind me and it was just a speck. I thought it was right behind me because my hearing was so sharp! And I was like, "Holy crap, I could hear that car way back there."

So, I was still kind of like adjusting to everything because my eyes were really bright. I mean, everything looked really bright. My hearing was really good and the same with my touch. I mean, like, every time I would come onto my bike, I would just grab onto my handles. Okay, these are handles. That's how I felt them. They were just handles, right? But I could feel, once that moment hit, I could feel every little texture rubbing against my thumb. I could feel every single groove that my skin could push into. I don't know. I could really touch. It was a more advanced feeling of just touching things. So, that was that.

From then on, I felt like my whole body was just a constant flow of positive energy that just always, I couldn't hold it in. I felt like there was energy that bursted out of my body and that was constantly flowing out of me. I would feel I could not resist smiling at all. Whoever saw me, if they were like very depressed, it was just, like, bam, they would just smile. I would feel good because I was making them smile without doing nothing at all. Effortlessly, just making people smile every single time they got near me. Yeah. It really was amazing.

Smell was all the same. The thing is, this is Oakland. At this moment, I wasn't really involved with too much gardening except my house garden. There is a lot of very unpleasant smells around when you walk around Oakland. So, all the smells were just, like, "Ugh!" You could smell disgust! Yeah, the smells weren't really pleasant. There was, like, a whole bunch of carbon dioxide floating in the air. I could really taste the carbon dioxide, so that was not very pleasant.

ILLÈNE: You were eating raw food and you had this heightened sensitivity. Did the food taste better?

NEO: Not with vegetables [*smiles*]. The vegetables stayed the same, really bitter and unpleasant. But every single time I bit into a fruit, I felt like it was so sweet and so delicious, it just made me smile. I would just burst smiling. Why am I smiling? Yeah, it's the best. It being the best didn't allow me to, like, continue eating it because I would smile so hard I was stuck. It was, like, a solid smile on my face and I couldn't relax my smile to take another bite. It was so hard; it wouldn't allow me to eat the fruit. The smile would stay on my face. It was so delicious. But that was that.

ILLÈNE: How long did this heightened awareness last for you?

NEO: For me, I was only a vegan for about a month. It was about two, no, a week and half that my heightened senses were like really active. Once I decided to not just focus on my diet, that was when they just faded away. So, the reason I stopped was because one day, I woke up and my whole body was completely swollen. My body, all my joints were really swollen and they hurt.

ILLÈNE: Had you never had lupus before?

NEO: Never had lupus, I didn't know lupus existed. I woke up sick one day and my mom said, "You're sick because you're being vegan; you're eating all that stuff and not eating meat." I was always arguing with my mom about my diet, telling her I got a balanced meal—I don't eat meat, but I eat protein enough eating peanut butter. Then I went to a doctor because this was like excruciating pain all over. They diagnosed me with lupus and they told me it was an autoimmune disease that my immune system was attacking my joints.

ILLÈNE: And did you tell them about this experience you had just eating vegetables?

NEO: No. I just told, like, students from my school and, I don't know, they felt really inspired.

ILLÈNE: I don't know what the diet requirements are for lupus. Are your doctors oriented towards nutrition?

NEO: Yeah, they just told me to try to eat healthy. That is what I was doing at the moment. So, the thing was because lupus was not being treated and the main problem was my immune system was attacking my joints. If you are on a vegan diet, your immune system is super pumped, powerful, just take any bacteria on, right? If your immune system was really, really strong, that is what is attacking you and like hurting you then.

ILLÈNE: That is so bizarre. Your experience is truly unique. Thank you for sharing it with me.

NEO: For me now [*takes a long pause*]. It's hard to say because I hardly feel this as a sense, I don't know how to describe it, a sense like smell or sight or touch, but whenever I feel like connected to, to… I am talking about more of a spiritual kind of connection or sense, where it just like an aura or you can connect to your environment. That is the strongest sense I have even though I rarely feel it. Because [I need] to be in a really, like, good, really strong, a vibrant environment.

ILLÈNE: A natural environment?

NEO: A natural environment!

ILLÈNE: You come here at the end of the school day and you work here for an hour or two. How do you feel at the end of the time that you are here compared to when you come in?

NEO: I feel like it's really late, and even though it is really late and I have to go home and do a whole lot of homework, I feel like these two extra hours that I spend out here knowing that then I have to walk home and it's really cold or dark or whatever, that kind of just like pushes me and makes me feel like everything is okay. Yeah, it changes my stress levels a lot because um… 'cause the thing is, most of the stress that I get is from my lupus, and the thing with lupus is because my body has to work with an upset stomach, with pressure everywhere, with tension everywhere, my whole body is just inflamed. And 'cause I take a whole of medication for this, there are all the side effects that come along with it. So, all that stuff just, like, fused all at once puts a lot of stress on my body and a lot of stress on me. So, I feel I have to push myself a lot to just make it through the school day. So, for me to know I made it through another day at school, feels like having made it through another [day], like, as if I was a soldier out there in Iraq. People don't see it. They don't see what goes on inside me in my body and my mind. They don't really understand. I try not to make it obvious that I feel like I am dying or that I feel like I am suicidal or any of that stuff. For me, to make it through another day, knowing I had suicidal thoughts because I was in so much pain, and to make it to this garden, takes a lot of that stress away, knowing I am going to be fine now. I don't have to think suicidal or I don't have to go and do drugs to relieve pain or whatever. So, coming to this garden affects me a lot. I am trying to keep myself from going insane.

ILLÈNE: So, you changed your eating preferences before you started gardening. Is there any difference now when you get to take food home? Do you find that growing the food or getting to take it home or eating it here in the garden changes your choices at all?

NEO: For me, I feel it hasn't changed much about me. It has changed a lot, but not as much as I wish to change myself. I know I can really push myself to limits that I wouldn't even expect myself to surpass. I take vegetables home and I tell my mom that these are at the garden, that there are corn or strawberries and to come pick up the food, and she will come pick it up. But it is not a huge difference because there is not a big variety of vegetables and fruit and there is not a whole lot and they all kind of just, they are not prepared as quickly. To grow them, to have them grow and then be on your table ready to eat is really a long process. I do benefit from it, just not as much as I wish it would.

ILLÈNE: Do you find that your capacity to focus changes as you garden?

NEO: Yeah, it changes a lot. So, my capacity to focus in the garden just feels a whole lot easier. I feel like there is not much I have to worry about. I know exactly what I have to do, so it is not, "Oh, I am confused about what I have to do." I look out for whatever is my next objective or priority. I just go and focus on that and then I go on to the next thing. There are just a lot of factors that come into how focused I am because I feel my brain can just function better because I am out here in the fresh air and sun. There is nice, warm sunshine instead of being inside the classroom where there isn't any sunshine and there is just a bunch of people crammed into one room and I feel like it's hard to focus. I feel like that puts a lot of stress on me because if I am not focused on the lesson, I miss something. I am stressing that I am missing an important piece of information.

ILLÈNE: Can you take the state you get into gardening when you go back to doing your homework? Does it last?

NEO: Yeah, I definitely feel it helps me. I feel energy carried on or a good positive emotion carried on for another decent hour or two.

ILLÈNE: What about your relationships with the other kids and adults you garden with?

NEO: My relationship with anyone that works at the garden is pretty good because I feel like we are just a team. It feels completely different than if we were a team in class working on an assignment or a soccer team. It feels like the people here at the garden, they have a lot of things in mind, they are making a change in the community, and that they are doing something to, like, improve themselves and learn more to benefit themselves. They have the potential to have more people involved in, like, the garden.

ILLÈNE: Your relationship with Grey and the other adults you work with in the garden, are they any different than your relationships with your teachers in a regular class?

NEO: Yeah, it's completely different 'cause in the classroom, I don't communicate much with my teachers. It's more like, "Oh, they are my teachers. They are just here to teach me and they help me learn whatever needs to be learned, right?" But here in the garden, I feel like not only, like, can I learn from my teachers, but I feel like I can teach the teacher as well. Like, here is this plant and it's spreading everywhere and I am guessing it is invasive. We conversate, we would conversate about the different features this plant has. Just because it is invasive, it doesn't mean we have to take it out. It might have some different purposes. So, we conversate and we learn about it. I feel like I get in a deeper level of understanding with the adults here because I don't feel like they are just some teacher. They are my friends and they are here to make a difference. I feel like we are here for the same reason. I feel more comfortable. We just conversate. It doesn't have to be about the garden. It could be about, "Oh, today, it was just harsh at school and my teacher gave me a hard time," or something or, "I learned something new," or just anything.

ILLÈNE: Do you think that gardening has changed your environmental perspective and awareness?

NEO: I do think that gardening has changed a lot of my perspective on the world and things that are going on around us. There is a lot of pollution and we are running out of resources and there just isn't a lot of stuff like this happening out in the world.

ILLÈNE: "Stuff like this," meaning, like, this garden here?

NEO: Yeah, and just like agricultural kind of stuff or just being educated about agriculture. So, that being said, gardening here gives us some tools you can use in the future. If they use a bunch of pesticides on your food, you know that you can grow it yourself so it is all organic and doesn't have pesticides on it.

ILLÈNE: Do you think that gardening here has made you more likely to take a stand on an environmental issue or to protect a natural place that is threatened?

NEO: I definitely would because I just don't think it is right for people to disturb nature like that for their own selfish need or whatever, so I personally would take a stand and I would try to have as many people on board with my perspective on why you should not meddle around with nature.

ILLÈNE: Has gardening helped you connect with people that you have never connected with before? Has it helped you to meet people you might not have met?

NEO: Yeah, it has definitely given me, like, this whole different network of people who think and feel the same as I do on our environment. They support me like Grey. He supports me. He always tells me that if I am ever, like, interested in dedicating more time into this kind of stuff, he always can help me out. He is definitely one of my favorite guys around here 'cause of the resources or the people or the connections he can [share]. I feel like I could get really far or he could help me get to where I want to be.

ILLÈNE: If the school board came to you asked you what you thought about them putting in a garden at another high school, what would you say to them after your experience in this garden?

NEO: For me, I would suggest that they make sure they have room to grow because I feel that if you have, I am talking about physically, if you don't have enough space, much space to work with, you can only do so much. If you have a really large place where you can grow a variety of things, you just have more space to just put everything you like into it. I think it would just serve a lot better.

ILLÈNE: Do you feel confined here?

NEO: A little bit because I feel that even though this looks like a lot over the last year, we could definitely grow a whole lot more, take on a whole lot more than this. But this is all we have, so I feel like we are not being pushed to our full potential.

ILLÈNE: Grey told me there is another piece of land nearby that might become available to grow a forest garden.

NEO: So I got really excited when he told me we were going to put a whole lot of fruit trees over there.

ILLÈNE: So why did you agree to let me interview you?

NEO: Well, I thought you would be really intrigued about how I got to where I am now and how I feel toward all these useful gardening skills and how just, like, being in the garden could affect you in so many different ways. I want people to know, like, a perspective of a teenager in a high school that does this kind of stuff in a city that is infested with so much violence and to find a beautiful place for beautiful things to grow in a really bad environment. To me gardening is, I don't know, it's really broad, but the first thing that comes to mind is trying to grow, just growing. Trying to grow something the best way possible and just trying as if you were kind of competing to grow, like, the best-looking tomato plant or the best whatever you were planning on growing and just hoping it comes out just beautiful and nice and green and tall and strong. I definitely feel I grow a lot by just studying the plant, by just learning.

ILLÈNE: Is there anything I have not asked you that you would like to share with the people who read this book?

NEO: I would say that, for me, another part that puts into my whole enthusiasm when it comes to gardening is don't look at it as work because that takes all the fun out of it. I feel that people when they grow up and they are told to mature and to act a certain way, they forget how to have fun. This whole garden—I see as a whole jungle gym just to have fun and jump around.

After saying that, Neo clambered up a nearby apple tree to pick an apple to give me and it was truly delicious. (His climb and gift of an apple grace this book's front cover.) As I ate the apple, I reflected on all that Neo had shared with me: his deep connection to nature throughout his life that he nurtures by gardening, his experience feeling all his senses heightened, and his struggle with lupus and how the garden comforts him when he struggles with pain and suicidal thoughts due to the medications he has to take. Neo experiences agency in his gardening work. Through his own observations and knowledge, he can make decisions about what to do next and accomplish it through his own volition. He mentioned every element of PERMA (Seligman, 2011) in his conversation: the positive emotions he experienced in relation to his senses and his companion gardeners, as well as the engagement with the work and his senses, including the positive, team-type relationships with Kolevzon and his fellow gardeners. He gained meaning growing food for the community and creating a safe space away from the surrounding violence. He experienced achievement in what he learned and what he grew in the garden and in himself.

Neo found a mentor in Kolevzon who has offered to help him find more food-growing opportunities, and he is thrilled that they will soon plant a forest garden. By coming to work in the garden after school, Neo finds his inner strength to keep going, his grit—those qualities identified as necessary for life success (Duckworth and Seligman, 2005). I am humbled by Neo's willingness to share so much personal information. His deep connection to nature reflects what biologist Edward O. Wilson (1984) named biophilia, or our innate kinship with nature that is perhaps hardwired into our genes because we evolved in nature.

Neo goes to nature for solace and finds the pain relief he needs from the lupus and the side effects of the pharmaceuticals he takes to treat the disease. Ulrich's (1984) study of hospital patients showed that those with window views of nature needed fewer analgesics and lower doses than those having had the same surgery and with no nature views out of their hospital windows. Neo has discovered for himself that gardening in nature gives him comfort and pain relief.

# 15

# HARVESTING RESPONSIBILITY

Garden shed at Castlemont built by Green Pioneers. Credit: Sione

In the midst of his second year gardening with People United for a Better Life in Oakland (PUEBLO), Sione, aged fourteen, came from sweeping up leaves for the compost to speak with me. During this interview, he draws on his Samoan heritage to weave a story describing a relationship to food growing and harvesting that spans the Pacific Ocean.

**SIONE:** What made me want to do this was actually because I was taking environmental science freshman year and I was very interested in certain bugs. I was curious about that. Then I started talking more about the environment, like, how the acid from the rain affects certain things. The plants we use around us help us and help the air. I didn't know that and so I wanted to learn more about it. And then my English teacher, she talked to me more about it. There was finally something that was positive at school that I wanted to get a part of. It was positive to show other youth it's okay to do something different. You don't always have to just hang out after school with your friends after work and sit around and do nothing. For my group of friends, I wanted to be a lead example and go do something positive to give back to the community.

ILLÈNE: Do you have any family members that garden?

SIONE: My grandmother, well, she likes plants. When you go in her house, there are plants everywhere. She plants a lot indoors, but, like, I got into the outdoor gardening by a lady named Willow. I forgot the garden name, but it is in Oakland, California. When I was, like, littler, she let me work there when I was seven, and I was selling produce. And she would show me how you would use, like, the urine. And you actually put urine on plants and that helps them grow. She showed me how to transplant the soils and the plants and all that. I actually got inspired by her when I was little.

ILLÈNE: What inspired you to get involved with gardening?

SIONE: There ain't too many youth enthused about doing stuff like that. I actually went to her [Willow] personally because I kind of knew her and I seen her around, like she stopped me and my friends. How I finally met her, we were walking down the street one day and we were eating chips and stuff and she stopped us and she introduced herself and we introduced ourselves. And then, like, she told us to come to the garden and then she gave us strawberries and apples and all types of fruit to eat.

She was telling us why it was not good to eat junk food, what the junk food can do to you, how it can destroy some part of your body and, like, you are not going to be as athletic or anything. 'cause she asked us which one of you liked sports and everyone said, "We do!" She started telling us about junk food. She started telling us about lessening our portions of junk food, like, if you eat it, don't eat it every day, like a certain amount.

I went to Lafayette Elementary. I went to that school and they had a garden outside and that was during the time when I was helping the lady down there by my house, Willow. So, I was learning in both ways. Last summer, we went down to Stockton, me and my mom, to visit our other family and there was a guy my cousin was working for, and he do gardening and he had us help him in his backyard in the garden and he paid us for that.

From my experiences in Samoa with my uncles, we got the food ourselves, hand-choiced food. My uncles, they were kind of aggressive and they would, like, do competitions. My grandma on my father's side, she always was finding how to make people do things, but make it in an enjoyable way, like, make a game out of it. So, like, you had to get in the water or whatever and catch the baby sharks. They aren't really as vicious as some might think. "Oh, they are sharks!" No. It would be fun, but the older guys, they tend to do it like their regular fishing because they are not really that young to be doing that again. So, like, after we ate it after my grandmother, she does all the cooking around there, so, like, after she cut it and made sure it was killed and all that and she gutted it and took everything out and made sure it was clean, she fried it 'cause you can actually fry shark.

ILLÈNE: So how big is a baby shark?

SIONE: About three feet. When you make the shark, you can make it like hamburger meat. So, she does that. When I ate it, I started asking different people, "Like, I don't get it. Why does it taste different [than when I eat it in the US]?" That's when my grandma on my dad's side, she was like, "Things are processed out there." I really didn't know that. I thought we got our food, like, straight from the farm, stuff like that. But some farmers, they don't feed their cows what they supposed to. They feed them corn so they can get more stubbier, fat. If you go to these fast food restaurants, it's not 100 percent meat. They just use commercials to attract customers to make you feel like, "Okay, I am getting this!" But you are not getting what they say you are getting. At McDonalds, for fries, they use the fat from the burgers in making the fries. And KFC meat, it's not really chicken. Well, it's chicken, but they pump it with acid and salt and water and some type of acid to make the chicken more plump and more bigger.

ILLÈNE: Did you grow up always in Oakland?

SIONE: Yes, but not this part of Oakland. The night my mom was coming back from Samoa after my dad and her got married, like she actually went into labor that same night, so her flight got postponed for a week later because she wanted to stay out there in Samoa so the family out there could see me. Then when I was a week old, we came out here to Oakland. Time to time, like for summer and major holidays, we go to Samoa.

My Samoan family, we tend to eat horse and pig. That is the main dish, like doing a Luau. That is the main portion. The pineapples always come in somehow. People who are biased, they always look at people that are Samoan or Tongan as always pineapple eaters because everything, like when my grandmother, when she makes pig, shark, deer, somehow, some way, there are pineapples in it. Also, like, as appetizers, you eat pineapple as shish kebobs with lime and cilantro. The pineapple out there is different, I gotta say. It's more sweeter and it has that more natural taste to it.

ILLÈNE: Here in Oakland near your home, do you get to see trees a lot?

SIONE: Yes, there are trees where I live, but, like, people planted them themselves in their yards. And I have a tree in my backyard, several trees in my backyard 'cause, like, my backyard is big. The block I live on is a bunch of elderly people. They are retired and some of them, they do landscaping now. The guy across the street, he do landscaping. I call him Mr. Lance because his name is Lance, but I call him mister as respect for an elder. He landscapes and he do that type of stuff even though he is up in age. He shows me the basics of growing things. If I am outside and I am not really doing anything, he will start giving me the history of plants. It will be random sometimes, but it is fun to know.

ILLÈNE: You told me that your grandmother in this country gardens, and your grandmother in Samoa, too?

SIONE: Yes. The majority of time when my mom has to work overnights, I go over to my grand-mother's house because she lives close by, and my granny, she goes on and on about garden-ing. So I say when I am learning myself, give me a chance to do something to show my grandma I did something myself without her telling me, "Do this, do that. Help me plant this, help me plant that." I actually, on my own time, did it myself.

ILLÈNE: Do you think that gardening has changed your environmental attitudes and awareness?

SIONE: I have to say, yes, because I was the type of person that just threw anything everywhere. If I was outside, I would litter. I littered. But ever since I got the concept of gardening, the main part of it, it made me start doing things quite differently. Like if I see trash by a plant or people throwing soda cans with soda still in it on a plant, if I am walking with my friends and I see it, I tell them to pick it up. And some of them are like, "Wow, are you really going to make me pick it up?" And I say," I am not going to make you, I am going to ask you." It made them look at me differently and give the plants more respect as a living thing.

In my spare time, like, if I get an e-mail about things going on, like cleaning up things in the neighborhood and community, I got to do it. Like OYDC [East Oakland Youth Development Center], they still e-mail me because I did the job training with the younger kids, so they still e-mail me about things going on, like, if they are going to clean up, up and down the streets like from 103rd all the way down to 73rd, like, I join them. Like that would be on a weekend. Like I said, I want to be known as my job ethic. Like at OYDC, I take that very seriously. If I am going to commit to something, I am a person of my word. You can't force people to respect people; you have to earn their respect. You have to respect people and by doing things that will get your respect in return. By making a stand, for a person my age—I wasn't even a freshman yet, I was in the middle of 8th grade—that made me stand out to others, that really made me be more responsible for my work ethic.

A couple of weeks ago with Beautify Oakland, I went and I did, some call it community service, I went and cleaned up the community all the way from San Leandro High back down to 98th. We cleaned up and then we got the respect and dues for things we did. It made me feel I am part of something. The things I do now, I feel like the things I do now can be some type of a better way for the future. So, like, if it wasn't for people like you and me today to stand up for Oakland and planting and giving back to the community, where would the future be at now?

ILLÈNE: Say that someone from the school board came to talk to you and they wanted your opinion on if they should put a garden in at the high school down the street, what would you say?

SIONE: When people make investments, I think it creates opportunity and space and it's also inspiring youth to get into things. If you ask someone, "Oh, you want to make money?" It is giving them another tool to do it without doing it illegally. Everybody needs to get some kind of money to say they earn it their own self. That is their accomplishment. Every time somebody cash a check, that is their accomplishment, what they made. I would tell the school board I think it is a fine idea. I have to say that for a youth in this community, it is opening new experiences and new doors. They can be taking fresh veggies and fruits home so they won't be going to the grocery store to get processed food that is not all that good. It will be healthy and affordable at the same time. How can you lose from that? You can't lose from that benefit and I think it would be good for others to do it.

ILLÈNE: You are getting paid to garden here after school. What about if you were taking a class in high school and it was part of your environmental science class and you were working out here and not getting paid. What would you think?

SIONE: That was a big chunk in our environmental sciences class. We were never indoors. We always came out here. We always used this garden. It always felt good. I had Miss H. When we came into the garden and were working in the garden, it made me feel more of a leader because stuff that people didn't know in my class that I learned from Green Pioneers that had me working here during that time, it made me step in and also be a teacher in a certain way and guide them and tell them why this plant was planted and the effects and benefits from it and encourage them to come out and share. If I wasn't getting paid, I really don't care because I am getting paid in a way, I am learning. A lot of people think you can profit from money, but you can turn your education, you can profit from education every day. The learning experience would be more of a payment at the end of the day for me.

ILLÈNE: Is there anything I have not asked you yet from your gardening experiences that you would like other people to hear and to read about?

SIONE: Yes. I contributed to building that shed right there [the new shed to replace the one inhabited now by bees]. We started it from the garden up. And Neo, he was a big, he was like, Neo, he brung it there. He helped it. Days that I wasn't there, he would double the work. So, days I was sick, the weather was off and on. So, I was getting sick a lot. That is why I actually admire him. I got to say, he put in the most work even though I was there, and the days I wasn't there, as a coworker and as a friend, he stepped up as a leader to help me. The days I wasn't there, he still came in and he helped me, like, he covered for me things that I was not able to do. That's why I really admire him for that.

I feel good 'cause every time I look at it [the shed] and every time I hear a teacher or someone comment on it. Oh, I was a part of that. It makes me feel good to say I was part of something positive and not negative, something that could benefit the garden. 'cause the old shed, it's, like, there's not really that much room, yeah, and a lot of bees were bothering people. It was so small in there, so cramped, and the wood was starting to tear down and break down until we built that. That is what really made us think of building that, [a shed] where it is wider and open, more space, not so cramped.

The shed that Sione and Neo built at the Castlemont High School garden.  Credit: Sione

**ILLÈNE:** So building is another skill you have learned with this garden project?

**SIONE:** Yeah, and also bike repair. I did that. I did the compost and I contributed a little bit with the pond over there by cleaning it out.

**ILLÈNE:** Why did you let me interview you?

**SIONE:** I let you interview me because I wanted to show other people about the garden and also give them an opportunity to see how much we accomplished for something that started out with nothing. I wanted to inspire other youth to stand up to make a change, to rise above all the negativity and come up with something positive. Look at everybody around and see when you have school, you actually have family. You spend more time at school than at home, so that is, like, your second-base family. So, since you are family, you can come up with some things you can do to make your surroundings better instead of complaining, "Oh, this isn't right!" Step up and do something to make things better. Basically, to let others know about Green Pioneers, knowing the details to know how much dedication and coworkers it took to do this.

Sione keenly expressed his enthusiasm for growing food with PUEBLO Green Pioneers and painted not just the new shed but a bigger picture of his relationship to nature and family and the many people who have mentored him. He acknowledged and honored all he learned from: his grandmothers, his elderly neighbor, his environmental science teacher, the community gardener, Willow, and his peers. Sione expresses gratitude for what they taught him, for the inspiring mentors who figuratively and, perhaps, literally opened the garden gates to him and taught him not to litter and be a youth leader. He admires Neo who modeled a serious work ethic. Sione has determined to serve his community and speaks proudly of his accomplishments. He, like many of the young gardeners, now has a new awareness of trash; he no longer litters and asks his friends not to litter. He has embodied what PUEBLO aims for: young people experiencing dedication and pride in growing food, building sheds, fixing bikes, building community, and making a positive difference for themselves and Oakland.

# 16
## YOUTH REACH OUT TO THE COMMUNITY

Rosanna and Neo harvest a carrot. Credit: Illène Pevec

Rosanna, aged sixteen, smiles with exuberance. She speaks openly even though we met just three days before. The People United for a Better Life in Oakland (PUEBLO) Green Pioneers team members work in the public realm: they make presentations, teach younger children what they have learned about gardening, and have a great deal of confidence to express themselves freely. Rosanna explains to me how she got involved.

ROSANNA: I had a friend and the founder of Green Pioneers was his science teacher. He told me, "Oh, there is this really cool program and you get stipends for working in a garden." So, I decided to check it out. So, my freshman year second semester, I decided to join it and I thought it was really fun and I just got the hang of it. So, over the years, I have been a member of Green Pioneers and the garden. Now, I am a junior and I am still part of it.

ILLÈNE: Are you paid for your work and what are your responsibilities?

ROSANNA: I was paid $250 per semester. We had to be here three days a week: Monday, Wednesday, and Thursday from three to five p.m. Basically, it is our responsibility to learn as much as we can, like gardening skills from teachers and from some gardening experts. And then, there were some days that we just did it for fun. We definitely did not just sit there not doing anything. We had to create projects, like end of the semester projects. And then talking about what we learned throughout the whole semester, like summarizing everything we learned on one poster board. Then, with that project, we would present it to local groups; anything related to gardens, like anything local, we would present it to people at events and stuff like that. This year, my schedule is different and I am working Tuesday and Thursday three to five.

In my freshman year, we worked with middle school kids and we helped them create a garden. It was after school. They had a bunch of empty beds and everything was just empty. I think it was four kids, including myself, we went to that middle school. We taught kids how to plant, how to grow their own produce. We taught them how to weed, anything that is garden related. And then, at the end, they were really grateful and they had a ceremony for us and then the kids made us little cards saying thank you. It was just really fun. It was fun 'cause, 'cause, like, being a student myself, for once teaching someone else younger than me for a change, I felt like a teacher. I felt really inspired because instead of the kids being at home doing nothing, watching TV, I am teaching them how to do something creative with their time. It was also a learning experience. I learned a lot from the kids that I met. Yeah, it was really fun.

It helped me realize what teachers struggle through; what it is like to actually teach kids that are younger than you. I felt their struggles being with kids that don't really want to listen to you. Not that I was a hard kid or a hard student, but I understood where they [the teachers] were coming from.

ILLÈNE: My research involves the sensory experiences people have while gardening. Are you aware of which sense you pay the most attention to while gardening?

ROSANNA: I think my strongest sense that I use when I garden would probably be my sight because I can definitely see and spot out a plant that is healthy or unhealthy. It's just, like, I kind of developed that skill from being in the garden for so long. I kind of just figure what is dying and what is not and what needs to be taken care of.

ILLÈNE: Now that you have attuned yourself to the needs of the plants so that you can see what they need, how does that make you feel?

ROSANNA: I felt a lot of things. I felt accomplished, but, at the same time, I felt discouraged because I figured out there are so many things I can do and so much things people can do and people can learn to do instead of doing nothing about it and just ignoring it. For example, there could be a dying plant in their home and they maybe wouldn't know—or wouldn't care—what to do with that plant. But being here, oh, I learned so much and it wants me to take on things that I learned farther.

ILLÈNE: You mentioned caring. Do you think you cared about plants in the same way as you do now, before you were in this gardening project and learned about plants?

ROSANNA: [*Laughs.*] Oh, no. At first, I didn't care about plants, but over the years, it becomes kind of a part of you. For example, I like the feeling of starting a little seed and then as it gets bigger, [it grows] into a plant and that plant produces fruits or vegetables or anything like that. You get a good feeling because your hard work turned into something wonderful. It's kind of like that's your child. You cared for that child, you watch that child, you protect

ILLÈNE: Did you ever see any of your parents or grandparents garden before you came here?

ROSANNA: Yeah, my grandma was a big gardener, but I didn't really pay attention to it. She had her own garden at her house and I would just pick the flowers and I wouldn't really care. And I didn't know something would happen if I did that and, like, damage stuff and destroy stuff, but now that I am older and I have been in the garden, I have kind of learned what I am supposed to do.

ILLÈNE: What about your sense of smell when you are gardening? Do you like to put your nose in a flower?

ROSANNA: I can smell compost. I did a project on compost my sophomore year. A lot of that had to do with my smell as well—my smell and my sight. And then I could smell a good soil of compost. It's kind of like gold to me when I see our finished compost. Yeah, I like seeing it. It smells good and it looks good. It feels really peaceful. It's really quiet here sometimes, aside from all the crazy stuff going on outside the garden that you can hear. If you pay attention to the leaves rustling and the chickens making noise and the water watering the plants, it's really peaceful.

ILLÈNE: What's it like for you watering something that you have planted from a seed?

ROSANNA: I feel it's good because it's my food. I mean, other people would just go to a grocery store and buy fruits, but sometimes, they don't really think how hard those farmers worked and how much work they put into that produce, just one piece of produce. We are here and we have our own produce and [when] we taste it, we get a sense of hard work and the dedication that farmers put into their produce and we feel proud.

At first, my taste buds were so used to what they sell at grocery stores, but then when I come here and I taste natural produce that we put in. You can really tell the difference. When you taste something that is right there and ripe, you can really tell the difference. I guess it tastes more natural. I mean, I don't really like vegetables personally.

ILLÈNE: What about a carrot picked straight from the ground?

ROSANNA: I don't hate it, but it's not my favorite. I will eat it if you ask me to. It's not my favorite snack. I am still into junk food, I guess. Shame on me! I still eat junk food. I can't help it. I am a teenager. For me, I wasn't into changing my food style. I was more, like, community outreach, like what it does to people when you become part of a garden.

I am interested in growing food, but I don't know, I just don't like vegetables. I just don't. But I try to eat it. I know it is good for me. I am more into, like, getting hands on and growing it than eating it. I like the fruits. Yeah, I love the fruits in the garden. This summer, we had a lot of cherries, plums, watermelons, squash, lemons. We had everything, almost everything. Now, our apples are getting ready. I kind of have this pattern where I will eat healthy for two weeks and then I get a taste of junk food and all the craving comes back. So, that is, like, my problem.

ILLÈNE: What is the difference? If you are eating healthy, do you feel different after those two weeks?

ROSANNA: I feel less stressed. I usually am stressed a lot because of school. Eating healthy plays a big part in lowering my stress levels. When I come out of school, of course, I feel really exhausted. When I come out [to the garden], I don't feel very different except more exhausted, but a couple of weeks later when I am away from the garden for maybe a week, I feel like I have to be here. I have to feed the chickens. I actually love being here. I want to be an example to my peers that I am not out there wasting my time on something useless.

ILLÈNE: Does gardening change your stress levels?

ROSANNA: Yeah, in a good way, in a positive way. Umm, well, it's the reason I like to be here and do my homework at lunch sometimes because it is so peaceful rather than being in a classroom filled with a bunch of kids talking too much. I just come here whenever I am having a bad day or whenever I have to do homework or just because I want to be here.

ILLÈNE: Do you think that being part of Green Pioneers has given you a chance to know people differently than in your classes?

ROSANNA: Yeah, the kids that participate in the garden, I am kind of surprised because when they are here and they start to learn and work, you kind of see what kind of skills they have, what they are good at. And in class, you see that too. I mean, you see a kid who is good at math or good at English, but you don't see a kid who is good at planting or weeding or seeing if the garden is okay. You don't see that. And being here, you can learn that from your peers and other students. It makes us feel a lot closer to each other. I made a lot of friends being in the garden. It brings us a lot closer. We have something to talk about and we have something to relate to whenever we are outside the garden because the garden is something we have in common.

ILLÈNE: What is the meaning of gardening for you?

ROSANNA: I guess the meaning of gardening is, when I think of the word, I think of fruits and vegetables and hard work, nature. Well, that is my definition of it. So far, I have just been a big part of the garden for, like, three years now. That is all I have been focused on.

ILLÈNE: One of the things you talk about is the caring you give to the plants and how that makes you feel. Are there other activities at school that give you the chance to care about someone or something other than yourself?

ROSANNA: Other students and my grades. [Laughs.]

ILLÈNE: So you care about your grades?

ROSANNA: Yeah. I am Filipino. I was there [in the Philippines] until I was nine. When I was nine, I came here. It's really dangerous around here. I lived in San Leandro. It was a little tinier, peaceful too, but since it is close to Oakland, whatever is going on there, it kind of happens around San Leandro. Then we moved to Oakland. Then I joined the garden. My favorite part of being in the garden is reaching out to my community because it is so dangerous for kids to be here and for kids to be around here and going to school and living here and stuff like that. I feel like being in the garden kind of distracts them from all that. I am happy because it is kind of like something about the plants makes me happy; the weather, the flowers, the trees, the plants, the chickens, the bees sometimes when they don't sting.

ILLÈNE: Do you have any family members that you have seen garden or farm?

ROSANNA: My dad built a little, kind of like tiny, really tiny garden kind of by our steps. There is, like, a table just full of plants. Like cactus, chiles, tomatoes, roses, stuff like that. And they are actually well taken care of. My grandma started it and my dad takes care of it.

**ILLÈNE:** Do you think your environmental awareness has changed as a result of gardening?

**ROSANNA:** Yeah. When I started [gardening] freshman year, I actually stopped littering. And then I would point to other people and say, "Hey, don't do that. Pick up your trash. Throw it over there." I don't know, it's just kind of like a habit. And then the chickens, I think about them whenever I am not in school; I am worried. Are they hungry? Are they cold?

**ILLÈNE:** You took a picture of the sunflower. Tell me why the Mexican sunflower.

**ROSANNA:** I have a boyfriend. He was here last semester and he planted that. I saw him put it in the soil; he prepared the soil. Yes, he planted the seed. I worked here during the summer. He had to do things in the summer because he had a scholarship, so he couldn't be here in the summer. I was here in the garden. I took care of his seeds. I took the seed, it got bigger and I planted it in the ground. Well, yeah, now it is all blooming and happy. He is at home doing homework.

**ILLÈNE:** He is not in Green Pioneers anymore?

**ROSANNA:** No, he wanted to do other things.

Mexican sunflower planted by Rosanna's boyfriend. **Credit:** Rosanna

ILLÈNE: Is there anything I have not asked you that you would want people to know about gardening for teens?

ROSANNA: Just something for a person to read this book to know; it's just really a great learning experience. This started as a program called Green Pioneers, which is a gardening program where you have to learn about urban sustainability. I have always wanted for Green Pioneers to be heard. So we would come out and reach other people, reach other gardens, and ask them, "Hey, we are here. We exist and we help the community too." And then we figure it out. We Google ourselves. I Google myself, I Google Green Pioneers, and you see all these links to Green Pioneers and you are so proud of yourself. "Hey, we are known. I am known!" It's like a happy feeling. You are so proud of yourself. It's like a happy feeling. I am getting tears. You see yourself. You are on the Internet. And people see the things you do, the great things you have done being a gardener, and from something so simple that can come something so big.

⁊ᴥ

Rosanna thrives creating gardens. A good student who cares about her grades, she also cares about nature and creating a safe, clean space where other people can come and thrive too. She has quit littering because she has gained new respect for the environment around her by caring for it through gardening. Like other youth interviewed, Rosanna describes how the plants that she grows feel like her children. She feels great accomplishment in all she has done with Green Pioneers. She does not mention any discomfort being the only girl in the fall program—the garden appears to foster equal footing for all without gender issues. Even though her boyfriend has moved on to other activities, her own choice remains with the garden.

Rosanna resumed her gardening tasks with Neo, and I interviewed Javier, Neo's sixteen-year-old brother who, like Rosanna, has been involved in Green Pioneers and the Castlemont High School garden for two full years. While we talked, I heard a lot of siren noise coming from the surrounding streets for the second day in a row.

ILLÈNE: How did you get involved in gardening?

JAVIER: During my freshman year, I met the founder of Green Pioneers, Miss Johnson, at this school. I was, like, really motivated to actually do good in the garden 'cause she pretty much inspired me. I am a junior this year. I've been doing it for two years. We had internships. If we worked for a semester, we got paid a certain amount. The first year, it was $500, but since more and more students started to join, it became less. But during my last year, since I was pretty much a leader in Green Pioneers, they promoted me and two other students to be leaders and caretakers and that is when they started paying us differently. We get paid by the hour by PUEBLO. We get paid $8.25 an hour.

ILLÈNE: Do you notice what you smell in the garden?

JAVIER: We have some very nice flowers to smell. You ever smell lemon verbena? I love smelling that. It's also my favorite plant. Usually, we had two lemon verbena bushes. One of them got taken away. We didn't really need it because we didn't have space for it. The other one, I pretty much persuaded for it not be taken away. I fought for it. I'm taking care of it. It's doing pretty well. You can use it in tea. [*After our interview, Javier picked me a lemon verbena branch with the heavenly, fresh-scented leaves for me to enjoy with tea with a friend.*]

ILLÈNE: How do the smells of the garden make you feel?

JAVIER: I'd say calm and relaxed.

ILLÈNE: What are the things you enjoy looking at when you are out here gardening?

JAVIER: Right here, I usually give attention to the bees because I want to see how they work. Then, when I am near that area, I face towards the mountains. I usually see the blue sky and the hills. And what we used to have was our pond and I just loved looking at that, but since we didn't have a permit, we had to take it away pretty much because if we kept on continuing it, they would just fill up the hole again. That was one view I enjoyed. First of all, it was one of my creations. I helped to make it. It was with a group of students. Once we were finished with it, it was pretty nice. It looked pretty beautiful. It had rocks at the bottom. It had a little fountain we added, we installed. It would make me feel relaxed and comfortable because, usually, when I am mad or something, I usually do some deep thinking, but when I put my mind on something else, I actually forget about the anger I had. That is what usually makes me comfortable and brings me back to a relaxed state. I start interacting with other people nicely instead of in a rude way.

ILLÈNE: And what about the tastes in the garden? Do you like being able to pick something you have been growing and pop it into your mouth and taste it?

JAVIER: [*Chuckles.*] Yes, I do. Especially when last summer when we had our cherry tree blossoming with lots of cherries, I used to like coming up there and eat a lot of cherries. They were very sweet. We also had our apples growing too, and those were pretty good, but I think we could have done better. We also had our corn, and we still have some growing.

And then our pumpkins, we only have a couple left because a lot of people would come by and decide to take one. And then we had our plum tree, and the plums were very sweet and then people pretty much took them all, but, then again, I did save some and I did enjoy that. Hopefully, I get to taste some tomatoes that are starting to grow.

ILLÈNE: How do you feel when you get to eat something you have grown?

JAVIER: I'd say I feel pretty excited because that satisfies me because I satisfied it. I am pretty excited and happy because, well, it's delicious. So, of course, that made me feel good inside.

ILLÈNE: What about touching things? You garden without gloves, don't you?

JAVIER: Sometimes. It's only when I am picking weeds that I do it with gloves because some have thorns and then they end up making you bleed. But, also, there are particular plants in here that are very soft. They feel like a piece of blanket and I just grab a piece of it and start playing with it or just rub it the whole time and keep it so I have something to do, keep my mind on something. But then, also, there is some stuff that is very rough. There used to be some thistles that we had. Even if you have gloves or not, they will pierce your gloves and stab you. I love touching the dirt with my hands because it feels like, well, it depends because if it is soft and wet dirt, it's like playing with Play-Doh if you ever played with that before. I am not sure what I feel, but it's like a sense of duty, I guess. It's, like, up to us to take care of what we need to take care of and to make this garden better than before.

ILLÈNE: Tell me more about this sense of responsibility. Do you have it because you are getting paid to do the job or because the plants are living things and you know they need your care?

JAVIER: Well, I would say because not a lot of us would want to take care of it because not much people are interested in gardening. They would rather do other stuff, like kick boxing or stuff like that. I would say I feel responsible because if we just leave this garden alone, it's going to end up dying and it would be like when we first saw it. There was nothing growing or anything like that. It was just weeds growing everywhere. It was pretty trashy. For it go to back like that would be the end of a dream. For it to end so helplessly, without even helping it. I want it to keep on living. I'm only going to have two more years here or one more year here and then it's in the hands of whoever is next in taking care of it, and I fear there are not much people interested in taking care of it. So, I hope that more people will get involved into helping in the garden.

ILLÈNE: Where do you think your interest for gardening comes from?

JAVIER: Well, I'm one who likes to learn a lot of skills. Especially since this is a skill that would help me actually survive in this area if I had all these materials. It's something school wouldn't really teach you. But if I know the skills and I have the materials, I could pretty much last off of what I make instead of just die in a week or so because gardening is like a key skill. You can learn how to grow stuff and also spend less money. Instead of going to a store and buying it, you could just make it in your backyard and have it for less that you would buy it for. I'd say it's like a benefit.

ILLÈNE: How does that make you feel to learn how to take care of yourself and these plants?

JAVIER: I would say I end up feeling pretty knowledgeable, having fresh foods come out of there. Instead of getting them from an organic store, knowing that is going to cost money, [I am] getting them from my backyard when it is right there. Usually, I would say, "Knowledge is power." So, I would say that would be pretty powerful to know how to maintain a garden. We actually helped start up two other gardens. The mayor came and I took a picture with her. There were a whole lot of people helping out. I wasn't the only one. It was fun. It was like a community thing. We pretty much started a new garden from scratch.

It was part of Green Pioneers. They wanted us to help out and we decided to go. It was on a Saturday, pretty much got it done. Now, it's better looking than before. There was also another one. They were sharing out beds and getting some fruits too. We helped them mulch, add soil to the box, helped them create schematics for how to plant stuff. Pretty much now, they are on their way too. I actually have helped at the Elmhurst garden too. They started out with a little area for the garden. It wasn't really much, but there were four or five of us that helped some 6th graders learn some skills for a little bit so they can know how to do some stuff, like what to do with some plants. We pretty much taught them what we know. Now, hopefully, their garden is going well.

ILLÈNE: You come out here after class and then you garden for a couple of hours, do you feel any different when you are done gardening than you did after class?

JAVIER: Well, I'd say I'm more energetic and getting more done in the garden because what school does is put me to sleep because, like, we have to stay in the class for an hour and then go to the next class and do the same thing. When it comes to the end of the class, I get excited and energetic just to finish and come here and do my work.

ILLÈNE: Do you think it changes your mood?

JAVIER: I would say it does. Usually, when I first wake up and there's a whole lot of cloudy, I am kind of in a sad mood, but if it's a day that's all sunny and bright outside, it gives me strength and energy. But, also, outside, I feel more calm and ready to work. Usually, by the time I am done here, I will be kind of exhausted depending on what I had to do. Say, if I was just to do a regular, not hard-working day [as opposed to] a day where I have to pull plants out of the beds and plant everything. Usually, I would be tired, just take a nap and just do my homework when I can, but most of the time, I finish my homework before I get to the garden because of the program we have now. So, I just feel, I just want to like feel relaxed and just go to sleep.

ILLÈNE: Do you find that gardening changes your ability to focus?

JAVIER: Well, I would say it would redirect my focus into actually helping the garden. Usually, when I am in school, I would just doze off and, like, daydream, but when I am here, I already know what I have to do and I accomplish what I have to do, just work. I am more the sort of person that wants to be active instead of sitting down in the classroom 'cause what it usually does to me if I just sit down and do nothing, it makes me go to sleep. When I am actually moving, it gets me motivated to keep on accomplishing.

ILLÈNE: Do you think your eating habits have changed any from getting to grow fruits and vegetables and take them home to eat?

JAVIER: I'd say usually in the summer, I had to come here at ten or twelve [in the morning] and sometimes, I would skip breakfast and just come here and eat any fruits and vegetables I could find. Usually, I would say that changed my diet. I wasn't interested in hot chips anymore. Sometimes, people would offer it and I wouldn't be actually eating it. I would prefer eating something else besides junk food.

ILLÈNE: Did you eat a lot of junk food before you started this program?

JAVIER: I actually ate a lot of junk food. I ate a lot of candy. I had a craving for candy and I couldn't stop. When it came to, like, 9th grade, I started learning what candy does to you, and also from Miss Johnson. She taught me a lot and she told me that pretty much we should learn what to eat and what is right to eat. So, I cut back on candy a lot from that day. I started eating less candy and junk food. I didn't completely stop eating it; I just eat it once in a while and have more protein and stuff.

I would say that I eat from this garden pretty well. I like it a lot, especially the strawberries. They are really sweet. Even though they are small, they are so good. Instead of actually growing it with pesticides, I would rather eat these.

ILLÈNE: What is the meaning of gardening for you?

JAVIER: I would say it would be a, like, skill. Yeah, I would say it is a life skill because it teaches you how to take care of plants and how to actually do stuff right. Doing stuff right is learning how to plant stuff or knowing how to treat it or learning how to make soil or compost for the plants. I'd say it is a pretty useful skill.

ILLÈNE: I am curious if what young gardeners see every day from their homes affects them. Where you live, from your apartment, can you see trees?

JAVIER: There are not a lot of trees except there are some trees beside our walk where they have planted some. I can see those, but besides that, I don't really see trees. But if I was going to more open space where I could see the mountains, then I could see a lot of trees up there. I would say it makes me feel that we kind of destroyed Mother Nature. Because even though we do know it is for us to improve and for us to protect the environment, I would say that having Mother Nature is pretty much like actually going to see a forest and just live there, go camping or something like that.

ILLÈNE: You like that? You like to feel close to nature?

JAVIER: Yeah.

ILLÈNE: What about your relationship with adults in the garden, are they different than your relationship to your teachers in the classroom?

JAVIER: Usually, they would see me as, like, "You guys, you kids, you teenagers did all this!?" Like this is really impressive, right? But in school, it's like, "You're doing your work. Good job." It's like pretty much going to work and not really doing much, not doing a change. That is how it feels in school. But here [in the garden], people are praising you because your team accomplished something.

ILLÈNE: So you get more recognition for what you accomplish out here?

JAVIER: Yeah.

ILLÈNE: I don't know all the adults you work with here. I met Grey. Sometimes he works with you, but sometimes you all work by yourselves. What about working with the adults in the garden?

JAVIER: Usually, since in the beginning we didn't know much, he would teach us how to do it, but now, since we already know the skill, we just get it done. Sometimes, he helps us out and we get it done faster. It makes me feel very responsible. It makes me feel like an adult for them to trust me to do my work without them actually supervising me the whole time. Makes me feel pretty responsible.

ILLÈNE: What do you find most pleasant about gardening? What do you like the best?

JAVIER: I like when I get to see all the stuff I planted actually grow and produce something because pretty much I put my work and the effort into that plant for it to grow up and do what it needs to do, and, in the future, it repays me by giving me fruits and vegetables.

ILLÈNE: Is there something that you don't like about gardening?

JAVIER: It's not really because of gardening, but there are some students that come by from other schools and vandalize the garden. For example, what they wrote right there [points to profane graffiti]. Pretty disrespectful. Sometimes, they come here and do illegal activity and stuff like that. They just tag up our shed. One time, we left that shed open and they took most of the tools and left a mess. We put our hard work into organizing and pretty much buying the tools and then it's just a waste. We have to work with it and deal with it.

ILLÈNE: Do you think that working in the garden has made you more aware environmentally? You would be more likely to take a stand for the environment in your community?

JAVIER: I would say it did because, usually, like before, I wouldn't be that active in saying, "Oh, you shouldn't destroy the forest like that." But now that I have all these skills, to destroy a forest, it's like taking away our lives because the forest gives us what we need to breathe. Take away the forest is pretty much saying you don't want to live.

ILLÈNE: Say the school board came to you and said that it was thinking about starting a garden at another high school, what would you say to them?

JAVIER: I would say, by all means, go for it. You would expect a lot of stuff. Usually, people, we have a lot of people who would come by during meetings or school events, and they come see the garden and they say, "Wow, this is really amazing." They give affirmations like that and praise the garden and have an event to help the garden. I am pretty sure they will be motivated to do it.

Something that you need to know for students that actually want to work in the garden is that you have to get them motivated or inspire them or pretty much persuade them to actually work in the garden. You have to get the right type of student to actually help you out in the garden.

ILLÈNE: What inspired or motivated you?

JAVIER: What inspired me? I was pretty amazed by, when I first saw this [garden]. I was like, "Wow!" When the founder of Green Pioneers told us about the garden internship with Green Pioneers during one of our planning meetings at school, I wanted to join because she gave us a lot or reasons why, like learn skills and stuff like that. It's pretty much an activity or pastime you do after school. Usually, I didn't really want to do things after school, but now I would rather do this than do nothing. So, you have to find people that actually want to do this. You can't force it on someone that doesn't really want to do it.

Since we did all this stuff with other people from other gardens or other schools, we found out it's a big community of gardens. So if people need help, or create something new in the garden, you can give a shout out to someone and they will come by and help us out. And, yeah, usually, you meet other people. Say people want to start their own garden and you have plants to help them start it, they will pretty much, like, need your help. Usually, we get a lot more gardening type of people, people who are a lot more interested in helping the environment and stuff like that. We get more interaction with them.

ILLÈNE: How come you let me interview you?

JAVIER: Well, I was very interested in actually reading your book when you finish it and see what it comes out to be, like if it has a greater impact on other people, see where it goes from there, see if it does good for other people or actually inspires people to be more involved in environmental activities.

ILLÈNE: It's your words that will inspire people.

Javier offers cherry tomatoes. Credit: Neo

Javier clearly explained all the ways he found purpose, pride, and achievement working to revive a school garden that had been abandoned to weeds. He met inspiring mentors, including his teacher who started Green Pioneers, Grey Kolevzon, and the other people who come out to help with community garden building, and he realizes he can call on these people for help when needed. He saw the tangible results of his efforts in the beauty created and the food grown in the garden. He discovered that he could calm himself when necessary by looking at the garden and working in it. He identified self-motivation as an important quality for youth gardeners. Javier, Rosanna, Sione, and Neo, Javier's brother, all discussed the positive emotions, the engagement, the positive relationships with peers and adults, the meaning they derive from their gardening work, and the achievement they feel. They experience gardens as places for personal and community flourishing and they are committed to their work helping to maintain and start gardens with others.

# 17

## A MENTOR GOES THE EXTRA MILE

"Do plants have sex?" In PUEBLO Castlemont High School garden. Credit: Illène Pevec

Grey Kolevzon, the project coordinator for People United for a Better Life in Oakland (PUEBLO), took a permaculture training course right after college and has been involved with youth, permaculture, and community gardens ever since. Permaculture (permanent agriculture) is the conscious design and maintenance of agriculturally productive ecosystems that have the diversity, stability, and resilience of natural ecosystems (Mollison, 1990, *ix*). Fruit and nut trees, berry bushes, perennial and annual herbs, and vegetables are inter-planted to maximize use of natural resources without depleting them or the energy of the human tending and harvesting them—an approach to living in tune within one's natural environment that has been practiced for millennia by indigenous people. Bill Mollison (1990, ix), an Australian, brought permaculture and its approach into international awareness and practice in response to the rapid rise of agribusiness modeled on industrial practices rather than on natural systems:

> Permaculture is a philosophy of working with, rather than against nature; of protracted and thoughtful observation rather than protracted and thoughtless labor; and of looking at plants and animals in all their functions, rather than treating any area as a single product system.

Reflecting on how much the movement for local healthy food has grown in recent years, Kolevzon observed that permaculture has rather quickly moved from the fringe and into mainstream community college classes. He brings its principles regarding healthy ecosystems and social equity to PUEBLO and to the high school classes he teaches.

KOLEVZON: My main job at PUEBLO is pretty unclear and pretty flexible. Basically, it is program development and that involves also supporting program directors. When we develop a program through whatever means and we hire someone to run it, sometimes they need support in the beginning particularly and I am that support person.

ILLÈNE: The youth gardeners all seem to know you well. What is your role in relationship to them and this specific program?

KOLEVZON: I played the same role last year. The program director last year was not someone we hired. She was someone who was here before we took it over. She was a volunteer for the founder and when the founder left, she took over. And the founder gave the program to PUEBLO, essentially. It was a small after-school program. It was small but growing, and she had raised money for it. A lot of the pieces were in place. They just needed an organization to cosponsor the program. Through my role with PUEBLO and with our move to Castlemont [High School], it worked out that I gave some support to the garden program. I was there a lot, and I volunteered every Wednesday in the fall after school. I have a lot of other responsibilities for PUEBLO too.

PUEBLO does not make a living for me, so I have other jobs. For the time being, I am a classroom teacher. I teach in a program called Sustainable Urban Design Academy [SUDA]. It's a class called Green Urban Design, and what it has mostly been so far is looking at food systems. We are doing projects that work towards healthier food systems and a little bit around the ecology of Oakland itself, like land, people, geography, history. I also teach at the community college and I work at the park service too.

I only get paid for some of it. I have about seventy paid hours a week now and that is why I am always tired and I don't have time. I am always stressed a little bit. The problem is we are a small nonprofit and our cash flow is good sometimes and not good other times. I am sort of the least important in a way. The programs are more important than the program developer. We have to pay the program directors—we have commitments to them. So, if there is a cash flow problem, I don't get paid, but I still have a lot of responsibilities. That has been the case for the past few months, but we just got a grant for a project that I will manage. I am already supposed to be the manager of it, but I am doing the minimum until the money comes in and I can get paid. It is from the government and they take a long time to pay. Once the money comes in, that will be my main job and I will pass on my high school job to a coworker so he will teach my classes and I will have a much more normal life.

ILLÈNE: What is the relationship of PUEBLO to SUDA?

KOLEVZON: PUEBLO is a fiscal agent and we are a partner of SUDA. It is an academic career and college preparation program, part of the high school. So, we are an affiliate of the high school, a partner with the high school. I also teach at SUDA because it was kind of a way of advancing our mutual goals. The program is about green job creation and training. That is one of my main goals too for PUEBLO, so there is a lot of overlap. So, essentially, the district created a position through SUDA, created a program through classroom teaching around the same goals we had set up at PUEBLO. So, it made sense to take money from the school district rather than from PUEBLO. But I have to work on their terms, so I have to be in the classroom every day and teach x number of students. It's sort of different working for the government than working for a nonprofit, and I have had to change my life a lot. It's affected PUEBLO a lot because I have to spend my time teaching.

ILLÈNE: One thing I was impressed with was that I watched you facilitate a discussion for the youth to choose their jobs for the week and the fall term, and you told them you would not be there for a few days because of other things you had to do. The next day, you were not there and the kids all did their jobs. Are they that self-directed? It really impressed me as I watched in between interviewing them one by one. I have not seen any youth gardening project where there has not been an adult present supervising the youth.

KOLEVZON: That's pretty unusual. Part of it is how the program was set up originally by the founder. She gave them a lot of self-direction and a lot of power to really feel ownership of the garden. That is part of the reason. The other reason is because we pay the students, and we have paid them for a while, so they have been around for a while. They really think of it as part of their job. They not only feel an investment in their job, they are rewarded for doing their jobs. And they know what they are doing. We have given them a lot of training. I, personally, have given them a fair amount of training. They had had a little before too. So, they have a background, they have a strong level of investment, and they get paid, so they feel compensated—so, the combination of those things. Also, they are really great kids. Some kids would take longer to step into that managerial type or staff-person type of role. Some kids, like all people, have higher levels of initiative and competence and all those things. So, they are sort of self-selected as young people who, although they have problems in their lives, also have great qualities that help them be leaders.

ILLÈNE: I have found amongst the kids I have interviewed who choose to engage in gardening programs a lot of responsibility and commitment, but I had never seen a group work by themselves. Perhaps, they work alone sometimes in other gardens, but I just was not present to witness that.

KOLEVZON: Oh, cool. They are an unusual group—well, hopefully, not. I think also it is the age. I think there is a certain age, if young people are given an opportunity, they care a lot about the world and they want to make a difference. They look for ways to express that if they are available. I think that one of the great things about garden programs is that it is a pretty clear, available, practical way for young people to do good in the world should they want to express that. Especially with more consciousness in society around the kind of issues that gardens solve, I think it is a natural way for them to do something like that. Not all young people are at that point in life in their teenage years, but if they get to be seventeen, eighteen, they start to think about the future and their lives. If they want to affect the world positively, this is a possible way for them to get into it.

ILLÈNE: Sione is fourteen, Rosanna is sixteen, Javier is sixteen, and Neo is eighteen. So, it is a range.

KOLEVZON: That's true. Also, that is the beauty too. They can be affected by older peers. The garden founder who started it really established a peer-to-peer leadership ethic. It was clear that as you got more experience, you got more responsibility. So that sets up a thing where the younger people are much more influenced by their older peers rather than feeling that they are in the young people's program that is run by adults. That kind of makes an easier transfer of responsibility over to the younger ones. Do you know what I mean?

ILLÈNE: Yes, I do, and I saw that. And I saw it in Oakland Leaf. Do you know Matthew?[1]

---

1. Matthew Linzner of Oakland Leaf and the two sets of brothers he mentors will be discussed in depth in Chapters 18 and 19.

KOLEVZON: Oh, yeah. Oakland Leaf, they do the same thing. I know everybody that works in school gardens in Oakland.

ILLÈNE: One of the other things I saw is that the people who take on mentorship of young people in gardens are natural mentors.

KOLEVZON: What I am noticing now with classroom teaching is that it is really a way for adults to thrive as well, like when they are in a position of mentoring young people. My classroom management skills are not the best. My management skills in general are not the best, but I am a really good mentor for small groups or individuals. I think that is true for a lot of adults. I think if we had more opportunities in society for adults to mentor young people, that adults would do better too. I think adults are not fundamentally different. They still have a desire to contribute to society, but I think the way workplaces are structured and families are structured, we are an economy of scale and a specialized society. There really are not mentorship opportunities. I think when they do exist, adults really thrive as well. Teachers, they got into [teaching] because they want to work with young people. They love young people, but they spend much of their lives stressed out and, unfortunately, most of the time spent during their day is spent in a role with young people that I think is much more challenging for them than their natural role, so gardens are a great opportunity for them as well. As a matter of fact, I know teachers who literally have stayed in the job because of their opportunities to work in gardens with kids.

ILLÈNE: Have you noticed how the kids have changed over time as you have watched them?

KOLEVZON: I wish I was around often enough to say that, to really testify to that. I ran into one of our graduates who was in the program for two years in a row. He was on the BART [Bay Area Rapid Transit] the other day, and I ran into him. He is now working at the zoo. He was telling me he really loves working at the zoo. He finds it really fulfilling. He enjoys the relationships he has developed there. It seems like he has made that transition to a potentially successful career. I don't know if it will be what he will do for the rest of his life. He was a young man and he was happy! When I run into other kids that I have known in the past, you just don't know if things are going to work out for them, especially in Oakland where there are a lot of things that can happen to you. To see a young person in that position in life just knowing that they are going to be successful and contribute to the community and to the world, they are doing something positive and at all levels. And that means the world to me. So, I think I get little glimpses of that. You get it more and more as they get older when they are in these programs. You can see those moments where you think,

"Wow! This could be this person's future. They could be all those things. They could be happy. They could be contributing. They could help make a more positive world." It's an overused word, but a more sustainable world, one where we could actually live here in a healthy way. Those are the moments where, as they happen more and more, you see that the program that is affecting the young person is also affecting the world around them, hopefully, on some level—the subconscious of the universe.

ILLÈNE: Yes, I know what you mean. How many kids in the course of a year are involved in the PUEBLO garden program and how many sites? Salina talked about working at Stonehurst. She was working at the zoo planting trees. Was that part of PUEBLO too?

KOLEVZON: It was. You know, we are a young and growing organization, so sometimes you have to be opportunistic. You have to hustle, especially because the school system changes a lot. For example, we started our partnership with an academic program called SUDA, but the school closed and that is why we moved down the hill to Castlemont. The garden we built before was a large school and community garden. That garden sort of got turned over to community members, but just Friday, I was up there at a new school up there. I was meeting at that school with the principal and their fiscal agent because an alternative school just moved in there because they needed a facility. They offered us a contract to run programs with their youth during the school day. It is an academic credit class. We are always creative in looking for opportunities; that is how we have to be. So, the gardens exist in different incarnations, continually transforming. It's a part of growth, and I think that sometimes in these developing phases, you have to be real creative. So, PUEBLO I could define in a general way. We work in partnerships with schools in East Oakland because it is the easiest way to access young people. It has an institutional component that is more sustainable. If we disappear, if we move on to other things or whatever, there is a continuing program with institutional support. I also feel that when there is a strong partnership, there are more resources brought to a common mission. At PUEBLO, we work with community partners. We don't really work in isolation. So, the way our partnership works at Stonehurst Elementary, we provide young people and adults with support for the development of their garden programs and with stewardship for the garden itself. So, the form that has taken is we actually helped build the garden two summers ago with a crew of young people. We worked on it this past summer too to develop the infrastructure a little more. We have provided young people during the year to help support an after-school elementary school garden-based program.

ILLÈNE: One thing Salina talked about was the aquaculture system she learned to build at Castlemont with fish and plants. Does that continue now with a science class program?

KOLEVZON: That was actually part of an after-school job-training program. Our after-school [program] is really a funded job-training program for our students who take academic classes through us. That is really what our garden-training program has become now too. They get paid with city job-training funds and during school, they take academic classes. All the students who are in job training are also in our academic classes.

ILLÈNE: Is it part of violence prevention and creating a healthier environment for youth?

KOLEVZON: You got it.

ILLÈNE: Almost all the kids I interviewed in Oakland talked about the streets and the danger and that gardening was their conscious choice to be involved to keep them off the streets. In these job-training programs, do you talk to them directly about these programs as an alternative to gang life? Is that part of a conversation the adults have with the kids or is this something the kids just know from living in Oakland?

KOLEVZON: I have never had a conversation with them like that. I mean, it is pretty obvious to everybody. There is no one who is not in that position or conscious of it. We don't really need to have that conversation with them. It isn't just gangs, actually. Most of the people who get involved with violence at some point are not in gangs. It is just something that affects a lot of youth in general.

ILLÈNE: I was reading the statistics on youth violence on some Web sites that Rashidah [Grinage] referred me to and I was appalled, but I did not personally feel at risk on the streets that I walked down in Oakland.

KOLEVZON: You probably are not. It probably would not affect you, but it is part of young peoples' world.

ILLÈNE: The kids mentioned it to me and they told me they did not want it in their lives.

KOLEVZON: I don't know how religious you are, but I think it is almost like an internal thing. You can really look at it externally. People tend to externalize things, especially when they are young, but you can look at it internally. They are making a spiritual choice. If they made a different choice, they would get involved with violence and gangs. Something would affect them. And maybe they wouldn't. Maybe they would be in another place where they would get involved with drugs or alcohol. At some level in life, you just have to make a spiritual choice. The way that comes out is, well, you could be a positive person and work for the good of the community, but there are forces around that could push you the other way or that will try to drive you out if you make that choice. That is true in the world. That is a choice human beings all have to make in life. I don't think it is endemic to Oakland.

ILLÈNE: But compared to Colorado, it is night and day. Kids in rural Colorado where I live are not faced with needing to make a choice to garden to protect themselves from armed youth gangs. The kids in Oakland are being faced at a younger age with more serious choices.

KOLEVZON: Definitely, it is true. They know that if they are not careful, their lives are at risk. And even if they are careful, their lives are still at risk. There are certain things they can do to definitely protect themselves. And if they have a positive attitude towards themselves and their lives, they will tend to do those things, whereas if they get depressed or don't have the will, there are more things that can happen to them.

ILLÈNE: You and the other people running youth gardens are making the container to hold these youth and make it possible for them to garden. You are doing the groundwork that has to be done. Are there things I have not asked you about the intention behind this youth program that people should know?

KOLEVZON: It's up to folks like yourself to make the world understand. It's the voices, it's the stories that make life meaningful and, ultimately, are the creative voice behind the world.

ILLÈNE: Do you have a story about kids and gardens that would be an enlightening story for people to hear?

KOLEVZON: I can give you one good story about one young person that when she was around fifteen, she was in my class as a freshman. Our class was a really special class, and it was the first time we had taught it. I co-taught it with a friend of mine. It was really about trying to connect the young people with the living world in the place where we live. We would have three hours a week and go on all these field trips. We did some creek restoration. We did some water studies. We would see the special places of the East Bay and learn the stories. She was actually the least interested of the twelve or fifteen students. She would show up every day, but she didn't do the work. She would never talk. She didn't participate, but she was around, but was really uninvolved. They had to do a final project. She chose to see all the creeks that come into Lake Merritt [a lake that is near downtown Oakland]. She wanted to see what they looked like and how they worked. She came to me the day before the project was due and she said, "Can you take me to see these creeks? Can you tell me where to go?" I told her it was really far up in the hills and it would be hard for her to ride a bike there. We had given some students bikes to use. So, she said, "Could you drive me?" It's totally illegal, right, so I can't believe I did this, but I actually borrowed the principal's car and I drove her up to several of the creeks way up in the hills above Oakland. One of the creeks we went to is in the back of a cemetery and I think they are turning it into a baseball field now. It had a long history, Blair Park. There are waterfalls there and a spring that comes out of the ground. It's a place where people go for picnics on Sundays. So, we went there. There are ancient oak and bay trees. We went up and we saw a family of deer wandering through the forest right where the stream was. Her eyes really lit up. I could tell this had a big effect on her. She did her project and she actually did a decent project. A year or two later, when she was graduating, she called me and told me she was graduating from school and asked me if I had a bike she could take to college. She was going to UC Santa Cruz. Yeah, well, she is an intelligent person. She just did that adolescent thing where she wasn't engaged with anything. But she ended up getting into Santa Cruz, so I helped her to put together an old bike that she could take to school. And she called me up a few months later and told me that the bike was great, she rode it all around and took her boyfriend with her and found all the creeks in Santa Cruz. And I was, like, "Oh, that's cool." It was a nice thing to hear. And two years later, she contacted me and she told me she was volunteering in this project called the Homeless Garden Project. It was a program started by students at Santa Cruz to help homeless people grow food. She had been helping in this Homeless Garden Project and she was majoring in environmental and community studies field. She said that my class had affected her a lot. It helped her always think about where the water was and the importance of the land and stuff like that in whatever we are doing and helping connect people to those kinds of things, like healthy food. She said that whatever she was doing or wherever she is, she thinks about those kinds of things and gets involved in those kinds of projects. Now, actually, she moved back to Oakland and is working on establishing those kinds of programs. She has been volunteering at Girls Inc., and I think they have hired her by now. I think she is going to end up working in a field helping young people doing those kinds of programs. Last year, her family had never been anywhere. Her father runs a café and her mother cleans houses. They had not been on any kind of trip since they got married thirty-five years ago. They are just struggling to survive. They have six kids. They live in this tiny place in Oakland. A lot of the kids are grown up. She called me up: "I would really like to take my family to Yosemite. Can you help? Can you help get a campsite and drive? My dad is a professional cook and he can cook, but can you help us get there?" They have a van they use for business. We took the van, we packed everybody in, and we rented another car. We drove to Yosemite. We went on a hike and stuff like that, and I could see her parents holding hands looking out over this valley. Deanna told me it was the first time they had been on a trip in thirty-five years. It was her desire to take them somewhere beautiful in California that caused us to go on this trip.

ILLÈNE: And your willingness, Grey, that she felt safe enough with you to ask you to do this for her family. That's a big deal, Grey, to ask someone to take your entire family on a vacation.

KOLEVZON: It is a big deal, but what was amazing to me was I could see her life path going in a really similar way to mine. She had gotten to the point in her life that she is doing the same things I was trying to do as a young adult. It makes me feel great. Actually, I went to her graduation last spring. She graduated from Santa Cruz and invited me, and so I saw her family again and met her boyfriend. I think they got married because they live together here in Oakland. I asked her what she was going to do after graduation, and she said, "My boyfriend wanted to go to Texas because his family is from there, but I really want to come back to Oakland. I am dedicated to my community and I really want to come back to be part of it and all the great things that are happening here." That's what she said.

ILLÈNE: Isn't that amazing? That's a beautiful story and a testimony to the highest level of mentorship in a young person's life.

KOLEVZON: I hope so. I always hope there are a few young people that I have really, really affected. Obviously, you can't really affect the hundreds or whatever that you work with every year. There is no way to, but I always hope there are a few I can affect a lot and that there's a bunch that maybe we can affect a little bit and that other people working with them can. Do you know what I mean?

ILLÈNE: All the kids I talked to in the gardening program are profoundly affected. Thank you.

The mentors I have met running after-school and summer gardening programs have been similar to Grey Kolevzon in their willingness to go more than an extra mile to support the young people they work with and to help them find their way into a fulfilling life. Kolevzon mentioned that school gardens appeal to teachers also because they would prefer their relationship to be one of mentorship with youth rather than the more authoritarian role teachers seem to have in classrooms. He talks about the stress he and other teachers feel in the classroom. The youth have said being in the garden relaxes them, and, most likely, the teachers feel their stress decrease in the garden too and feel more able to relate as mentors.

# 18

# LOVE CULTIVATING SCHOOL YARDS

Ascend School children and intern take compost to their garden under the BART
train track. Credit: Illène Pevec

The Love Cultivating Schoolyards organization focuses on creative education to nurture strong youth and families. The young director, Matthew Linzner, arranged to meet me at the garden that he developed and maintains with youth interns at Ascend School, a charter school serving 347 children, 80 percent of which are Hispanic, in grades kindergarten through 8th. The first new school built in Oakland in many years, Ascend has an attractive building, interesting design, lots of color, and it sits right by the Bay Area Rapid Transit (BART) track. When an elevated train goes by every seven minutes, the noise stops all conversation and very well could impact people's hearing. The lights even went out in the cafeteria on the one afternoon I was sitting in there speaking with the young gardeners.

Two sets of brothers, ranging in age from fourteen to nineteen, serve as interns to teach the younger children to garden in an after-school program. They also do the heavier gardening work that small children can't do. Matthew mentors the interns in the broadest way possible, and they all work together with the first and second graders every Wednesday afternoon.

Matthew and his interns gave me a short garden tour before the elementary children arrived full of enthusiasm to get to work gardening. That day, they were working in the garden that runs below and just at the edge of the BART track behind the school and the school parking lot that is behind the cafeteria. They also created and tend a garden in front of the school, but the vegetables they are growing now and quite a few fruit trees are in this back area, a permaculture forest garden thriving near the school cafeteria door. They also have room for a large pile of shredded bark mulch and a compost pile.

A bright mural painted by students with the guidance of a professional artist decorates the cement walls of the school's outbuildings. Planters made by the garden interns from reused Styrofoam hang on the wall of a storage shed—part of an effort to make new and usable things from a product that is ubiquitous and either goes to waste in landfills or can be retooled to make a planter to green the urban environment. Matthew hopes these up-cycled planters can create a program income stream as well as cut down waste and make barren walls into living walls.

One intern showed me one of his favorite plants, a huge pineapple sage that appeared to be about six feet tall. Covered in red blooms, it exuded a delightful scent. We met with the seven-year-old gardeners in the lunchroom at three p.m. While three interns headed outside with Matthew to guide the younger children in harvesting carrots, mulching part of the garden, and doing some planting, I spoke with Ramón, aged seventeen. We went inside the school in an attempt to get away from the rattling cacophony each passing BART train made. Ramón is younger than his brother, Genesis, who also gardens here and whom I spoke with after Ramón.

RAMÓN: I am currently a senior at Fremont High School [in Oakland]. I got involved in the gardening program after middle school. I started after my 8th grade summer. I started participating with Matthew when I was thirteen. The first summer, I was learning the basics about the flowers, the weeds, the compost, the plants that we wanted, and the plants that we didn't want. After that summer, I think it was during the spring, where Matthew told me about the internship possibility. That sounded like a good idea because I really liked working outside, working with the plants. I had my own little garden at home. I had it before I started the program, so I kind of knew a little bit, but once I joined the program, I learned a lot. And my plants, like, it reflected on my plants the love they got afterwards. They grew so much bigger and they were so much sweeter and everything was nicer. Because at first, my plants would be between green and yellowish, and I wouldn't have enough time to water them, but in the garden, we made, like, a juice that came from the worms and the plants— I don't know what it's called.

ILLÈNE: Compost tea.

RAMÓN: Compost tea. And Matthew would give us bottles, and I would just take it home and add more water, and I would water my plants with that. And it really helped my plants. Yeah, and it also improved our soil at our house. And my neighbor would ask, "What do you do with your plants? What do you do with your plants?" Because he would have a tree that would always die. He would plant a tree every year, but it would always die. And he asked if I would plant the tree for him, and I said, "Well, I could try." And I planted the tree for him, and it is still there to this day.

ILLÈNE: That is wonderful. Your neighbor must have been grateful. You must be so proud. So, you learned a lot that you could use at home. And why did you start your garden at home? Did your parents help you?

RAMÓN: I come from a family that worked the land before, like my grandparents and my parents worked the land in Mexico. They cultivated fruits and vegetables. And, like, I got inspired by that. It's like a good example, a good leadership, like something to look up to. You don't always have to buy the fruits and vegetables at the store where they are polluted and some have, like, a lot of bad things that harm our health. And it's like, I'd rather just grow it. I know what I am putting into the dirt. I know the love I am putting into the plant. And reflecting on that, that's why I do it.

ILLÈNE: You talk about the love you put into the plant a couple of times in talking about your plants and how you garden. Is that something Matthew taught you or your parents or something you feel innately yourself that you are giving love?

RAMÓN: I think in both ways. With Matthew and in my family, we talk about, like if we don't water the plants or if we don't respect them or we step on them or we, like, break off the branches when we are not supposed to or prune them when they are too small or if we cut the main stem of it, the plant is going to get harmed and not get the full attention. If we don't water it, it's going to die. That's the love I was taught to give the plants, like to water it and not soak it, but give it enough water, give it enough time to absorb it.

ILLÈNE: So you have learned it and you have felt it?

RAMÓN: Yeah, I learned it and I felt it.

ILLÈNE: When you garden, is there one sense more than the other senses that you get the most information from?

RAMÓN: I think my nose, and I like the air I breathe in. Everything is much richer and everything is pure and healthy. Rather than if I am walking down the street and a bus passes by and you're, like, "Oh, the nasty air," and we breathe all that in. And I think also, like, my eyes. I like to draw and that inspires me to come out with something creative, like a flower with the nice, bright colors, and also, like, the contrast of the colors. That has helped me a lot with developing my skills inside the garden and outside. It has taught me other skills. It has also helped me to use my hands more, like to be sensitive with some plants and then the ones we have to pull them out by the roots, like the weeds, when they are bad for our plants. Those are some of the main things I have with my senses.

ILLÈNE: How does it make you feel to go out in the garden and smell something you have planted?

RAMÓN: I think it feels good. It feels like that it is helping out the community because sometimes, we give it [the produce from the garden] to the cooking class and they make something out of it and they really enjoy that. And it's just a good thing that we are doing something not just for our own good, but for the community's good. We are doing something to help out the people and that we as young people [are helping]. You don't see that too often, like young people involved in this program. It feels good that I am a part of it. I am hoping that being a role model for other people, like for the little kids, also [for them] to like trying to do something like that in the future, to try to get involved with something like this.

ILLÈNE: So that is a sense of feeling good because you are giving to the community?

RAMÓN: Yeah.

ILLÈNE: How about your body, do you get more relaxed, tenser, more energized? How does your body respond to getting out there smelling the pineapple sage, lemon flowers, or cilantro?

RAMÓN: I think I feel like more relaxed. More energetic and more like, I get more inspired to, like, do things. If I come from school and I am sitting in a class for two or three hours and [then] I get to the garden, I am just like awakened by everything that is going on because of all the bees, all the butterflies, all the flowers, and different colors. I wake up, and that is really nice to have green. It wakes up my eyes and my whole body feels better, more energized.

ILLÈNE: Does time spent in the garden help you focus on something?

RAMÓN: I think it does. I think it is like a break from all the other work, from all the other stressful things. [*A huge noise from the younger kids in the school yelling and shrieking interrupts us and we have to stop a moment. This is the after-school program time, and there are many kids of all ages involved in a wide range of activities.*] It's a break from everything. It's a break from all the stress. I'm a senior already. I am starting to feel like a senior. I am not trying to get senioritis, like they say, none of that. I am trying to stay on top of my work. It's always something, like, stressful because I have to get home, do my homework. And, like, coming here helps me to have a break once a week, have a break to relax, to spend time in the garden, be with the kids, like play around, have fun.

ILLÈNE: Do you think it is easier to do your homework after you have worked in the garden?

RAMÓN: I think it is because I get home, I eat, and then I am more focused, I am more relaxed, less stressed because when I get home from school, I usually get home stressed. I have to walk [home] and I am tired and I just want to take a nap. But when I get home from the garden, I am awake. I am full of energy, like full of life. I want to draw. After I am done, I want to do other things. I want to go play soccer, like do something.

ILLÈNE: So, do you hope to study art more in the future or is it a hobby?

RAMÓN: I want to major in architecture. I really like that because it has to do with math and I found myself good at math and then I also like to draw. And I like different types of architecture. I have been in programs that are helping me get there. I don't know if you have heard of a program called ACE [ACE Mentor Program of America, Inc.]. It has to do with architecture, construction, and engineering, and it has helped me with that because it teaches you what an architect does on a daily basis and we get to work with them. We get to do things. It's something I look forward to, the art. It's not a mural or something like that. It's different kinds of art, that is, like we get to sit down and draw and make figures and abstract buildings.

ILLÈNE: And real buildings too?

RAMÓN: Yeah, and, like, build them. That's what I want to do in my future.

ILLÈNE: Tell me about getting to eat food that you grow. The food that you grew at home, does the food go into your family meals?

RAMÓN: I would plant, like, the basics, like radishes and carrots and cilantro and things like that. Once when my cilantro was nice and big, my mom would make a special meal and we would all eat it together. The taste of the cilantro is much stronger; that's what my mom really liked about it. And she also liked that the radishes were spicier and had more texture. That made me feel good about myself because I am contributing to my family. We come from a middle-class family, like low-class family. I am helping them in a way that I can. I really like being helpful. And also from the garden, from right here, we would have, like, tomatoes or grapes and a lot of little things like carrots and beets and different squash. And we would take them home, and my mom would do something with them and we would use it, like for a snack, or she would make something or bake it; we would eat it. We would use everything we take from the garden.

ILLÈNE: Has gardening changed your eating habits?

RAMÓN: I think it really has changed the way I see things. I am more open-minded now. I would think about fruits and vegetables, and think, "Oh, that is nasty," or I would see a salad and I would be, "Oh, that is not going to taste too good." The things I would grow would be like cilantro and carrots. Carrots are something I always liked because they are sweet and they have a good texture. I don't really like radishes, but my mom does. I really am close to my mom, and she really likes them. The thing that really [changed] I think was because I would eat, like, a lot of hamburgers. Instead of eating, like, a salad, I would eat a hamburger or I would eat junk food. Like, I would go out and we would buy food at Jack in the Box or at another junk food place or Chinese food, but now I would rather eat what my mom makes, like chicken soup, salad, fruit salad, or, like, chicken salad. I am trying to play soccer for my high school. I want to be in shape. I want to be healthy and ready for that. It's a big competition with the other high schools. It's my last year. I want to finish it strong.

ILLÈNE: Are you on the varsity team?

RAMÓN: Yes. This is my first year on it, but we are going to make it.

ILLÈNE: I just read that a lot of the Olympic athletes are drinking beet juice for endurance. They have discovered there is something in beets that helps for endurance in the muscles. It might be great for a soccer player to drink that.

RAMÓN: We have lots of beets in the garden. We have a bed full of beets.

ILLÈNE: Has being in this program increased your environmental awareness and improved your environmental attitudes?

RAMÓN: I think it has because, like, at school, we have a small garden. At Fremont, we have a small garden and it is, like, fenced off and no one would take care of it or people would go and run through it. [The people who would run through it] would be like people who wouldn't listen to their teachers, but coming from a student, they would say, like, "Why? Really? He just told me that?" and they would pay more attention.

ILLÈNE: Did you tell someone not to run through it?

RAMÓN: Yeah, I did. It's like in a courtyard between some portables. So, people would just run through it as a shortcut. I would sometimes call their attention to it and say, "That's not cool. Someone spent time on that. You are ruining someone's project or their next meal that would feed people." They would take it more deeply than if a teacher would have told them that, like, "Don't go through there because you are messing up a plant." But when a student tells them that, they would wonder why I would care about it. It's not mine, but it's the whole environment's. And it's helping, I mean, it helps the pollution and all that. Before, I wouldn't really pay attention and I would be eating something, and I would just throw it away, but now, if I come, I take everything back with me. I would take it to the nearest recycling or trash can. I would go to school and buy, like, a granola bar, and I would eat it and I would put it in my pocket. The gardening class has helped me with all of that. I think if I wouldn't have been in the gardening class, I would have not noticed, but just thrown it away because everybody is doing it. It has really opened up my vision. I would rather just keep it in my pocket and then throw it away later.

ILLÈNE: That's very interesting that you have had the courage to tell your peers at school that they should not run through the garden.

RAMÓN: A lot of them would be rude. They wouldn't listen, but I have noticed that then they wouldn't do it again. I would tell them and they would say something back. At Fremont, we have a lot of violence. They would say something bad, but then they would not do it again. I felt like it was something good I was doing.

ILLÈNE: Congratulations! It takes courage to tell people to stop doing something they are doing. If you had someone in the school board come to you and say, "We are thinking about putting in a garden at another high school and we would like your opinion as to whether you think it would be a good idea for students to have access to garden at high school," what would you say?

RAMÓN: I think that would be more than a good idea. I think that would be a great idea because that would also keep kids out of the streets, keep them out of trouble, keep them, and it would also change their whole mentality: eating healthy foods, thinking about what they eat, thinking about what they put in themselves. And I think it would be a great idea that we have more gardens at high schools and elementary schools because once you go to kinder[garten] and then you start to see that all the bigger people are doing that, all the cool kids and all the kids are eating carrots and eating something sweet, like strawberries, you feel that, you feel happy just seeing that because they are doing something. You have to start when they are small so they can keep doing that. You don't see a lot of high schools with gardens. I think that is where it falls off; in middle school and in high school, it just falls off. I have heard about gardens a lot at elementary school, but I don't really hear about them at middle schools or high school. I think that is really the point where everything vanishes. I think that nobody touches that point no more. Nobody goes there. I think that would be a great idea.

ILLÈNE: So you are on your high school soccer team and doing this garden as an intern. Is there some overlap in what you feel and what you learn being on a soccer team and being a gardening intern?

RAMÓN: I think leadership in the garden. You come and you have to show leadership, like whether it is with the little kids or with your teammates. You can't have a team without teamwork. Like, right here at LCS [Love Cultivating Schoolyards], we are a team. We are a team and if one of our teammates gets hurt, we are going to advocate for them, stand up for them. We make sure we are all on the same page. We are thinking we are all focused on the same thing. And I think that is one of the things that is a big responsibility. It's like if we come to take care of the garden only when we want to, or, oh, we don't have time today, we have to do this, we start slacking off, we start falling off on the garden, it is just like being on the soccer team. If you start hanging out with other people, people that are going to tell you to do other things or just stop going to soccer practice because you have something better to do, you are going to start falling off little by little. You are not going to get the same work, the same... the reflection of your work is not going to be the same. I think gardening has brought us all closer. Like Matthew, I don't seem him as a friend, I see him as a role model, someone to look up to. Like Julio and my brother, Genesis, I also see them as role models, and Julio's little brother, Marcos, I want to be a role model for him. I want to be a role model for the next generation. We are like family members, a family where we share our problems. We share our responsibilities. We share, like, everything. We are connected. Not like any other friend, not like any other role model. We hang out out[side] of the gardening class. We get together. We go hiking. We always go where there is nature, whether it is the soccer field [or] something that is good for us and our health. Like, we will go and play soccer or we will go to the hills or the mountains and we will hike or camp or go swimming. Matthew takes us. I think that has really also changed how I see the world, how I see everything.

ILLÈNE: You are lucky that you have such a rich number of activities to do together that are all healthy. Is there something that I have not asked you that is important about the gardening experience to you that you want people to know about, such as the benefits of gardening to you and other young people?

RAMÓN: That young people should be more involved. It should be more of a priority for them, not like an option. Not like should you play this or do this? It should be something you grow up with. The land is what is feeding you. The land is what is keeping you alive. Everyone should be more into gardening, more into cultivating their own fruits and vegetables, more involved with the community. To take the role model, be that role model. Be the change you want to see.

ILLÈNE: Do you feel that you are being a mentor for these little children?

RAMÓN: I think I do. I think I am a role model for other little kids because this is our second class and today when I came in, they started smiling and like, "Oh, hi Ramón."

ILLÈNE: Today is only the second class with these kids?

RAMÓN: Yeah. They are like, "Hi Ramón." They remembered my name. They are happy to see me just like I am happy to see them. I feel like they look up to me because I am not a full adult yet, and it's like I am a young person. I think that is what motivates them more to keep coming. It is not like a lady or a guy telling them, "Oh, you have to do this, this, and that." It's a young person. They have brothers and sisters and they might be like, "Oh, my brother and sister might be doing this, this, and that, but you guys are doing something good for us." We are there for them—whatever they need, whatever they ask for we are going to be there for them. I think they appreciate that. They show their appreciation.

ILLÈNE: What did you photograph in the garden?

RAMÓN: I took a picture of corn. I took a picture of corn because my family, we come from Mexico. For Mexicans, it is like a basic thing that we eat tortillas. We eat tamales. All of that comes from corn, like masa, and we do bread. We do a lot of things. That is a really important food for us because it's not only my family, but my ancestors; the history of my country is based on that. Corn is the best symbol for me. I thought it was a good symbol for me because it represents me. It represents where I come from and it represents why I am doing it. I feel like it's something that represents me because it has fed me for a very long time. It means a lot to my ancestors and my family in Mexico; my mom and my family used to harvest it. They would work on plantations and grow corn and that is what they lived on.

ILLÈNE: It will be fun to see that picture and print it and send it to you. Tell me why you let me interview you?

RAMÓN: Because it is like a good opportunity and I wanted to let you know what we have learned with this program and the knowledge that I have gained. When I started in 8th grade, I didn't know about corn. I didn't know about it. I thought it grew on a vine or something. I

Fresh corn from the garden. Credit: Ramón

didn't really pay attention. I didn't think there were different types; I thought it was all trees. I learned a lot of plants that you eat the roots, like jicama and beets and carrots. I learned a lot of things, like all those things I learned, [that] I don't think if you asked somebody else they would be able to respond. That is why.

Everything that Ramón said about how valuable Matthew is to him as a mentor and how he came to be on this garden path to a healthy life he now shares with the young children that he mentors in the garden. His commitment to making the world a better place, where more people connect to the earth and care for it through gardening, gives meaning and direction to his life (Seligman, 2011). He has learned the importance of perseverance and staying focused for success (Duckworth and Seligman, 2005).

I interviewed Ramón's older brother, Genesis, aged nineteen, next since he needed to leave early for his other job. Genesis began by telling me how long he has been with the program and how he had become involved.

GENESIS: This is my fifth year. I was in 7th grade going into 8th grade. A lot of people just went out in the streets. There is still a lot of gang activity now, but, at that time, there was a lot of gang activity and I didn't want to be one of them. So, I decided to do something better with myself. What better than to help out with a garden? I always wanted to help in a garden. It would have been nice, you know, working with people. We met Matthew because of Urban Promise Academy; he was our soccer coach. He worked here as well. He was the head of the garden. We got together with him. He said he would get us an internship, and we were all happy to do it.

ILLÈNE: Did you ever see your parents plant a garden?

GENESIS: Plant a garden like this? Not really, but just plant trees, like fruit trees and roses and all that. A big garden that we got things out of? No, but an apple tree, a rose garden, just fruits. My mom loves roses. Every time we had a little money, we would get her roses because we knew she loved roses. We liked her being happy, so we kind of contributed to that.

ILLÈNE: How nice. Does your mom like the fact that you bring home vegetables?

GENESIS: She loves it. She loves it. She loves the fruit because it is organic because it doesn't have a lot of chemicals. Then, at the same time, she loves it because she knows we are not out there doing bad things. She knows we are doing something good. We are helping some other people. She is happy that we are doing this. The last class we had was about three years ago. So, this is our second year.

ILLÈNE: The second year you have worked with the younger children? So, what it is like for you to be mentors to younger children the way Matthew has been for you?

GENESIS: It's just a great feeling, you know. It is just joy to come here and work with little kids. Like two years ago, we used to see the little kids and how their faces got all happy. They used to get happy. We just came here and they all crowded around us: "Oh, what are we going to do today? What are we going to do today?" I think that is one of the best feelings somebody could ever get because you are setting a good example for the little kids to follow in the end. It's a good-ass feeling. It's a great feeling we can get from the little kids.

ILLÈNE: Your garden has all different kinds of food. Has the chance to grow fresh fruits and vegetables changed how you eat over the last few years?

GENESIS: I was always like a healthy person, you know. I was always in shape and everything. And yeah, it has. I would rather eat fruits and vegetables over hot Cheetos and that all the time.

ILLÈNE: I hear a lot about hot Cheetos in Oakland.

GENESIS: Yeah, trust me, a lot of people in Oakland, that's all a lot of people do. I would rather eat fruits and vegetables. I am not too big on vegetables, but there are certain ones I eat of course. It has helped a lot because, you know, instead of taking a break and going out to a store to buy something to eat, we just eat from the garden. It's good for our health and everything.

ILLÈNE: You have been doing this all the way through high school. Do you find that gardening helps to focus your mind?

GENESIS: Yeah, it does. It helps me focus my mind and it helps me, what you call, if I have, if I have problems and everything, it helps me get rid of them. Or just, it makes the problems seem easier. I work with little kids; they like, they help me. And after that, I just, my girlfriend, we share, like, a little thing. And, yeah, after that, the problem doesn't seem all that bad. Or I look at it in another way than before that I was thinking so we can fix the problem.

ILLÈNE: Do you think that ability to stand back from your problem and see it in a new way; does that come from having quiet time or from interacting with the little kids and having their energy and enthusiasm?

GENESIS: It's their energy pretty much. They help me lift it up and forget about it. I focus on them, and they make me forget about it. I focus on them. They make me forget about it. They always come with a positive attitude. I have to come to them in the same way. I can't have them all happy and me depressed. I like to see them smile. I like to see them happy. I try to do the same thing. That's how I think. We lift each other up. If they have a problem, you know, I'm not too into that, but I tell them, "If you need anything." I tell them, "What's wrong?" I am there for them. If they are confident to tell me, they will tell me, but if it's not me, it can be somebody else. If they are not comfortable with someone, that is how it is. We each help each other. That is how it's always been. [*We are sitting in the cafeteria talking when a BART train goes by, making a huge, loud, long noise and causing the lights to go out for a moment. I am wondering what the impact is on children's learning to hear so much noise and see lights going off when a train goes by.*]

ILLÈNE: Do you find that gardening changes your stress levels?

GENESIS: Yeah, it reduces them. I am not really a stressful person. I am not stressing all the time, but when I am in the garden, I forget about it. I give my garden all my 100 percent. At the end, I know it's good for me and it's good for the school. I'm helping them. I like helping them. I like helping the school. If I come here, the whole stress goes away. If I am stressed, I don't bring all the bad energy. I just put all the effort into the plants. My grandpa used to tell me, "If you are feeling bad, the plants feel it." My grandfather used to grow corn. So, he's like, "If the plants know you are upset, if you are doing just a crappy job, it is not worth it. You know, 'Why is he doing it?' You got to take your time." You got to do everything with courage. Not courage, you got to do everything with love, you know. So, yeah.

ILLÈNE: You got a good lesson from your grandfather. Now, you are in a program with the same theme. You have a long family tradition of relating to the land and taking care of things. Do you think being in this program has increased your environmental awareness? Would you be more likely to be an environmental activist as a result of this work?

GENESIS: Yeah, 'cause the garden, all the trees and all that, they give us oxygen. We got to take care of that. That is pretty much it. We got to take care of that 'cause if we don't do it, we are not going to survive. It's not just for us. You know, when we are older, the little kids are going to do it. So, if we chop down all the trees, that might not matter to us, but to the other generations, it probably will make a big difference. That's why if we start now working with the little kids, it helps us a lot. If we start now, then they start. So, we are going to keep it going. One day, if we are not here, they are going to do it and teach other kids and other kids and other kids.

ILLÈNE: What are you doing in college?

GENESIS: I am doing civil engineering.

ILLÈNE: Has doing gardens influenced you in a way to study civil engineering?

GENESIS: There is not really a big tie like that. Since I was little, I wanted to be an architect, but then after I got into it, and I got into talking with engineers and learning what they did, that pulled my attention even more. But every time since I was little, I used to take care of the plants and everything. I think in elementary [school], we were part of the garden class.

ILLÈNE: Really? So, you started this very early in your life?

GENESIS: It was probably just a year. I don't remember that well, but we used to be part of the garden class. I think it's beautiful, nature and everything. If we work and do something about it, it's even going to be better.

ILLÈNE: Do you notice if one of your senses more than any other pulls your attention in the garden?

GENESIS: It's probably what I am smelling. And I think it is a little bit of everything 'cause, you know, if I am down there pulling roots, I feel it. You know, I feel it. If I have to, when I want to take a break, I just go smell some flowers or something. If we have fruit, we go eat something. It's pretty much everything. At certain times, certain things more than others, but pretty much everything pops out at one point.

**ILLÈNE:** How do these direct sensory experiences make you feel in the moment?

**GENESIS:** To be honest with you, they make me feel very good because I feel like I put a lot of effort into it and that is like a little reward. Getting a little reward. When we were here, there was nothing. All the paths, there was nothing. We had to bring in compost and throw it on top and we had to mix it and everything else. Oh! The first two years, all we did was dig all this garden and the south side garden [located on the other side of the school], but after that, it was worth it. I was looking back, I think Matthew has some pictures if he wants to show you, but looking back at both gardens, it's a good feeling. Even though I didn't come, this wasn't my school, I feel good. I am doing something good for some people. I am not out there doing something bad. I am doing some good. I am not wasting my time. I am doing something that is beneficial for the youth and me. I am doing something good. I am doing something good for other people too.

**ILLÈNE:** What did you take a picture of?

**GENESIS:** I took a picture of the fence because it took us a summer to build it. It was the first time and we didn't bring nobody. It was just us. I kind of had an idea 'cause the only thing I knew was how to cut boards, cut boards and everything because I had my class.

**ILLÈNE:** You had a carpentry class in high school?

**GENESIS:** Yeah, in high school. And I loved that class. I used to make checker boxes and everything. I got into it. So, let's just do it. He's [Matthew] like, "All right. Let's do it!" I cut up all the pieces, we all did. We took our time, but, at the end, it was good because every summer, we came, and during summer school, they used to step on the plants. We don't want that no more. We want these gardens to last. That's why we put up our fence. We set up our barrier. You know, we are going to be here.

**ILLÈNE:** Is there anything that I forgot to ask you about the value of gardening for young people that you would like people to read about in this book?

**GENESIS:** Just that if they would take the time to come and do what we are doing, they are going to understand that it is hard work, but, at the end, they are making someone's life, they are putting a smile on someone's life. It doesn't matter who it is, they are making someone happy.

Listening to these brothers both speak of the love they bring to their gardening work touched me deeply. They value their Mexican agricultural heritage, their grandfather who taught them to care for their plants with love, and Matthew who gives them the opportunity to experience Love Cultivating Schoolyards and the smiles and happiness it brings to children. This is the only program where I interviewed two sets of brothers working together in one garden. Genesis expresses exactly what positive psychology has found: if you do something good for someone else, it will make you feel good too. Doing something good for others also takes away your own problems by giving you a new perspective and purpose (Seligman, 2011).

Ramón and Genesis discuss the change in their eating habits towards healthier foods and the pleasure in sharing this healthy food not only with the young children they mentor but also with their own family. They express the energy, joy, relaxation, and pride in what they achieve as food growers and mentors to younger children. We will see these same elements expressed by the next pair of brothers who complete the Oakland Leaf youth gardening team.

The Ascend garden fence the brothers built. Credit: Genesis

# 19
## BUILDING A GARDEN BUILDS US

The Oakland Leaf program interns are two sets of brothers. Similar to Genesis, Julio, aged eighteen, has been gardening with Matthew through Love Cultivating Schoolyards since he was thirteen. He and Genesis have worked together all that time and brought their younger brothers, Ramón and Marcos, into the program too. I asked Julio what kept him gardening for the past five years.

JULIO: I am really close with Matthew, you know. I think he has influenced me a lot. And just nature, in general, is a good thing in our environment. So, just working with our garden and dealing with the soil and the earth is a great experience. I am really motivated to learn new experiences and new things with the garden and the plants. At first, I couldn't distinguish between a weed and a plant. Now, I can probably say I can master the difference between a weed and a plant. Even just with that, it feels good to be helping the environment become more natural with the plants. I think it helps in this environment with such a tremendous amount of buildings.

ILLÈNE: When did you become an intern?

JULIO: It was actually three years ago. I was still learning. I am still learning now. And just dealing with kids at high school, I wasn't aware of their energy and our energy and how we could manifest with that energy. This year will be our second year teaching this class.

ILLÈNE: How do the hands-on activities of gardening—shoveling, planting, etc.—make you feel when you start and then when you are done after an hour or two?

JULIO: It's just a great feeling. You know, at first, you see the visual of this pavement where you could create a beautiful garden. So, at first, you know it is going to be hard work, but you know with dedication and hard work, you are going to accomplish so much. For instance, the garden outside—that was just all dirt and really hard soil. Seeing it now, it is a good feeling you get. I am proud to say I was part of that accomplishment. And, you know, even by just seeing this tiny flower, it means a lot, especially if it's your first one to plant.

ILLÈNE: Were you involved in planting that lemon tree that is totally covered in flowers?

JULIO: Yeah, sure. Everything that is out there, we all participated in. And, you know, we all worked together to try to create beautiful gardens. Over the years, we have worked with different people, interns, roughly at the age of high school students. Now, me and Genesis are the ones that have been in this program for the longest.

ILLÈNE: Are you aware of your sense of smell when you garden?

JULIO: I think it is just a great feeling when you smell something you are attracted to. For example, we have a flower that is called the pineapple sage. It smells so good, you know. At first, I wouldn't know what it was called, but now I am aware of that plant and it smells so good. And to the younger kids, we teach the children and tell them about the pineapple sage, and they seem very attracted to it. Just to share the same feeling with them feels so good. You know, we try to teach the younger kids what we know. That way, they can grow and teach it to the younger kids. That is the evolution we are trying to have, the cycle. Hopefully one day, we can reach that goal.

ILLÈNE: Well, you are already one of those younger kids who is now older teaching other kids. That has been your evolution already as a gardener and young man. What about the stuff you get to taste that you have grown?

JULIO: Two years ago, we had this food stand where we would harvest all the fruits and vegetables and sell them on this [Fremont High School] campus for a cheaper price than they would be in the store. It was a huge success in my point of view. Every child and every parent would buy carrots and tomatoes. It just feels good. We are helping the people in our community and the environment not only by providing them healthy food, but telling them the great things that could be done by building a garden.

ILLÈNE: Has growing food changed your food choices?

JULIO: Yeah, tremendously. At first, growing up, I would eat fruits and vegetables, but not as much as I do now. I can see it is a big impact in my life, eating healthy. I would rather tell the children to eat an apple or banana rather than eat candy. Growing up, you have the mentality to teach the younger kids about eating healthy, just learning through the years.

ILLÈNE: Do you come here from school? Are you a senior?

JULIO: I am in college.

ILLÈNE: Congratulations! You come here from having had some classes? Have you noticed if coming here changes your ability to focus?

JULIO: Well, honestly, it just feels good. I feel relief coming to the garden, actually, from all the stress of school and everything dealing with that. Just coming to the garden just feels more peaceful. I like the feeling of being in the garden. It just opens my mind. Smelling the plants in the garden and the soil, it just feels so right, so relaxing. So, I think it is a huge, a big factor, you know, coming to the garden. If I were to be in the garden and then go home and do homework, I would be a little more motivated to do my homework than just sitting home. For some reason, I don't know how to explain it, just keeping your mind busy, just being active by going to the garden and then going home to do homework [makes it easier to focus]. But every now and then, I believe every human should have some type of rest. But the garden is just another world.

ILLÈNE: Sometimes gardening is hard work, but not always. If you've worked hard outside, you're breathing deeply. You're sweaty. How do you feel?

JULIO: Personally, I like to workout. So, I see no negative point of view in that. If I get sweaty working in the garden, I get two positives: working out and helping the garden. So, I just get home, take a shower, eat, do homework, and on to the next day. But it just feels good. It's tough, no doubt, but it's good to workout.

ILLÈNE: Do your parents garden?

JULIO: Not too long ago, I asked my mom about her childhood and what it was like. And [I found out that] the majority of my family worked in the fields in Mexico and that, honestly, never came into my mind. I wasn't really processing that. Like, okay, she worked in the fields. I never asked myself what it would be like or how it would feel like until now. It's not as tough, but I can have a picture of what it would be like in huge fields. It's intense. But I got to appreciate what we have.

ILLÈNE: Did your mother express that she found some pleasure in it or only that it was hard work?

JULIO: There is always a positive and a negative. The positive was that she was working in hard times. Just working with the earth, that is probably a positive for everybody. The negative was that it would be hard work and low pay. So, yeah, it's kind of different from now.

ILLÈNE: If someone on the Oakland school board came to you and asked you about putting in a garden at another school and if you thought it was worth the money, what would you say?

JULIO: Yeah, definitely. It's not even just the garden, you know. It's dealing with the kids and showing them the positive things of building a garden. I think it is a tremendous effort and a great work building with the kids at a young age. At first, you know, you have to deal with the younger kids. You know, as a high school intern, I noticed it was much more attractive for the younger kids to work with high school students than with adults for some reason—I can't really explain it. If students and older students could work together, environmental-wise and community-wise, it would be a whole better place.

ILLÈNE: Does it feel good to have the younger children look up to you?

JULIO: It feels good for sure! Even outside school, you are walking by somebody and they say, "Hey, you are that guy that works at the garden. I like your program." It just feels good hearing that from a young kid. If it keeps them from the streets and more involved with gardening or just after-school programs, I feel good about it.

ILLÈNE: Do you think your environmental attitudes and awareness have changed as a result of gardening?

JULIO: Oh, yeah, tremendously! At a young age, you know, out here, it was tough for me, for a lot of us. And just being involved with Matthew and his program, it was a great experience! It has changed my perspective in a whole lot of ways. It kept me out of the streets and [brought me into] gardening. As the years went by, I have applied that to my family and I taught them. And they were proud of me. Not only was I not on the streets, but I was doing something positive for my community.

ILLÈNE: Would you take an environmental stand? If this garden were to be threatened, would you talk to the mayor or the governor?

JULIO: Oh, yeah, definitely. Even if it wasn't the garden, if I had worked on something and someone was just going to come and try to take it away, I would stand up for it. All of us, as interns with Matthew and everybody else, building this garden was building us, our friendship. If someone came and tried to destroy this garden, we would all come together and deal with it in a positive way.

ILLÈNE: Is there anything else in your everyday life that allows you to have these collaborative relationships and activities with others?

JULIO: You know, I am an athletic guy, and Matthew was not only my gardening boss, but he was also my soccer coach since middle school. That is how I met him. We have grown so much. We kind of combined soccer with gardening and nature. Me and him, we are really close and with our other intern, Genesis. And I have my brother here too. It just really feels good because we are all a big family. Hopefully, we can make it bigger. It still is one of our goals. As we teach the younger children, maybe they can influence their parents, like [have] them do what we are doing and what they are doing in the garden, and have an impact on their families.

ⵣ

Gardening has given Julio an appreciation for what his mother experienced working in the fields in Mexico when she was young. He recognizes how different his experience is creating a school garden and helping the younger children engage in gardening compared to hers working all day in a huge field for low wages. He notices how much the younger children look up to older youth and identify with them and hopes they will emulate this work to teach their families and other children. Even though he is already in college, he has stuck with this program, helping make gardens and teaching younger children to be the next garden makers.

During the closing circle with the younger children once the tools were put away and hands washed, one seven-year-old boy went around and offered each of us a carrot that his group had dug up and washed that afternoon. Marcos, aged fifteen, had spent his afternoon harvesting carrots with these children. His shy, big smile spoke clearly of a sweet nature, and we spoke together after the young children went home.

MARCOS: This is my second year. When I was going to high school, that summer I started. This is my first time with little kids.

ILLÈNE: What is it like for you to garden outdoors with this friendly group of young men?

MARCOS: Well, it's my brother and my friends, so I know Genesis and Ramón. I know them, so I feel comfortable with them, especially Matthew. I know him for a long time now. I don't have to worry about what they'll say, so I just do my thing, like have fun while I do it.

ILLÈNE: Had you eaten fruits and vegetables before you started gardening?

MARCOS: Before that, I didn't really like them. Well, I liked how they tasted, but I wasn't, like, "Oh, they are good for me. I know they are good for me." I didn't know that, so I didn't really eat them. But then I started working, and I was, like, "Oh, they are good for me, I know how to grow them now." I know everything about them now, so I started eating them more.

ILLÈNE: Are you eating less junk food now that you are eating more vegetables?

MARCOS: Back then, I didn't really drink water either or eat vegetables or fruit either. Just chips! Especially with the soccer team with Matthew—it's, like, fruit and vegetables, just good meals.

Carrots the children harvested in the Ascend School garden.  Credit: Illène Pevec

ILLÈNE: Do you feel better?

MARCOS: I feel better. I feel, like physically, I feel better.

ILLÈNE: Have you noticed that if you come to the garden from school, that you feel different after you leave than when you had arrived?

MARCOS: Before, like in school, I feel tired and, like, I want to get home, but when I remember I have sports, I get excited again. Or like, at the end of the period, like I am just thinking about coming gardening, planting, or something, I get excited about it. And after [gardening], I feel good about what I did, what I have done, like what I planted so far that day, what I did.

ILLÈNE: Do you notice if gardening changes your stress levels?

MARCOS: It, like, distracts me from other stuff. I work after school, so that helps me stay off the streets. It distracts me. Like when I am gardening, I am thinking about that, what I am going to do next. What I am planting now? What I am planting next? What I am going to grow? Stuff like that.

ILLÈNE: Do you find that gardening changes your ability to focus in general?

MARCOS: It makes me focus more on one thing. Like, in school, if they are teaching me one certain thing, I used to daydream a lot, but, now, I like really focus on it, just like here at work. When I get to eat the vegetables, it makes me happier and makes me want to do everything and then just relax and then probably eat more fruit.

ILLÈNE: Did your family talk much about their farming background in Mexico?

MARCOS: No. Well, my mom shared with me, like, once when she would go with her sisters and aunties, with her father, my grandpa, when they would go up the mountains in Mexico planting things.

ILLÈNE: What does she think about you gardening in the city?

MARCOS: She is happy. Like I said before, [I] stay off the streets. Also, because it's my brother and Matthew, and my mom knows them. And Genesis and Ramón, and she knows them too. She is happy that I am with them and doing something good for the community and for myself.

ILLÈNE: Are you aware of your senses when you garden?

MARCOS: I always want to smell stuff. I smell everything more. It smells good, so it makes me feel good. The colorful plants, the colorful flowers; they really stand out. But, like, the flowers in the big garden over there, just seeing different colored flowers, I feel everything is brighter, nicer. I feel relaxed. Like, just walking in there, I feel like I am in a different world, all garden world, all plants and flowers, just better, different than being in the street all the time.

ILLÈNE: How does it make you feel to be so young and be a mentor to the younger kids?

MARCOS: It feels good teaching them what I know, what Matthew taught us, and just teaching it to them. Probably, they can grow up and be like me and teach other little kids, just keep it going, just growing, growing, growing. You see their smiles always. It makes me happy. If they are happy, I am happy. I try my best to make them happy. I just play little games with them, like when I tell them to cover their eyes and surprise them. I just smile all the time. That's cool! It helps me think more about the community and what we can do together, what we can make, what we can grow!

ILLÈNE: Did you feel that way before you did this or has gardening had an impact on that for you?

MARCOS: Back then, I was more shy and wouldn't interact with many other people, like in the community, just my family and friends, let's say. But now, [I interact with] the community with little kids now. I teach my little cousins now, like at home sometimes or when I can. It's good.

ILLÈNE: Has your confidence changed to talk to other people?

MARCOS: Like in big groups? Kind of. Like in my little group or small little groups, it helps a lot. I can actually lead stuff. If I know what I am doing, I can like lead people, but before, I couldn't. Before, I'm like the one being taught. It feels nice like, leading people.

ILLÈNE: That's great to have developed that strength. If someone from the Oakland school board came and told you that they were thinking of putting in a garden at a high school and wanted to know what you thought of what it would do for high school students, what would you say to them?

MARCOS: I'd say, yeah, 'cause it distracts them from other things, like bad things that happen living in Oakland, all the bad things. It distracts them from that. Putting work in the garden takes time, that's like stuff you can do besides being in the streets.

ILLÈNE: Do you find that your energy level changes when you garden?

MARCOS: At school, like after my last period, I feel tired, but when I get here and I get started and I get in it, I get all my energy back and I want to do more and more and more, all I can. And the next week is the same, just try and put all my effort and all the energy I can.

ILLÈNE: What did you photograph in the garden?

MARCOS: I took a picture of an empty [garden] bed—like with nothing, just dirt—with corn growing on the sides. That represents to me that we start off with nothing and then we have to work with patience, like grow something big, something cool, something good for us.

The picture that Marcos took representing going from nothing to something big, cool, and good reflects what he also discovered inside himself by mentoring the elementary school children in the garden: the leadership he now exercises through teaching gardening to the younger children. Marcos's improved diet includes more fruits and vegetables and comes with a desire to be healthy, reflecting what he has learned with the Love Cultivating Schoolyards team. Marcos and the other young men on the Love Cultivating Schoolyards team are working to change their community for the better. They have committed their adolescence to making Oakland a more peaceful and healthier place for everyone and are very proud of their work. They learn to be mentors themselves by teaching and nurturing the little children as they all care for the garden together.

When I finished interviewing the four interns, it was about five p.m. I attempted to leave the school by the school's front door, but I found it locked. The janitor cleaning the hall told me there had been a school lockdown because someone had shot a child in Oakland. He directed me to go out the back door and through the parking lot to leave. I could not figure out how that was safer than using the front door, but I followed those directions back to where the garden is. Matthew, Julio, Ramón, and Marcos were all getting into Matthew's pick-up truck to leave. They didn't know anything about the shooting. While I walked from the back of the school to the main street that went through the Fruitvale neighborhood to wait for my bus, I wondered what child had been shot and why. Was this child alive? I watched carefully for signs of danger, but I saw nothing alarming.

Garden bed: going from nothing to something good.  Credit: Marcos

Wall mural at the Ascend School garden expresses the garden program's spirit. Credit: Illène Pevec

## 20

# GAME THEORY,
# OPTIMIZING A FOOD BUSINESS

In 2012, Game Theory Academy, an Oakland nonprofit, launched West Oakland Woods (WOW) Farm, a new urban farm project that integrates game theory, financial management, and a business operation. Through the running of a food-growing business, its aim is to give youth the opportunity to train in food growing, money management, and business skills. This particular orientation to growing food, particularly using game theory, is unique in the programs I encountered. I did not have a chance to visit their urban farm, but I was grateful that I could speak with some of the people involved by phone. Sara Weihmann, the program's farm manager, explained the program's first year's operations to me by phone in November of 2012.

SARA: A man named Philip Krohn had been the caretaker of this land for nearly ten years. This is a private piece of property. He had worked with a couple of organizations in Oakland that do urban agriculture projects, like City Slicker Farms and Oakland Based Urban Gardens. He wanted to do something different that was more business oriented and worked with high school youth. He teamed up with Patricia Johnson, the executive director of Game Theory Academy, to start the program. Game Theory Academy teaches youth personal financial management—what to do with money when you have it, what the credit system looks like, why it is advantageous to have a bank account, how to save up for things you want, how the economy works, that sort of thing. I was invited to get involved because of my direct experience with farming and with urban agriculture projects. I came in as farm manager and have been leading and writing the curriculum for the program. So that is how it got started: our three brains working together on what to do with this land and how to incorporate youth and business training.

I got my masters in sustainable business and administration from Dominican University [of California]. I started a business called All Edibles, an edible landscaping company in the East Bay that does mostly residential edible spaces. I worked on a farm in San Leandro for a year as farm manager and I have been on the board of City Slicker Farms for the last five or six years. So, I have sort of been in the urban agriculture scene, but this is my first experience with young people running an urban farm. We currently have six youth between the ages of sixteen and eighteen.

ILLÈNE: How did you enlist youth to participate?

SARA: We had an open application process. We distributed applications like wild fire to get our first round of youth. We went to local high schools, networked with teachers, and handed out applications with a description of our project. We went to food justice and urban agriculture groups in West Oakland. We were specifically seeking youth who lived in West Oakland, went to school or had family here.

I think probably two of our first cohort of youth had prior exposure to gardening, but the primary reason a lot of the youth were interested in this opportunity was because it was so new to them and they didn't have a lot of experience. A few of them had school gardens at the schools they were coming from, but I don't know how involved they were. It was a pretty new experience for all our youth. They are not taking on the risk. They get paid a wage of $9 an hour. The program is about business education, where they are earning their money and keeping track of their revenue, cost of goods sold, what their net income is. The finances are different for the cost of the program and the finances of the business.

ILLÈNE: Do the youth gardeners get the profits from their businesses or does it go into the program?

SARA: Some of the profits. We haven't figured out exactly what this looks like yet. What we have discussed is that a percentage of what is earned when cost of goods sold is taken out and probably some labor costs (we are not entirely sure) would be split with a percentage going back to the program and a percentage split between the youth to access like a scholarship fund so that if they want to buy a computer or put it towards college, they would have the ability to do that. They are all collaborating on a business that sells the produce they grow to local restaurants. WOW Farm is one cohesive business where the youth are working together.

ILLÈNE: Did you already have some customers or did the youth go out and find them?

SARA: This particular group had a really unique opportunity to forge the way with establishing these initial relationships with restaurants. I don't know how we will simulate that in coming years. There were no previous relationships before now. I had personally talked to a couple of chefs, but nothing was set in stone. We trained the youth on professional communications and business relationships, preparing them to present a message about our farm in a two-minute sound bite. We set up interviews and meetings with different chefs and the youth presented who we were and what our product was, what our prices would be, etc. I think it was a really interesting experience for them. They were initially very nervous about talking to the chefs because they had seen Hell's Kitchen and these shows where the chefs are mean and don't want to give anyone the time of day. I think they were pleasantly surprised to see how the chefs here were open to hear their message and to work with them and collaborate.

ILLÈNE: When did the youth begin?

SARA: They started in February 2012 and will be working on the farm until Thanksgiving 2012.

ILLÈNE: Have they been able to make a profit?

SARA: That is something that is difficult to know because the program is taking care of their labor, so their cost of business is just water and seeds. They are making quite a lot of money. They are making a huge profit. I think we are going to talk about next year having it so that it reflects the cost of labor too. We have talked about keeping track of the time they spend working on the farm and the time in class learning, and the program pays for their time in training in business skills and agriculture and their businesses pay for their time spent farming. I think we knew our program was unique in the beginning, and we are considering having two cohorts next year for a shorter duration rather than just one so we would have the ability to work with more youth. It's been great to have this deep mentorship model that we have this year, but the more opportunities we can create, the better!

ILLÈNE: Is it two of you working with the youth?

SARA: It's all three of us. Philip is a sculpture artist who has a lot of various projects going on. He is often at the farm and serves as a mentor both on the farm and also in the business sessions. Trish [Patricia Johnson] specializes in the classroom education, the personal finance, and the administrative functions with the youth. As the farm manager, I implement the farm training and operations. I also have created many of the business lessons and arrange for guest speakers from the community to present to our youth. Yesterday, we had a man who works as a planner for the City of Oakland. That was really exciting for them. They are clearly inspired by all the different types of jobs there are and the various role models we have in our community. I think the farming leadership is really strong in this program, and these youth are interested in growing food, but they are also compelled by the business aspect quite a bit. I have been trying to bring in lots of different kinds of business owners for them to learn from. It has also been interesting to hear them draw parallels between what happens on the farm and what happens in life. The other big thing for these guys has been being outside more. Someone was saying the other day that they felt like they noticed the hints of the season changing more than they ever had before because they are connecting with the same space each week.

৪১

The seasonal changes in the San Francisco Bay Area in California are not as dramatic as they are in places where winter gets much colder and there is snow. The fact that the youth notice the seasonal changes more now that they are gardening and observing the natural progression of plants through their life cycle shows that they are more tuned in to their natural environment than they ever were before. These are cycles humans have observed while seeking food, planting, and harvesting for as long as they have been on this earth—changes urban dwellers may not notice if they spend their time indoors looking at media. The WOW Farm teaches the youth applied business skills and also connects them with the broader natural world.

Sara told me that WOW Farm has a similar challenge with noise as I experienced at Ascend School. BART comes by every seven minutes, and they have learned to deal with the loud, invasive noise by breathing deeply and suspending conversation. I found it troubling from a health perspective that two of the Oakland youth garden projects were right by the BART tracks. The rapid transit serves a very important mass transportation need in a broad urban area, but it certainly presents a noise-level challenge that could cause irreversible hearing loss for anyone repeatedly exposed to the noise (Brody, 2013). I wonder if the local public health department is doing any studies to determine whether there is hearing loss for people habitually exposed to the BART noise. To me, it sounds much louder when I am outside near a passing train than riding inside one of the trains. It concerns me that so many children have this intense noise assaulting them daily while they are at school and after school attending programs like WOW Farm and Oakland Leaf.

During my next WOW Farm interview by computer phone, I met Akira, aged sixteen, and she explained to me how she got involved with urban farming and WOW Farm.

AKIRA: I worked with my mom. She started a garden two years ago through City Slicker Farms. And from City Slicker Farms, I got an internship with them through a youth court organization where I participated. So after that, they were sending me different e-mails about different opportunities. I got an e-mail from them about a program that was half working with the garden and half learning how to run a business. So, it was kind of like a word-of-mouth, networking type of experience, and since I worked with my mom, I thought I would be perfect with it.

ILLÈNE: Had you ever done some gardening at school programs before that?

AKIRA: I had done some, but not specifically at a school. It was with a gardening program for West Oakland residents with City Slicker Farms. One of the things they do is they try to reach the healthy food need in West Oakland by offering people backyard gardens. And through that, they have gardens throughout West Oakland. Some have chickens so they can provide people with eggs, some have squashes, some have collards, depending on the garden. So, that way when they are not building backyard gardens, the people who are not eligible for backyard gardens still have access to the fresh food. They were offering this program for eight weeks throughout the summer. They were offering paid internships for youth. So, every week for eight weeks, I worked with them putting in backyard gardens with my supervisor and a coworker. Then, on Wednesdays, we were working at a greenhouse doing start-up plants to put in the backyard gardens we were building on Saturdays.

ILLÈNE: So you were doing a lot of gardens? How did you begin this program in February?

AKIRA: In February, we did the applications, and then Sara called us back for interviews and she told us if we got the job or not. So, Sara, she is the farm manager, she called us up and she told us we got the job and she told us our first day of work at WOW Farm in West Oakland. It was on a Saturday. This was when we were working from ten to four. They had planned to hire eight of us, but only seven could do it. [On our first day,] we did ice breakers; we organized ourselves with little games by age, whose birthday was first, whose last name was the closest. It was like ice breakers since we would be working with each other. Then, for the rest of the day, we took a large pile of mulch and spread it across the gardens. It is a 3,000-square-foot garden, so we spread it around. Either Monday or Wednesday, we would come in and talk about the business aspect. So, the first couple of months, we partnered with the Game Academy. We worked with Trish and we learned game theory. And she would teach us about business and economics and best self-interest and how the choices we make gardening would affect the income we bring in. So, after we learned about the business aspect, we started choosing different customers because, of course, we have to sell what we grow. We have ten production beds and two kitchen beds. Our kitchen beds are like our beds. They are kind of like stuff where we try things out and where we eat what we grow. We had ten different beds that all had a clover crop [a green manure crop] on top of it. So, we started out one Saturday to cut the clover cover crop and turned it into the bed so the bed could get as much nitrogen as possible so that it could be nice and fertile. From there, we started our basic stuff. I think the first [beds] we did were mustard greens and purple frilly mustard, which are some of our biggest sellers. They have a lot of space, but they don't take a lot of time. We started with that.

After we got that out, our first round, we decided to choose who we would sell our things to. At first, we talked to a chef from Hibiscus, but he went in his own direction and started a catering company. So, we started finding different places to sell to. Sara really got us involved in this process. She got us a couple of different options. There was Café 15, something like that, and then we have Flora, which is our biggest customer, and then Brown Sugar Kitchen, so we had those three restaurants. Two of us, me and a coworker, Paul, we went to Flora, and with Sara, we talked to them. The two chefs could choose. They don't own the restaurant. Their names are Yoni and Riko. We talked to them one day during off-business hours. We talked to them about our program and what we do. They loved the aspect of it being youth-run. Since then, they decided to partner with us. We explained to them how our business works. Because we have a small farm in relation to other farms, we can't produce as much food as a bigger farm, so we try to put out as much as we can in as little a time as possible. We try to do all our gardening in a thirty-day time period. So, we will plant something that is in the ground thirty days. Whereas something like carrots is in the ground for sixty to ninety days. And tomatoes are in the ground for ninety days. We eventually did those just as an experiment, but we learned that based on the economics part of our job, they don't give us as much revenue, so is it worthwhile to do stuff like that. So, we explained to them that we only can grow this much. We started on Wednesdays. When we were working, we would call them and say, "Hey, we have this, that, and the other, and this amount, and this is what we will sell to you come Saturday." They came by to see us. This is when we were having our first open house for the farm. Riko and Yoni are our biggest customers. We sell the majority of our product to them. Sometimes, we will sell to Brown Sugar Kitchen if we have a little extra. Sometimes, we sell to Cafe 15. It just depends on how much we have and what they want. We explain to them that we have radishes, purple curly mustard, mustard greens. At the time, we had carrots, but carrots did not make us a lot of money because they take a lot of time in the ground, so we stopped doing carrots. Arugula was a big one. Pea shoots was one of the first things we did because it was wintertime and springtime and we had a lot of pea shoots and we could grow them in tree rings so that gave us a lot of profit.

ILLÈNE: What do you mean by growing them in tree rings?

AKIRA: We grow our food in beds primarily. When we come back to the business office, we will count how much space we planted and how much product we got out of that area and then how much money we can make from the product we sold. And we calculate how much profit is in each square inch and each plant so we know how much we are making and what is the best profit. But, sometimes, we have extra space around the farm, and that is the tree rings. At WOW Farm, we have a bunch of different fruit trees, so what we will do for the pea shoots, we plant peas around them [the fruit trees]. We are utilizing the extra space we have at the farm. It is not necessarily to make us a profit, but it could make us a profit because pea shoots were able to grow around the trees just as well as in a bed. We had these three large extra quantities of pea shoots that made us extra revenue.

ILLÈNE: How fantastic! Are you primarily focusing on the greens?

AKIRA: Greens are really fast. They go in the ground and they come out. You can eat them at any stage of development. So, sometimes what we do is, we will harvest something like radishes while they are sprouts. You know how when you are gardening sometimes if something is too clumped up, you thin them so other things can have more room? So, sometimes what we do is, we take those thinnings and we sell them.

ILLÈNE: So you sell the radish greens for stir fries?

AKIRA: Yes, exactly. So, we will have different kinds of sprouts, greens. You can't sell carrot sprouts. You don't eat the green part of the carrots. You only eat the actual large fruit, I could say. So, you can't make extra revenue off of carrots. So, we plant a lot of greens because they are quick and we can harvest them in different stages. And, also, we did spend a lot of time [thinking], what stuff do we utilize the most?

Sometimes, we had this pest problem. Wow! Originally, we had a gopher problem, but then we kind of solved it. The gopher kind of went away. But on one half of the farm, there

Harvesting salad greens at West Oakland Woods Farm. Credit: West Oakland Wood Farm

is this one large tree full of little birds. They come and eat all this area. It will be a whole half bed gone because of all these birds. Some mustard greens, in particular, they can stay in the ground, and we know that if we put a whole bunch of seeds in that area, we know that some will come up and some will get eaten. But carrots weren't like that. We tried lettuce, but the birds ate a lot of that. On top of that, they were a big home for bugs.

**ILLÈNE:** How did you use game theory?

**AKIRA:** We kind of strategized using the things we learned from game theory, which would be [what would be] the best to plant, and by figuring out our profits, we learned, overall, that greens were the best thing we could grow. Partially because of the price we charge. And they [the restaurants] love the way we work and they love the youth aspect, so they are willing to pay a little more extra for our produce.

   We use wine cases to sell, like old wooden wine cases with our logo on them, to sell our produce. The big ones are around sixteen by twenty-four inches, three dimensional, like a box, and one that is half that, the same type of thickness or width, I should say, but it is half, and a third one that is mainly used for radishes and it is flatter and smaller. For the big cases, we charge $23 per case for kale, arugula, and purple frilly mustard. That's a big one. One big case can be maybe a quarter of a bed. Our beds on average are twenty-three feet long and four feet wide.

ILLÈNE: Do you plant your beds solidly? Is it just a solid mass of greens?

AKIRA: Originally, the first couple of months, what we did, we usually planted four to six rows of one produce, but then we realized that because we are a team, it can be tedious to be harvesting one type of produce for a couple of hours at a time. Some of them are really difficult to clean. Particularly, the purple curly mustard; the top is kind of like a bush, so it can get dirty if you don't clean it well and then that causes even more cleaning. And we had a problem: bruising. So, we were taking so long to harvest the stuff, and by the time it came to deliver, it had this bruising problem. So, then we came up with this other solution, that maybe we should do half and half. So, we will put radishes in a bed. We will put two different types of radishes in a bed or put radishes with arugula because they have the same growing time. Or we will put carrots with them because the thing is, when we plant and after we take something out, in order to replant it, we have to go through the process of turning the bed. In order to turn the bed, we have to put in buckets and buckets or wheelbarrows of compost, turn it and edge it, shape it, and fork it out so that it goes back to its bed shape so it can get that healthiness. If we don't have two things with the same growing time, you have half the bed that is harvested, that is barren and desert, and the other side that is still growing, so we are kind of not utilizing all the space. We have to make the money we need or want. Eventually, we realized we needed to break it up into half and half. This was more in the summer that we decided to do half-and-half beds. So, we just recently started doing half-and-half beds. But for pea shoots, we do a whole bed specifically for pea shoots because you don't plant pea shoots like you would kale. Where for kale, you can put a line of seeds side by side each other, but for pea shoots, you have to plant a seed every inch or two, so we use a whole bed for pea shoots. So, in general, we will do half and half now. But for our kitchen garden, we will mix it up. Right now, we are growing broccoli, and we can put chard in back of broccoli because we are not necessarily selling that stuff for revenues, so we can mix it up as much as we please.

ILLÈNE: You really have figured out what works best for you based on what you have studied! Very impressive! How much money are you each earning a month doing this?

AKIRA: We work, originally, we were assigned to work two days a week and our starting pay and our ending pay is $9 an hour. During the weekdays, we work two hours. On Saturdays, we work four hours, so that is six hours. But halfway through the program, one of the people working with us, she had to resign for personal and location issues. Because we get grant money, the pay that was allocated for her was an extra earning opportunity for the rest of us to work overtime. So, now we have this schedule where we come in on Thursdays. We do business meetings. On Saturdays, we work every single week. Then half of us will work one Wednesday and then the other half of us will work the next Wednesday. So, instead of working six hours a week, we have this chance to work eight hours a week. We get paid every two weeks at $9 per hour, $9 times six hours. So, technically, we get paid $54 per week if we are always on time. So, $54 times two is $108. If it isn't your extra week, you will make around $108 for two weeks, but if it is your extra week, it is $116. But we have to take out money for taxes, such as social security and Medicare, stuff like that. So, on average, you can come out with $104. On a good pay period, you can come out with $110.

ILLÈNE: I understand that, at the end, you are going to do some profit sharing from what you are selling as well.

AKIRA: We started a couple of months ago. We started deciding what we were going to do with this extra money we had because we had grants. So, we were thinking about doing scholarships for us if ever there was a time we needed extra money for books or tuition. Two of us, well, three of us, take college classes, and the rest of us are in high school. We were thinking of doing scholarship money. This is our second-to-last business meeting to decide what we are going to do with it, so we are still deciding, but I think school scholarships will be it.

ILLÈNE: What kind of schooling are you doing? Are you in high school or taking community college classes?

AKIRA: I go to ASTI, Alameda Science and Technology Institute. The way my school is set up, they give students the opportunity to graduate with an AA degree or graduate with UC [University of California] credits. That means that if I graduated with all the credits or I did my AA while I was in high school, those units can be transferable. Some students earn so many units in high school through my school that they can go to UC Berkeley and start as a sophomore or junior instead of as a freshman. Freshman and sophomore year, I did all my high school classes, and now I am in my junior year. I am ending my first semester of college classes. I am taking three classes at Laney [College] and one at College of Alameda. By the time I am done this year, I will have taken eight to ten college classes.

ILLÈNE: That's fantastic! It sounds like a wonderful opportunity. So, I am going to change the nature of our questions from all these practical issues with your program because I am curious also about your personal experiences and your feeling level as a gardener working with the soil and growing plants. I am curious about what you are experiencing in the garden. Are you aware of all the things you are smelling when you garden outside? And how do the smells of a garden make you feel?

AKIRA: Well, I personally like working at the garden because it has come to teach me about appreciation. My mom shops at Berkeley Bowl and Whole Foods and then she will do farmers' markets, and there are all these expensive prices, and you are kind of like, "Why are these all these expensive prices?" I am so used to the cheaper prices based on the way our society works because of not having expensive stuff because we pay workers so cheap. But actually, sitting here tediously cleaning all these vegetable taught me that gardening, farming, is extremely important in our country, but it is not appreciated. It taught me to appreciate what people do to get me the food that I need to survive. It is not easy at all. It is not a common practice, but it is extremely worthwhile. I think it is extremely necessary. So, just in general, it has taught me appreciation, especially [when it comes to] where I choose to spend my money now. I like to find small local places to spend my money. The other day, I realized, instead of going to McDonalds, I found myself walking ten minutes to buy a bottle of ginger ale from a local market rather than from a corner store. So, I am finding myself learning to appreciate things that are local, things that take time and a lot more energy. I think they are better and they should be appreciated. When it comes to smell in the garden, I don't necessarily notice any type of smell. I think the air is very clean, very fresh. The only thing is our garden is next to a mechanics shop, so sometimes there are all these revving motorcycle engines and we get all this gas and the exhaust, so those are the kinds of smells we sometimes smell. Sometimes, when we get fresh manure that we have to turn into our compost pile, we have to mix that. Manure is a very common smell. Some people don't like that, but I don't think it is a bad smell. Our compost doesn't have a smell; it smells just like soil to me.

ILLÈNE: Do you find your environmental awareness has changed as a result of gardening?

AKIRA: Definitely, especially because sometimes we do perimeter clean up. We go around and clean up the trash on our block. There is all this trash, and I am looking and thinking there is a trash can right here and I wonder why people can't take the extra time and couple of steps to throw it away. Sometimes, people don't appreciate the environment we live in. In the type of classes I choose to take, I have learned that the earth is kind of recycling itself. If we are not careful, it will end up recycling us and we will be gone if we don't really take care of what we have. It kind of makes me think. I feel the earth is my home. If I go home and I don't want this gum anymore, I am not going to throw it on the floor in my own house. I am going to take the time to walk to a trashcan, or if not, I am going to leave it in my hand until I get to a trash can. So, I feel like when I am outside, it is the same as when I am in my own home. In my opinion, the earth is my home and we need to treat it better. I find myself correcting people when I see them throwing something away. If someone has dropped something on the floor, I will take the time to pick it up because I don't think it is necessary and I think people should be aware that they are sharing the space with others and that they should leave it clean.

ILLÈNE: So you have become an activist in helping other people develop the same awareness you have?

AKIRA: Yes.

ILLÈNE: The work of gardening can be precise. Has it changed your ability to focus?

AKIRA: I think it affects my ability to focus on details. When it comes to academics, I am still working on focusing in different areas and learning how to focus. I can focus in class, but it is just learning how to focus when I get home. When I am on the farm, I have to focus on these specific tasks, but, at the same time, the fact that I am getting a paycheck can guide my focus. Whereas when I am not at work, focus does not necessarily come to me as easy. I think I am getting better at tedious tasks and learning how to be patient. I am learning to do it slowly, slowly, and, eventually, you get to your goal. Overall, I think it is something that is helping me, but it is going to take a while for me to completely get it down.

ILLÈNE: Does the physical work of gardening change your stress levels?

AKIRA: Definitely. Overall, I am an active person. I have been in dance since I was four and I run track, so, overall, I am very active. In general, I find that when I go to work, when I come home, I just feel so happy. It's just physically working at the farm. Especially when we are on compost days or we are on building beds days when it is hot. That is when you get the most out of your physical workouts. It just alleviates all your stress. It just makes me want to lie down and look at the sky.

ILLÈNE: That's a lovely image. Has working on the farm increased your vegetable consumption compared to before?

AKIRA: I ate a lot of vegetables before I went to WOW Farms, but now I think I am choosing different types of vegetable to eat. Where instead of regular lettuce and tomatoes, I am trying different things and mixing it together to create new types of salads. Before, I ate the same stuff. Now, a friend of mine eats a lot of okra and I am trying it, and it is actually not so bad. I am still getting over the slimy kind of liquid feelings. I think by working in a garden, I have explored variety.

ℰᔕ

Akira emphasized the appreciation she now has for the work it takes to grow good food and the value reflected in local, organic food's price. What a fascinating use of game theory to introduce youth to business strategy and food growing at the same time! Their strategies to figure out the best crops to plant to gain maximum use of limited land and optimum financial profits will surely have applications to any other small business ventures the WOW Farm participants may choose to pursue in their futures.

    Along with growing food, urban farms serve to create mini oases in the midst of urban pollution, such as the trash left by unconscious pedestrians or fumes and noise from engines as Akira related. Despite these pollutants outside the garden, Akira wanted to just lie down in the garden and look at the sky to feel the peacefulness there. Her experience learning to farm and run a food business while she goes to school has given her practical life skills and business acumen along with greater variety in her food choices and better focus. She has worked within a positive youth development environment that provides safety both physically and psychologically

West Oakland Woods gardener transplants seedlings. **Credit: West Oakland Woods Farm**

and a mentorship for her to work with others towards a common goal (Eccles and Gootman, 2002). She has needed to exercise self-discipline in order to arrive on time and thus receive the full pay that goes with her allotted work hours each week. Given how important self-discipline is for life success (Duckworth and Seligman, 2005), these youth are lucky to have this experience that rewards them for cultivating self-discipline along with other necessary life skills. The whole experience makes her happy. Akira feels that the earth is her home and she will care for it.

I also spoke with De'Andre, aged eighteen, another WOW Farm gardener. He told me that he loves Asian pears because of their wonderful smell and that the smell gives him "a nice, warm, and happy feeling inside." I asked him about whether the seed-to-harvest experience had affected him in any particular way.

DE'ANDRE: Yes, it has because when you first plant something, you put water on it and you think, like, "I wonder when it is going to grow?" Then, the next day, you come back to work and it has sprouted. And then, before you know it, you come back, and back, and back, and it gets taller, taller, and after a while, it is ready to harvest. It has given me, how can I say, the recognition that everything is a process. So, it takes time for stuff to grow just like it takes time for something good to happen. It has definitely given me more patience because I think more about stuff. I think about stuff more now before I do it. Just being outside is a peaceful feeling. When I wake up in the morning, I be very sleepy and just kind of out of it, but then when I get to the farm, it just, it gives my body a very ready feeling. Like just being there, being outside with nature, it, like, brightens up your life.

ILLÈNE: Has gardening affected your environmental awareness and attitudes?

DE'ANDRE: It definitely has made me more environmentally aware. When I am walking down the street, I used to just see green stuff hanging out on the sidewalk, but now I can identify it: "Oh, that's a weed." Or it is this and that. When I go to the grocery stores in the local areas and look at the food and it doesn't look very fresh as if it came from the farm, I notice. Like, "Oh, yeah, it looks very brittle, it doesn't look as fresh as it should be." It opens my eyes to what I am eating and how stuff is supposed to look and stuff like that

ILLÈNE: It's great that you are thinking about what is in the food you are eating. Since we are on the topic of wanting to know what is in your food, what did you think of Proposition 37 [California's 2012 ballot measure on labeling genetically modified organisms that the agribusiness giants poured millions of dollars into defeating] in the state elections this past November?

DE'ANDRE: The proposition about labeling the food and knowing where food comes from made me want to vote yes on it. I think people should know where their food is coming from, what is in their food before eating it.

ILLÈNE: And did you talk to any friends or family about that GMO proposition and food labeling?

DE'ANDRE: Yes, I talked to my mom about it and told her what it was all about and why she should vote yes on it.

ILLÈNE: Did you see a lot of those ads from the agriculture industry on TV against it?

DE'ANDRE: Yes, they came on TV a lot from time to time. When they did, I saw a lot of them. If you really don't know what they are talking about, it is kind of easy to not really understand that you should vote yes on it and why you should not just ignore it because the way they word stuff and the way they try to make you perceive; they make stuff seem like it would not actually be good for you. I didn't know, I never really thought too much about voting and why it was so important. I really didn't know. It was just so intense.

ILLÈNE: What else do you think you have gained from participating in the WOW Farm?

DE'ANDRE: When I first thought about asking about this job, I was thinking about more sort of the future: if I wanted to have my own garden in my own place and learn how to grow healthy vegetables. I think knowing the business stuff that I learned so far will help me more in the future because I already know a little bit, but it is giving me an advantage over people who haven't learned it yet. They have to wait till their third year in college to take a business class to learn stuff.

ILLÈNE: What would you say to other youth considering of applying for the WOW Farm program?

DE'ANDRE: Being outside instead of, like, being inside a condensed room just with the TVs and all that electronic stuff, just being outside with just nature and the bugs and the dirt and the sun, it makes you look at, it makes you realize things that you didn't realize before because you were too busy looking at your phone or watching TV or playing video games or something. It just makes you look at stuff more, more in a different light. It makes you more enlightened about things. I feel that learning skills like this puts you more into, puts you more enlightened to your environment and how things work, and I just feel that a lot of people who did not get this opportunity to learn how to grow fresh vegetables and to learn business skills should try to take advantage of programs like this.

ℒ

West Oakland Woods gardener harvests arugula. Credit: West Oakland Woods Farm

Working at WOW Farm has given De'Andre insight into an important political measure regarding food and the power advertising has to confuse issues. Not only has he gained valuable life experience, but now he feels he is more enlightened, particularly in relation to the environment.

In May of 2014, Patricia Johnson, cofounder and director of Game Theory Academy, sent me via e-mail the following information regarding the 2012 Young Farmers' group that included Akira and De'Andre:

> In 2012, we sold $4,711 worth of vegetables. Rough volume was: 75 pounds of lettuce, assorted greens, radishes, and pea shoots; 443 bunches of radish, carrots, and herbs; 91 wine crate cases of lettuce, assorted greens, and beans; and 16 baskets of tomatoes.
>
> To teach the youth about profitability, over the course of the year, we have facilitated conversations about how to maximize revenue: through marketing, planting efficiently, harvesting effectively, pest management, and minimizing costs (through water conservation, seed conservation, caring for farm tools, etc.). To make the numbers real for them, we have established a formula to calculate costs of goods sold, or the direct costs of production, and each month, we discussed what our costs have been and why. At the end of the year, what was left, after subtracting costs of goods sold from revenue, was split in half, with half being reinvested into the program, and half put into a scholarship fund for this group of farmers, who could request funds for

educational expenses. Each farmer had up to $215 available in a scholarship fund. Only two of the farmers ended up drawing on these funds. WOW Farm has not continued a profit-sharing program in subsequent years because we found youth were more motivated by the chance to beat the previous week's/year's revenues as a team rather than by personal gain.

According to the Census for Agriculture (2012, 1), the number of American farmers numbered 2,109,303, 4.2 percent less than the number of farmers included in the last census in 2007. The average farmer is 58.8 years old, with the greatest number of farmers in the 55-to-64 age bracket (ibid.). In 2015, the Census for Agriculture (2015, 1) reported that 2014 sales of organic farm products rose 72 percent from the last census in 2008 and that 688 farms were transitioning to organic farming. Today, the fastest growing group of professional farmers is organic farmers (ibid.).

Given the mature age of professional farmers and the heavy physical demands of the occupation, we are fortunate that so many young people are becoming interested in farming even in big cities thanks to programs similar to the ones highlighted here. A renaissance in farming is happening in America's urban centers where the majority of the US population now lives. As more people become aware of problems in industrialized food systems, city governments are beginning to adapt their planning and zoning policies to support this growing urban farming movement. In 2014, the City of Oakland made the following statement regarding its zoning regulations related to urban agriculture:

> The City of Oakland is updating its zoning regulations related to urban agriculture. These regulations are being updated to reflect Oakland's vital urban farming movement, and to encourage and facilitate local food production. Urban farming, the small-scale cultivation of crops and animals, has become increasingly popular throughout Oakland and the United States. The current rules require a comprehensive revision to keep up with the latest urban farming practices.
>
> On March 15, 2011, the City Council adopted new residential and commercial zones for the entire City. The new zones allow "Crop and Animal Raising Agricultural Activities" with approval of a Conditional Use Permit in all residential and commercial areas in the City. This change is intended to be an interim measure until the City can conduct a comprehensive update to address all aspects of urban agriculture.

Not all cities have as ideal a political and meteorological climate as Oakland has for year-round growing, but all over the world, town planners and food activists are collaborating to change the urban landscape and social scape by rewriting zoning laws to make food growing, even when it involves chicken and bees, possible, including for commercial purposes as it is at WOW Farm (Lim, 2014). These young people's experiences in three distinctive Oakland youth, food-growing programs have born personal and political fruits for them in their self-awareness and political knowledge of the role food and food growing plays in a healthy life and, to a certain degree, the role multinational corporations play in food growing, labeling, and processing. These youth participate in an international movement towards local food sovereignty and sufficient local production, enabling communities to be not entirely reliant on imported food resources from other states and countries thousands of miles away (Lim).

Oakland has many organizations devoted to food justice and easy access to affordable, healthy, and culturally appropriate food for all citizens, including groups that work on policy such as the Oakland Food Policy Council, groups that focus on food-growing education such as People United for a Better Life in Oakland, Oakland Leaf, and WOW Farm, and a myriad of other groups that support access to healthy food for all residents. When Jerry Brown was mayor of Oakland in 2006, the Oakland City Council, Life Enrichment Committee passed a resolution that the city would strive to produce 30 percent of the food consumed locally and develop a plan to assess the food system in order to improve equitable food access (Unger and Wooten, 2006, 3). The Oakland Mayor's Office of Sustainability soon collaborated with the University of California's Planning Department, and the resulting document, "A Food Systems Assessment for Oakland, CA: Toward a Sustainable Food Plan," written by Unger and Wooten (2006), now guides Oakland's efforts to eradicate food deserts and develop more agriculture in the city.

We need school systems nationwide to catch up with city planning departments similar to Oakland, where the master plan has created more agriculturally friendly guidelines. Oakland recognizes the importance of growing food for community well-being in terms of health, economics, and the environment; this is the ecological approach to creating health: develop environments where healthy food grows and is accessible to all!

# 21

## TAOS
### ANCIENT TRADITIONS, YOUNG FARMERS

Native Americans were the original agriculturalists on the North American continent, the people to whom Americans owe the first Thanksgiving. Had the American Indians not shared their seeds and knowledge of how to grow corn and other local plants with the European colonialists, it is very possible none of the colonists would have survived. I wanted very much to include Native American youth who grow food in this research and book, and so I headed to New Mexico and its ancient agricultural traditions.

My family spent many Thanksgivings and Easters in Taos, New Mexico, because my parents appreciated the American Indian culture and natural beauty there. I grew up surrounded by images from this region where Native American, Hispanic, and Anglo cultures meet and mix. The Taos Pueblo has been inhabited for more than a thousand years. The earth-colored adobe walls of the pueblo rise softly from the sagebrush-filled valley. Taos Mountain reaches its forested slopes to the sky, a powerful and sacred presence. I had an opportunity to drive to New Mexico in July of 2013. I called Farm to Table New Mexico, FoodCorps, and the New Mexico Acequia Association to inquire about youth gardening programs, and I learned about several, including in Taos, Chamisal, and Albuquerque. Shirley Trujillo from the Taos Pueblo agreed to meet with me first and introduce me to the youth she mentors in the market garden project she runs through the Taos County Economic Development Corporation (TCEDC), a nonprofit dedicated to creating local agricultural opportunities TEDC has with farm fields and an industrial kitchen at their Taos headquarters.

On a hot July afternoon, I climbed into a car with one of my lifelong friends, Jane Katz, and we headed to Taos, our first road trip together since we were eighteen. Jane was attending the

Mural on the Taos County Economic Development Corporation headquarters. Credit: Illène Pevec

same conference in Albuquerque that I was, so we had planned to spend some extra time together after it ended. Since she is a teacher and a very experienced gardener, she also was interested in these young people's experiences growing food. Jane even offered to drive her rental car, for which I was grateful, as the air conditioning was not reliable in my old Saturn. New Mexico was experiencing a drought and the high temperatures felt very uncomfortable.

The 2013 National Drought Mitigation Center maps showed New Mexico's drought situation as "severe, extreme and exceptional" all summer. This weather pattern has a big impact on everyone who is growing food. Mercifully, it rained a bit the night we arrived in Taos so that the morning dawned cooler than it had in the previous weeks, which had averaged in the nineties. We arrived at the TCEDC building, with its stunning garden mural gracing the building's front, at nine a.m. to meet Shirley and her young garden crew. First, we heard the history of the TCEDC from the two women who founded it, Terry Bad Hand and Patti Martinson.

Bad Hand and Martinson, both Native Americans but not from Taos, were hired from the Denver Indian Center Development Corporation three decades prior by the Taos Pueblo to start an economic development process for the community. A local mine had recently closed, and many people were out of work with no job prospects. Since tribal government changes annually, the TCEDC ended up being a countywide organization rather than simply tribal. It has since become a grassroots development model for sustaining health in native and rural communities.

When they began, Martinson and Bad Hand went door to door with surveys to find out what the community desired. They discovered that people wanted their youth to be able to come home to northern New Mexico from college and military service and find a viable economic and social system that provided them with work and a future within their home culture. Northern New Mexico has two land-based agrarian cultures that share the land and many blood ties after five hundred years in the same area: ancient traditional Pueblo Indian culture and Hispanics descended from Coronado's expeditionary explorers who came in the 1500s and those that followed them north from Mexico (Mann, 2005).

The 2014 US Census estimates the 2013 population of New Mexico to be 2,085,287. The Native American population is 10.2 percent, nine times that of the national average, while the Hispanic population is 47 percent and the white population is 39.8 percent (US Census Bureau, 2014c). New Mexico is unique in the United States with this vibrant cultural mix.

The TCEDC mission became "supporting the land, food, water, and the cultures of the people of northern New Mexico," explained the directors. They brought in resources to the community to put back together an "interrupted" food system and raised the funds to erect the beautiful building that houses their offices, a 5,000-square-foot kitchen that provides space for added-value food businesses and food education for youth and elders, and a daycare center and preschool. The farm field lies directly behind the TCEDC building.

Bad Hand and Martinson explained that for Native Americans, the transition from agrarian trade to a cash economy has presented many challenges, one of them being a disruption in the food system. The TCEDC works with people of all ages to redevelop ties to traditional food growing and preparation as the basis for health. In 2012, the TCEDC began working with the First Nations Development Institute to start the Native American Food Sovereignty Alliance (NAFSA) to revive local food systems with Indian tribes across the US. This is a Native American-driven and -controlled alliance that supports tribes to develop agricultural programs to integrate all generations in restoring traditional knowledge and crops so that diets are balanced and not processed-food based.

The young people growing food at the TCEDC farm create a model for a healthy, local, sustainable food system. Corn, beans, and squash grow together in the traditional Three Sisters garden—a combination that provides the plants' growing needs and the nutrients for good human health. The TCEDC farm crops include not only the traditional Three Sisters (corn, beans, and squash), but also greens, such as kale and various lettuces, as well as the hot chilies so important in New Mexican cuisine. The growing season is short at the 6,767-foot elevation, but plenty of tomatoes grow in their greenhouse, where they are protected from the cool, high-altitude nights.

A unique component to the Taos county local food economy is the Matanza, a mobile, humane, animal harvesting unit that allows farmers to slaughter their bison, yak, cattle, pig, sheep, and goats on the farm where they are raised and sell this meat from a US Department of Agriculture-approved facility. Bad Hand and Martinson proudly explained that the Matanza was the second mobile slaughter facility in the United States and that it serves all the local tribes that have bison herds and redistributes the meat to all tribal members, providing healthy, traditional meat.

According to the *Albuquerque Journal*, 66 percent of New Mexican children qualify for free or reduced-priced school lunch and out of the forty thousand New Mexicans per week who seek help from food banks, 40 percent are children (Linthicum, 2013). Besides a high rate of food insecurity, New Mexico also has a high rate of diabetes, particularly in Native American and Hispanic populations. New Mexico Department of Health (2013) statistics present the state's health disparities: "The NM American Indian population had the highest diabetes death rates; the NM White Non-Hispanic population had the lowest rates; the Hispanic rates were in the middle. The 3-fold difference between Native American and White rates, and the 2-fold difference between Hispanic and White rates, has been unchanged since 2000."

Martinson and Bad Hand told me that a survey carried out by TCEDC in their service area showed that many Taos county residents either were diabetic or had someone in their family with diabetes. In response to these findings, TCEDC provides healthy living education with cooking classes to prevent diabetes and for people already living with it. The youth garden provides food for the cooking classes in the TCEDC kitchen. The youth also learn to eat the vegetables they grow as a form of diabetes prevention.

Martinson and Bad Hand informed us that the garden frequently has volunteers needing to do community service and that some youth volunteers come from residential addiction treatment centers. The medical personnel accompanying the youth say that the youth need less medication when they garden, but this is simply an observation on the part of the supervising adults and not something that has been measured as part of any research with them.

After learning about TCEDC, Jane and I sat down with Shirley Trujillo in the beautiful lattice-roofed courtyard that separates the offices from the daycare center and preschool to learn about the program she leads where youth learn to grow food and save seeds. Garden beds planted both by the teens and the young children line the walkways leading to the farm field and two greenhouses behind the TCEDC. Swallows swooped in and out with their graceful double-

Taos County Economic Development Corporation courtyard.  Credit: Illène Pevec

pointed tales and shared their songs with us while we talked. Shade, a slight breeze, and a view to the gardens made it a lovely place to be.

**SHIRLEY:** I am from the Taos Pueblo. I am also part Diné.

**ILLÈNE:** Does that mean you are part Navajo?

**SHIRLEY:** Yes. I've been here [at the TCEDC] around six or seven months now. Before that, I was with Red Willow Growers in the Taos Pueblo. It's called growers because, for me, it was the students who were the growers, so it should be named after the people who were growing, so we called it Red Willow Growers. I actually helped start the program there and that is basically where a lot of what I am doing started. I enjoyed planting.

**ILLÈNE:** How did you learn about farming?

**SHIRLEY:** I was raised by my grandparents. I still had my parents, but I loved staying with my grandparents. My grandfather spent a lot of time with me irrigating the fields, a lot of time outside bailing alfalfa with me helping him in his gardens and the cornfields. A lot of what I got interested in had to do with my grandparents. Also, when I was living on the Navajo reservation with my parents, I babysat for a woman who did dye charts. I got interested in native plants because while I was watching her kids, I was also learning about native plants that dye wool. That's another thing that got me into learning about native plants and gardening, a lot of outside work. I'd rather be outside than in an office. I love working with the youth, especially probably junior high or high school age. I've worked with youth for about seven years.

I started working in a commercial greenhouse. When I left there, I went to Red Willow Growers, and we started putting up greenhouses. So, I also construct greenhouses. At Red Willow Growers, or Red Willow Farms as it is called now, we actually put alternative energy into the greenhouses. So, we had all-year-round heat using a biomass heater, which is basically a giant wood heater and solar [photovoltaics] for the pump. And a couple of the men from the Pueblo were helping us out too with the construction. A lot started from there. We had a really good team and we worked together really well. From there, it really boomed working with the kids, and I love working with them. Some of them come in, you know, not wanting to do anything. Youth nowadays, some people say, are hard to get along with, but I think I get along with them better than I do with some of the adults. [*We both laugh.*] Some of them do have attitudes. It's really great. But since I have been working with a lot of them, a lot of them seem to grow up a lot while they are working with me. They find out how important it is for our food system. We need to work on our food system. I see these big corporations that are trying to take over our seeds. To me, that is all control. For me, all our heirloom seeds at the Pueblo, we need to preserve them. Those have been handed out from one generation to the next. A lot of the kids that I work with have grandparents from the Pueblo who have given them seeds. We need to preserve those. I tell them, "Grow them out. You've got to keep that lineage going or we'll lose it." I think that is so important for the Pueblo and for any culture. Our food system is one of the most important ones. If you don't have that, you really don't have much of anything because we find that connection between the generations. You also find it with yourself and the land. We have lost a lot of the connection with what is around us. What is there and what is given to us as a gift. We misuse it. We don't think about it very much. The modern world is so much around us and it moves so fast. There is so much to take in, but we really need to get back to our hands-on work with the earth.

ILLÈNE: What are the traditional foods specifically of the Taos Pueblo? I'm assuming that is a big part of what you are teaching the kids.

SHIRLEY: Yes. A big part is our corn. There are certain types of corn. A flour or flint corn that we use for grinding for making tortillas that is kind of like cornmeal bread. Different types of corn, different colors of corn for traditional use. We have a bean that, as far as I know, originated from the Taos Pueblo called the Taos Pueblo red bean that was actually getting very, very rare. Then I started giving it out. I just give it out to Pueblo growers. If they need something, we should be able to grow it out. That's what I have been telling the kids. It's so important to keep that community effort, that community giving, giving back to the community. I think once they see it from others, it will be kept in their mind that they are giving back to their community. There are different varieties of squash we use at the pueblo. It's a type of blue Hubbard-type squash.

ILLÈNE: I have a question about squash. Since they cross-pollinate and then you don't get the fruit true to the parent plant, what do you do?

SHIRLEY: If we are going to grow a specific [squash], the one from Taos Pueblo, we just grow that one for that year. If we are going to grow other squashes that we don't use traditionally, then I grow several kinds that year. They say beans don't cross, but I have seen some beans cross. So, if we are going to grow the red beans, we only grow those that year. We try to keep it as pure as possible.

ILLÈNE: What about the corn?

SHIRLEY: It's really hard with corn because so many people around the area grow corn. Corn pollen can travel several miles. It's hard with corn. We still use it as much as we can. We need to grow it even if it does cross-pollinate. As long as there are no GMO seeds—that would be really bad. We try to inform the community, especially the youth, about just how wrong it is to manipulate our heirloom seeds. It's just wrong. We talk about that too. I think that it's so important, that the knowledge of keeping these seeds going is so important, but also the knowledge that we can still work with our hands with the earth. As a Taos Pueblo member and as a native from Taos, I think it's so important that I personally stay connected with the earth. I think there is no greater connection. It's just so important. I want the youth to know that too. No matter what we have with technology, I don't think there is any other connection than being part of what is given to us.

ILLÈNE: Does it change you to work with the earth?

SHIRLEY: It does in a way. Sometimes, I feel like when I am doing stuff, I am in a whole different place. I don't know if you call it spiritual. You see things grow, you see things emerge. I don't really know how to explain it. It's like I am actually here, I am part of the earth, and that is who I am. I could do without all this technology. I would rather be out in nature just listening and watching, just being out there. I really don't know how to explain it, just being there is part of what we have on this earth. It's just important to me to be part of it. I think it is so important, especially for the youth to know about it. A lot of them, it's kind of sad, I've worked with a lot of groups that come to Taos. Especially with Red Willow Growers, we have had groups of young kids that have come from California, from North Carolina. A lot of these young kids don't know how to work with the earth or even to feel it. Nobody spends the time to just listen or observe what's going on. It was kind of sad to see some of them that didn't even know what a corn plant was. That is shocking to me. They don't know where their food comes from. They eat all this food, but they don't know where it comes from, how it's grown, what it is, what's put on it. I think it is so important that they know how to grow food.

ILLÈNE: Are there traditional Navajo or Taos ceremonies related to planting or harvesting food that you have taught the kids?

SHIRLEY: Most of the kids I teach are Taos Pueblo. I mainly stay in Taos. Navajo is quite different. There are a lot of ceremonies we use, but I really don't go into it. If it's traditional, I try not to get too much into that. I'll tell them what it could be used for. A lot of the traditional stuff I try to stay away from that.

ILLÈNE: Do you mind if I ask you why?

SHIRLEY: Out of respect. A lot of things get exploited. I am part of the community, but I don't believe in exploiting what is there as in ceremony or in traditional use.

ILLÈNE: The reason I asked that is that I know that throughout Central and North America where corn came into being, many cultural groups have ceremonies to honor corn and the life-giving capacity it has for people. We don't have that in the modern world outside of indigenous traditions and aside from saying grace to say thank you for food, but it's not quite the same as a ceremony around a particular food. It seems to me that we have lost a sense of sacredness around food. You are from a culture that still has sacred traditions around food.

SHIRLEY: We do, like as you say [about the] corn. I think all food is sacred. A lot of the native foods; I try to get into that sometimes. In a way, we are losing that knowledge. In a way, I would like to bring that back. I want the kids to understand that they can live off the land. For me, tomatoes are modern. I want them to know the traditional native foods they have around them. We are surrounded by all kinds of native food, but people don't know or remember how to use it. I think, traditionally, we do have that spiritual part. Food is sacred.

Food is part of every culture in the world. I myself, I give thanks to what I am growing when I start a garden—I'll throw some corn meal out just thanking the earth for what it is teaching me. As an individual, for me, it comes from the heart. Just growing up and learning from my grandparents who give thanks every day for everything they have. Food is one of them.

ILLÈNE: The kids are lucky to have a program and a teacher like you.

SHIRLEY: Thank you. They are pretty neat. Sometimes, we talk about the food and the GMOs, but I really just want them to put their hands in the earth and work with it and see what they can produce from what they started. We start everything by seed. I use organic seed or seed that I have stored. I have seed saved throughout the years. I have a lot of seeds that I have saved for as long as I can remember [*laughs*]. I tell the kids, "Keep those seeds going!" That's one of the main things we need to keep going. Especially since we are from Taos Pueblo and a lot of that is a part of our culture.

ILLÈNE: Do you do seed saving with the youth in the fall?

SHIRLEY: Yes, I do usually with the squash and pumpkins and the corn. A lot of the ones that I like to save and keep for the next year are the ones the kids love. I like to save what the kids like. They have come to like a lot of the foods that they had never even known about. They have come to love a lot of the kales.

ILLÈNE: Anita [one of Shirley's students] told me when I arrived that the prairie dogs have eaten a lot of kale.

SHIRLEY: Yes, they have eaten some of it. We are working on live-catching them and moving them. There are a lot of challenges. Every day is a challenge, so we take it one day at a time and keep going forward.

ILLÈNE: Is there anything I have not asked you about that you think is important for people to understand who will read this book?

SHIRLEY: Listen! Tell them [the youth] the truth! Be honest with them! I work with a lot of them who have some challenge in their lives. They are only teenagers, yet they have gone through so much already. I think a lot of us grow up that way because of this modern society. It's been a challenge for them. I look at my life too when I was growing up. It was a challenge too. Talk with them. Listen! They want to learn. They want to understand, but they also want to be understood. They want someone to listen to them, to talk with them. I think doing the gardens; I think it helps a lot. I have students who come back and they are totally different. And they come back. It amazes me that they come back, but they do. They want to do the work.

**ILLÈNE:** Do you have some really good conversations with them when you are just weeding?

**SHIRLEY:** Yes, we do. Some of us come up with the strangest things. They bring up things that interest them that they want to learn more about. If I can help them just a little bit to keep going with what interests them—a lot of them are interested in environmental science and animals and nature. If I can just spark that spark a little bit for them and help them on their way, that just makes me excited. That fulfills me. I have seen seven or probably eight of my students who have gotten scholarships so their first year of college is free. A lot of them are also talking out more. A lot of my students, when they first came, they didn't say a word. They started speaking out! I think you learn about yourself too. I still learn each day, every time I talk to a student. I take my students to see different farms, to see different projects. I tell them everyone does things differently. Another farmer might do things differently from me. Something might work for someone and not for someone else. That's why I want them to see other farmers and differences in everyone and everything. I think each and every person is different. Even if they are teenagers, they have their own traits and their own knowledge they can share with everyone. I tell you, they have some knowledge they can share. A few years ago, I went to the Terra Madre conference [the international biannual Slow Food conference] in Turin, Italy, and I met people from all over the world. That was really wonderful. It connected me to many people.

I think it's important that the kids take home the food they grow and share it with their parents. It's a big thing for them to do that, to show they can do something. Some of our kids at the high school were in a class where the teacher said they would start to compost, and the kids jumped up and said, "Let's do it!" They knew from working here. The other kids in their class were surprised. This knowledge is with them forever. Just working together, learning to speak out and ask what they want to know; they had a hard time at first, but now they jump in and ask. It brings out a lot in the young people. It stays with them forever.

Shirley's connection to the land and growing food as part of her experiences with her grandfather echoed throughout the interviews I did from Taos to Albuquerque. In Taos, I spoke with three gardeners in the TCEDC program, and all had connections via family to agricultural traditions. One, Luis (pronounced Lewis) Trujillo, is Shirley's son. He has been growing food at his mother's side since he was a small boy. Now, he is eighteen and preparing to go to college at the University of Northern New Mexico in Taos for one year and then transfer to Fort Lewis College in Durango, Colorado, to study environmental sciences and forestry. Fort Lewis College is one of only two US colleges that provide free education to American Indians who belong to federally recognized tribes.

Luis's description of growing up in the Taos Pueblo gives a glimpse of the unique life this community offers all generations and what he has learned from his mother while she helped to develop Red Willow Growers and the TCEDC garden where he works now. Luis was a baby when his great-grandfather passed away, so his mentor has been his mom.

LUIS: She [Shirley, his mother] has helped me to learn a lot of things throughout the years: how to grow my own food and cultivate the land, how the seeds are important and they are really our future for developing and growing our community. Use what we have; use our land and resources to help us grow.

ILLÈNE: Did you work in the Red Willow Growers project with your mom?

LUIS: When I was first there, there was only one greenhouse and one field covered with weeds and thistles. It was really hard to get it all started, but we had a lot of volunteers to come help. That is what Red Willow was all about: volunteer work, getting the community to come together, making sure our people keep growing and getting kids back into cultivating, farming, harvesting, everything.

At my old house at the [Taos] Pueblo, that's all we would do [farming]. We would grow raspberries, strawberries, blueberries. But, now, we live in town because we don't get the water we used to have. We would have ditches throughout the Pueblo. As long as we would keep the ditches clean, we could have the water. It came straight from the river right down to our houses.

ILLÈNE: What was it like to grow up in the Taos Pueblo?

LUIS: It was like a whole different experience. Everywhere I went, everyone around you cares about you, knows who you are. They look out for you. They really try to help you grow as a person. Everywhere I went, I knew the people that were around. I felt I was safe all the time and no worries. Everyone around was my friend. Everyone was related to me or knew me somehow. I wouldn't want to grow up anywhere else.

ILLÈNE: I have not had a chance to see the Red Willow Growers garden yet. When you were growing there, did everyone garden together or in individual plots?

LUIS: My mom started one greenhouse, and we would do all the seedlings there, start everything there. When the plants got big enough, we would go plant them in the fields. We would keep that rotation going. My mom did an amazing job. They put up another greenhouse and also a biomass heater that keeps the soil heated and keeps the seeds and plants warm. You can produce product in the winter or any time of year since everything was all natural light.

ILLÈNE: Have you been growing food all your life? You have been helping your mom since you were thirteen or even earlier, right? Have you noticed whether your sense of smell is heightened when you garden? Do you pay attention to what you smell more than when you are walking around town?

LUIS: When I am in town, all I smell is smoke and exhaust from the cars, but when I go into the garden, it's, like, fresh. Everything is nice. Everything my mom uses, like no GMOs, all she wants is to help the kids grow some food and keep that going so we don't have to depend on supermarkets so much. Yeah, I really do think it heightens our senses, or my senses at least.

ILLÈNE: How does it make you feel to smell all these smells in the garden?

LUIS: It feels so good. It makes me feel alive every day. It makes me active. It makes me want to get up and do something. When I am in my house, it is really cool and I don't really want to do anything, but when I am outside and everything's all green, it's totally different. I don't know, like I go into somebody else. I become like this person who wants to get things done and help people understand what my mom wants to help and do. It brings out another thing in me. It makes me feel good because it makes me think, like I did something else. I am putting my time to where it really counts. It really grows on you because you see it growing; you see it growing more and more and it makes you feel really good because you are helping nurture it and, later on, it is producing something really good.

ILLÈNE: When you were working at Red Willow Growers, did some of the food go into the school lunch?

LUIS: My mom would distribute some [produce] to the school, she would take some to restaurants actually, and to Sid's Grocery store, and she would take some to senior citizens. She would take some to the day school in the Pueblo. It is kindergarten to 8th grade and there is a daycare. I went there too. I went to kindergarten to 8th grade there too. Then I went to the Santa Fe Indian School, which is in Santa Fe. It really opened me up to all sorts of possibilities. It made me want to join more activities and know more people. They really helped me there. They really helped me with my grades. They really want you to succeed. They provide you with all this extra tutoring. They go the extra way for you. They try to get all the [tribal] governors involved. They want to know when all the feast days and all the traditional activities are going on so the kids can make it back and still stay in school so they won't be held back for it and won't be left out of their own traditions as well. They teach US history, world history, Native American history. They have a broad perspective in what they teach.

ILLÈNE: When we are outside in the garden, we get to smell things and see things that are different from when we are inside. Do you notice when you are outside that you hear more?

LUIS: I actually notice a lot more things, like what's going on around me. When I am outside, I am much more aware of what is around me than when I am doing nothing. It makes me cautious, makes me want to do a good job. I want to make sure I do a good job the first time so I don't have to do it over again 'cause it gets really hot out here.

ILLÈNE: I am so relieved we have this cloud cover today so that it's comfortable. Yesterday was so hot!

LUIS: It's really nice this morning.

ILLÈNE: You must feel you are making a very important contribution with this work that you all are doing.

LUIS: I really think that we can change everything. We can change the way we eat and change the way we show things to other people and how we can grow from that—how we can come together as a community and get the youth involved in these events so that they won't be getting into trouble, so they won't be doing, uh, basically, they won't be getting into trouble.

[Being in the garden] really helps people to get out of that kind of [bad] situation. Being away from peer pressure in a free environment; there is no pressure [in the garden]. There is no demand for you to do anything. You are there on your own to learn what you need to learn.

ILLÈNE: I've had quite a few young people tell me a garden is a free environment. How do you perceive that a garden is free?

LUIS: The thing that makes me feel it is free is that everything around me, like all the work I have done, I know that I did with my hands because I got all these blisters. The work really shows on you. It helps. Even the sunburns; it keeps your mind off of things. It clears your mind. That's how I see it.

ILLÈNE: It clears your mind? So, you feel like your mind is free?

LUIS: My mind is free. It's no worries. I don't have to worry about everything. It gets me away from society. That's how I see it. Being back with the earth, I guess. Being Native American, we have a lot of duties, a lot of things we have to do in order to keep our traditions going. Everything, everything is connected. We have to all see that in some way. I am really proud of where I am from. It's a nice place.

ILLÈNE: Have you ever gone to speak at any of the youth garden conferences?

LUIS: I have been with my mom at some of the seed exchanges, where they have a big variety of seeds that they just give out to the community. It's really amazing. It's really cool because everybody barters. They want to trade, but they only trade to people they know are going to nurture it. They only trade to people they know that are good growers. Like mom, she is really known way down south, so she'll get seeds from everywhere. She brings them over here mostly because that is what she used to do at the Red Willow. She used to bring all of those seeds together, and we would plant them all in the fields.

ILLÈNE: If you had a chance to talk to a group of kids about this, what would you tell them that you want them to understand about this experience?

LUIS: I would want them to understand that, to me, it is not about the money, it is about growing as a person. Once you know where your food comes from, you don't have to rely on society that much or you don't have to rely on food markets to stay healthy. There are different ways to help you grow as a person, I guess. What I would really want them to take is to know how to grow their own food and know that seeds are really important to every person in the world. Companies, now, are trying to buy every seed because if they own all the seeds, they have all the food to produce. My mom, she doesn't really like the big companies and everything like that. She told me if they get all the seeds, like all of the seeds, and they put trademarks on them, they will own them and the land. If we want something, we will have to trade with other people to get things. I just want people to be aware of what is happening.

ILLÈNE: If you had the chance to talk to grownups about school gardens, what would you say?

LUIS: I would say it's a stress reliever. It helps cope with different types of problem situations. Yeah, it's been really a stress reliever for me. It helps to get my mind off of other things. I'm here every week. It helps me stay out of trouble really. It makes me more aware. It makes me more alive, I guess, is how I could say it.

Luis's experience of feeling more alive from the experience of working outside to grow food reverberates in what youth say all across the country—more evidence for the deep engagement and meaning that gardening affords youth and their flourishing.

The other male intern working the day I visited TCEDC, Ed, was going through preparations for a tribal ceremony and because of that, he was unable to speak with me. The newest member of the team, fifteen-year-old Marta, learned about the program through her father who works at the TCEDC. She told me that her little brothers also come sometimes to help. I asked her if she planned on applying to Fort Lewis College, and she told me she has Navajo ancestry on both sides of her family, but probably not enough to qualify for the Indian tuition waver. She is saving her $8-per-hour wages to buy a car, and then she will save for college. She told me her grandfather always has a vegetable garden every year.

**MARTA:** What Shirley has been teaching me is how much to water and what to do with the plants when you are transplanting them—that you have to be careful and everything. Every day, she chooses something different, like different plants. She gave us this paper on how to manage a farm or garden, what plants could destroy your crops, and what pesticides you could use, stuff like that. All of this stuff she is showing us is pretty new to me because I have never done anything like this. That is why I am really interested.

**ILLÈNE:** Do you feel any different after a time working in the garden?

**MARTA:** I feel really tired after [gardening] because, usually, it is really sunny and when we are making the rows, it is really hot. After, I feel really good because we finished a lot during

Marta and Luis transplant seedlings from the greenhouse to the field. Credit: Illène Pevec

the day. With this, I feel like I did something that is helpful. Everything that is grown here or in your own garden, you know how you take care of it and you are getting everything from it that you need. You are getting all the nutrients and everything and there are no preservatives, so it is fresh and it's a different taste from processed foods. I prefer eating stuff from the garden than buying food from somewhere else because you don't know what they have put inside it. I usually eat from my grandpa's garden, and that is really good. After working here, I know this is a better choice. My mom cooks [from scratch] most of the time.

ILLÈNE: Is there anything you would like other young people who might read this book to know about your experience growing food this summer?

MARTA: It is an amazing experience. You come and you learn so much in a certain amount of time. It's a lot to learn. It's, like, really amazing to know how to grow your own food and all these different things that Shirley tells you. You are outside and you are hearing all these different things and you are working with the ground and nature and everything. It's really interesting. A lot of people don't get to do that, but I am lucky that I can. I like it. It's really relaxing, and I like it. Yeah, just seeing everything growing is just really amazing. We did all that work and something is actually happening. It's all growing! We are all really happy that we could do something like that. When we planted all those flowers, I didn't think they would grow, and then a week later, we were all, "Yeah!" We got really happy!

ILLÈNE: Have you told your grandfather what you are learning?

MARTA: Yeah. He said that it is really good for me and he knows that I will love it. I told him I do [love it], and he told me, "That's great!" and said maybe I would help him in his garden next time, and I told him, "Yeah!"

Even though Marta had watched her grandfather plant and grow food, she had not actually gotten involved in gardening before working in the TCEDC garden with Shirley. Now with her new skills, a multigenerational bridge for sharing knowledge and life experience has grown. The next person I spoke with was Anita, aged sixteen, who had greeted us when we arrived at TCEDC. She lives with and is very close to her grandfather.

ANITA: Last year when I was a freshman, I needed a job really bad. My brother was working with Shirley at the time, and he asked her if there was a job for me, and she said, "Yes," and she got me to work that same day. I started off and I really didn't know anything that was going on, but after a while, I started learning. I just thought it was really interesting, like how things grow, what you have to do to get them to grow, and I stuck with it. It was really interesting. We got laid off from that job because the money ran out. I was looking for another job, but I really didn't want to work inside in an office, sitting at a computer, answering phones all day. I liked what I did outside. I was waiting and waiting and waiting. Finally, Shirley came to my house. She asked me if I needed a job, and I said "Yeah." I waited a long time, but it was worth the wait. It's the only job I have ever had since I started working. It's pretty cool.

ILLÈNE: What is it that you like about growing food?

ANITA: For me, it was growing it—watching it grow, helping it grow, selling it to people knowing it's healthy and knowing they are going to go home and eat it. It's healthy for them. It's healthy food, and we are selling it to people.

ILLÈNE: So, you are helping them improve their health?

ANITA: Yeah, that's what makes me like it.

ILLÈNE: Has growing food changed your own food choices?

ANITA: Yeah, it has. I have actually stopped eating candy, as weird as that sounds. I don't like candy anymore. I'd rather eat a carrot or something like that. It's just like that knowledge. I've learned a lot about what's in plants. It's pretty cool, like with medicine especially, it showed me a lot. We don't grow a lot of medicinal herbs here, but at other places that I have seen, I have learned a lot about the herbs and how they heal. It does change you a lot. It makes your view of gardening different. I never thought I would be a gardener. I never thought I would do all of this. I thought I would be doing something different, but it's just what I like to do. Some people think it's weird, but I don't care what other people think. If I like it and that is what I want to do, then I will do it.

ILLÈNE: Do you notice if working in the garden changes how you feel?

ANITA: Yeah, with me, I will come to work if I am sick. I'll come to work if I don't feel good, and I will still do it. I know we are not supposed to do that, but I can't resist it. The only time that I won't come to work is only if I am extremely sick and I can't do anything. Or if I have other things I have to do that are, I would not say more important, but things I have to get done. It's really changed me as a person. I feel more responsible because when I first started out, I was the one being taught. Other people were teaching me what to do and telling me what to do, but now I have to teach them what to do and tell them how to do things and make sure they are doing it right. If not, then I get the blame for it. I have to make sure they are all working. It's a really big responsibility. Like you wouldn't think it is, but when she [Shirley] is gone, and then she gets back, the kids get so scared: "Oh, my God, she's back, what are we supposed to do?" And I am like, "I told you. You should have been working."

ILLÈNE: So, Shirley gives you all a lot of responsibility to get the work done when she has to be somewhere else, she expects you to get the work done?

ANITA: Yeah. I usually do. The only time I don't is when it is hotter than crap outside, and then we can't work that long.

ILLÈNE: What do you notice about the things you smell when you are out gardening?

ANITA: You mean like plants?

ILLÈNE: Or the soil, anything. Do you notice your senses when you are out there working?

ANITA: Yeah. Like with the compost, especially if it's dry on top and you can't tell, you can put your finger in to tell.

ILLÈNE: Do you smell it then? Put your finger in and then smell?

ANITA: Yeah, it's a weird, really a musty, smell. I really don't know with the plants and stuff. It's pretty easy to tell what they are by their smell, like with basil and cilantro. A few other different plants, if you didn't know what they were and you went and smelled it, you wouldn't be able to tell, but if you know what it is, they have their smell. Like with cucumbers and the melons. There is this weird, like, sense of… I don't know how to explain it.

ILLÈNE: You can identify the plants by their smell?

ANITA: Well, not exactly that. Some of them I can, but not all of them. There is this weird kind of sense you get after you have worked like this for a while, you know what needs to be done, especially, like, with watering. That is one of my big jobs here. Things can't be over-watered or under-watered. I have to teach all the kids how to do that. You have to be right there. They don't all take all the steps you need to take to make sure the watering gets done right. So, I have to check it. We get a lot of moss on our flats in the greenhouse if you over-water.

ILLÈNE: That's amazing that you get moss in Taos. The greenhouse is really holding in a lot of moisture. That's impressive. How do the smells of the garden make you feel if you have been sniffing the cilantro or basil?

ANITA: Sometimes, it gets to me. It makes my stomach hurt sometimes. I can't be around the cilantro and basil for a long time. I can plant it, but I can't be touching it all over. I can just smell it, and it makes me feel not good. I'll eat it. I can eat it, but the smell of it after working with it for a long time, like if I do two flats, the seventy-two plants per flat gets to me after a while.

ILLÈNE: What do you feel when you see a seed sprout when you plant it?

ANITA: It's so cool. That's one of the things I really like, seeing it come out of the dirt. I'm like, "Oh, my God, I planted that. The plants are alive and it's growing." That's one of the things I like. It's like bringing a new life into the world, but it's a plant. It's really interesting. There was a flower out there the other day, and it was closed and the sun barely came out and it opened up. I was like, "Whoa, that was cool!" I had never seen a flower open up so fast. It was so amazing. Some people don't think about plants being alive. They just think, "Oh, that's just a plant or a tree." But it's not just a tree. There is life in there. It is green. It's alive. It's not like this pole here [*gestures to the log holding up the shade structure under which we sat*], you know.

ILLÈNE: That was once a tree, and it gave its life to be part of this building.

ANITA: Yeah. See, it's weird, a lot of my coworkers kind of get weirded out because I'll say, "It's weird how plants grow, but it's cool." They'll go, "I guess."

ILLÈNE: How do you feel when you pick something that you have planted from seed and watered?

ANITA: It's kind of sad sometimes. You see it grow, you water it every day, you see it there, and then it's gone in someone's stomach or someone's house. But it's a good thing to know they are eating it. But you get a bond with these plants when you are growing them. If you really enjoy doing this gardening, you have a bond with these plants. If they look sad, you'll feel sad. If I see a plant that's all sad and droopy, I'll feel sad.

ILLÈNE: Because somebody forgot to water it?

ANITA: Yeah. I'll get all sad, and I'll go water it or fix it or something.

ILLÈNE: Sometimes, I think my plants are calling to me, "Come and water me!"

ANITA: I talk to plants sometimes.

ILLÈNE: Do you know that people have done research on that?

ANITA: Yeah, and it helps them. It's a good thing. It sounds weird, but I talk to them. Sometimes, I come in the evening to make up hours and I'll be alone in the greenhouse and that's when I do it. But I don't do it when I am around people because they will think I am weird.

ILLÈNE: So, you have a conversation when you are on your own with them? I am sure they enjoy it. Do you notice that any one of your senses is stronger than another in giving you information when you are working in the garden?

ANITA: I think I use sight and touch the most. Like, a lot of places that sell food to stores do stuff with machines. They grow their stuff with machines, but we do all of ours by hand. I think that when you do it by hand, it gives you a connection with the earth and yourself. I don't know, it's just weird; it connects you with the earth. You are feeling the dirt. You are planting it in there. You know the roots are going to go into the soil.

ILLÈNE: How does it connect you to yourself?

ANITA: It just makes me feel like a really better person. I've been the type to get into trouble. When I was small and all through middle school, I was just a bad kid, you know. I ran into tons of trouble. I was always in the office. I was always getting in trouble. I would get in arguments, fights, telling people off. I mean, I have a really short temper. I don't like it. I'm going to tell you that right now. I hate that it is short and I can get mad at anything. But when I am here [in the garden], it's like it calms me down. I could probably stay in that greenhouse all day and just do stuff in there. I don't know, sometimes when I'll be home, I will get into an argument with somebody and I will wish I were here. And I wonder why, but I know why. It's just a really relaxing place to be. The plants can't talk to you; the plants can't give you any crap. It really calms you down, especially me. I don't know, but it really calms me down. When we are weeding, some people think it's a really hard job, but I like it. I can take my anger out. A weed is a plant too, but they are a nuisance too and you have to take them out. I can just take all my anger out on the weeds. It helps instead of taking it out on people 'cause I do that a lot. It's just really cool. That's something I never really thought I would do!

ILLÈNE: Have you ever heard of horticulture therapy? It's a way to take care of a hurt or a psychological need by taking care of plants. It's what you are doing naturally for yourself here.

ANITA: I went to this conference in Texas, a job-training program. I met a lot of cool people there. There was a guy from this place called CoBank, in Denver, I think. They are like this really big organization that deals with gardening stuff. They give out funds to start gardens. They have this program somewhere and they got convicts and people who are in trouble with the law, and they got them all together in this program and they have them cooking healthy food, and he said that 85 percent of the people in that program didn't go back to doing what they used to, like being a bad person with violence and all that. It actually helped them overcome it.

ILLÈNE: Was there gardening in the program or were they just cooking?

ANITA: I think he said there was some gardening, but I am not too sure. But I don't know what got into me that day, but it made me want to start a program like that. I don't know, just like with the people I work with here, they are really, like, I don't know, I would not tell them this personally because they wouldn't think of it the way I do, but when I come to work and work with them, they are like my family. Like me with Shirley, I can tell her anything and she will help me out, whatever I need. If I need a ride somewhere, she will take

The Taos youth farmers with Shirley in their hoop house. Credit: Illène Pevec

me. She is like family to me. It is really cool. I just met that girl, Marta. She is really cool too. We talk a lot. We are friends, you know? And Luis and Ed, I have known them forever. I went to school with Ed. Luis was my brother's friend, and I used to hang out with him when I was small. We all know each other and it's awesome.

ILLÈNE: You might be surprised. They might say the same thing.

ANITA: I don't know. They don't enjoy doing it [working in the garden] as much as I do. But I don't know, I wouldn't say they are here for the money, but the paycheck does help to get on working. I could come to work here and not get paid. I wouldn't care because it helps me out. That's as good as pay to me because it helps me. And see, I am going to college for agriculture. And I know I am! I am going to make that happen. A lot of people have told me that I can't do it. I've been put down a lot. What people have seen me do, getting in trouble and all that, people think that is all I can do.

ILLÈNE: It's wonderful that you have found Shirley who encourages you in your work ability to learn and that you can talk to her when you are over here gardening.

ANITA: She really understands. And knowing that I actually accomplished this, I got to go to Texas for job training. I'd never been to Texas. I'd never been to anywhere. It's a big accomplishment.

ILLÈNE: It's a wonderful accomplishment. Do you get to take food home to your grandpa that you grow here?

ANITA: Not now because it's not ready yet. I don't know, I am just really proud of myself knowing that I have done this because I waited for two months to get this job and now I've got it. And it's something that I like to do. I work for a different garden now, but I am Shirley's, I don't know what you call it, but she called me her next-in-hand.

ILLÈNE: Congratulations. That is a huge accomplishment.

ANITA: Heck, yeah, it is!

ILLÈNE: You know what? There are more and more programs in sustainable agriculture in colleges around the country now. People finally understand that this country has to give the opportunity to young people to learn about sustainable agriculture so they can feed themselves and the country because it has to change from industrial agriculture.

ANITA: It's really cool knowing there are people out there that actually enjoy doing the same thing I do. When I went to the conference, I met so many smart people who love gardening and love doing exactly what I do. I was the only high school intern there. The rest were all college students. I was like, "Wow!" It was so cool. It's just really good to know there are people out there who care about what we are doing. Some people think it's really dumb and a waste of time, but they won't be saying that when they have to pay $10 for a head of lettuce at a store [*sighs in disgust*]. It actually gets me really mad sometimes when I think about it, but as long as I know that I am doing good and I know what I am doing, that's all that matters.

ILLÈNE: What you are doing is extremely important. You are making a very positive contribution.

ANITA: And it's changed a lot with me getting in trouble too. I don't get in trouble anymore. I could, but I don't. It's not what I want to do. It's just changed me as a person. If you had known me for a really long time, then you would really see it.

ILLÈNE: Congratulations for all you have accomplished being a youth worker in the program. Thank you for trusting me and telling me your story.

ANITA: It's one thing I'm not afraid to tell people anymore. I used to be uptight about it, but it's my life. I have to deal with it either way.

ILLÈNE: If you had to explain to a bunch of school principals why youth gardens are important, what would you say to them?

ANITA: I would probably tell them that there are other ways to learn besides being in a classroom and learning about plants from books. It's not right. You can get out there and be hands on with things. It's really good for kids to know about what's going on in our whole food industry and the purpose of planting your own food. That's why I support it. Even for kids like me who have been in trouble and in hard places, there is help. You can't just let it take you over. You can do this [gardening] and feel good about it or live your life trying to get into trouble again. People think this [gardening] is a bad thing sometimes—well, not a bad thing, but that it's dumb. It's not dumb. It's really interesting. We learn a lot—not just about plants, but about life itself. You learn a lot about life. You learn to really cherish your life. I have. I definitely have. I would just tell them it's something people have to figure out now while they are still young so that they will know this forever. We are not always going to have things the easy way. This [gardening] does get tough. It gets really tough. You can get sunburn. You can get really tired. It's just really hard work, but you don't think about it as work. You think about it as an activity. Just go plant a carrot. You can eat it when it grows, and it's cool.

I was actually really thinking about the [CoBank] program that guy, Elliot, told me about, where people didn't go back to being violent. Well, I want to do something like that, but with kids my age. Growing your own healthy food and the way they have the kitchen here, you can go make something good out of the healthy food. But some people when you think of healthy food, they think it will taste gross, but what I want to do is make it taste good, but healthy.

ILLÈNE: And as soon as you get it from a garden, it is both.

ANITA: So, I don't know, but you know what I mean, like putting flavor into it.

ILLÈNE: Yes, of course.

ANITA: It's just an idea.

ILLÈNE: It's a wonderful idea! I'm sure you will be able to do that someday. You have the experience to do it and you know how important it is to do it. Thank you for sharing your dream with me.

ANITA: You are welcome. Better to share it with more people now so when I do it, you'll know.

&

Anita's life was transformed from anger and hurt to joy in working with others to grow food by participating in this garden. She found a mentor in Shirley and a life purpose: growing food sustainably for her own and others' good health. She has found peers with whom she can work and pride in what she does and harvests. She no longer gets in trouble and now grows food and strives to prepare for an agriculture degree and career. She has transformed herself and her life by working with the earth.

# 22

## SEMBRANDO SEMILLAS:
### COMMUNITY IRRIGATION, ANCIENT TO MODERN

When I finished interviewing Anita, the Taos farmers left for lunch. Jane and I retreated from the hot midday sun to a shady courtyard for a picnic. What a gift to meet the people at Taos County Economic Development Corporation and learn about their comprehensive programs for promoting community health, economic development, local food system advancements, and a new generation of farmers to keep the traditional seeds growing. This program wedded community and culture, youth and elders, food and health, and education and action. What would we find at the next farming program?

Refreshed, we drove a winding road south through low mountains, pine forest, and sagebrush to Chamisal to meet the people in Sembrando Semillas, the youth-farming program that is part of the New Mexico Acequia Association. Acequias are the community-dug and community-maintained irrigation systems that farming depends on in the New Mexican desert. Sembrando Semillas means "sowing seeds."

We stopped at the Peñasco post office to ask if they knew how close we were to the farm we sought in Chamisal. As soon as I gave the postmistress Juliet's name and address, she told me exactly where the farm was because she knew the family personally. Chamisal has a population so small that the most current US Census does not report it as a searchable town name. However, 301 people lived in Chamisal when last it appeared in the official census report (US Census, 2003, 28), and most live on small farms as we saw many along the road.

Hand-built horno adobe oven. Credit: Norberto

As we pulled into the driveway, a Hispanic gentleman came out of his adobe house to greet us. Juliet's father, Maximiliano Garcia, welcomed us in Spanish. I responded in Spanish and told him I had come to speak with Juliet and the youth who were part of the food-growing project. He proceeded to tell me about his family's history. What an amazing story he shared. Their family descends from Coronado's drummer, a Moor named Estefanico, who decided to stay in New Mexico on the very property where we were currently standing rather than continue on with Coronado's expedition in the 1540s. The family's ancestors are buried in the two cemeteries very close to the farm.

I stepped back in time listening to this story. How extraordinary that the family has been on that very same piece of land for almost five hundred years growing food and children! A horno, a traditional circular New Mexican adobe oven, graced the front of the property.

Behind the house, I could see the farm field and fruit trees and the various piles of equipment that occupy and define farmyards. Juliet's father explained to me that acequias have, from the beginning, been dug and managed communally to ensure that everyone has fair access to water. Maximiliano gestured towards a nearby hill and told me that all their acequia water came from that watershed and that the winter snows accumulate there to feed the spring that provides their water. His ancestors had been involved in digging the ditches that are the acequia system. He also told me a story about a woman lighting a huge fire up the mountain that blew apart the rocks to allow the water to flow—the fire had heated the water in the stones to steam, making the rocks split. The word acequia comes from Syria, and the Spanish learned this way to distribute water from the Moors who had occupied Spain and influenced Spanish culture. The Spanish conquistadores brought the traditional acequia system with them when they explored and brought New Mexico under Spanish rule.

Before he said good-bye to let Juliet give me a farm tour, Juliet's father told me that he could no longer find piglets to buy. Their absence was a mystery and loss to him. He asked me to keep my eyes open as we drove back to Albuquerque and let him know if I saw any signs advertising piglets for sale. (We looked carefully on the way back, but saw none, and I felt sad that I had no good news to send him about available piglets.) His request made me remember the impressive pig that had starred in *The Milagro Beanfield War*, a 1988 Robert Redford film made just a few miles south of Chamisal in Truchas, New Mexico. I asked Mr. Garcia if he had seen it. He had, and we laughed together at that big, fabulous pig. The film portrays this region, how an acequia carries water, and how integral family farming and irrigation water rights are to the local culture.

When Juliet took us out to meet her husband, Edward, and his brother, Cristino, she told me that I was lucky to hear so much from her father since he was not always so forthcoming with family history. I indeed felt blessed to have had a conversation that covered almost five centuries of family history and culture in a Spanish that had the sound of a different era—a time when families dug irrigation ditches together from mountain tops to valleys.

The corn, beans, and squash grow in a field together behind Juliet and Edward's frame house and her parents' adobe house. The hoop house that Edward built shelters a rich mix of salad greens, tomatoes, and cucumbers. Their daughter, Donne, offered us tastes of arugula and herbs that she clearly took pride in growing.

I could see the alfalfa already starting to bloom in the fields all around them and asked Juliet if people in that area were alarmed at the GMO alfalfa that had been launched into the agricultural market with US Department of Agriculture approval recently. Juliet assured me that thanks to the acequias and the way they operate communally with a dedication to local food culture and education, they were all doing seed saving and avoiding the GMO-potential pollution in the region. The New Mexico Acequia Association (2013) vision statement makes clear a dedication to nurturing traditional agricultural values, including seed saving, and recognizes the importance of resisting any "commodification and contamination" of water and developing "querencia through a strong connection to land and community." Querencia is a metaphysical concept in Spanish that describes a place where one feels safe and at home and is derived from the Spanish verb *querer*, meaning to desire or to love.

I found querencia growing abundantly in the Sembrando Semillas project. After our farm tour that included the orchard with Donne and her parents, we went into Juliet and Edward's home so that I could interview Donne and Noberto, another youth who participated extensively in the agricultural program. While it sprinkled rain outside, cooling the July heat and watering the thirsty ground, I heard from them about what tending the land and caring for their deeply rooted culture means.

Norberto, aged nineteen, has gardened three or four years with Sembrando Semillas. He attends Northern New Mexico College in Española, studies accounting, and wants to go into business. He still comes to participate on the farm in the summer. Like many people in New Mexico, he is a descendent of both American Indians and Spanish settlers.

ILLÈNE: Why did you get involved in Sembrando Semillas?

NORBERTO: Well, I first came over here because Juliet's son, Torivio, is my best friend and this is what they did, and I got involved and I realized that this is our culture, this is our heritage; it is something that we should always know. No matter where we are in life or how far along things go, this is something that we should always have in life. My culture would not have survived if it had not been for agriculture.

ILLÈNE: Are you a person who liked vegetables before you started growing them?

NORBERTO: No.

ILLÈNE: Do you like eating them now?

NORBERTO: Yes, I do.

ILLÈNE: So, has it changed your eating habits?

NORBERTO: It definitely has, for sure. I do take things home. I have learned how to cook things in the horno, how to make chicos [young, green field corn baked in an horno overnight and then reconstituted with water; chicos obtain a unique, distinctive, smoky taste from roasting in the wood-fired oven], how to re-mud it [the horno]. I've learned a lot of things.

ILLÈNE: How long does it take to fire the horno?

NORBERTO: It takes all day. You leave it overnight. It's ready in the morning. Everyone has to get involved. Everyone has to help. It's pretty nice. For Thanksgiving, we have made the turkeys that they have here. We beheaded the turkey and plucked it here. I feel like it makes you respect what's around you more because you know the hard work that was put into growing what you eat, that someone broke their back out there to pull all the weeds so that you can have food on the table. I feel like it is something that no matter how hard you work for it, you have to work hard for it because it sustains you. It sustains your life. It sustains me mentally because I feel more connected with the earth and with what God gives us and the things that we have outside.

ILLÈNE: Do you notice that your emotions change when you are gardening?

NORBERTO: They do. I feel like I am in a better mood. Even if I am tired, it's not a bad tired. It's a good tired because you actually worked on something. I think it is the community, the sense of community, because we all go outside to do it. We work together to accomplish one thing.

ILLÈNE: Do you notice that your focus changes when you are gardening?

NORBERTO: I feel like it does because I feel like, after working on something, you are putting your energy into one thing all day. Because you are working so hard on that one thing, you are practicing how to focus.

ILLÈNE: What does your family think of you growing food over here?

NORBERTO: I think they enjoy it because I take them home fresh food. I take them lettuce, tomatoes, and other things, and so I think they enjoy it.

ILLÈNE: If you had a chance to talk to the superintendents of schools, what you would tell them about the importance of gardening for children in schools?

NORBERTO: I feel like they need to teach kids to garden, especially in New Mexico, especially the traditional way. I think it is something everyone should know how to do. If it wasn't for gardening, our families wouldn't even be around. We probably wouldn't survive without gardening, without agriculture. I feel it is something very important that children should know. It is very important to culture, to everybody's culture. It doesn't matter who you are, where you are from, or what your skin color is, your ancestors gardened at some time and it's important to know how to do.

ᏼᎦ

Norberto is the only youth who used the expression "practicing how to focus" to describe gardening. Indeed, from what others have said not so directly as Norberto, focus developed during gardening can be seen as an inner practice of mindfulness, an awareness of being fully present in the moment. Norberto has grown up embedded in the local culture with close friendships to the Garcia and Gonzales family where traditional agriculture is the way of life. In a region where one has to drive many miles to get to a grocery store, knowing how to grow food is particularly valuable to not only feed the family but save money and carbon emissions on the transportation costs involved in obtaining it elsewhere. His own experience learning farming with this family that embodies the values of Sembrando Semillas makes him see how important this knowledge is for all New Mexican children and all children in general to honor the land and the work for life itself.

I spoke next with Donne Gonzales, also called Donita, Juliet and Edward's eighteen-year-old daughter and Mr. Garcia's granddaughter.

**DONNE:** I have really been planting all my life—my grandparents, my parents—it's really just been a traditional thing. If you don't plant, you don't eat. That's what it comes down to. I used to not like working in the field. It was boring to me. And then I realized it was pretty cool. I was like, "We have our own seed. We can watch it grow. We can eat it. What else is there?" It's pretty amazing. Since I was a baby, definitely everybody, my parents, grandparents, my brothers, aunts and uncles, cousins, everybody has always helped work in the field and cared for animals: pigs, chickens, even cows. We buy cows to slaughter them. We have meat during the whole year. We go to slaughter at my uncle's property. He lives closer to the mountain. He has cattle, so we buy the animal from him. We butcher up there.

Swiss chard, lambs-quarters, mustard, and mallow planted by Donne. Credit: Donne Gonzales

ILLÈNE: When did your awareness shift that growing food was worth your time and effort?

DONNE: I want to say maybe eleven or twelve. I found out it was really cool to have a culture, to have a background, to know your ancestors, to know where you are from, where your roots are. That's when I realized it was cool. Not everyone knows, not everyone has someone to ask about your past: your grandma or your great-grandma. My family has actually been here for thirteen generations, right here on this land. What more can I say? My dad's side of the family has always been farming or ranching. That's how they lived. They hardly went to school because they were so busy with the land, with the sheep. But my mom's side of the family, they were always really busy too. My grandpa never let us be bored or be lazy in the summer: "You have to get to work, you have to *escaldad*." [Donne's father, Edward, explained to me that escaldad is a colloquial expression meaning that when you are hoeing, you have to pay attention to your plants and take care of them properly.]

ILLÈNE: Your grandfather told me that his family is descended from Coronado's drummer. That is very cool. Does your family still have a tradition of drumming?

DONNE: It is very cool. It's awesome. I wouldn't say we have a drumming tradition, but we do like to get together once in a while and we have a little music fest. We bust out with the guitars and drums and rattles and stuff. It's really fun, but we don't go all out. But it's really cute. We get around the campfire too.

ILLÈNE: You all have a horno too. What do you cook in the horno?

Edward, Juliet, Donne and Cristino in the hoop house.  **Credit:** Illène Pevec

DONNE: That depends. For Thanksgiving, we will do our turkeys in the oven. We'll do bread or even pies sometimes. When harvest comes around, we do pumpkins. We'll cut them in half and put spices and brown sugar and put them in there and bake them, and then we take them out and dry them, and they are so delicious. We do chicos. We take corn, get the husks wet, and bake them in there. And we do a lot of meat in there. When we butcher animals, we will put them in there overnight to cook them, but that is pretty much it.

ILLÈNE: Did you help make that horno?

DONNE: Yeah, I did. We usually plaster it once a year to maintain and keep it in good shape. With our youth group, we built a horno at our community center. It is actually really lovely. It was about a two-week process. We made the adobes [hand-made bricks made from clay and straw that are the traditional building blocks for construction in northern New Mexico], and we had to let them dry. We made the base and we filled the middle with rocks and plastered it. Then we made the actual horno—the round shape. It was really interesting to see how it all fits together. It's actually really tricky when you are building the adobe. It's not an actual square, but it curves in. The back is square, but the front curves in, so when you are building it, everything curves in and when you get to the top, you just have to put one on top. We can use the soil and we add some hay to it and some sand and a bunch of water [and dry them in the sun].

ILLÈNE: Where are you going to college?

DONNE: Right now, I have a scholarship with an organization that is helping seasonal farmers. They accepted me because I work more than seventy days on a farm, and so it is worth $21,000, and I am attending University of New Mexico in Albuquerque main campus, and I am looking into political science.

ILLÈNE: That is very exciting for you. Are you thinking of joining a campus community garden when you are there?

DONNE: Yeah, definitely. I have friends there actually, and there is El Centro de la Raza. They are an organization there to help immigrants. For me, it's more about being such a country girl and moving to the city: [*changes her voice to that of a frightened child to make fun of herself and acknowledge her real fears*] "I don't want to go to the city: it's stinky and polluted and there are people everywhere!" But it's okay. I have a scholarship and I can stick it out. And they are like, "It's okay. We will help you. We've got your back. We will feed you. You can come to us for whatever you need." And there are community gardens there. With the organization that I got the scholarship with, I will be working in gardens.

ILLÈNE: Oh, that's great. Tomorrow, I am going to meet the young people with Project Feed the Hood in Albuquerque. When you are outside, do you find that your sensory awareness is heightened? Do you pay more attention to the sensory experiences in the garden?

DONNE: Yeah, I definitely think so. I feel like you hear everything. You are in touch. You are not disconnected or paying attention to your phone or the computer or TV. You are there and you can feel the dirt, feel Mother Earth. You can smell it and touch it and feel it. It's amazing.

ILLÈNE: Do you feel there is one sense you pay more attention to?

DONNE: I really feel like smelling and touching are pretty big because everything smells so good. Especially after the rain and everything is blooming and you can smell the flowers and it's amazing. And the way the rain smells, it's really yummy, I think, and touching is amazing too. Everything, knowing that it is real.

ILLÈNE: Do you find that it changes you? If you go outside and you are annoyed because you have too much homework, does going outside to work change how you feel?

DONNE: Yeah, definitely. When I am outside, I feel more calm and more at peace myself. I can think and be more in tune with my body and not having crazy thoughts.

ILLÈNE: That's a really wonderful thing for you to already have that experience when you go off to college. College can be overwhelming for anyone, but knowing you can go outside and get your hands in the dirt, even for just a little while, and that it will help will be a wonderful personal resource you can take to the city with you. It will be a big help. Is there anything I have not asked you about Sembrando Semillas that you would like people to know about?

DONNE: One cool thing I have done with Sembrando Semillas: they have created leaders. I guess they have made me into a leader. We get to go on trips and meet different organizations, and within that, my brother and I and some other kids have created a Food Bill of Rights. We went to a conference with about one hundred kids from all over the country, and so we all got together to create this new Food Bill of Rights. It's been three years. And we got supported by this organization called RIC, which is Rooted In Community. They were supposed to take it to the president and see what he thought about it. It was so many different bills, a big bill of rights.

We thought it would be good for us and for the earth for being sustainable people. What really got me into farming was knowing that there is still modern-day slavery. I have so many friends who are immigrants. It doesn't happen here, but it does in Florida. There are so many kids that are hurt and families that are hurt so badly because of modern-day slavery [*begins to cry as she speaks*].

ILLÈNE: So, families that are immigrating into Florida are getting imprisoned on farms to work?

DONNE: Yeah, like some of the fast food restaurants are a huge buyer of these tomatoes [and] they pay workers like $10 a day to pick thousands and thousands. They are not giving them a just wage to make it through life. They just give them a shack to live in. It hurts so bad and that is why I really started paying attention. I decided I wanted to grow and pick my own food.

ILLÈNE: Did you meet some young people from Florida?

DONNE: Yeah, I did. I met kids. I met this guy named Hedarto from Florida from Immokalee. He started a big movement for more benefits for farm workers there because he is an immigrant and that is what he went through.[1]

ILLÈNE: Like Cesar Chavez?

DONNE: Yes, definitely. America is about freedom, and we abolished slavery, but nobody knows there is still modern slavery out there. I am not studying political science for law, but I want to protect my seeds and land and water.

ILLÈNE: So, this is very personal for you and about public policy!

DONNE: Yes, definitely!

ILLÈNE: Well, that is a big view and an important goal. The good thing is that there are a lot of young people waking up now to food and a growing awareness in this country. You are not alone in this. There are a lot of good people involved in this work. Have you heard about the Food Policy Council in Santa Fe? They are doing really good work and you could call on them for help. You already have a really big goal in life. If you get fed up with all the work, remember you have a really big reason to go to university. If I can be of any help in connecting you to people, let me know. If you had a chance to talk to the superintendents of schools about the importance of school gardens, what would you say?

DONNE: I would tell them that it is a really good idea. I think it is really good for kids to know, first of all, where their food comes from. And it's also really healthy. So many kids these days even have diabetes. It's because of all the junk food because it's not real food. If you have a garden, you can eat healthy and eat and live [food with a living content, unprocessed]. You can learn so much culture from having a garden or from being outside, [learning] from your grandparents. Every culture in the world has gardened and it is not all the same, but it is all for the same reason: to live.

---

1. The Coalition of Immokalee Workers continues their social justice work for fair wages and decent working conditions for farm workers.

⁊ꝺ

Donne feels deeply about the social justice issues she sees tied to food growing and harvesting. She has been brought up with family local awareness and has participated in a national conference that exposed her to the national agricultural labor injustices affecting human lives. It's frightening for her to leave her close-knit family to go to Albuquerque, New Mexico's biggest city, to attend college, but she wants to learn in order to engage professionally in creating new food policy that is in accordance with health and social justice values. She understands on a very deep level what saving seeds is all about and how important it is to everyone's health and well-being.

Juliet Garcia Gonzalez and Edward Gonzalez work closely with their children and their community's youth to nurture a deep regard for the land and teach traditional farming skills. Edward and Cristino were busy working outside, and so Juliet talked with me about the family's shared mission with Sembrando Semillas, for which both she and Edward work.

JULIET: I have been gardening, I am going to say, at least forty years. My dad would get up early in the morning, and he would have this field out here always with corn, and I was the one of the children, I want to say the other ones were forced, they felt forced, but I loved it, just to be out there with my dad, and we would just pull weeds. I would always pull weeds while the others were doing homework. To me, it was easier because you always have to have that. Someone is pulling weeds and getting really close to the roots. Someone is tending the corn. I've always loved it, yeah!

ILLÈNE: Do you know why you have always loved it?

JULIET: I don't. I am going to blame it on being a Taurus. I was born in May. It is my favorite season. May comes around and I am a new person. I don't know how real that is, but, for me, that is how it feels. I wait all year for the green grass.

ILLÈNE: How did you get involved with Sembrando Semillas?

JULIET: Sembrando Semillas was a project of Paula Garcia, who is the executive director of the New Mexico Acequia Association. And she was working with Miguel Santistevan, who was a mentor. He got my son involved. So, Torivio has been involved with Sembrando Semillias since its inception. So, they have been part of the project for a long time. They asked my husband to be a mentor. I want to say there were at least five sites. There was Mora and Pecos and Urraca and Embudo and then Taos. And then, over the course of the years, some of those sites dissolved. It's hard to get the kids engaged or to make time as a mentor. And so, at the time my husband started mentoring, he is the hands-on guy. He will go out there and teach you how to do things, but I was always stuck writing reports: "I need this done, babe. I need this report written, can you get it done?" So, one day, they said, "Hey, do you want a job?" So, I have been working for the New Mexico Acequia Association full time now for two years this August. Working with youth, writing reports—simple things about our activities, what we have done, what we accomplished, what they learned, what went into the ground.

ILLÈNE: Tell me the two stories on how your acequia system got built that your father talked about when we were in the field. I want to make sure I understood all he said since he was telling me in Spanish.

JULIET: I have heard the stories, but I can't remember from whom. I have heard it many times: that the first time it got engineered, the water didn't come down, and a woman went up there and she engineered it and it went through. You have to light fires to get through the rock. That's it right there. They would make fires and throw water on it, and the heat busts the rocks, and that's how they get through the rock. But last year, my dad told me a different history. We did an activity up in the watershed, and my dad told me it took thirteen families thirteen years full-on working all summer each year to build the system. They would camp up there at the base. They start at the base. The springs emerge naturally. They need to run off somewhere, but they are giving them direction. The water comes from the snowfall on the mountain, from the watershed.

ILLÈNE: I saw that you have a watershed protection area here from the road signs posted.

JULIET: Yes, that is the Chamisal Mutual Domestic Water Consumer Association. That is different. My dad sat on the board for thirty years, but he just came off it last year because I was willing to do it. It's a community system. It's our drinking water and it comes from a deep well. It's from an artesian well. We don't have to purify it. We probably have 200 to 300 families in town, and the association has only 120 memberships sold. Right now, the organization could probably hold another 100 families. I know in the 1950s, they appropriated the water from the state. I don't know when they dug it. It's a big deal. New Mexico is the driest state in the nation. I know in my whole life, we have had really good water. It has to continue. We are real careful in that area. Right now, we want to educate the community like California does: "Don't spill your paints. Don't spill your gasoline. Don't spill your oil." Because the closer you get to the well, it's this big around [*makes a big circle with her arms*] and the well is in the center. It's important to keep it clean.

ILLÈNE: Do families have septic systems?

JULIET: Yes. A lot of people have septic systems, and my dad has been on that committee for twelve years trying to figure out a sanitation system, like one big area.

ILLÈNE: Has anyone around here figured out how to use your grey water to put on the farm fields?

JULIET: No. We do it, but we just throw it outside. It's no fancy system.

ILLÈNE: I was just thinking in a place like this, probably with no building code, I would think there would be a way to plumb your showers and bathtub so that the water went through a gravel bed to the acequia or to the chickens.

JULIET: Or to the fruit trees. We have to figure it out. In all my life, this is the first time we have had a problem. The last drought we had was fifty years ago. So, this year, people are talking about it—how to reuse the grey water. We have never struggled in Chamisal. When I say we have acequia water running all year, we have acequia water all year. Whenever you need it, you can use your water. This year has been different. So, it's a good thing that people are thinking about it now.

ILLÈNE: There is a New Mexico Acequia Association. Does that mean there are many places that there are these springs where water comes from a higher collection area? Is it specific to this region of New Mexico?

JULIET: No, it's the entire state. I don't know how everyone gets their water. I think in some places, they divert it off a river, but in Chamisal, it comes from our watershed. I am sorry I don't know about the whole state. I have only been with the association for a little while.

ILLÈNE: Can you tell me what the most rewarding part is for you in doing this work with young people, mentoring them, setting up mentorships, and sharing an enormous amount of your own experience with them?

JULIET: [*Chokes up with tears.*] Oh, that I know my kids have querencia, the truest querencia. When it was time for Torivio to go to school [university], he didn't want to go. Now that it is time for Donne to go to school, she doesn't want to go. She knows the importance because I push them and I tell them the importance of education, but they already have that balance. They already know it. Sorry [*for her tears*]. They already know what it means to come back home. I always tell my kids, "It doesn't matter where you go, when you come back, this is where you belong." I am not leaving. I am not going anywhere. I have never left in forty-three years. I am not going anywhere. This is where we are rooted. To me, that is the most important thing: that they understand where they are from and that there is no shame in farming and just that they love it. And they have loved it. They know the amount of hard work that goes into it. And they belong. They just have that sense of appreciation for who their ancestors are. When we hear our grandmothers talk, our *viejitos*, about the work, they can relate. They know what it means. Some people are so disconnected, even [people] from around here. They don't know what it means. What does it mean to make acequias, what does it mean to make chicos, to slaughter an animal for food? To me, that's the most important: that my kids know these things and their friends know these things because that is who we mentor [*sighs with relief for having spoken her truth*].

ILLÈNE: They do. They told me they know it.

JULIET: [*Laughs.*] Good! Good! Good! It's very empowering that they know those things. They know the importance. Anywhere they go! When my kids went to those Rooted In Community conferences, I didn't get to go, but I got the report back that my kids were teaching.

ILLÈNE: I heard that your nine-year-old did a presentation! That's really impressive! It's wonderful! Congratulations to all of you!

JULIET: They are really great! They are confident because they are doing it. It *is* so wonderful. Thank you. It has been a lot of work.

ILLÈNE: Your work has grown deep roots. Your kids have gotten the nurturing they need to stay strong.

JULIET: It's true. It's true. That's why, one day, I am going to paint. My husband and I made the agreement that we were going to raise kids. It's been about the family. Everything else will come. Everything else is going to come. Since I was four, I have wanted to paint. I went to school to paint, but then I couldn't finish because I had a family. My kids hear me say it all the time. One day, I want to paint. I still dream to paint. I want to paint!

ILLÈNE: You will.

JULIET: Yeah, I will. I really will! Right now, we are raising kids, good kids, good, strong healthy kids.

ILLÈNE: It's been such a pleasure to be here today and meet you all and hear your father's wonderful telling of family history.

JULIET: Yeah, remember the story because he doesn't always come out. We get lots of visitors. I don't know why he came out today. We had FoodCorps here yesterday.

ILLÈNE: I was telling your daughter that she would be an ideal applicant for FoodCorps with all her experience. You know, they get so many applicants, more than one thousand, for a few positions because so many young people want to learn to grow food now.

JULIET: I think there are only sixty positions throughout the country. One of our Sembrando Semillas participants is a FoodCorps member, so he brought them by to see us to show them what we are doing.

ILLÈNE: That's so wonderful that you are already represented in FoodCorps. That is so great!

What would you like to tell all the people who are going to read this book about the value of what you are doing right here? You are growing kids here, but it goes broader than just your own kids.

JULIET: The importance, I guess, is just to love kids, to be forgiving of kids, being available to youth all the time. That is the hardest thing we do some times. We go to bed, my husband and I, and we cry [*she begins to cry*]. There are a lot of things going on, a lot of dynamics that the kids are dealing with. So, we have to really try and help them, to walk them through things. They aren't even our kids [the youth they mentor in Sembrando Semillas], but they need that. It's important to be open to somebody, to be really open so you can be friends with somebody. Know that these kids really appreciate it. They appreciate it. They are like, "Wow! Someone is listening. Somebody cares!"

ILLÈNE: I realized in thinking about the different kids across the country and the different adults I have talked to, that what is happening is that all of you who are mentors, all of us who are mentors to kids, what we are planting is seeds of love inside them. That's what's growing. That's what is so powerful. We are planting the seeds of love right along with the carrots and lettuce.

JULIET: It's not about the garden, it's about what is in here [*she touches her chest*].

ILLÈNE: The garden makes it easier. I don't know why, but the garden makes it easier to plant the seeds of love.

JULIET: The kids show up. They want to be part of the group. It doesn't matter what you are doing. They want to help. It's wonderful. I have a big group. There are fifteen youth.

ILLÈNE: I'm sorry I can't stay longer to meet and interview everyone.

The warm welcome the Garcia and Gonzalez family extended to us to hear about their work mentoring youth to respect and cultivate the land to grow good food touched me deeply. Querencia entered my vocabulary to capture the love that guides a mentor to support a youth to grow in the best way possible. Before Jane and I left, we walked around the area near the house with Edward and Cristino, who showed us how they make hoop houses to extend the growing season by cutting in half the metal frames of old trampolines that are no longer useful to make the half circle frames necessary to support the plastic that covers the hoops and protects the plants from cold weather. Inside this basic framework, they use willow branches lashed together as the center supports to hold up the roof. Their handy work saves thousands of dollars in material costs and provides at least an extra couple of months for food to grow each year. They are the kind of farmers who know how to take what is at hand to make what's needed. They are not down the street from a hardware store. They have the skills to be self-reliant and teach the youth the same.

They also had a large pile of bicycle parts, and I begged them to figure out how to make a pedal-operated compost shredder. Every community and school garden in the country needs one, as do home gardeners, to shred the inedible stalks and vegetation debris so that it will compost faster. Edward gave me a big grin and said he would work on it!

Reluctantly, we drove away. They had things to do and we had miles to cover to return to Albuquerque before dark. We saw the approaching thunderstorms that could quickly bring flash floods to the dry desert. I knew there was much more to learn here in Chamisal. I was grateful for what we had heard from three generations in this farming family that mentors their own children and others. Once again, we witnessed the internal latticework that adult gardeners provide the youth to support their personal growth as skilled and caring humans. At this family farm, it's called querencia.

# 23
## FEED THE HOOD

Albuquerque, New Mexico, sits at the base of the Sandia Mountains and has miles of high desert around it, but it's very much a bustling urban environment. The 2010 US Census estimated the 2013 population in Albuquerque would be around 556,495 and relatively youthful with 24 percent under 18. In 2010, the city population was 46.7 percent Hispanic, 42.1 percent white, and 4.6 percent American Indian, half the percentage of American Indians living in Taos County (US Census Bureau, 2010).

Since the Spaniards marched into New Mexico almost five hundred years ago looking for gold, they have intermarried with the Native Americans. The youth and adults that I interviewed in Albuquerque with Irish and Scottish last names had black hair and dark eyes, so the statistics cannot really be understood just in numbers. A person may self-identify as Latino or white and still carry the genetic heritage of the Pueblos or Navajo or another Southwest tribe and have Celtic ancestors too. New Mexico has not just multicolored soils and rocks that glow in the high desert plateau sun, but a beautiful mosaic of human cultures and colors. New Mexico's modern capital reflects this life dance.

On my last day in New Mexico, I headed to an Albuquerque farmers' market early in the morning to meet several youth and the mentor and director of Project Feed the Hood, Travis McKenzie. Travis uses a Spanish pronunciation of his first name. The youth and adult gardeners from Project Feed the Hood greeted us with enormous smiles from behind their farmers' market table laden with colorful produce. Three adults and three youth were not only selling their

Project Feed the Hood table at an Albuquerque farmers' market. Credit: Illène Pevec

purple, red, orange, and yellow carrots, white Japanese turnips, rainbow chard, and early hot habanero peppers, but also displaying the wild weed plants that are edible and grow between the rows. The lamb's-quarters and purslane, both higher in nutrients than spinach, sat next to the more familiar domestic vegetables.

In my own garden, these wild, very nutritious self-seeding plants survived the grasshopper plague I had that summer while my milder tasting leafy greens that I planted and watered did not. Offering education on the value of what weeds to eat is very wise. Knowing what these nutritious wild plants look like and how many nutrients they have may encourage people who don't even have a garden to eat wild, free greens.

I interviewed Travis by phone the month after my visit to the farmer's market where we met, and I include his history of Project Feed the Hood here to provide context for what the youth he mentors told me in person that day we all met in Albuquerque:

TRAVIS: In January 2010, I was asked to meet up with Rodrigo Rodriquez to meet with one of our colleagues and mentors, Joachin Lujan, at a coffee shop that has old-school New Mexican food. We had breakfast and talked about creating a garden to promote social justice and positive social change. Rodrigo and I met a couple of times and started Project Feed the Hood. We partnered with city councilor, Rey Garduño. He actually was able to help us get some space. The space of our community garden is actually on an emergency landing strip with the aviation department. It worked out for us because the space can't be developed because of that and it's perfect for a community garden. We got some start-up money from the [W. K.] Kellogg Foundation to start addressing issues of childhood obesity and diabetes. So that's what helped us to start at the beginning, and now it's grown the last couple of years into what it is now. We started with turning that lot into a community garden. We partnered with the city, and they brought in some compost and mulch. We also partnered with a veterans' group to build some raised beds for the elderly people and people in wheelchairs. In that space itself, we pulled thirty wheelbarrows of trash out. The space was an empty lot that was being used for substance abuse. We had people tell us it was used for drug deals too. A couple of people told us fights would go on there after school. It wasn't a very productive space for the community. That was part of the idea too: to take something that was somewhat detrimental for the community and transform it into something positive and beneficial. Since then, we have had direct testimonies from community members saying there is no more substance abuse, no more drug deals, no more slow cruise-bys. So, it has kind of transformed that whole part of the neighborhood. We did start in a low-income community, very diverse, transient. There are a lot of different ethnicities. There is a large, urban Native American community, kind of urban-displaced Native Americans. It was a good place for us to start; a community like that being so transient. We have seen some sad things too. Some kids have moved out of state to get work. Some got addicted. It's that kind of neighborhood. At least, we could be there for them while they were there. Besides that, we have had a lot of successes from that space too. A lot of neighbors decided to grow food in their backyards. We were able to work with a couple of youth, do some youth internships. The whole idea was to create a community garden where everyone works together and everyone shares in the harvest.

**ILLÈNE:** So, people don't have their own garden plots, they all work together communally?

**TRAVIS:** Yes. That was strategic. Like I said, our mentor, Joachin Lujan has an old *dicho*, a proverb, "*Quien pone, saca.*" That means, "Who puts in, can take out." That has been our dicho that guides the space. So, anyone who comes in and works can take home food. When the staff is there working with the kids, we always try to send them home with bags of veggies and fruits. The space is really an educational space. Not only did we want to grow food, but we wanted to use the garden as a community organizing tool. SWOP [SouthWest Organizing Project] isn't really an agriculture organization. SouthWest Organizing Project is a mass-based community justice organization that has been doing community organizing for a long time. That was kind of more of our focus. We wanted to grow food, teach people how to grow food, talk about food, but we also wanted to have meetings there, organize people, talk about issues we could address, empower people to want to make positive social change. That part of the community garden has been extremely successful. That led to groups wanting to come in and see what we are doing, school groups. We had at-risk youth come in so that instead of doing community service on the side of the road, they can work beside our food justice organizers and work in the garden and learn skills that they can take home and apply with their own family members. A big partnership happened with school groups coming in and that led to being invited to schools to create gardens with a social justice emphasis. That was a great project for me because I was already working with schools and school gardens. Now, we are working with seven or eight schools partnering. Now, we call them school cohorts. We have groups of students, nurses, councilors, teachers, principals, and parents at each school. We have them be part of a group that then could advocate for food policy changes too because like I said, SWOP is more of a mass-based community social justice organization. We are trying to use the gardens for social justice and promoting being involved in creating positive social change so we have an environmental justice sector and food justice. We have a mass-based political sector where they try to get people to vote; try to get the word out about things. During the legislative session, they are targeting people whose representatives support the things that we are working towards. SWOP throws an annual youth summit, YES, Youth Engagement Summit, that is for youth in Albuquerque and around the state. They come and talk about youth and the power of engaging in social change. That is really cool.

We are getting ready for our twentieth annual chili and art festival called Fiesta del Sol. We do a big festival every year to support chili. We do a chili cook-off. We do a pumpkin smashing festival for people to recycle their pumpkins. We do it at the community garden. We smash them all, then pile it all up and mix it with leaves and make compost out of it. It's just a fun way to recycle pumpkins that are getting all wrinkled up and compost them. We partner with the schools to see which class can bring in the most pumpkins. Like, the first year, we had a kindergarten class where a dad brought in more than sixty pumpkins, so they won. We give a party to the class that wins. We do pizza with a healthy salad from the gardens, and we give away seeds to all the kids. We try to make it a fun way to get people involved with recycling while using the resources we have. We are so trained to use our jack-'o-lanterns and then throw them out or bag up our leaves and throw them out, but these are a resource we can use again.

ILLÈNE: Tell me what engaged you in this work that made these other people come to you to help start this program?

TRAVIS: I grew up in the East Mountains [an area comprised of Tijeras, Cedar Crest, Sandia Park, Edgewood, Moriarty, and other surrounding communities in New Mexico], so I always kind of had a reverence for nature. We had a lot of fruit trees growing, and my mom always grew little things like tomatoes. It really started when I came to the University of New Mexico [UNM]. I was going to be a teacher, but I wanted to change the education system, and when I got into the [UNM] College of Education, I realized that was pretty much the beef that I was trying to fight, that I was going to have to go through, and so I decided not to go that way. Then I didn't know what I was going to do. I learned about the Bachelor of University Studies [BUS] from one of my mentors in the UNM Service Corps, Karen Patuta, and I totally changed my major. Basically, the BUS is a custom major, and I got to choose my concentrations of study. My main focus was sustainable agriculture with alternative education and media anthropology. I signed on for the UNM Service Corps that is kind of like AmeriCorps where they help students get meaningful jobs in community settings. I got a job with El Centro de la Raza. They were really supportive of me, nurturing my passion to work with kids, and I met people who had gardens doing after-school programs with kids. Then I met my agriculture mentor, Miguel Santistevan, and I spent a whole season with him growing at La Placita Gardens, a newly formed community garden space in the South Valley. So, he was the first person that I did some serious food production with planting corn, garlic, beans, lentils, and all sorts of native New Mexican crops. I spent the whole summer shadowing him. I met him through the Sembrando Semillas program. I went up to the Sembrando Semillas Winter Encuentro in 2007 and the following season, I worked with Miguel and learned all about that. He was my first mentor in the food scene. It became a life style, and I loved it and just learned all I could. I started going to conferences and presenting at conferences. Miguel funded us to go to the Native American permaculture course that is held for two weeks every year with the Traditional Native American Farmers Association and the [New Mexico] Food and Seed Sovereignty Alliance. So, we got to do two weeks of an indigenous permaculture course at an agricultural school at Camino de

Paz in Española. That was base camp for us, and then they took us on different field trips every day to see what was going on in different places. We got to go to the Tesuque Pueblo to see what they are doing, to the Santa Clara Pueblo to see gardens at people's home, and to see some people in Embudo. That was just awesome. Then I moved in with the other guy Miguel sponsored to go there, Casey, and we created a big community garden in our back-yard in Old Town [Albuquerque] and that was pre-Project Feed the Hood, and since that came up, I have been funneling all my garden work through there.

ILLÈNE: So, you had a very organic development of your skills?

TRAVIS: Yes, a very natural germination. Yeah, I thank Miguel because he took the time to take me under his wing and teach me. I honor him as my first mentor in agriculture. I planted corn with him for the first time and that is a pretty spiritual thing in New Mexico. He took me to Hopi land to see agriculture out there. We have seen some cool things around the country. So, we are trying to be a network of food justice and a catalyst for that work. I am studying educational leadership for my master's degree and studying how gardens impact students. I am going to be researching that. I appreciate what you are doing, gathering everybody's stories and testimony and bundling it up in a good way.

I guess that is how I got started in Project Feed the Hood. It has been a perfect outlet for Rodrigo, Joachin, and me to help people know about food and cultivate a relationship with the food they eat and grow. I have always loved to work with youth, so it is a perfect set up for me to continue to work with youth and be there for them as a mentor the way other people have been there for me, like Joachin. He is from another time back in the fif-ties when he was working on the early Chicano movement, fighting for social justice. I think intergenerational mentorship is valuable in whatever you are doing because you learn a lot.

ILLÈNE: I am going to ask a question that is perhaps politically incorrect. When I lived briefly in Albuquerque forty years ago, I heard there were animosities between the three cultures in New Mexico: American Indian, Hispanic, and Caucasian. I did not experience that myself, but I wondered. From what I have seen here, it seems the sustainable agriculture movement is bringing together people that perhaps did not traditionally work together in the past.

TRAVIS: Definitely. I agree. New Mexico has a history with a lot of conquest and colonization, anywhere from the Spanish first coming in and trying to colonize native peoples to the United States government coming in after the treaty [the Treaty of Guadalupe Hidalgo that ended the Mexican–American War] was signed.[1] With both cases, there was stolen land. There was a lot of cultural genocide and attempts at cultural assimilation. There were the boarding schools. Joachin is about sixty. When Joachin went to school, he went in Joachin and came out Jackie. They didn't like [the name] Joachin and so they named him Jackie. Those kinds of things. Like Joachin was forced not to speak Spanish at school, and now we are trying to get kids to speak Spanish in school. We have come a long way, and I think you are right: food justice, agricultural sustainability, and caring for the earth are definitely bringing people together. We like to promote that everyone, no matter what the color of their skin, has some kind of agrarian heritage. Somebody's great, great-grandma or grandpa stewarded the land and liked to provide for the family with what they stewarded. Definitely, I think that it is bringing people together. With the whole Spanish-Native American conflict, there were some tensions, but, now, since we have seed exchanges and group blessings of seeds and different cultural practices shared, we are bringing the two cultures together. But, traditionally, there was not just conquest. There was camaraderie too. If one village was hungry and needed food, another shared. It's important to not lose that. In modern society, these things seem to be strategically removed from our cultures and that is why I am thinking our cultural agrarian heritage; that we are here to take care of the land and each other; it's important not to lose that. I think food is something universal that brings all of us together. Like in all faiths or religions, we all eat food. It is the thing that brings people together because we all eat food. When we hear Joachin talk about how it was in the day, how he remembers the acequias thriving and gardens everywhere, we try to do both. You see it happen in the garden when people work together, and every chance we get, we provide little lessons for the kids. It happens in different settings. We do workshops. It could be in a classroom presentation or school assembly or just on our social media. We try to keep the history alive. We are shifting. We are losing the older generation that had more of an agrarian upbringing. People talk about how we have a lot of elderly farmers and not a lot of youth wanting to take their places. We are supporting youth to steward the land. We want

---

1. The Treaty of Guadalupe Hidalgo gave land that the Spanish had taken from the Native Americans to the US government when the US won the war with Mexico that was fought over who would "own" Texas. The treaty's land agreement also included all or parts of New Mexico, Colorado, Arizona, Nevada, California, Utah, and Wyoming, essentially ceding lands that the Spanish considered theirs, but were really Native American lands, to the US government.

it to be viable for youth for future jobs for kids. We are trying to be a think tank for food justice. What possible positions could we create?

ILLÈNE: You sure have amazingly articulate young people in your program. I don't know if they went into the program so articulate, but I think your level of discourse in the program must be terrific because not all young people will be so forthcoming with total strangers as your interns were with me.

TRAVIS: Since I am studying education, I see that sometimes schools don't allow young people to speak their minds. We empower them to speak their minds and think so they are not just regurgitating what they have heard. We take them to conferences, and they get experience in different settings. We try to get them involved in opportunities like that so that they can just go for it and succeed at what they want to do. We have some amazing young people, and they are prepared to face the world.

ILLÈNE: I think the work you are doing is adding to their preparedness. I have seen this in all the youth I have met here in New Mexico. You are all doing such a great job! Is there anything I have not asked you about the program that is important for people to understand?

TRAVIS: Policy work. The work we do in the garden is tied to what is going on with food policy in the legislature. SWOP encourages participatory democracy and people being involved in local issues, local government, meet and greets with elected officials. We are using the gardens and local food as a vehicle for social justice and policy work. It's a good mix. We see hundreds of people at the farmers' markets and can talk to them about policy issues. That has been successful for us. We have a seed library, where we give out seed with the hope that people will grow the seed and then give us some back to share with others. It's not the capitalist model of a seed bank, where you just save something. We share it out and ask others to do the same: grow it, save the seed, and give back some seed to the library. The library is a living entity. We can give out more seed the following season.

Travis spoke eloquently about how important his own mentors had been in helping him find his way into agriculture, food justice, education, and media to create a meaningful life for himself where he can learn by collaborating with many other people. What appears on the surface to be just about growing food, herbs, and flowers really has deep roots in land use policy, social justice, and democratic processes. The fact that old political divides can be bridged by growing gardens together speaks to the power that growing and sharing food has to transform people, land, and social divisions. The young gardeners I met at Project Feed the Hood explained that further to me. One of these young gardeners is Alicia, aged fifteen, a young woman who has the social justice awareness that Project Feed the Hood nurtures.

ALICIA: I've been working with gardens for about two and a half years now. My mom was doing a collegiate internship for social work, and when she got involved, she discovered they had a youth program and gardening stuff and so she got me involved, and then I later became their youth intern.

ILLÈNE: Did you grow up here?

ALICIA: I grew up in the North Valley, and my grandpa has been a farmer his whole life. So, yeah, I have a lot of memories of being a child and farming and gardening. That is just an important part of my life and important part of my culture to me. He mostly grew food to supplement, but also because we just enjoy fresh produce. And it's so nice to just go pick your salad greens from your backyard. My grandma was raised on a ranch in Mexico, and she was raised that you ate what was from your garden and that was just what you ate, and my grandpa as well. That carried on to my mother and I who obviously come to buy organic food and still plant in the garden. At Project Feed the Hood, anyone who volunteers can take home food.

ILLÈNE: Did your grandpa teach you to plant seeds?

ALICIA: Yes. I learned that as a very small child. I remember when he showed me about all the different ditches and the acequias and water systems and then he did teach me how to plant and how to make the rows; things you learn by watching. Definitely!

ILLÈNE: How does it make you feel to grow food for the broader community?

ALICIA: I think it is great. I love food justice. I am very passionate about it because it affects everyone regardless of gender, race, class, all that good stuff. Food affects you. I think food is also a very uniting factor. I think growing food for the community is a great thing and it brings people together.

ILLÈNE: Do you find amongst your high school friends who are not involved in a gardening project that they have an awareness of food justice and talk about it together here in Albuquerque?

ALICIA: No, not really. For starters, I don't think most teenagers think about, "Hey, where does my food come from and how does the food getting here impact everybody else?" I think that, as teenagers, it is difficult for us to get that outer-worldly view and bring it back to us. We are just in our little world. But to see the bigger, broader picture for me is important. But I think it's not something all teenagers grasp at this point in time.

Those guys down there are some of my best friends! [*She gestures to the Project Feed the Hood team at their farmer's market table down the hill from us.*] They are like my brothers and my uncles. I have built those relationships with them, and they are lasting relationships. Whether we have a garden next year or not, I know I can still call one of those guys and ask them, "Hey, can you help me with so and so?" We build lasting relationships, and gardening definitely has helped.

I think for one, gardening is a team effort. Everyone has to be on the same page and kind of know what they are doing. I think there definitely has to be pretty good communication, and for there to be good communication, we have to be comfortable with each other and know each other as a team. Gardening is like a team effort.

ILLÈNE: Have you ever noticed that working out in the garden changes your emotional state?

ALICIA: Definitely. Just when I see people who come for the workshops on Saturdays, as soon as they get their hands in the dirt, they look like a little three-year-old kid making a mud pie. They look so happy that they are getting connected to the earth. Definitely. When I look at the garden outside, I feel at peace or like I am doing something valuable. That is why I do it.

ILLÈNE: Are there other things you are learning in this program?

ALICIA: I have learned to multitask, working with these guys and having to go to the farmer's market and figure out scheduling and stuff like that. So, I think you definitely learn to multitask and problem solve really fast.

ILLÈNE: Do you help Travis with the scheduling for what people are going to do what job?

ALICIA: That is generally something that we all discuss as a group. It is usually a group decision we all make.

ILLÈNE: So, you are learning collaborative decision making too?

ALICIA: Definitely.

ILLÈNE: Do you do other things at school that help you learn collaborative decision making?

ALICIA: At school, not so much, but I think within the organization, I have learned a lot of team building and being able to make decisions together. That is *not* something I have picked up at school, but something I have picked up working outside of school because, I don't know, school is just not my thing. I think there are lots of opportunities because we do lots of gardens in schools. That is such a good thing. It connects in so many ways. What better way to teach biology than to go sit out in a garden? There are just so many ways to plug in. I wish more schools would utilize gardens to be a teaching tool.

ILLÈNE: Does your school have a garden?

ALICIA: It does, but it is inactive currently. There was a garden at some point, and then the person who ran it, the teacher, left.

ILLÈNE: Do you think if a group of students at the school went and talked to the principal, you could have a garden again?

ALICIA: I can't say. It hasn't crossed my mind. Every time I walk by it, an empty garden always makes me sad. I think it is more a budgeting issue, and there has to be a teacher sponsor. So, if there is no teacher sponsor, there is no club.

ILLÈNE: Does this experience make you want to go and talk to your favorite teacher and say, "Wouldn't you like to sponsor the garden?"

ALICIA: Definitely. I have done it before. I would love to spread food justice and what it means to me to other kids my age. And to also teach it from the perspective of food justice and that perspective would be a very good thing.

ILLÈNE: So, you have this unique perspective of having a mom starting out in this work before you did, who is involved in social work and food justice and who invited you to join her in it. You have a broader perspective perhaps than other kids at fifteen might have and you could share it.

ALICIA: I was just on the radio about a week ago on the university radio station KUNM talking about food justice. SWOP and this garden have given me so *many* opportunities to go places and to talk to people. I feel like it's my job to come out here, to not make them look good, but to highlight what they are doing and show that it is a very positive thing and that it is truly opening doors for youth.

ILLÈNE: Do you notice that your senses are more active when you are in a garden? Do you pay more attention to all the sensory stimulation in a garden?

ALICIA: I think so, yes. I mean, when you look at a plant, you don't know if it is ready just by looking at it. You may need to touch it or feel it. You have to use all your senses to help you decide what is fresh and not fresh. Sometimes, you just have to be logical about the garden. We have been growing food from the beginning of time, so it is ingrained in us. We just have to find it.

ILLÈNE: Do you notice if those sensory experiences, like smelling the basil before you eat it, change your state of being?

ALICIA: I think it resonates with you. Like that smell and that memory resonates with you. I know in our backyard, I can still smell fresh corn. Those things that resonate with you create those long-lasting memories that you tell your children. I think, for me, the garden is comforting because it is something I have been seeing since the beginning of my life. That's normal for me. It's a source of home and comfort for me. I think gardens are such a great healing tool. It's so nice just to be at peace with the land and be connected. It's such, like, a peaceful thing for people.

ILLÈNE: I agree with you. Is there anything I have not asked you about your experiences gardening that you want people reading this book to understand?

ALICIA: I think the main thing is just start by thinking about where your food comes from and how that food coming over here impacts everybody else and realize that you literally are what you eat and that when you are putting toxic chemicals into your body, it is not good. But, definitely, buy locally and buy organically. That small business opens many doors for people like me.

Alicia is only fifteen and already has a comprehensive understanding of food justice and the cultural importance of food, an indication of the excellent educational opportunity Project Feed the Hood provides. The next young farmer I spoke to, Ian, is twelve going on thirteen. He is the youngest person I interviewed for this book. He wanted so much to tell me about his experiences that I made an exception to my fourteen-to-nineteen age range for interviews. He has a Celtic name, but the physical appearance of a multiethnic New Mexican and beams a brilliant, enormous smile.

IAN: I got so excited when I heard I might be able to talk with you. Before I came to Project Feed the Hood and SWOP, I really knew nothing about gardening. But once I got with SWOP and Project Feed the Hood and Travis, I learned so much more about it and I want to share with everyone how much fun it is to garden, how fun it is to raise crops. I worked on it a little last summer, but more this summer. I am more engaged with it this summer now that I know more. I have gone with Travis to school gardens and backyard gardens. The community garden also is fun. I live right by it, so I can just stop in and help. Not too long ago, Travis and I went down early in the morning to the farm, and we planted some bell pepper and chili. Then there is another plant, but I can't remember what it was though.

ILLÈNE: What is it like for you when you have planted something and you see it growing?

IAN: I feel, I think it is awesome. I feel a connection towards it. It sounds a little weird, but when

I have planted something, it is like me and the plants are friends now a little. When you are planting, you grow a connection with the plant.

ILLÈNE: Had you seen anyone in your family garden before you began to garden?

IAN: I had planted with my dad. I pretty much watched him and did what he told me to do back when I was a little boy, like four or five, but I don't really remember it. At my mom's and Travis's house, we actually have planted a garden. It is really cool watching it grow. I know we are growing some squash and some carrots, and I think we might have some lettuce. Because when we moved in, there was dirt, so now we have repurposed it into a garden. It is really cool!

ILLÈNE: When you are outside in the garden, do you pay more attention to your senses?

IAN: Sometimes. Like, if I am by a plant, I can smell it or feeling senses or whatever, I can feel the texture of the plant. Not so much what I see or what I hear, but mostly what I smell and what I feel. This morning, Travis and I were down at the farm, and we were harvesting peas. Every once in a while, we would grab a pea pod and eat it. It tastes amazing. It doesn't taste like any of the artificial stuff. It tastes like amazing. I love it. You don't have, like that frozen taste. They are more fresh. You can taste a big difference because they are fresher and they have just come out of the ground instead of going from first being sprayed with pesticides, then traveling to somewhere, then traveling somewhere else. You can taste it coming fresh out of the ground where you live instead of from all over the world.

ILLÈNE: Did you like vegetables before you started planting them? Did you eat vegetables?

IAN: Not as much. I did not like carrots at all. But now, like the carrots we grow, there are different colors, like red dragons [carrots]. I enjoy carrots now because they are fresh and they are out of the ground instead of artificial. Well, not really artificial, but not sprayed with pesticides and stuff.

ILLÈNE: Does it make you think about what you will eat when you want a snack?

IAN: Yes, it has. Whenever I go to a store, I want to look at the ingredients or nutrient facts and make sure I am eating something healthy. Once in a while, I eat some junk food because it tastes good, but the vegetables and the fresh fruits taste good *and* they are really good for you.

ILLÈNE: What is your favorite vegetable right now?

IAN: My favorite vegetable? I kind of like the salad turnips. It's kind of like a mix of a radish and a jicama. Well, that is what it tastes like. This one is a little sweeter, I heard. I have not tasted another type of turnip, but I really like the salad turnip. I like the squash. The squash is good. Last Tuesday, when we were here and we were harvesting, we had just picked a squash.

ILLÈNE: Well, turnips are really good when you cook them in the winter too. If you roast them, they get super sweet.

IAN: One of our volunteers here used to boil and mash them and they were really good. And they have little leaves on them and you can sauté those too. Usually, we take some vegetables home to cook for dinners and stuff.

ILLÈNE: It sounds like Travis has been a great food mentor for you.

IAN: Yes, he has.

ILLÈNE: What would you say to the school principal if he asked you about the value of having a garden at your school?

IAN: I would say, definitely. All the school gardens I have seen, it helps a lot it seems. Not only are kids eating healthier, it teaches more kids how to garden and then they can take that information home and start a garden at home and share it with others. We are moving to a new school campus and it is much bigger, so maybe I could start a garden there. I am going into 8th grade. At my school, they also have a high school on the same campus. I might go there, but my dad wants to move to Denver and so I might go to high school in Denver.

ILLÈNE: What has been the most exciting thing this summer about the garden for you?

IAN: I think meeting new friends. This summer, I don't really talk to my friends from school in the summer, but knowing my friends from the garden, I can just go hang out with them. It's been really fun. With my friends from the garden, we kind of, like we connect more. We are better friends. But with some of my friends at school, some of them aren't good friends. But every friend I have made at the garden, they don't take a couple of days to get to know you or they don't try and stay away from you. Once you start talking, you are friends right away. Maybe it is because we are a community and we are doing something we both enjoy and we are doing it at the same time.

ILLÈNE: Do you think about the contribution you are making to the broader community, do you think that is part of it?

IAN: Yeah. One of our community gardens is in the international district and it has a lot of low-income houses there, and I love to think about how we are helping the community over there. Last Tuesday, we interviewed for *Al Jazeera* and we went to one of the supermarkets over there and it was terrible. There was so much junk food and the jalapeños were so wrinkled and terrible and the bananas were like $6 a bundle.

ILLÈNE: So, you are doing a huge community service providing food for people. How does that make you feel?

IAN: It makes me feel great. Even if they don't know that I am providing food for the community, I like to know that I am still doing it and that other people can eat healthy too and they don't have to pay much. Pretty much what we do at the community garden is you can come and help and you leave with some vegetables.

ℰↃ

Ian is only twelve, but he has already learned to plant food and work collaboratively on important food justice issues and, in the process, has gained close friends. He identified the difference in the way people make friendships while working together on a common cause. Having close bonds with others is key to a healthy life, as are the positive emotions and meaning these engaged gardeners discovered as they planted and harvested together (Seligman, 2011). He has already had the chance to speak up for growing food locally on international television with the Al Jazeera interview. His enthusiasm for working in a garden with his peers and mentors has no bounds!

I bought the salad turnips Ian recommended that Project Feed the Hood was selling to take to my friends in Colorado. They tasted mildly spicy and had a great crunch. Turnips are one of the few things deer won't eat, an issue for any gardener living near them. But even more important than any specific crop Project Feed the Hood harvests, this group cultivates knowledge and social commitment in its participants.

Ricardo, aged sixteen, was the last Albuquerque gardener I interviewed that July morning. I used his phrases, exactly as he spoke them, to end these youth interviews on a poetic note, as I often felt the young gardeners spoke in poetry as they expressed their love for what they do.

## Ricardo's Garden Harvest

*I love working with them.*
*I love meeting new people.*
*That's my favorite part.*
*I wouldn't have met any of them*
*If I hadn't joined the garden.*

*My grandpa, he has a chili garden.*
*I love eating his chilis.*
*They are spicy. He has different varieties,*

*Red ones, green ones.*
*My favorite ones are the red ones.*
*Every Christmas, he makes tamales.*
*They are delicious.*

*My mom told me my great-grandpa was one [an Indian].*
*He had a lot of Indian in him. He had a garden too.*
*And he just loved to do what he did.*
*I love to garden too, so she told me I got his blood.*
*I am into the gardening.*
*I love to be outdoors.*
*I just love it.*
*Very happy! Knowing that all the vegetables*
*And fruit are coming out perfect,*
*And the people are noticing and come and get them,*
*And we come and sell them at the farmers' market.*
*I think they enjoy the fruits too. We give them samples*
*To taste, and they love the samples and come back for more.*

*We teach them how to plant,*
*Like not to plant too deep*
*So the seed won't grow.*
*But some kids already know how*
*Because they have gardens at home,*
*And we go to their house and help them out*
*By giving them soil if they need it and seeds too.*

*I am relaxed. You know you are going to*
*Grow something real good.*
*I haven't thought anything bad at all,*
*Just fun stuff. We have music classes*
*There sometimes. We play music there too.*

*A lot of people come to take yoga to relax there,*
*And they love the smell of the garden.*
*Sometimes they buy stuff because they*
*Love how it smells and looks and tastes.*
*I just love being with them.*
*I would have a boring summer*
*If I didn't have the garden.*

These New Mexico youth gardeners learn from mentors who teach ancient traditions in relation to earth, water, food, and family. The mentors also offer hope and an example of healthy eating habits so that the young generation that learns and practices these skills handed down from grandparents will not fall prey to the obesity, diabetes, and depression plaguing modern society. All the young gardeners introduced here express deep appreciation for the meaningful engagement gardening offers them and for the strong relationships they develop with their adult mentors and their peers. Their smiles glow with life and accomplishment. They are flourishing where they are planted and where they plant.

# 24

# PHYSIOLOGICAL AND NEUROLOGICAL RESEARCH
## CLUES TO WHY GARDENING BENEFITS THE GARDENER

In World War I trenches, World War II Japanese internment camps in the US, and World War II ghettos in Europe, soldiers and prisoners of war created gardens as ways to cope with danger and fear (Helphand, 2006). An innate need for a relationship with nature, the biophilia that Wilson (1984) identified, appears to be universal amongst humans and forms part of our shared biology as living creatures on earth. Perhaps the act of caring for something that is both alive and growing from the earth on which we depend soothes us, and that is why we turn to gardening and other encounters with nature in stressful times. We give to the earth our time and energy to care for it, and it gives us our well-being in return.

## THE NURTURING HORMONE: OXYTOCIN

In considering my own feelings while gardening and what youth related to me about theirs, I wondered if perhaps caring for plants stimulates the production of oxytocin in people. Oxytocin is the peptide hormone that female mammals, including humans, produce abundantly in pregnancy, during and after birth, and while nursing. It promotes mother/infant bonding, milk production, and relaxation. It is also being investigated for its overall capacity for creating intimacy and bonding (Carter, 1998).

Since I could not find any published research on human-plant relationships and oxytocin, I e-mailed researchers investigating oxytocin's effects on bonding to inquire whether they knew of any research on oxytocin production by humans caring for plants. I sent them these youth gardener comments indicating that plant nurturing is fulfilling to the gardener: Sage from Colorado Rocky Mountain School related her experience planting seeds and seeing them sprout: "If I planted the seed, it's like my baby. If I didn't plant it, it feels like little relatives, like my niece." Sage, like many others, also said gardening made her feel "calm and tranquil." One of the teen mothers at Yampah Mountain High School mentioned that she felt similarly when caring for plants as when she cared for her own baby, but "less stressed." Two seventeen-year-old boys who had both worked in daycares with preschool-aged children experienced a similarity in caring for small children and for plants.

Dr. Inga Newmann at the University of Regensburg in Germany replied to my query via e-mail in 2008:

> This is a very fascinating topic. Of course, our knowledge of the wonderful effects of oxytocin mostly comes from animal studies. They don't garden, but eat what grows there. . . . We know that social/physical stimulation (touching, stroking) activates oxytocin. Gardening is, I believe, something that lies very deep in our genes; we were so much dependent on it, and sure enough, there must be strong neurobiological roots for this kind of behavior. Seeing young plants/seeds grow may be very well comparable with the joy to see a child or a pet grow and develop. Although we cannot give evidence for it, I can very well imagine that basic neuroactive substances like serotonin and oxytocin are involved. Lack of evidence is not evidence of lack.

Regarding animals and oxytocin production, a recent review of sixty-nine original studies examining human and animal interactions, most specifically people petting animals, showed that these interactions benefit people in social attention, social behavior, interpersonal interactions, and mood, as well as lowering blood pressure and cortisol levels (Beetz et al. 2012, 11). The Beetz et al. (2012) research team believes the evidence for these benefits points to oxytocin production as being a principal factor in improved well-being, and lists some of oxytocin's known behavioral results as empathy, trust, social skills, positive self-perception, and generosity, as well as decreased depression—all things that we have heard the youth describe in their gardening experiences. The physical effects of lowered blood pressure and cortisol after gardening have been measured and were cited previously (van den Berg and Custers, 2011). It seems reasonable to consider that if oxytocin is involved in the well-being people feel when petting animals that is may also be involved in similar feelings that come from tending plants.

A team of women researchers at University of California at Los Angeles revealed that 90 percent of existing research on stress and the flight-or-fight response was done on men. In fact, they discovered that women produce oxytocin, not testosterone, in response to stress and have a tend-and-befriend response rather than a flight-or-fight response (Taylor et al. 2000). They found that "Both men and women show higher affiliative (i.e., befriending) behavior when induced with oxytocin. Also, women show higher oxytocin levels than men during a stressful situation" (ibid., 411). They further postulate that it behooves women evolutionarily to seek social protection for their offspring in times of crisis and stress to ensure their children's survival, and so their bodies produce the hormone that helps them bond to others (ibid.).

Dr. Shelley Taylor, principal investigator in the Taylor et al. (2000) study, e-mailed me in 2009 in response to my questions regarding people and plants: "That's a very interesting idea. I suppose it could be, but I'm pretty sure there is no evidence for it yet. The pets part is true, but nobody has done the plants part."

Do we have any physiological evidence for possible oxytocin production while gardening? Not any that I have found. Would it behoove us to have some physiological studies done on gardeners to see if oxytocin does indeed increase while people garden? Yes, it would be extremely valuable for educators and physicians to know if gardening has this physical effect on people as oxytocin's benefits are many, including supporting healthy immune response (Beetz et al. 2012, 11).

Dr. Christopher Lowry heads the Behavioral Neuroendocrinology Laboratory at the University of Colorado. His research, though not on oxytocin, intrigued me. When I spoke with him, he had just identified the neuroendocrine responses of mice to a common soil bacteria called *Mycobacterium vaccae* (Lowry et al. 2007). Lowry injected mice with M. vaccae, and the resulting increase in serotonin[1] levels indicate that perhaps inquiry into soil bacteria and human exposure to it will prove fruitful in understanding gardening's beneficial effects on humans. This line of inquiry is beyond this book's scope, but Lowry's ongoing research does indicate that both obesity and mental health are impacted by exposure to certain common bacteria during pregnancy and childhood (Rook, Lowry, and Raison, 2013).

I also asked Dr. Lowry about the possibilities of oxytocin being involved in creating the feelings of well-being and connection to the earth and each other while gardening that the youth reported to me. Dr. Lowry explained to me in an e-mail in 2010:

---

1. Serotonin is important in regulating mood.

Oxytocin is a fascinating peptide. I think your idea is very reasonable. I don't know either if another kind of nurturing, other than maternal, can induce the release of oxytocin, but it is certainly possible. These peptides are, at one level, under control of parts of the brain that are involved in very cognitive functions and perhaps a "feeling" of nurturing is able to influence oxytocin.

Perhaps because a garden needs the gardener to give it life, it calls out the nurturing instinct in us whether we are male or female. The plants, like pets, need us to survive, so we respond. And when the adult leading the youth gardeners showed the plants and the youth care and respect, as was the case in all the garden programs, the youth had a chance to immediately put into practice what they were receiving and learning—care and respect for life.

In considering oxytocin and bonding, let us reflect on a Greek myth. Myths are stories used in cultures all over the world to explain phenomena, human behavior, and relationships within and outside the human realm. This story of the goddess of grain and agriculture, Demeter, and her daughter, Persephone, perhaps gives us some insight into our own love for our earth.

One etymology of Demeter's name is *gê meter*, meaning mother earth. Her story is often told to children to explain the seasons. Demeter's job is to care for the earth and teach people to care for all that grows from the soil. Like human mothers, she adores her daughter, Persephone, who is a young maiden at the time this story occurs. Persephone was out one day, picking flowers with her friends out of sight of her mother. She saw a beautiful narcissus blooming and went to pick it to bring to her mother, but the earth opened beside her and a black coach with black horses emerged from the chasm. The driver of the coach, also dressed in black, grabbed her and plunged back into the earth with Persephone screaming. Demeter did not hear her daughter's screams, but felt that something was wrong and went looking for her. She was grief stricken when she could not find Persephone anywhere and neglected her job caring for the plants, even setting fire to certain regions in her despair. Plants withered and died as Demeter searched the earth for Persephone and did not tend to them. She went to the sun god, Helios, as he rode his chariot across the skies and could see everything. He told her that Persephone had been kidnapped and taken to the underworld by Hades, its ruler.

Hades had kidnapped Persephone because he was lonely living in the darkness below the earth and had wanted a beautiful queen by his side. Evidently, Zeus, the ruler of all the Greek gods and goddesses, Persephone's father, and brother to Hades, had promised her to Hades. Trapped in the underworld, Persephone longed for her mother and pined for the beauty of the earth's surface, refusing to eat because she knew that if she ate food in the underworld, she would have to stay forever. Demeter went to Zeus and demanded that he make Hades release Persephone so that she could return home to the earth's surface and be in the sun once again with her mother. Zeus sent Hermes, the messenger god, to tell Hades to release Persephone, but Hades tricked Persephone and offered her a pomegranate saying it would give her energy for her return journey. Persephone ate three seeds, or perhaps six, depending on the teller of the tale. Persephone returned to the earth's surface, and when she did, the flowers bloomed and the grain grew. However, as a consequence of eating the pomegranate seeds, she must also return each year to live for three to six months underground with Hades, and when she does, the plants die and whither during winter.

One can understand why some storytellers fix their attention on this story's capacity to explain the seasons, but it holds many meanings. Persephone's time in the underworld can also represent the fallow time a person may need before bursting forth with new ideas after a long winter's rest below ground. I also see this story as a story about motherly love for her creation: her beautiful daughter, her earthly gardens, and her realm of responsibility for agriculture. We can see it as a story of the deep love humans innately have for the earth and her fruits, or biophilia, and our need to tend the earth on which our very life depends. If we are separated from our relationship with the earth, we are bereft, as was Demeter when she was separated from her daughter.

The story of the loving mother, Demeter, and her beautiful daughter, Persephone, reflects those qualities of bonding and love that research identifies with oxytocin. Donne, in Chamisal, expresses this aspect of our relationship with the earth that is so fundamental to human well-being: "You are in touch. You are not disconnected or paying attention to your phone or the computer or TV. You are there and you can feel the dirt, feel Mother Earth. You can smell it and touch it and feel it. It's amazing." When we garden, we regain this relationship that we may have lost in relating to modern technology for so many hours a day—we become Demeter when she is reunited with her daughter and can once again serve the earth and people as the goddess of agriculture.

The Gaia hypothesis, a scientific theory, proposes that all life on earth is one living organism living in balance with the atmosphere and that we humans are also an element of this biosphere; all elements work together to maintain life in balance. The biologists, Lovelock and Margulis (1974), chose the name Gaia for their biosphere theory because it is the name of the primal, original Greek earth goddess, she from whom life emerged, the universal earth mother.

From ancient times, humans have conceived of the earth as the mother of all life, including us. I suggest that the myth of Demeter and Persephone speaks to our human physiology and psyche. It reflects the bonding and caring that oxytocin facilitates in our bodies, and it explains the profound relationship humans have with our planet, our earth, and our soil, on which we rely for all we need for living. The earth, in turn, relies on us to care for it and not destroy it. When we are tending the earth as we do in gardening, we are in harmony with this fundamental relationship. Brain physiology, where oxytocin creates beneficial bonding effects, has more functions that explain the well-being we experience when gardening.

There is another ancient story that speaks to our deep connection to the earth that gardening allows us to feel and express. When Buddha was sitting beneath the Bodhi tree waiting for Enlightenment Mara, the god of material things and power, appeared to Buddha and tempted him. Buddha put his hand down onto the earth itself and called on Tara, the goddess of the earth, for help to resist temptation, and Buddha became enlightened. Tara is often depicted as green in Buddhist paintings. This profound relationship of an enlightened human to Mother Earth/Tara/Gaia speaks to the human need to touch the earth and be united with its essence. An enlightened mind results according to this Buddhist story.

## LEARNING, HUMAN PHYSIOLOGY, AND WELL-BEING

Dr. John Medina, a developmental molecular biologist, investigates learning environments and brain genetics. He heads the Brain Center for Applied Learning Research at Seattle Pacific University and is an affiliate professor of bioengineering at the University of Washington School of Medicine. Medina (2008) explains that the human brain evolved in the outdoors, seeking safety first, and his research has identified safety as the foremost qualifier for a healthy learning environment.

As food gatherers for most of human evolutionary history, our ancestors sought green spaces because those environments could provide food, water, and security. Research shows that our bodies and minds relax in green spaces and our cognitive function improves, probably a direct result of millenniums living in natural areas (Hartig et al. 2003; Kaplan and Kaplan, 1990; Kaplan and Berman, 2010). As mentioned earlier, Medina (2008) points out that the human brain evolved primarily in motion, solving problems in a direct relationship with the earth.

The industrial revolution pushed adults inside to work in factories beginning about 250 years ago. Children, instead of following their parents around and learning by watching and doing what their parents did at home on the farm, had to go to school. For the first time in human evolution, children spent most of their hours inside sitting down. They continue to have to learn to sit still and obey directions, as well as to learn whatever subject matter is required. Human lifestyles in rapidly industrializing countries have changed dramatically and quickly away from outdoor physical work, but our bodies and brains cannot evolve with the same rapidity.

Dr. Daniel Lieberman, a Harvard professor and evolutionary biologist, coined the word dysevolution to describe the modern diseases that come from our bodies not being able to live healthfully due to the disconnect between the built and cultural environment and how we have evolved while hunting and gathering food over eons (Wheelwright, 2015). His work gives an evolutionary perspective to the research by medical doctors on obesity that examines sedentary behavior, food consumption, and media discussed in Chapter 12.

Not only do most modern children go to school and spend the day sitting, but 84 percent of American households have computers, which are used for entertainment as well as for work (Rainie and Cohn, 2014). A recent study shows that teens in the United States use media (computers, tablets, smart phones, and iPods) for entertainment purposes an average of nine hours per day (Common Sense Media, 2015). Adults and children spend a great deal of the day seated, both working and being entertained, and Lieberman believes that, as a result, we suffer from obesity, diabetes, heart disease, backaches, insomnia, nearsightedness, and carpal tunnel syndrome, amongst other modern maladies (Wheelwright, 2015).

Dysevolution doesn't mean that we are going backwards evolutionarily, but that our activities are not in tune with our bodies' needs. Lieberman identifies the lack of vigorous physical activity as one of the major causes of diseases ailing modern humans (Wheelwright, 2015). Sitting indoors does comparatively little to make us feel well or to stimulate our creativity. Recent research at Stanford used tests that measure creative problem-solving capacity to see if sitting or walking produced the most creative thinking. The research showed that walking, both indoors and out, produced about 50 percent more new ideas and insights than sitting, and concluded by stating that "Walking opens the free flow of ideas" (Oppezzo and Schwartz, 2014, 1142).

Darwin (1871) ventured a theory on the importance of bipedalism in human evolution. He suggested that when we stood up, we freed our hands for more creative activities, such as tool and weapon making, and we grew our brains to handle all these new uses that we found for our hands (ibid.). We didn't develop more brute strength to hunt mastodons; we developed bigger brains with greater problem-solving capacity so that a group of humans could communicate and collaboratively hunt animals bigger than themselves. We grew new neural pathways that resulted in brains twice the size, relevant to our body mass, of other mammals (Medina, 2008). We learned to communicate with our hands. We learned to make blankets, houses, clothes, and fire. We learned to gather food and, eventually, to plant and care for plants and animals that could provide us with food and warmth—all with the coordination of hands and mind. Until very recently in human history, all of us did all these things on a regular basis. Medina (2008) admonishes us to move, be outside, and solve problems to continue to learn and be healthy, both mentally and physically.

## THE NEURAL PATHWAYS MEET THE GARDEN PATHWAYS

Dr. Kelly Lambert is the Macon and Joan Brock Professor of Psychology at Randolph-Macon College, where she teaches neuroscience and psychology, chairs the psychology department, and maintains a behavioral neuroscience laboratory. She studies the relationship between using the hands for intentional action and for general well-being, and her research with rats examines how using the hands impacts depression and what might prevent depression.

Dr. Lambert (2008) identified in rats' brains a system that links the nucleus accumbens (the pleasure or reward center) with the motor system and the limbic system, which is involved with emotions and learning. We humans have the same brain structure as rats: the accumbens serves as a connector to the pleasure center, the motor system, and to our prefrontal cortex, where we think and make decisions. This system links movement, emotion, pleasure, and thinking, and Lambert (2008, 32) calls it the "effort-driven rewards circuit." (You may remember from the Preface that Dr. Mark Dubin, also a neuroscientist, suggested that the positive experiences youth relate to gardening may have to do with stimulating the brain's pleasure center, and he encouraged my line of inquiry about gardening youth and their sensory experiences.)

Physical activities that we decide to do, especially ones that involve our hands to produce a result that we can see, feel, and touch, such as knitting, cooking, making clothes, making art, doing crafts, or tending a garden, result in elevated well-being. Lambert's (2015, 22) research shows that when rats search for a hidden treat and dig it up with their paws (hands), they show healthier stress hormone levels and "enhanced emotional regulation" in comparison to the rats who did not have to dig to get their treats. These digging rats have engaged the effort-reward circuit in their brains and experienced the pleasure of finding and consuming a food treat.

We do not have comparable neurological research to show the physical effects on human brains from digging a hole and planting a tree, but doctors in the nineteenth century noticed that making things with the hands often relieved a patient's symptoms of depression and would prescribe knitting to depressed patients (Lambert, 2008, 87). Nearly 80 percent of the brain's neurons are in the cerebellum that governs motor coordination, and throughout human history until only recent decades, we used our hands and whole bodies for almost all our work. It is very possible that our recently developed sedentary and consumption-oriented lifestyles accounts for the 400 percent rise in the use of antidepressants from the 1990s to the 2000s (Lambert, 2015).

Lambert's (2008) research leads one to think that people today need more work to do with their hands that requires motor coordination and the visible completion of a task. She suggests that recent neurological research shows evidence that do-it-yourself hobbies and doing arts and crafts may offer more benefits to brain health than pharmacological treatments (Lambert, 2015, 22). Add to that evidence Medina's (2008) work on human evolution and brain function that suggests that working and solving problems outdoors helps the brain to thrive, and we can see where gardening offers benefits to bodies and brains.

Research with war veterans with post-traumatic stress disorder shows that working in gardens and with nature helps them recover from trauma (Westlund, 2014). Gardeners work hard with their whole bodies and their hands by digging, planting, or building a rose arbor or some other garden feature, and they do this work out of doors or in greenhouses with living plants.

Rose, from the ¡Cultiva! garden, shared the fact that she was diagnosed with clinical depression and described her gardening experience as therapeutic: "I can see my work right in front of me. I can see what I have accomplished." Could this important connection of active hands to brain health play a role in the photos youth took? About 10 percent of the youth gardening in Colorado photographed their hands or a peer gardener's hands when I asked them to photograph something meaningful to them in their gardens. Some of the New York and California gardeners also included hands in their photos. We can see these as pictures of their accomplishments

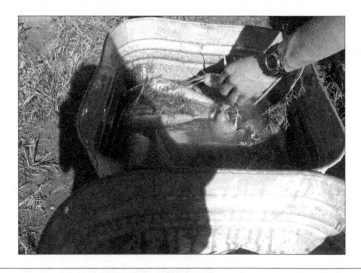

Washing the day's carrot harvest at Colorado Rocky Mountain School
Credit: Colorado Rocky Mountain School student

and perhaps as a statement on how important it is to their mental health to have their hands actively at work producing valuable food.

## THE NEED FOR PHYSIOLOGICAL STUDIES OF YOUTH GARDENERS

As discussed earlier, we do have evidence in studies with adults that show the beneficial physiological impacts of being in nature. One study with adults showed that smelling the essential oils of rosemary and lavender lowered cortisol levels (Atsumi and Tonosaki, 2007) while another showed increased memory formation for those smelling rosemary and enhanced mood for those smelling rosemary or lavender in comparison to a control group that smelled neither (Moss et al. 2003). These sorts of studies have not been done on adolescents. If they were, what would we discover?

High school and university biology students could be co-investigators in the study on the impact of smelling herbs, scented flowers, and finished compost on brain function and health. Knowing if essential oils and many living organisms in healthy soil could benefit memory and learning for children and youth would be invaluable information and provide further evidence on the efficacy of learning in garden environments.

Medina (2008, 207) explains that functional magnetic resonance imaging shows that the brain integrates multiple sensory experiences: "The brain cut its developmental teeth in an overwhelmingly multisensory environment. . . . [L]earning abilities are increasingly optimized the more multisensory the environment becomes." A garden offers a rich multisensory learning environment.

The thalamus is the control tower for the senses inside the brain. All of our senses, excepting the olfactory, send information through the thalamus for rerouting to other brain areas for perception and reactions (Medina, 2008). What a person sniffs, such as a rose's scent or garden compost, goes directly to the olfactory region between our eyes and then to the amygdala, the brain area that supervises emotional experience formation and the memories those emotional experiences create. Smell also goes to an area behind the eyes that is involved in decision making (Medina, 2008). Smell is very important in memory formation, retention, and recall, and, therefore, should be recognized as an important element in a learning environment.

Several youth said that the earthy smell in a garden reminds them of time spent with a parent or grandparent outdoors and makes them feel and recall the well-being they experienced as a child. I am guessing almost everyone reading this has had an experience of smelling something and being transported through time to a vivid childhood memory. Since memory needs to be acute while learning, Medina (2008) suggests integrating more sensory experiences with the presentation of material to be learned in a class to better optimize memory formation. I personally encourage teachers to keep herbs, such as rosemary, lavender, mint, and thyme, in their classroom windows for students to get up and touch and smell to assist in memory formation and relaxation, two other important factors in successful learning.

# 25

## CULTIVATING HEALTH, HAPPINESS, AND PEACE

Let us return full circle to New York, where I went in 2012 to interview Stephen Ritz's students after I saw him in a TED Talks. Those conversations on an East Harlem rooftop garden opened this book. In that week I spent meeting his students and the three young men he had worked with already for several years, Ritz was so busy that we only talked as he drove, showed me parks, and planted with his students. I wanted a conversation with Ritz that did not involve a myriad of other activities so that I could fully understand how all his greening work with youth began.

In 2013, I made another spring trip to New York, and though school was still on and Ritz's weekdays were full, he offered to pick me up at 7:30 on a Sunday morning to go see a new urban plant store under the elevated Metro track at 116th Street and Lexington Avenue, where he was finding employment for some students. Ritz brought his eighteen-year-old daughter, Michaela, with him, and we went to a Puerto Rican café near the plant nursery to have breakfast and talk while we waited for the plant store to open. We were the only customers and the café was quiet. I had watched this man's physiognomy transform in the brief sixteen months since I had first seen him on a video screen, and I wanted to understand more about what transpired to make him change into the person he had become, an internationally known youth mentor and gardening guru from the South Bronx.

ILLÈNE: Tell me what started you gardening with kids.

RITZ: Someone sent me a box of bulbs. They were literally daffodil bulbs, and I didn't know what they were. I thought they were onions.

ILLÈNE: I am glad you didn't eat them because daffodils are poisonous!

RITZ: Well, we contemplated it, but what I did was I hid them behind the radiator. I hid them because I didn't want the kids to throw them at each other. And the radiator was leaking, and with the moisture and heat, the bulbs got forced. And lo and behold, I went back behind the radiator one day looking for something else and there were hundreds and hundreds of flowers. The boys wanted to give them to the girls. The girls wanted to give them to their parents. And everyone wanted to sell them. That was the beginning of all of this.

ILLÈNE: [*I am laughing very loudly and am glad the little restaurant has no other customers at the moment!*] That is amazing. These were high schools kids?

RITZ: Yes, and they were bad kids! [*I had never heard Ritz use the word "bad" in relation to his students, but he said it with affection for kids who had the potential to be juvenile delinquents and instead became gardeners.*] And now, the story gets a little better. That year, I planted with those kids 25,000 bulbs across the Bronx to commemorate 9/11. We then went out to plant 250,000 bulbs, and I got the Golden Daffodil Award from the City of New York without knowing a thing about planting. So that is really how it started; with me going around the Bronx with all these crazy kids planting. So I had this incredible labor force. And these are some tough kids.

ILLÈNE: Where did you get the first money? Where did you get money for 25,000 bulbs?

RITZ: People sent me a box of bulbs, and we just kept taking pictures and sending them, and people kept sending more. There was no shortage because there was a project called the Daffodil Project in New York City. And they were trying to get kids involved planting daffodils to commemorate 9/11. And the more people gave me, this funny thing, the more I got done.

ILLÈNE: It sounds like a fairy tale.

RITZ: Yeah, it was like a fairy tale. The kids really liked it because it got them out of school to plant daffodils. I had a group of kids that no one was really enamored with except for me and my wife and Michaela.

MICHAELA: I really didn't comprehend what their issues were then.

RITZ: They were just nice kids, and they were very nice to Michaela because she was little and cute and the teacher's daughter.

MICHAELA: And I got my nose in everything. I was in 3rd or 4th grade.

RITZ: So I took a love for these kids. The kids took to it. And, of course, everybody in the school despised these kids because they were really tough, so they just kept giving me projects to keep the kids out of school. But I really found a niche for them. And then we met this gentleman, Russ, who said, "Wow, you've got twenty really strong kids. I've got a project." And lo and behold, we gave birth to Bissel Park.

**ILLÈNE:** Did he own that land?

**RITZ:** No, it is city property. It was a decommissioned city street.

**MICHAELA:** It was his vision.

**RITZ:** Part of it was his and his wife's vision. He lived in the area. He's a longtime resident of that neighborhood. In his lifetime, he saw the rise and the rapid decline of the neighborhood, particularly related to drugs and property values with everything that was going wrong in New York in the nineties, so they wanted to reclaim that as a place to do good things and reclaim the neighborhood because what was going on there was an epicenter of everything that was wrong in New York from drugs to prostitution to illegal dumping. It was counter-intuitive to everything that he and his wife and many decent people in the neighborhood believed in, but they didn't know how to do it all. These were older people. Russ was in his sixties, and most of the long-term residents were in their sixties and seventies. Physically, they did not have the strength. Here I was with these incredibly nutty, energetic kids who were dying to get out of school, but needed to go to school, who needed to get credit, and I had a bunch of teachers who did not want to engage with these kids. So, the more I could keep these kids out of school, and reading about it and writing about it, it was kind of like a match made in heaven. And what happened is that the kids really became successful.

Ritz concluded by telling me that he had found a job for Darrell installing green roofs, which he would start after high school graduation the next month. We went to check out the plant store and its resident chickens clucking away under the elevated trains. On our walk over, I also learned that Nathli had completed his AA degree in criminal justice that spring, and that Monroe College, where Nathli was studying, had offered him a scholarship to continue and get his bachelor's degree.

Ritz and I stay in touch. Nathli has since graduated and has his first criminal justice job now in Pennsylvania. Mateo from the East Harlem high school has a job at the urban plant store under the train tracks. Jonathon works at Home Depot and sees Ritz regularly. In 2015, Ritz renovated a classroom at Community School 55 in the South Bronx to be a Seed-to-Table program for youth. He calls it the National Health, Wellness and Learning Center. It opened in January of 2016 and is filled with white towers growing food hydroponically and has a kitchen where children can prepare and eat what they grow. Darrell has become Ritz's second right hand.

Ritz's successful work with youth has earned him a visit to the White House and many awards. The Green Bronx Machine youth are broadening their worlds and moving up in their lives thanks to a lot of love from Stephen Ritz and his family and all of the job opportunities and training they have experienced.

All the mentors in this book and all the young gardeners I have had the privilege to hear speak about their experiences have touched me deeply with their openness and their willingness to tell the world about how much their gardening experiences mean to them. When I seek to understand the essence of something intangible, such as how one person can give so much to so many as these adult mentors across the country who nurture youth and gardens do, I often turn to poetry and poets, including a national poet laureate, Stanley Kunitz.

## CULTIVATING LOVE

*Why is the act of cultivating so compelling?*

*All my life, the garden has been a great teacher in everything I cherish. As a child, I dreamed of a world that was loving, that was open to all kinds of experience, where there was no prejudice, no hatred, no fear. The garden was a world that depended on care and nourishment. And it was an interplay of forces; as much as I responded to the garden, the garden, in turn, responded to my touch, my presence.*

*The garden isn't, at its best, designed for admiration or praise; it leads to an appreciation of the natural universe and to a meditation on the connection between the self and the rest of the natural universe.* —STANLEY KUNITZ (2005, 13)

Stanley Kunitz, one of the most celebrated poets in the United States,[1] wrote the above words at age ninety-eight. His garden was located in Provincetown, Massachusetts. His words mirror what the young gardeners said in all twelve gardening programs about their experiences in their gardens.

----

1. Stanley Kunitz won the Pulitzer Prize for Poetry, the National Book Award for Poetry, and the National Medal of the Arts, was appointed Poet Laureate Consultant in Poetry to the Library of Congress twice, and taught at Columbia University for twenty-two years.

Norbeto from Chamisal echoes Kunitz: "[Gardening] sustains me mentally because I feel more connected with the earth and with what God gives us and the things that we have outside." Salina in Oakland describes how transformative it could be for her city to have a garden on every block where people could work together in safety and clear their minds. Luis in Taos declares that gardening "makes me more alive." Rose and Barclay in Boulder call the ¡Cultiva! garden a sanctuary. Justin in New York City explains that the "fresh oxygen makes you feel better, more calm." Maria in Carbondale, eight decades younger than Kunitz when she spoke with me, mirrors his observations: "Gardening helps me care more about the earth. Working with nature has helped me to see that nature works with us to give us what we need. We need earth to survive and it gives us so much; we should give back."

These experiences in peace, reciprocity, and connection in relation to gardening transcend age, place, gender, ethnicity, socioeconomic status, and educational attainment. A garden provides a common learning ground where nonagenarians and teens and children and parents can share experiences, knowledge, and feelings. A garden in its oneness with natural cycles unites us with nature's wholeness. I began my inquiry with three purposes: (1) to better understand the affective experiences of adolescent gardeners; (2) to identify gardening programs' impact on youth development; and (3) to discover how gardening may impact brain function and health. All of these elements relate to human well-being. What have we learned by listening to these youth?

The young gardeners have revealed that gardening provides them with focus, happiness, calm, peace, well-being, meaning, achievement, and close relationships with adult and peer gardeners. Their experiences provide abundant evidence that gardening programs with caring mentors meet adolescent developmental needs. This chapter summarizes the mental and physical health implications in the youths' gardening experiences and outlines the need for policy in health, food, education, and public land use to support garden access.

## THE ROLE GARDENS CAN PLAY IN YOUTH HEALTH

Research on youth gardeners could well have been framed in the context of educational achievement, community sustainability, climate change, or the existing agricultural system. I chose to frame it primarily in relation to health because we have such a serious health crisis involving both mental and physical health in the US and around the world that seems solvable when one considers all we know about food and exercise in relation to human well-being. Statistical evidence in the US cites mental health problems during adolescence in 20 percent of youth (Centers for Disease Control and Prevention, 2013); and 17 percent of youth are obese, approximately 12.7 million children from ages two to nineteen, (Centers for Disease Control and Prevention, 2015b, 1). Other developed nations have similar rates (World Health Organization, 2000). The gardening programs profiled provide evidence that gardening with mentors provides critical resources that promote mental and physical health.

The social-ecological approach to health frames health as an integral part of the social and physical environment and requires that the planning, education, and health professions work together to examine all possible amenities to engage people in active, healthy living, including easy access to healthy, affordable food (Sallis et al. 2006). Gardens are a vital component of the environment and afford people access to nature. The research evidence discussed throughout the book shows the many physical and mental health benefits nature contact provides boost immune system function and lower stress. Hansen-Ketchum and Halpenny (2011, 558) studied Canadian families with young children to see how they engage with nature as restorative places to support health and suggest that

> inter-sectoral governance with active citizen engagement in research, decision-making, and action may be essential to develop the ecological citizenship and communal norms and strategies that promote the health of people and their shared restorative places.

Youth in all four states in my study spontaneously shared personal mental and physical health challenges. They also described vividly how much gardening helps them feel healthier, both physically and emotionally. They enjoy the outdoor activity, access to healthy foods and food knowledge, and working with others in a safe, peaceful environment. Several of the teens identified time spent gardening as self-therapy. While this was not quantitative research that had youth fill out food consumption surveys before and after being in gardening programs, many youth described improved diets because of what they learned and could access in the garden.

"Eating from a garden is an experience that never gets old," said April, aged sixteen. Rosemary, aged eighteen, adds, "[Food from the garden] seems to give it a whole different taste, a whole new meaning, so you appreciate it so much more that it seems to taste better." From the many things that the youth gardeners discussed, it is clear that they overwhelmingly consider the food they grow to taste better and are more likely to eat vegetables as a result of growing them. The three young men in New York who had already gardened several seasons with the Green Bronx Machine happily told me how many vegetables they now eat and how much weight they have lost as a result. Even students just recently engaged with gardening testified to the changed habits that resulted, including eating more vegetables and fruits.

Research shows that including adequate vegetables in daily diets is important for a healthy lifestyle—vital nutrients are found in vegetables and fruit, and the fiber and water in vegetables can help control weight (Rolls, Ello-Martin, and Tohill, 2004). Gardening develops young people's taste for vegetables and encourages them to try new ones. Their photographs of their own hands next to the vegetables that they had harvested illustrate vividly their connections to what they grow.

Studies show that ease of access makes vegetable consumption easier (Libman, 2007; McArthur et al. 2010; Pothukuchi, 2004). Many gardeners described stopping or lessening junk food consumption, eating more vegetables and fruits, and losing weight, thus benefitting their health. Andrew explained, "[The vegetables are] right there [in the garden]. I can just pick it whenever I want to." A study of high school youth to determine what they considered healthy and what they chose to eat indicated that lack of access to healthy food choices at school made it difficult for them to choose well there (Croll, Neumark-Sztainer, and Story, 2001). A garden at a school provides easy access to better choices. "When you are working in a garden, and tomatoes hang on a vine in front of you, it's really easy to pluck and eat one," Rose explained about the tomatoes she grew at ¡Cultiva!, "I used to hate cherry tomatoes; now, I love them!"

Julieta, aged eighteen, was influenced also by the films on industrial food production that her agricultural biology class watched:

> I don't eat much fast food anymore because I know what's in the hamburgers and chicken nuggets after those movies we've watched. I don't want to put that in my body. I don't want those things going in my body. They taste good, but the things that make them are disgusting. My habits have definitely changed.

## POSITIVE RELATIONSHIPS AND EMOTIONS

All of the garden mentors I observed provided clear instruction and friendly guidance to the young gardeners. Many youth described their close relationships with their garden mentors. Those youth who were most at risk due to societal or personal situations found exceptional support from their garden mentors who extended the garden experience to other activities, including camping trips, vacations for their families, jobs and job training, and opportunities for making presentations at professional conferences in their capacities as youth gardeners.

The psychological structure identified for human flourishing by Seligman (2011), PERMA (positive emotions, engagement, positive relationships, meaning, and achievement), that is referred to throughout this narrative highlights how youth thrive psychologically while gardening. The positive relationships grow right along with the vegetables. Garden friendships cross ethnic and social lines. As they share work towards a shared goal that provides meaning, youth and adults meet each other on common ground. What they achieve, they achieve together.

Oakland Leaf's Love Cultivating Schoolyards program's name identifies the most important element needed for growing healthy youth and sustainable communities: love. Stephen Ritz and I discussed the love grown right along with the vegetables. Even when the other programs did not include love in their names, I saw a lot of love in practice. Whether the youth were twelve or nineteen, they focused on this element of human caring that made their gardens so important to their well-being. "We have more of a bond 'cause we all are together doing the same thing, the same job, so we actually connect more," said Damian, aged sixteen, of East Harlem. And Ian, aged twelve, of Albuquerque told me:

> Every friend I have made at the garden, they don't take a couple of days to get to know you or they don't try and stay away from you. Once you start talking, you are friends right away. Maybe it is because we are a community and we are doing something we both enjoy and we are doing it at the same time.

Over and over, in all twelve gardening locations, the students described their pleasure in gaining the skills necessary to grow food collaboratively. Rodrigo, aged eighteen, from Roaring Fork High School said in relation to building a hoop house with his class: "If we all work together, it helps make the world a better place." They perceive their actions as being for the general good, not just for themselves.

Not one teen gardener described any negative emotion when I asked how they felt about gardening. Most experienced a link between gardening, total focus, and stress relief. Virginia, aged seventeen and a teen mother at Yampah Mountain High School, explained, "I go back (to class) with less stress, and I can concentrate." Rodrigo at Roaring Fork High School echoed her:

"It's like taking a little break. You come here and work and learn. You come back to class more refreshed, more into work."

Courtney at Roaring Fork High School explained both the meaning and achievement in gardening as, "getting fulfillment out of hard work. And, yeah, growing something on your own is self-fulfillment. Like, it takes a lot of hard work to water and be responsible and check on it every day. It's a beautiful feeling." Youth found their gardening experiences fulfilling regardless of their ethnicity, geographic location, or their socioeconomic status.

Youth also gained meaning from honoring their families' culture of origin. In New Mexico, all the youth gardeners came from long histories of working the land whether they were Native Americans or descendants of the Spaniards who arrived as explorers in the sixteenth century or both. Many youth across the country had happy memories of being in gardens with grandparents or parents; gardens and parks held ties to family and childhood.

Their own hard work gave the youth gardeners a new respect for farmers and for naturally grown food in comparison to processed food. They delighted in eating and sharing the literal fruits of their own labor. I will always remember Neo in Oakland climbing the apple tree to get me an apple from a tree he had helped to nurture and handing the fruit to me with an immense smile (which can be seen on this book's cover). A few miles from that garden, the second graders proudly handed each one of us present with them that afternoon a carrot they had just harvested with Oakland Leaf youth mentors. This after-school gardening class ended with a delicious carrot crunch in their closing circle that completed the day. They were so proud and happy with their efforts to mulch garden beds and harvest carrots.

What good are these positive emotions beyond the time period in which they are experienced? Experiments have shown that positive feelings allow children to solve problems more creatively and effectively (Masters, Barden, and Ford, 1979). Positive emotions serve an important evolutionary purpose by making others want to be around us and cooperate with us and by giving us internal reserves to call on when things are difficult so that we can endure (Fredrickson, 1998; 2001). Some youth commented that they look forward to gardening days with pleasure, so it is clear that youth can experience positive emotions even before they enter the garden to work. Research shows that people who experience positive emotions, such as happiness, on a regular basis enjoy an optimistic outlook and expect that things will turn out for the better (Aspinwall, Richter, and Hoffman III, 2001).

A study comparing 220 adult gardeners to 223 adult non-gardeners showed a 20 percent difference in life satisfaction related to energy levels, optimism, zest for life, and physical self-concept—the gardeners self-reported higher satisfaction in all of these areas (Waliczek, Zajicek, and Lineberger, 2005). These gardeners also reported higher physical activity and health levels than non-gardeners (ibid.). It is fair to assume that similar results would come from teen gardeners compared to teen non-gardeners. A survey study with the same questions given to adolescents would provide valuable information to those seeking to design programs for positive youth development. These gardeners reflect what Rachel Carson (1998, 87) wrote: "Those who contemplate the beauty of the earth find reserves of strength that will endure as long as life lasts."

## GROWING AN ENVIRONMENTAL AND SUSTAINABILITY ETHIC

Our health depends on our planet's health. Many youth developed a sense of reciprocity with the earth through caring for it and using what it produced. They became aware of social justice in relation to food through their class readings, films, and discussions and by observing their own communities through a food access lens. At the end of their year-long, school-wide community sustainability study, Yampah Mountain High School held a community meal to represent the world's access to food. The greens served for that shared meal were from the school greenhouse and had been grown by teen mothers. For this luncheon, students drew lots to represent different world populations (i.e., those living in poverty or with plenty); thus, only a few students representing prosperous nations got to eat the greens. Most diners had only a small portion of rice to illustrate how little the world's poor eat. The gardeners did not necessarily get to eat the food they grew at that meal, but they experienced food injustice where some eat and many have little to no food.

The youth came to understand Aldo Leopold's (1966, 6) regard for farmers and farms: "There are two spiritual dangers in not owning a farm. One is the danger of supposing that breakfast comes from the grocery, and the other that heat comes from the furnace." The students understood photosynthesis not just as a vocabulary word in science class; they knew that the sweet flavor in a freshly picked pea came from the process in which a plant turns sunshine, water, and carbon dioxide into sugar molecules. They can taste the stored carbon.

The individual act of growing food and personal health takes on a broader meaning when one shares it with the community as all these programs showed. Sharing the food they grow gives youth the chance to help create sustainable communities that not only have adequate access to healthy food but also aid in caring for all the people and the environment.

Most programs where I interviewed youth gardeners included education regarding community sustainability even when the gardening was not part of an academic class. In the Colorado gardening programs, there tended to be a focus on environmental education, particularly in developing energy-saving techniques through improving the local food supply and in lowering the community's carbon footprint. In New York, New Mexico, and California, where there were more social and financial challenges in the gardeners' communities, the programs focused on caring for the environment and on strengthening food access, social networks, community safety, and economic opportunities through gardening.

The opportunity to engage in critical thought and action related to agriculture gave the gardeners experience in scientific inquiry and the political process and prepared them to be active members of a democracy through civic engagement (Schusler and Krasny, 2008). De'Andre in Oakland probably understood more about the GMO labeling ballot measure than he would have had he not been engaged in growing food and had the chance to discuss it with his gardening teachers and his mother. Active engagement with the environment while young and having the guidance of a caring adult encourages future environmental activism (Chawla, 1999). Many youth gardeners made it clear that their environmental commitment has grown. The youths' actions, knowledge, and personal commitments were integrated through gardening.

The gardening experiences that began as deeply personal, such as changed diets and attitudes, grew beyond to greater community consciousness, such as when the youth saw their food served at school and given to community elders and when they learned about the food system and its impact on people's health and on global warming. These profoundly positive human benefits harvested through gardening lead us back to the question that initiated this inquiry: What is happening in the brain and body while youth are digging and planting that helps create these healthy outcomes for youth? What is this organic brain fertilizer that gardens seem to provide?

## POLICY

During his time as the Chief Scientific Adviser to the United Kingdom from 2000 to 2007, Sir David King (2011, 744) oversaw Foresight project reports on obesity and soon came to realize that "We need collaborative societal changes in many aspects of our environment to avoid the morbid consequences of overweight and obesity. This change will require global political leadership across public policy, considerably broader than that of health policy."

King calls for a multidisciplinary, holistic approach to forming policy to create healthy communities. The experiences of the young gardeners I interviewed provide evidence that community and school gardens play a valuable role to enrich health. Community planning conversations need to include public access to places to garden, and gardens need to be integrated in blueprints for improving overall community health. Gardens as part of public policy to improve access to healthy food and exercise can be part of the needed holistic approach to societal change.

Publicly accessible gardens, such as those at schools and on other public lands, require political willpower, policy, and funding to support them. The American Planning Association continues to publish materials to help city planners integrate food growing within city master plans (Raja, Born, and Russel, 2008). Like King, the World Health Organization (2000) has encouraged countries to develop and implement policy that addresses the complex health issues obesity reflects, including food sources and types of food consumed, and it continues to call on government, business, media, health care providers, and consumers to work together to address the physical and psychosocial problems manifested in obesity. The American Heart Association (2016) has recently launched a Teaching Gardens program to involve more children in growing and eating vegetables as a health promotion activity.

If we see health and learning as an integrated whole, we must encourage our local and state school systems to write educational policy and legislate funds dedicated to school gardens as California has to get children outside and growing and eating fresh fruits and vegetables as part of their school day as the United States School Garden Army did almost one hundred years ago. Without policy and funding to support school gardens as places for learning and health promotion, they are at the whimsy of the personal preferences of school personnel with no guarantee that they will be maintained for the long term as an integral part of education to improve learning outcomes and student health.

Gardens are not expensive interventions to create engaged, healthy, committed youth. The fully fenced, one-third-acre garden at Roaring Fork High School that includes a forty-two-foot-diameter greenhouse dome cost about $80,000. Most of the labor involved in the construction of the garden was donated except for the greenhouse, where the construction labor was paid. Roaring Fork High School's garden has now been in use for five years, and all the food grown in the garden when school is in session goes into the school lunch at no cost to the school. A garden without a greenhouse or deer-proof fence can cost very little and require only the purchase of tools, seeds, organic soil amendments, and a means of irrigation, as well as the people and time needed to prepare soil, plant, and irrigate. These garden learning grounds are an investment in both education and health, and the benefits extend for years beyond graduation.

We have learned from what these young people say that human hands and energy given to creating a garden helps grow community and friendship. The good habits in nutrition and exercise cultivated at an early age can prevent the spending of some of the billions of dollars currently going toward treating obesity and mental illness. Through gardening, youth learn how to grow food and care for themselves, their families, their communities, and the planet. Gardeners can conceivably be outside planting and harvesting from ages two to one hundred. Growing food and flowers can bring joy for a lifetime.

I trust that the new evidence provided by the youth gardeners in this book on gardening's contribution to well-being will put garden plots and urban farms into school superintendents', planners', parents', and health professionals' vocabularies and tool kits as they work together to plan healthy environments for all citizens. These young gardeners provide a great deal of evidence to show that physical activity outside doing something with a tangible outcome—a beautiful garden with fresh food to pick and eat—results in happy, healthy youth.

We build confidence in young people by giving them real situations in which to learn, act, and see their results as these gardeners have demonstrated. The psychologist Albert Bandura (1997, 103) wrote: "The reciprocity between self-produced action and environmental events lies at the heart of the development of a sense of competence." Each garden portrayed in this book reflects that necessary self-produced action of youth who have gained competence to work with the environment for mutual benefits. Hunger and obesity, warfare and global warming, drought and nuclear waste—these are all challenges that young people face every day in the news, their classrooms, and their communities. After relatively brief periods of formal education, young people enter the working world. The world situation requires that we educate youth in the most effective way possible to bring their intelligence, skills, hands, will, and compassion forward to creatively solve these serious local and global problems!

Neuroscience and evolutionary history show us that our bodies need to move and solve problems outside and our hands need to achieve things that we set out to do. Ecological psychology provides a theoretical framework to help us understand the intimate interplay between people and nature. Gardens, with all their potential affordances for interaction with nature through observation and tending, provide a place for us to learn to integrate human health with planetary health. Environmental psychology, myths, and poetry help us understand our relationship with the earth. And poets help us to express the truth: "Find your place on the planet, dig in, and take responsibility from there" (Snyder, 1974, 101).

I find inspiration and joy in all these gardeners and their gardens. The gardens grow hope for the future along with food. I hope that these garden paths we have explored together will carry the reader to more garden paths, perhaps holding the hand of a child or sharing a shovel with a teen.

Youth inspire us to act for the common good. Maria, aged eighteen, a gardener at Roaring Fork High School, sums it up: "I can see that it's not just me that cares about healthy stuff, but others do too. If they don't care now, seeing us maybe they will."

*one word to you, to*
*you and your children:*
*stay together*
*learn the flowers*
*go light*

# REFERENCES

Agee, Janice, and Sheila Bruton, eds. 2002. *A Child's Garden of Standards: Linking School Gardens to California Education Standards*. Sacramento, CA: California Department of Education.

Alaimo, Katherine, Elizabeth Packnett, Richard A. Miles, and Daniel J. Kruger. 2008. "Fruit and Vegetable Intake among Urban Community Gardeners." *Journal of Nutrition Education and Behavior* 40 (2): 94–101.

Alvarado, Adriana, Quamrun Eldridge, Sonia Jain, and Janet Brown. 2011. *Project New Start Report 2011*. Oakland, CA: Alameda County Health Department.

American Heart Association. 2016. "About Teaching Gardens." American Heart Association. https://www.heart.org/HEARTORG/HealthyLiving/HealthyKids/TeachingGardens/About-Teaching-Gardens_UCM_436619_SubHomePage.jsp.

Ashe, Marice, Lisa Feldstein, Samantha Graff, Randolph Kline, Debora Pinkas, and Leslie Zellers. 2007. "Local Venues for Change: Legal Strategies for Healthy Environments." *Journal of Law and Medical Ethics* 35 (1): 138–47.

Aspen Historical Society. 2015. "The Utes: Pre 1879." Aspen Historical Society. http://aspenhistory.org/aspen-history/the-utes-pre-1879/.

Aspinall, Peter, Panagiotis Mavros, Richard Coyne, and Jenny Roe. 2013. "The Urban Brain: Analysing Outdoor Physical Activity with Mobile EEG." *British Journal of Sports Medicine* 49 (4): 272–6. doi:10.1136/bjsports-2012-091877.

Aspinwall, Lisa G., Linda Richter, and Richard R. Hoffman III. 2001. "Understanding How Optimism Works: An Examination of Optimists' Adaptive Moderation of Belief and Behavior." In *Optimism and Pessimism: Implications for Theory, Research, and Practice*, edited by E. C. Chang, 217–238. Washington, DC: American Psychological Association.

Atsumi, Toshiko, and Keiichi Tonosaki. 2007. "Smelling Lavender and Rosemary Increases Free Radical Scavenging Activity and Decreases Cortisol Level in Saliva." *Psychiatry Research* 150 (1): 85–96.

Bandura, Albert. 1997. *Self-Efficacy: The Exercise of Control*. New York: W. H. Freeman.

Barker, Roger G. 1968. *Ecological Psychology*. Stanford, CA: Stanford University Press.

Beetz, Andrea, Kerstin Uvnäs-Moberg, Henri Julius, and Kurt Kotrschal. 2012. "Psychosocial and Psychophysiological Effects of Human-Animal Interactions: The Possible Role of Oxytocin." *Frontiers in Psychology* 3:234. doi:10.3389/fpsyg.2012.00234.

Bell, Anne C., and Janet E. Dyment. 2008. "Grounds for Health: The Intersection of Green School Grounds and Health-Promoting Schools." *Environmental Education Journal* 14 (1): 77–90.

Beresford, Larry. 2014. "Legacy Emanuel Medical Center Plants with Purpose." *Healthcare Design*, November 12.

Berman, Mark, John Jonides, and Stephen Kaplan. 2008. "The Cognitive Benefits of Interacting with Nature." *Psychological Science* 19 (12): 1207–12.

Berman, Sheldon H. 1997. *Children's Social Consciousness and the Development of Social Responsibility*. New York: State University of New York Press.

Berry, Wendell. 2009. *Bringing It to the Table: On Farming and Food*. Berkeley, CA: Counterpoint Press.

Bianchi, Suzanne M. 1994. "The Changing Demographic and Socioeconomic Characteristics of Single Parent Families." *Marriage & Family Review* 20 (1–2): 71–97.

Blair, Dorothy. 2009. "The Child in the Garden: An Evaluative Review of the Benefits of School Gardening." *The Journal of Environmental Education* 40 (2): 15–37.

Brody, Jane E. 2013. "What Causes Hearing Loss." *New York Times*, March 25.

Bronx-Lebanon Hospital Center. 2013. *2013 Community Health Needs Assessment*. New York: Bronx-Lebanon Hospital Center.

Brownell, Kelly D., and Katherine B. Horgen. 2004. *Food Fight*. Chicago: Contemporary Books.

Burrus, Jeremy, and Richard Roberts. 2012. "Dropping Out of High School: Prevalence, Risk Factors, and Remediation Strategies." *R&D Connections* 18:1–9.

Cammack, Carol, Tina M. Waliczek, and Jayne M. Zajicek. 2002. "The Green Brigade: The Educational Effects of a Community-Based Horticultural Program on the Horticultural Knowledge and Environmental Attitude of Juvenile Offenders." *HortTechnology* 12 (1): 77–81.

Carmona, Richard H. 2004. "The Growing Epidemic of Childhood Obesity." Testimony before the Subcommittee on Competition, Infrastructure, and Foreign Commerce Committee on Commerce, Science, and Transportation, United States Senate, March 2. http://www.surgeongeneral.gov/news/testimony/childobesity03022004.html.

Carolan, Michael S. 2007. "Introducing the Concept of Tactile Space: Creating Lasting Social and Environmental Commitments." *Geoforum* 38 (6): 1264–75.

Carson, Rachel. 1998. *The Sense of Wonder*. New York: HarperCollins.

Carter, C. Sue. 1998. "Neuroendocrine Perspectives on Social Attachment and Love." *Psychoneuroendocrinology* 23 (8): 779–818.

Catalano, Richard F., M. Lisa Berglund, Jean A. M. Ryan, Heather S. Lonczak, and J. David Hawkins. 2004. "Positive Youth Development in the United States: Research Findings on Evaluations of Positive Youth Development Programs." *The ANNALS of the American Academy of Political and Social Science* 591 (1): 98–124.

Census for Agriculture. 2012. "2012 Census Highlights: Farm Demographics—US Farmers by Gender, Age, Race, Ethnicity, and More." US Department of Agriculture. http://www.agcensus.usda.gov/Publications/2012/Online_Resources/Highlights/Farm_Demographics/.

———. 2015. "Sales from US Organic Farms Up 72 Percent, USDA Reports." News release, September 17. http://www.agcensus.usda.gov/Newsroom/2015/09_17_2015.php.

Centers for Disease Control and Prevention. 2009. *Obesity: Halting the Epidemic by Making Health Easier*. Atlanta, GA: National Center for Chronic Disease Prevention and Health Promotion.

———. 2013. *Ten Leading Causes of Death by Age Group, United States: 2013*. Atlanta, GA: National Center for Injury Prevention and Control.

———. 2014. *National Diabetes Statistics Report: Estimates of Diabetes and Its Burden in the United States, 2014*. Atlanta, GA: US Department of Health and Human Services.

———. 2015a. "Attention-Deficit / Hyperactivity Disorder (ADHD)." US Department of Health and Human Services. http://www.cdc.gov/ncbddd/adhd/.

———. 2015b. "Childhood Obesity Facts Prevalence of Childhood Obesity in the United States, 2011–2012." US Department of Health and Human Services. http://www.cdc.gov/obesity/data/childhood.html.

Chawla, Louise. 1999. "Life Paths into Effective Environmental Action." *Journal of Environmental Education* 31 (1): 15–26.

———, ed. 2002. *Growing Up in an Urbanising World*. Paris: UNESCO.

City of Oakland. 2014. "Urban Agriculture Citywide Update." City of Oakland Planning and Zoning. Accessed May 8. http://www2.oaklandnet.com/Government/o/PBN/OurOrganization/PlanningZoning/OAK029859.

Clinebill, Howard. 2013. *Ecotherapy: Healing Ourselves, Health the Earth*. New York: Routledge.

Coleman-Jensen, Alisha, Mark Nord, Margaret Andrews, and Steven Carlson. 2012. "Household Food Security in the United States in 2011." *United States Department of Agriculture: Economic Research Service*, ERR-141.

Colorado Department of Public Health and Environment. 2011. *2011 Youth Risk Behavior Survey Results: Colorado High School Survey*. Denver: Colorado Department of Public Health and Environment.

Colorado Rocky Mountain School [CRMS], 2013. "About." Colorado Rocky Mountain School. http://www.crms.org/.

Common Sense Media. 2015. *The Common Sense Census: Media Use by Teens and Tweens*. San Francisco: Common Sense Media, Inc.

Confessore, Nicholas. 2014. "How School Lunch Became the Latest Political Battleground." *New York Times*, October 12.

Coon, Katherine A., and Katherine L. Tucker. 2002. "Television and Children's Consumption Patterns: A Review of the Literature." *Minerva Pediatrics* 54:423–36.

Croll, Jillian, Diane Neumark-Sztainer, and Mary Story. 2001. "Healthy Eating: What Does It Mean to Adolescents?" *Journal of Nutrition* 33 (4): 193–8.

Csikszentmihalyi, Mihaly. 1997. *Creativity: Flow and the Psychology of Discovery and Invention*. New York: Harper Perennials.

Darwin, Charles. 1871. *The Descent of Man, and Selection in Relation to Sex*. London: John Murray.

de la Monte, Suzanne M., and Jack R. Wands. 2008. "Alzheimer's Disease Is Type 3 Diabetes—Evidence Reviewed." *Journal of Diabetes Science and Technology* 2 (6): 1101–13.

DeNavas-Walt, Carmen, and Bernadette D. Proctor. 2014. *Current Population Reports, P60-249, Income and Poverty in the United States: 2013*. Washington, DC: US Government Printing Office.

Dennison, Barbara A., Helen L. Rockwell, and Sharon L. Baker. 1998. "Fruit and Vegetable Intake in Young Children." *Journal of the American College of Nutrition* 17 (4): 371–8.

Dietz, William H. 2011. "Reversing the Tide of Obesity." *The Lancet* 378 (9793): 744–5.

Dietz, William H., and Steven L. Gortmaker. 1985. "Do We Fatten Our Children at the Television Set? Obesity and Television Viewing in Children and Adolescents." *Pediatrics* 75 (5): 807–12.

Discovery Channel. 2009. *Gang Wars: Oakland*. DVD. Silver Spring, MD: Discovery Channel.

Doak, Colleen D., Tommy L. S. Visscher, Carry M. Renders, and Jaap C. Seidell. 2006. "The Prevention of Overweight and Obesity in Children and Adolescents: A Review of Interventions and Programs." *Obesity Reviews* 7 (1): 111–36.

Dubin, Mark. 2001. *How the Brain Works*. Malden, MA: Blackwell Science.

Dubois, David L., Bruce E. Holloway, Jeffrey C. Valentine, and Harris Cooper. 2002. "Effectiveness of Mentoring Programs for Youth: A Meta-Analytic Review." *American Journal of Community Psychology* 30 (2): 157–97.

Duckworth, Angela L., and Martin E. P. Seligman. 2005. "Self-Discipline Outdoes IQ in Predicting Academic Performance of Adolescents." *Psychological Science* 16 (12): 939–44.

Durkin, Erin. 2013. "'Diabetes Epidemic' Declared as New York City Deaths Tied to the Disease Hit All-Time High." *New York Daily News*, June 10.

Eccles, Jacquelynne S., and Jennifer A. Gootman. 2002. *Community Programs to Promote Youth Development*. Washington, DC: National Academies Press.

Eccles, Jacquelynne S., Carol Midgley, Allan Wigfield, Christy Buchanan, David Reuman, and Constance Flanagan. 1993. "Development during Adolescence: The Impact of Stage-Environment Fit on Young Adolescents' Experiences in Schools and in Families." *American Psychologist* 48 (2): 90–101.

Economic Research Service. 2016. "Vegetables & Pulses: Potatoes." US Department of Agriculture. http://www.ers.usda.gov/topics/crops/vegetables-pulses/potatoes.aspx.

Edible Schoolyard Project. 2006. "Our Work." The Edible Schoolyard Project. http://edibleschoolyard.org/our-work.

Engdahl, Todd. 2008. "Sodas Expelled from Colorado Schools." *Examiner*, December 11.

Erikson, Erik H. 1968. *Identity, Youth and Crisis*. New York: W. W. Norton & Co.

Faber Taylor, Andrea, and Frances E. Kuo. 2008. "Children with Attention Deficits Concentrate Better After Walk in the Park." *Journal of Attention Disorders* 12 (5): 402–9.

Feeding America. 2014. "Map the Meal Gap 2014: Overall Food Insecurity in New Mexico by County in 2012." Feeding America. www.feedingamerica.org/mapthegap.

Finkelstein, Daniel, Elaine L. Hill, and Robert C. Whitaker. 2008. "School Food Environments and Policies in US Public Schools." *Pediatrics* 122 (1): e251–9.

Flanagan, Caitlin. 2010. "Cultivating Failure: How School Gardens Are Cheating Our Most Vulnerable Students." *Atlantic Monthly*, January/February.

Fleischhacker, Sheila E., Kelly R. Evenson, Daniel A. Rodriguez, and Alice Ammerman. 2011. "A Systematic Review of Fast-Food Access Studies." *Obesity Reviews* 12 (5): e460–71.

Food Trust. 2008. *Healthy School Toolkit*. Philadelphia: The Food Trust.

Foster, Gary D., Sandy Sherman, Kelley E. Borradaile, Karen M. Grundy, Stephanie Vander Veur, Joan Nachmani, Allison Karpyn, Shiriki Kumanyika, and Justine Shults. 2008. "A Policy-Based School Intervention to Prevent Overweight and Obesity." *Pediatrics* 121 (4): 794–802.

Fredrickson, Barbara L. 1998. "What Good Are Positive Emotions?" *Review of General Psychology* 2 (3): 300–19.

———. 2001. "The Role of Positive Emotion in Positive Psychology: The Broaden-and-Build Theory of Positive Emotion." *American Psychologist* 56:218–26.

Fudge, Tom. 2009. "California Bans Soda in Schools." *KPBS*, July 1.

Gantz, Walter, Nancy Schwartz, James Angelini, and Victoria Rideout. 2007. *Food for Thought: Television Food Advertising to Children in the United States*. Menlo Park, CA: Kaiser Family Foundation.

Gibson, James. 1979. *The Ecological Approach to Visual Perception*. Boston: Houghton Mifflin Company.

Gluckman, Peter, Sania Nishtar, and Timothy Armstrong. 2015. "Ending Childhood Obesity: A Multidimensional

Challenge." *The Lancet* 385 (9973): 1048–50.

Gogolak, E. C. 2013. "New York City Graduation Rate Remains Steady." *New York Times*, June 17.

Gortmaker, Steven. 2008. "Innovations to Reduce Television and Computer Time and Obesity in Childhood." *Archives of Pediatrics and Adolescent Medicine* 162 (3): 283–4.

Grandbois, Will. 2014. "Solar Array Will Power Roaring Fork High." *Post Independent*, September 11.

Greenaway, Twilight. 2012. "A Grocery Store for the People Planned for the West Oakland Food Desert." *Grist*, November 12.

Growing Gardens of Boulder County. 2011. "The ¡Cultiva! Youth Project." Growing Gardens. http://www.growing-gardens.org/the-cultiva-youth-project.

Guerino, Paul, Paige M. Harrison, and William J. Sabol. 2011. "Prisoners in 2010." Revised on February 9, 2012. *U.S. Department of Justice Bulletin*, NCJ 236096.

Guthrie, Joanne F., Biing-Hwan Lin, and Elizabeth Frazao. 2002. "Role of Food Prepared Away from Home in the American Diet, 1977–78 versus 1994–96: Changes and Consequences." *Journal of Nutrition Education Behavior* 34:140–50.

Hale, James, Corrine Knapp, Lisa Bardwell, Michael Buchenau, Julie Marshall, Fahriye Sancar, and Jill S. Litt. 2011. "Connecting Food Environments and Health through the Relational Nature of Aesthetics: Gaining Insight through the Community Gardening Experience." *Social Science & Medicine* 72 (11): 1853–63.

Hansen-Ketchum, Patricia A., and Elizabeth A. Halpenny. 2011. "Engaging with Nature to Promote Health: Bridging Silos to Examine the Evidence." *Health Promotion International* 26 (1): 100–8.

Harnack, Lisa, Jamie Stang and Mary Story. 1999. "Soft Drink Consumption among US Children and Adolescents: Nutritional Consequences." *Journal of the American Dietetic Association* 99 (4): 436–41.

Harper, Elaine. 2007. "Making Good Choices: How Autonomy Support Influences the Behavior Change and Motivation of Troubled and Troubling Youth." *Reclaiming Children and Youth: The Journal of Strength-Based Interventions* 16 (3): 23–8.

Harris, Harry, and Natalie Neysa. 2012. "Boy, 11, Struck by Hail of Bullets Fired at East Oakland Home." *Oakland Tribune*, September 20.

Hartig, Terry, Gary W. Evans, Larry D. Jamner, Deborah S. Davis, and Tommy Garling. 2003. "Tracking Restoration in Natural and Urban Field Settings." *Journal of Environmental Psychology* 23:109–23.

Harvard School of Public Health. 2014. "Economic Cost: Paying the Price for Those Extra Pounds." Obesity Prevention Source. http://www.hsph.harvard.edu/obesity-prevention-source/obesity-consequences/economic/.

Hayden-Smith, Rose. 2006. "Soldiers of the Soil: A Historical Review of the United States School Garden Army." *University of California Monograph*, Winter: 1–19.

Heft, Harry, and Louise Chawla. 2005. "Children as Agents in Sustainable Development: The Ecology of Competence." In *Children and Their Environments, Learning, Using and Designing Spaces*, edited by Christopher Spencer and Mark Blades, 199–216. Cambridge, United Kingdom: Cambridge University Press.

Heim, Stephanie, Jamie Stang, and Marjorie Ireland. 2009. "A Garden Pilot Project Enhances Fruit and Vegetable Consumption among Children." *Journal of the American Dietetic Association* 109:1220–6.

Hellmich, Nanci. 2011. "USDA Calls for Dramatic Change in School Lunches." *USA Today*, January 12.

Helphand, Kenneth. 2006. *Defiant Gardens*. San Antonio, TX: Trinity University Press.

Henderson, Nia-Malika. 2010. "President Obama Signs Child Nutrition Bill, a Priority for First Lady." *Washington Post*, December 13.

Heschong, Lisa, Roger L. Wright, and Stacia Okura. 2002. "Daylighting Impacts on Human Performance in School." *Journal of the Illuminating Engineering Society*, Summer: 101–14.

Hollands, Simon, M. Karen Campbell, Jason Gilliland, and Sisira Sarma. 2013. "A Spatial Analysis of the Association between Restaurant Density and Body Mass Index in Canadian Adults." *Preventive Medicine* 57:258–64.

———. 2014. "Association between Neighbourhood Fast-Food and Full-Service Restaurant Density and Body Mass Index: A Cross-Sectional Study of Canadian Adults." *Canadian Journal of Public Health* 105 (3): e172–8.

Huh, Susanna, Sheryl Rifas-Shiman, Chloe Zera, Janet Rich-Edwards, Emily Oken, and Scott Weiss. 2012. "Delivery by Caesarean Section and Risk of Obesity in Preschool Age Children: A Prospective Cohort Study." *Archives of Disease in Childhood* 97 (7): 610–6.

Jacobson, Michael F. 2005. *Liquid Candy: How Soft Drinks Are Harming America's Health*. Washington, DC: Center for Science in the Public Interest.

Jaslow, Raymond. 2014. "World Health Organization Lowers Sugar Intake Recommendations." *CBS News*, March 5.

Kane, Will. 2012. "Bullet Injures Sleeping Oakland Boy, 11." *San Francisco Chronicle*, September 20.

Kaplan, Rachel, and Stephen Kaplan. 1990. "Restorative Experience: The Healing Power of Nearby Nature." In *The Meaning of Gardens*, edited by Mark Francis and Randoph T. Hester, 238–43. Cambridge, MA: Massachusetts Institute of Technology.

Kaplan, Stephen. 1995. "The Restorative Benefits of Nature: Toward an Integrative Framework." *Journal of Environmental Psychology* 15:169–82.

———. 2000. "Human Nature and Environmentally Responsible Behavior." *Journal of Social Issues* 56 (3): 491–508.

Kaplan, Stephen, and Marc G. Berman. 2010. "Directed Attention as a Common Resource for Executive Functioning and Self-Regulation." *Perspectives on Psychological Science* 5 (1): 43–57.

Kell, John. 2015. "The Fortune 500's Biggest Food, Beverage, and Tobacco Companies." *Fortune*, June 22.

Kessler, Ronald, Patricia Berglund, Olga Demler, Robert Jin, Kathleen Merikangas, and Ellen Walters. 2005. "Lifetime Prevalence and Age-of-Onset Distributions of DSM-IV Disorders in the National Comorbidity Survey Replication." *Archives of General Psychiatry* 62 (6): 593–602.

Kim, Geonwoo, Bum-Jin Park, Dawou Joung, Dong-Geol Yeom, and Shinya Koga. 2015. "Healing Environments of Major Tree Species in Kyushu University Forests: A Case Study." *Journal of the Faculty of Agriculture Kyushu University* 60 (2): 477–83.

King, David. 2011. "The Future Challenge of Obesity." *The Lancet* 378 (9793): 743–4.

King, Stanley. 1989. *Co-Design: A Process of Design Participation*. New York: Van Nostrand Reinhold.

Kingsolver, Barbara, Steven L. Hopp, and Camille Kingsolver. 2007. *Animal, Vegetable, Miracle*. New York: HarperCollins.

Klemmer, Cynthia Davis, Tina M. Walliczek, and Jayne M. Zajicek. 2005. "Growing Minds: The Effect of a School Gardening Program on the Science Achievement of Elementary Students." *HortTechnology* 15 (3): 448–52.

Kummer, Corby. 2008. "A Papaya Grows in Holyoke." *Atlantic Monthly*, April.

Kunitz, Stanley. 2005. *The Wild Braid*. New York: W. W. Norton & Co.

Kuo, Frances E., and Andrea Faber Taylor. 2004. "A Potential Natural Treatment for Attention-Deficit/Hyperactivity Disorder: Evidence from a National Study." *American Journal of Public Health* 94:1580–6.

Kuo, Frances E., and William C. Sullivan. 2001. "Environment and Crime in the Inner City: Does Vegetation Reduce Crime?" *Environment and Behavior* 33 (3): 343–67.

Laird, Fiona, and Tavia Teitler. 2015. "Drugs, Sex, and Alcohol: Healthy Kids Survey Results Revealed." *The Rampage* 8 (4): 1.

Lambert, Kelly. 2008. *Lifting Depression: A Neuroscientist's Hands-On Approach to Activating Your Brain's Healing Power*. New York: Basic Books.

———. 2015. "Do or DIY." *The Royal Society for the Arts Journal* 1:20–3.

Lantieri, Linda. 1999. "Hooked on Altruism: Developing Social Responsibility in At-Risk Youth." *Reclaiming Children and Youth* 8 (2): 83–7.

Larson, Reed. 2000. "Toward a Psychology of Positive Youth Development." *American Psychologist* 55 (1): 170–83.

Leopold, Aldo. 1966. *A Sand County Almanac*. San Francisco: Sierra Club.

Levine, Susan. 2008. *School Lunch Politics: The Surprising History of America's Favorite Welfare Program*. Politics and Society in 20th Century America, edited by William Chafe, Gary Gerstle, Linda Gordon, and Julian Zelizer. Princeton: Princeton University Press.

Li, Qing. 2010. "Effect of Forest Bathing Trips on Human Immune Function." *Environmental Health and Preventive Medicine* 15 (1): 9–17.

Libman, Kimberly. 2007. "Growing Youth Growing Food: How Vegetable Gardening Influences Young People's Food Consciousness and Eating Habits." *Applied Environmental Education & Communication* 6 (1): 87–95.

Lim, CJ. 2014. *Food City*. New York: Routledge.

Lindström, Martin, Bertil S. Hanson, Elisabet Wirfält, and Per-Olof Östrgren. 2001. "Socioeconomic Differences in the Consumption of Vegetables, Fruit and Fruit Juices." *European Journal of Public Health* 11 (1): 51–9.

Linthicum, Leslie. 2013. "Hunger in New Mexico is for Real." *Albuquerque Journal*, October 9.

Litt, Jill S., Mah-J. Soobader, Mark S. Turbin, James W. Hale, Michael Buchenau, and Julie A. Marshall. 2011. "The Influences of Social Involvement, Neighborhood Aesthetics and Community Garden Participation on Fruit and Vegetable Consumption." *American Journal of Public Health* 101:1466–73.

Loring, Belinda, and Aileen Robertson. 2014. *Obesity and Inequities: Guidance for Addressing Inequities in Obesity and Overweight*. Copenhagen, Denmark: World Health Organization Regional Office for Europe.

Lovelock, James E., and Lynn Margulis. 1974. "Atmospheric Homeostasis by and for the Biosphere: The Gaia Hypothesis." *Tellus* 26 (1–2): 2–10.

Lowry, Christopher A., J. H. Hollis, A. De Vries, B. Pan, L. R. Brunet, J. R. F. Hunt, J. F. R. Paton, E. Van Kampen, D. M. Knight, A. K. Evans, G. A. W. Rook, and S. L. Lightman. 2007. "Identification of an Immune-Responsive Mesolimbocortical Serotonergic System: Potential Role in Regulation of Emotional Behavior." *Neuroscience* 146 (2–5): 756–72.

Ludwig, David, and Steven Gortmaker. 2004. "Programming Obesity in Childhood." *The Lancet* 364 (9430): 226–7.

Ludwig, David, Karen Peterson, and Steven Gortmaker. 2001. "Relation between Sugar-Sweetened Drinks and Childhood Obesity." *The Lancet* 357 (9255): 505–8.

Mann, Charles C. 2005. *1491: Revelations of the Americas before Columbus Arrived*. New York: Knopf.

Masters, John, Robert Christopher Barden, and Martin Ford. 1979. "Affective States, Expressive Behavior, and Learning in Children." *Journal of Personality and Social Psychology* 37:380–90.

McAleese, Jessica, and Linda Rankin. 2007. "Garden-Based Nutrition Education Affects Fruit and Vegetable Consumption in Sixth-Grade Adolescents." *Journal of the American Dietetic Association* 107 (4): 662–5.

McArthur, Jacqueline, Walter Hill, Guy Trammel, and Carlton Morris. 2010. "Gardening with Youth as a Means of Developing Science, Work and Life Skills." *Children, Youth and Environments* 20 (1): 301–17.

McCurdy, Christine. 2014. "Textbook, Research Study Highlight Legacy's Gardens." *Lund Report*, January 1.

Medina, John. 2008. *Brain Rules: 12 Principles for Surviving and Thriving at Work, Home, and School*. Seattle, WA: Pear Press.

Mollison, Bill. 1990. *Permaculture: A Practical Guide for a Sustainable Future*. Washington, DC: Island Press.

Morris, Jennifer, and Sheri Zidenberg-Cherr. 2013. *Nutrition to Grow On: A Garden-Enhanced Nutrition Education Curriculum for Upper Elementary School Children (2nd Edition)*. Sacramento, CA: California Department of Education.

Moss, Mark, Jenny Cook, Keith Wesnes, and Paul Duckett. 2003 "Aromas of Rosemary and Lavender Essential Oils Differentially Affect Cognition and Mood in Healthy Adults." *International Journal of Neuroscience* 113 (1): 15–38.

Muntel, Sarah. 2012. "Fast Food—Is It the Enemy?" *Obesity Action Coalition*, Spring.

National Alliance on Mental Illness. 2016. *Mental Health Facts: Children and Teens*. Arlington, VA: National Alliance on Mental Illness.

National Center for Education Statistics. 2015a. "The Condition of Education: Status Dropout Rates." US Department of Education Institute of Education Sciences. http://nces.ed.gov/programs/coe/indicator_coj.asp.

———. 2015b. "The Condition of Education: Public High School Graduation Rate." US Department of Education Institute of Education Sciences. http://nces.ed.gov/programs/coe/indicator_coi.asp.

National Drought Mitigation Center. 2013. "US Drought Monitor." University of Nebraska-Lincoln, the United States Department of Agriculture, and the National Oceanic and Atmospheric Administration. Accessed September 10. http://droughtmonitor.unl.edu/.

National Gang Intelligence Center. 2011. *2011 National Gang Threat Assessment*. Product No. 2009-M0335-001. Washington, DC: Federal Bureau of Investigation.

Nestle, Marion. 2007. *Food Politics: How the Food Industry Influences Nutrition and Health*. Berkeley, CA: University of California Press.

Neumann, Inga D. 2002. "Involvement of the Brain Oxytocin System in Stress Coping: Interactions with the Hypothalamo-Pituitary-Adrenal Axis." *Progress in Brain Research* 139:147–62.

New Mexico Acequia Association. 2013. "About Us." New Mexico Acequia Association. Accessed September 22. http://www.lasacequias.org/about/.

New Mexico Department of Health. 2013. "Taos County Health Highlights: Diabetes Death Rates." New Mexico's Indicator-Based Information System (NM-IBIS). Accessed September 12. https://ibis.health.state.nm.us/community/highlight/DiabDeath.Cnty/GeoCnty/55.html.

New York City Department of Health and Mental Hygiene. 2007. *Diabetes in New York City: Public Health Burden and Disparities*. New York: New York City Department of Health and Mental Hygiene.

———. 2008. "Mental Health of New York City Youth." *NYC Vital Signs* 7 (2).

———. 2013. "New York City Community Health Profiles." New York City Department of Health and Mental Hygiene. http://www1.nyc.gov/site/doh/data/data-publications/profiles.page.

New York City Economic Development Corporation. 2015. "Hunts Point Peninsula Project." New York City Economic Development Corporation. Last updated July 2. http://www.nycedc.com/project/hunts-point-peninsula.

Newby, P. K. 2007. "Are Dietary Intakes and Eating Behaviors Related to Childhood Obesity? A Comprehensive Review of the Evidence." *Journal of Law, Medicine and Ethics* 35 (1): 35–60.

Newman, Christopher, Elizabeth Howlett, and Scot Burton. 2013. "Implications of Fast Food Restaurant Concentration for Preschool-Aged Childhood Obesity." *Journal of Business Research* 67:1573–80.

Ng, Marie, Tom Fleming, Margaret Robinson, Blake Thomson, Nicholas Graetz, Erin Mullany, Stan Biryukov, et al. 2014. "Global, Regional, and National Prevalence of Overweight and Obesity in Children and Adults during 1980–2013: A Systematic Analysis for the Global Burden of Disease Study 2013." *The Lancet* 384 (9945): 766–81.

Nielsen, Samara Joy, Anna Maria Siega-Riz, and Barry M. Popkin. 2002. "Trends in Food Locations and Sources among Adolescents and Young Adults." *Preventive Medicine* 35 (2): 107–13.

Noddings, Nel. 1992. *The Challenge to Care in Schools: An Alternative Approach to Education.* New York: Teacher's College Press.

Oakland Food Policy Council. 2015. "Glossary of Terms." Oakland Food Policy Council. Accessed January 29. http://oaklandfood.org/resources/glossary-of-terms/.

Office of Disease Prevention and Health Promotion. 2015a. *Scientific Report of the 2015 Dietary Guidelines Advisory Committee, Part B. Chapter 2: 2015 DGAC Themes and Recommendations: Integrating the Evidence.* Rockville, MD: Office of Disease Prevention and Health Promotion.

———. 2015b. *Scientific Report of the 2015 Dietary Guidelines Advisory Committee. Part D. Chapter 6: Cross-Cutting Topics of Public Health Importance: Added Sugars and Low-Calorie Sweeteners.* Rockville, MD: Office of Disease Prevention and Health Promotion.

Office of Minority Health. 2013. "Diabetes and Hispanic Americans." US Department of Health and Human Services. Accessed October 17. http://minorityhealth.hhs.gov/omh/browse.aspx?lvl=4&lvlID=63.

Ogden, Cynthia, Margaret Carroll, Lester Curtin, Molly Lamb, and Katherine Flegal. 2010. "Prevalence of High Body Mass Index in US Children and Adolescents, 2007–2008." *Journal of the American Medical Association* 303 (3): 242–9.

Open Voices. 2013. "Natural Design for Better Health: An Interview with Dr. Roger Ulrich." *Nature Sacred*, September 24.

Oppezzo, Marily, and Daniel Schwartz. 2014. "Give Your Ideas Some Legs: The Positive Effect of Walking on Creative Thinking." *Journal of Experimental Psychology: Learning, Memory, and Cognition* 40 (4): 1142–52.

Oregon Commission on Children and Family. *Best Practices: Positive Youth Development.* Manhattan, KS: Midwest Equity Assistance Center.

Ozer, Emily. 2007. "The Effects of School Gardens on Students and Schools: Conceptualizations for Maximizing Healthy Development." *Health Education Behavior* 34 (6): 846–63.

Paeratakul, Sahasporn, Daphne Ferdinand, Catherine Champagne, Donna Ryan, and George Bray. 2003. "Fast-Food Consumption among US Adults and Children: Dietary and Nutrient Intake Profile." *Journal of the Academy of Nutrition and Dietetics* 103 (10): 1332–8.

Peterson, Karen, and Mary Kay Fox. 2007. "Addressing the Epidemic of Childhood Obesity through School-Based Interventions: What Has Been Done and Where Do We Go from Here?" *Journal of Law, Medicine and Ethics* 35 (1): 113–30.

Pevec, Illène. 2005. *A Child's Garden of Peace.* DVD. Directed by Myra Margolin and Illène Pevec. Carbondale, CO: Sustainable Solutions.

Pollan, Michael. 2006. *The Omnivore's Dilemma.* New York: Penguin.

———. 2008. "Farmer in Chief." *New York Times*, October 12.

———. 2009. *The Omnivore's Dilemma for Kids: The Secrets behind What You Eat (Young Readers' Edition).* New York: Dial Books.

Pothukuchi, Kameshwari. 2004. "Hortaliza: A Youth 'Nutrition Garden' in Southwest Detroit." *Children, Youth and Environments* 14 (2): 124–55.

Rabin, Anne, Tatjana Vasilaras, A. Christina Moller, and Arne Astrup. 2002. "Sucrose Compared with Artificial

Sweeteners." *American Journal of Child Nutrition* 76:721–9.

Rainie, Lee, and D'Vera Cohn. 2014. "Census: Computer Ownership, Internet Connection Varies Widely across US." *FactTank*, September 19.

Raja, Samina, Branden Born, and Jessica Russel. 2008. *A Planner's Guide to Community and Regional Food Planning: Transforming Food Environments, Facilitating Healthy Eating*. Chicago: American Planning Association.

Reed, Edward S. 1996. *The Necessity of Experience*. New Haven, CT: Yale University Press.

Reedy, Jill, and Susan M. Krebs-Smith. 2010. "Dietary Sources of Energy, Solid Fats, and Added Sugars among Children and Adolescents in the United States." *Journal of the American Dietetic Association* 110 (10): 1477–84.

Rideout, Virginia, Ulla Foehr, and Donald Roberts. 2010. *Generation M2: Media in the Lives of 8- to 18-Year-Olds*. Menlo Park, CA: Kaiser Family Foundation.

Roberts, Donald, Ulla Foehr and Virgina Rideout. 2005. *Generation M: Media in the Lives of 8–18 Year Olds*. Menlo Park, CA: Kaiser Family Foundation.

Robinson, Thomas. 1999. "Reducing Children's Television Viewing to Prevent Obesity." *Journal of the American Medical Association* 282 (16): 1561–7.

Rolls, Barbara Jean, Julia Ello-Martin, and Beth Carlton Tohill. 2004. "What Can Intervention Studies Tell Us About the Relationship between Fruit and Vegetable Consumption and Weight Management?" *Nutrition Reviews* 62 (1): 1–17.

Rook, Graham, Christopher Lowry, and Charles Raison. 2013. "Microbial 'Old Friends', Immunoregulation and Stress Resilience." *Evolution, Medicine, and Public Health* 2013 (1): 46–64.

Ruiz-Gallardo, José-Reyes, Alonso Verde, and Arturo Valdés. 2013. "Garden-Based Learning: An Experience with 'At-Risk' Secondary Education Students." *The Journal of Environmental Education* 44 (4): 252–70.

Sallis, James, Robert Cervero, William Ascher, Karla Henderson, M. Katherine Kraft, and Jacqueline Kerr. 2006. "An Ecological Approach to Creating Active Living Communities." *Annual Review of Public Health* 27:297–322.

Schlosser, Eric. 2001. *Fast Food Nation*. New York: Houghton Mifflin.

Schor, Juliet. 2004. *Born to Buy*. New York: Scribner.

Schor, Juliet, and Margaret Ford. 2007. "From Tastes Great to Cool: Children's Food Marketing and the Rise of the Symbolic." *Journal of Law, Medicine and Ethics* 35 (1): 10–21.

Schusler, Tania, and Marianne Krasny. 2008. "Youth Participation in Local Environmental Action: An Avenue for Science and Civic Learning." In *Participation and Learning: Perspectives on Education and the Environment, Health and Sustainability*, edited by Alan Reid, Bjarne Bruun Jensen, Jutta Nikel, and Venka Simovska, 268–84. Dordrecht, Netherlands: Springer Netherlands.

Schwartz, Marlene, and Kelly D. Brownell. 2007. "Actions Necessary to Prevent Childhood Obesity: Creating the Climate for Change." *Journal of Law, Medicine and Ethics* 35 (1): 78–89.

Scott, Virginia, John Ascher, Terry Griswold, and César Nufio. 2011. *Natural History Inventory of Colorado: The Bees of Colorado (Hymenoptera: Apoidea: Anthophila)*. Boulder, CO: University of Colorado Museum of Natural History.

Seligman, Martin. 2011. *Flourish*. New York: Free Press.

Skowyra, Kathleen, and Joseph Cocozza. 2006. *Blueprint for Change: A Comprehensive Model for the Identification and Treatment of Youth with Mental Health Needs in Contact with the Juvenile Justice System*. Delmar, NY: National Center for Mental Health and Juvenile Justice.

Snyder, Gary. 1974. *Turtle Island*. New York: New Directions.

Spiering, Charlie. 2015. "Michelle Obama: Eleanor Roosevelt My Idol." *Breitbart*, February 9.

Stebbins, C. A. 1920. *A Manual of School-Supervised Gardening for the Western States, United States School Garden Army*. Washington, DC: US Government Printing Office.

Stokols, Daniel. 1992. "Establishing and Maintaining Healthy Environments: Toward a Social Ecology of Health Promotion." *American Psychologist* 47 (1): 6–22.

———. 1996. "Translating Social Ecological Theory into Guidelines for Community Health Promotion." *American Journal of Health Promotion* 10 (4): 282–98.

Stone, Michael. 2009. *Smart by Nature: Schooling for Sustainability*. Healdsburg, CA: Watershed Media.

Struble, Mary B., and Laurie L. Aomari. 2003. "Position of the World Dietetic Association: Addressing World Hunger, Malnutrition, and Food Insecurity." *Journal of the American Dietetic Association* 103 (8): 1046–57.

Swarz, Susan W. 2009. *Facts for Policymakers: Adolescent Mental Health in the United States*. New York: National Center for Children in Poverty.

Taylor, Shelley, Laura Klein, Brian Lewis, Tara Gruenewald, Regan Gurung, and John Updegraff. 2000. "Biobehavioral Responses to Stress in Females: Tend-and-Befriend, not Fight-or-Flight." *Psychological Review* 107 (3): 411–29.

Tough, Paul. 2012. *How Children Succeed: Grit, Curiosity, and the Hidden Power of Character*. New York: Houghton Mifflin Harcourt.

Trasande, Leonardo, Jan Blustein, Mengling Liu, Elise Corwin, Laura M. Cox, and Martin J. Blaser. 2013. "Infant Antibiotic Exposures and Early-Life Body Mass." *International Journal of Obesity* 13:16–23.

Ulrich, Roger S. 1981. "Natural versus Urban Scenes: Some Psychophysiological Effects." *Environment and Behavior* 13:523–56.

———. 1983. "Aesthetic and Affective Response to Nature." In *Human Behavior and Environment, Vol. 6: Human Behavior and Natural Environment*, edited by Irwin Altman and Joachim Wohlwill, 85–125. New York: Plenum.

———. 1984. "View through a Window May Influence Recovery from Surgery." *Science* 224:220–1.

Ulrich, Roger, Robert Simons, Barbara Losito, Evelyn Fiorito, Mark Miles, and Michael Zelson. 1991. "Stress Recovery during Exposure to Natural and Urban Environments." *Journal of Environmental Psychology* 11:201–30.

Unger, Serena, and Heather Wooten. 2006. *A Food Systems Assessment for Oakland, CA: Toward a Sustainable Food Plan*. Oakland, CA: Oakland Mayor's Office of Sustainability and University of California Berkeley, Department of City and Regional Planning.

United Health Foundation. 2014. *America's Health Rankings Senior Report, 2014 Edition*. Minnetonka, MN: United Health Foundation.

University of California Board of Regents. 2016. "California's Landmark School Garden Legislation." Division of Agriculture and Natural Resources, University of California. Accessed February 11. http://ucanr.edu/sites/thevictorygrower/Whats_New_Public_Policies_that_Work_/Californias_Landmark_School_Garden_Legislation/.

University of California at Santa Cruz. 2010. *Teaching Organic Gardening and Farming: Resources for Instructors*. Santa Cruz, CA: Center for Agroecology & Sustainable Food Systems, University of California at Santa Cruz.

University of Groningen. 2012. "The Letters of Thomas Jefferson 1743–1826: Letter to John Jay, August 23, 1785." American History: From Revolution to Reconstruction. http://www.let.rug.nl/usa/presidents/thomas-jefferson/letters-of-thomas-jefferson/jefl33.php.

Urban Strategies Council. 2011. *Violent Crimes in Alameda County: A Fact Sheet*. Oakland, CA: Urban Strategies Council.

US Census Bureau. 2003. *New Mexico 2000: Population and Housing Unit Counts*. Washington, DC: US Census Bureau.

———. 2010. "State & County QuickFacts: Albuquerque (city), New Mexico." US Census Bureau. http://quickfacts. census.gov/qfd/states/35/3502000.html.

———. 2013. "Table C8: Poverty Status, Food Stamp Receipt, and Public Assistance for Children under 18 Years by Selected Characteristics: 2013." America's Families and Living Arrangements, 2013: Children (C Table Series). http://www.census.gov/hhes/families/data/cps2013C.html.

———. 2014a. "State & County QuickFacts: USA." US Census Bureau. http://quickfacts.census.gov/qfd/states/00000. html.

———. 2014b. "State & County QuickFacts: Boulder (City), Colorado." US Census Bureau. http://quickfacts.census. gov/qfd/states/08/0807850.html.

———. 2014c. "State & County QuickFacts: New Mexico." US Census Bureau. http://quickfacts.census.gov/qfd/ states/35000.html.

———. 2014d. "Income: Families." US Census Bureau. http://www.census.gov/hhes/www/income/data/historical/ families/.

———. 2014e. "State & County QuickFacts: Bronx County, New York." US Census Bureau. http://quickfacts.census. gov/qfd/states/36/36005.html.

———. 2014f. "State & County QuickFacts: Carbondale (town) Colorado. US Census Bureau. http://quickfacts. census.gov/qfd/states/08/0812045.html.

US Department of Agriculture. 2013. *National School Lunch Program*. Washington, DC: US Department of Agriculture.

———. 2014. *Food Deserts*. Washington, DC: US Department of Agriculture.

———. 2015. "National School Lunch Program: Participation and Lunches Served." US Department of Agriculture. Accessed February 11, 2016. http://www.fns.usda.gov/sites/default/files/pd/slsummar.pdf.

US Department of Education. 2013. "High School Graduation Rate at Highest Level in Three Decades." *Homeroom*, January 21.

US Government Printing Office. 2007. *Child Nutrition and the School Setting*, US Senate, One hundred tenth Congress, First Session Sess. 127. Committee on Agriculture, Nutrition and Forestry, US Senate.

Utter, Jennifer, Diane Neumark-Sztainer, Robert Jeffery, and Mary Story. 2003. "Couch Potatoes or French Fries: Are Sedentary Behaviors Associated with Body Mass Index, Physical Activity, and Dietary Behaviors Among Adolescents?" *Journal of the American Dietetic Association* 103 (10): 1298–305.

van den Berg, Agnes, and Mariëtte Custers. 2011. "Gardening Promotes Neuroendocrine and Affective Restoration from Stress." *Journal of Health Psychology* 16 (1): 3–11.

Ver Ploeg, Michele, Vince Breneman, Tracey Farrigan, Karen Hamrick, David Hopkins, Phillip Kaufman, Biing-Hwan Lin, Mark Nord, Travis A. Smith, Ryan Williams, Kelly Kinnison, Carol Olander, Anita Singh, and Elizabeth Tuckermanty. 2009. *Access to Affordable and Nutritious Food-Measuring and Understanding Food Deserts and Their Consequences: Report to Congress*. Administrative Publication No. (AP-036). Washington, DC: US Department of Agriculture Economic Research Service.

Vespa, Jonathan, Jamie M. Lewis, and Rose Kreider. 2013. *America's Family and Living Arrangements: 2012*. Washington, DC: US Census Bureau.

Waliczek, Tina M., Jayne M. Zajicek, and R. Daniel Lineberger. 2005. "The Influence of Gardening Activities on

Consumer Perceptions of Life Satisfaction." *HortScience* 40 (5): 1360–5.

Ward Thompson, Catharine, Jenny Roe, Peter Aspinall, Richard Mitchell, Angela Clow, and David Miller. 2012. "More Green Space Is Linked to Less Stress in Deprived Communities: Evidence from Salivary Cortisol Patterns." *Landscape and Urban Planning* 105:221–9

Waters, Alice. 2008. *The Edible School Yard: A Universal Idea.* San Francisco: Chronicle Books.

Weinstein, Netta, Andrew K. Przybylski, and Richard M. Ryan. 2009. "Can Nature Make Us More Caring?" *Personality and Social Psychology Bulletin* 35 (10): 1315–29.

Weitoft, Gunilla Ringbäck, Anders Hjern, Bengt Haglund, and Måns Rosén. 2003. "Mortality, Severe Morbidity, and Injury in Children Living with Single Parents in Sweden: A Population-Based Study." *The Lancet* 361 (9354): 289–95.

Westlund, Stephanie. 2014. *Field Exercises: How Veterans Are Healing Themselves through Farming and Outdoor Activities.* Gabriola Island, Canada: New Society Publishers.

Wheelwright, Jeff. 2015. "Days of Dysevolution: Can We Adapt Our Way Out of Them?" *Discover* 36 (4): 33-39.

Whitehead, Margaret, and Paula Holland. "What Puts Children of Lone Parents at a Health Disadvantage?" *The Lancet* 361 (9354): 271.

Wiecha, Jean, Karen E. Peterson, David Ludwig, Juhee Kim, Arthur Sobol, and Steven Gortmaker. 2006. "When Children Eat What They Watch: Impact of Television Viewing on Dietary Intake in Youth." *Archives of Pediatrics and Adolescent Medicine* 160:436–42.

Williams, Dilafruz, and Jonathan Brown. 2012. *Learning Gardens and Sustainability Education: Bringing Life to Schools and Schools to Life.* New York: Routledge.

Willis, Judy. 2007. "Cooperative Learning Is a Brain Turn-On." *Middle School Journal* 38 (4): 4–13.

Wilson, Edward O. 1984. *Biophilia.* Cambridge, MA: Harvard University Press.

Wohlwill, Joachim, and Irwin Altman. 1983. *Human Behavior and Environment, Vol. 6: Human Behavior and Natural Environment.* New York: Plenum.

World Health Organization. 2000. *Obesity: Preventing and Managing the Global Epidemic: Report of a WHO Consultation.* Geneva, Switzerland: World Health Organization.

———. 2014a. "Adolescents: Health Risks and Solutions. Fact Sheet #345." World Health Organization. Last updated May. http://www.who.int/mediacentre/factsheets/fs345/en/.

———. 2014b. "WHO Calls for Stronger Focus on Adolescent Health." *WHO Department of Communications*, May 14.

Wu, Chih-Da, Eileen McNeely, J. G. Cedeño-Laurent, Wen-Chi Pan, Gary Adamkiewicz, Francesca Dominici, Shih-Chun Candice Lung, Huey-Jen Su, and John D. Spengler. 2014. "Linking Student Performance in Massachusetts Elementary Schools with the 'Greenness' of School Surroundings Using Remote Sensing." *PLoS ONE* 9 (10): e108548. doi:10.1371/journal.pone.0108548.

Yee, Vivian. 2012. "No Appetite for Good-for-You School Lunches." *New York Times*, October 6.

Youniss, James, and Miranda Yates. 1997. *Community Service and Social Responsibility in Youth.* Chicago: University of Chicago Press.

Zeder, Melinda A. 2008. "Domestication and Early Agriculture in the Mediterranean Basin: Origins, Diffusion, and Impact." *Proceedings of the National Academy of Sciences of the United States of America* 105 (33): 11597–604.

CPSIA information can be obtained
at www.ICGtesting.com
Printed in the USA
LVOW02s0323300816
502286LV00006B/10/P